PARTS OF A LIFETIME

MILOVAN DJILAS

Parts
of a
Lifetime

EDITED BY

Michael and Deborah Milenkovitch

New York and London

HARCOURT BRACE JOVANOVICH

Burgess
DR
359
.D5
A28
1975

Library of Congress Cataloging in Publication Data

Djilas, Milovan.
Parts of a lifetime.

Includes index.
I. Title.
DR359.D5A28   1975   949.7′02′0924   75–1307
ISBN 0–15–170969–6

First edition

B C D E

CONTENTS

Part IV. Doubts and Searches

Part V. Reality and Imperfection

Part VI. Utopia and Bureaucracy

Preface

The editors wish to explain how they came to prepare this collection of Milovan Djilas's political and literary writings. Their reasons were both scholarly and personal. Both editors are scholars—one a political scientist, the other an economist—interested in the socioeconomic development of Yugoslavia. They have been deeply aware of the consuming interest of their students in revolution and of their efforts to understand it. Both believe that Djilas—because he had been just such an idealistic revolutionary student himself—has something to tell these young men and women. This conviction was confirmed when Djilas, during his brief visit to the United States in 1968, spent a day at Herbert H. Lehman College of the City University of New York. In his occasionally bitter and polemical dialogue with the students, he emerged—more so in person, perhaps, than in his writings—as one who understood their frustrations. He, too, had been frustrated by the imperfections of an existing order. But unlike them, he had also experienced the deeper frustration of sacrificing everything for the revolution and of bearing the moral responsibility of urging others to sacrifice as well, only to be bitterly disappointed and profoundly disillusioned by the results.

These experiences and thoughts reinforced the determination to bring to fruition a project that had been conceived several years earlier by Michael M. Milenkovitch and John William McDonald, Jr.: to compile an anthology from Djilas's works, from early years to the present, and often from obscure sources. By becoming more aware of Djilas's unique experience as a revolutionary who had survived to reflect upon the outcome of the revolution, it was felt, a deeper understanding of this revolutionary figure would emerge. Like his brother Montenegrins, Milenkovitch has idealized the traits of honor, pride, courage, steadfastness, and dedication to justice. As an embodiment of these national ideals, Djilas was an ethically and emotionally appealing subject of study. William Jovanovich, after seeing an outline, took great interest in the project. Unfortunately, McDonald left New York to teach at Washington and Jefferson

College, and, because of the geographical separation and his inevitable absorption in his new teaching duties, he was unable to continue work on the project. This was a deep loss; he has a thorough knowledge of Djilas's writings and had had fine training in political theory.

Michael Milenkovitch appealed to his wife's professional and personal interests. Fully aware of her husband's background—he had spent the first twenty years of his life in Yugoslavia—and of his desire to understand better the Yugoslav socialist revolution that was the dominant event of his youth, Deborah Milenkovitch agreed to join him in the project. Her interest in Yugoslavia, both past and present, had emerged before she met her husband; it was intensified when she realized how much, directly and indirectly, the ideals for which Djilas stood influenced some of his personal decisions. He had come to the United States to study, and was thereafter faced with the difficult decision of whether to return to Yugoslavia or remain. This question was resolved when the Yugoslav government sentenced Djilas to jail for his writing. Milenkovitch decided to remain in the United States to study politics. Thus the fate of Djilas influenced one of the most important decisions of his life.

The roles played by the editors in assembling and organizing this book were both complementary and specialized. One of the most crucial and sensitive tasks was to achieve a balance, which was done by tempering the strongly pronounced Slavic romanticism of one with the Anglo-Saxon rationality and pragmatism of the other. Milenkovitch procured the original materials, compiled the bibliography, and made initial and subsequent selections for inclusion. They jointly translated the pieces from Serbo-Croatian, edited them, and tried to achieve a smooth transition in those articles from which major portions had to be cut. At all stages the editors worked together on organization and content. Numerous changes were made in the course of preparing the final version, which is truly a joint product. The Introduction, based on an article, "Continuity and Change in the Thought of Milovan Djilas," which appeared in *Review* (London) is also a collaboration.

All articles in this volume have been translated by Michael and Deborah Milenkovitch, unless otherwise indicated.

There are many persons whom Michael Milenkovitch wishes to thank for their assistance, especially in the initial phase of his work. Because of the theme of the book and the official Yugoslav attitude toward Djilas, several of the sources of funds for study in Eastern Europe were effectively closed. However, he was able to obtain certain financial assistance, which he gratefully acknowledges, from Hunter College of the City University of New York and from The American Philosophical Society. A sabbatical leave from Lehman College enabled him to spend eight months in Yugoslavia in 1971 and to compile the final version of the manuscript.

His thanks go to the staff of the Svetozar Marković Library of Belgrade University, where he did preliminary research in the summer of 1968 and more thorough research in 1971, and to the staff of Djurdje Crnojević Library in Cetinje, where he was able to locate some of Djilas's early works. Nor can he neglect the countless Yugoslavs who talked to him freely, some critically and others admiringly, about Djilas and his ideas. These included many ordinary citizens, some scholars, and even some persons in power. Without their comments, which he collected during his stay in Belgrade and his trips to Montenegro in 1964, 1968, 1971, and 1972, he would not have been able to understand how Djilas is perceived in his native land, in Montenegro, and in the national capital, Belgrade. His thanks go as well to the Yugoslav authorities for permitting him to work unhindered.

The help of several persons was invaluable in completing the manuscript. Both editors thank the late Hiram Haydn of Harcourt Brace Jovanovich, for his patient assistance, and Professor Leigh Winser, of the English Department at Seton Hall University, for advice and consultations. Special thanks are due to Patricia Chick, who, while taking care of our lively two-year-old son, Andrew, and keeping house for us in Belgrade, managed to find time to edit and type a sizable portion of the manuscript, and to Susanna C. Escoffery, who typed the last portion.

The editors wish also to thank Štefanija Djilas—who stood stoically by her husband during his darkest hours and who was left to raise their son, Aleksa, alone while her husband served almost nine years in jail— for her help in understanding the man Djilas.

And, most important, the editors express their thanks and gratitude to Milovan Djilas, romantic revolutionary, statesman, and humanist, for providing a wealth of published and unpublished material and for his willingness to answer our questions openly and honestly. This was of invaluable assistance in comprehending his personality. Perhaps, too, the most useful advice they received came from him. Upon being asked his opinion of a particular item, he replied that he preferred not to answer because it might influence their interpretation. He warned: "One must be wary of the opinions of former politicians, including myself, about their past. Politicians have a tendency to beautify their past."

The editors also must thank the many others who helped with their criticisms and comments. Of course, all omissions, commissions, and other deficiencies are the result of their failure to make the best use of the ample material at their disposal or the consequence of a well-known Serbian and Montenegrin trait—stubbornness—which has left its indelible mark on one of the editors.

PARTS OF A LIFETIME

Introduction

When his sense of the way the world worked first came into reliable focus, Milovan Djilas was torn between his desire to be a writer and his sense of duty to work for a society of social equality, economic justice, and personal freedom. The idea of revolution early won out in this conflict. He became a clandestine Communist, then a Partisan leader, a senior statesman in the new Yugoslavia, and, finally, a harsh critic of the results of the revolution. Then, while still in power, this rebellious Montenegrin chose the path that he knew would not fail to lead to confrontation after confrontation with his old comrades.

To understand what made Djilas follow this course—relentlessly striving for social change through the Communist revolution, then relentlessly criticizing the failure of the Communist revolution to achieve its aims and refusing to recant or keep silent—is our complex challenge. In an interview on January 1, 1967, upon his release from his third prison term, Djilas gave a partial explanation: he noted that he had always been strongly influenced by his Montenegrin heritage of honor, courage, loyalty, dedication to justice, and righteous indignation. These, and other Montenegrin traits—love of freedom, devotion to truth, romantic idealism, and a dualistic view of life and man—shaped his thoughts and actions. Thus, Djilas is a romantic revolutionary. The term is used here to disclose the character of the young Djilas, who committed himself to a revolutionary rather than an evolutionary theory of socioeconomic change. His convictions were shaped by his early exposure to Montenegrin romantic nationalism, a nationalism that had nurtured for more than five centuries a determination to preserve Montenegrin freedom from persistent Turkish invasion. In addition to being influenced by the exaltation of the struggle against the oppressor, Djilas embraced the fundamental ideals of freedom, truth, justice, and commitment to one's family and country that saturated the Serbian folk-ballad tradition. The works of Njegoš and Marko Miljanov, two self-educated nineteenth-century Montenegrin statesmen, further served to mold his character to commitment to the search for truth and justice. He had learned all of Njegoš's famous ode to freedom, *The Mountain Wreath,* by heart, as well as hundreds of folk ballads. Indeed, even today tears come to his eyes when he recites some of the most stirring passages.

In school, in the gymnasium, Djilas learned that European romanticism was, among other things, a protest against the enslavement of man and society to the mere method of science. Rousseau's proclamation that reason deceives conscience, the "true guide of man," and Kant's idealism reinforced Djilas's commitment to a romantic view of history. When Rousseau blamed social institutions for enslaving and debasing the common man, the themes of pessimism and despair in his work served to increase Djilas's hatred of the injustices in his own society. Perhaps the salvation of mankind lay in rediscovering nature, in respect for the common man, and, most important, in revolutionary social change. The suffering of the common man, his hopelessness, became even more apparent to Djilas when he read the graphic account of oppression in Marx and Engels's *Communist Manifesto.* This bold call for revolutionary action to all who wanted to improve the lot of the working class brought Djilas one step closer to Communism. Dostoevski's moving portraits of the misery and decay in corrupt tsarist Russia, moreover, carried Djilas further toward the romantic vision of revolution as the final step in eradicating injustices.

In addition to romantic nationalism, the most vital catalytic agent that helped fuse Djilas into a romantic revolutionary was romantic literature itself. The young Djilas had chosen literature as his profession. Through the writings of Pushkin, Goethe, Schiller, Hugo, Byron, Shelley, and, especially, Njegoš, he absorbed the value of the past, learned about love, nature, the emotions, and the importance of the subconscious. A sense of the mystery of the unknown and a hope for a brighter future for mankind attracted him to the romantic poets. He expressed his own romanticism by writing lyric poems, then poems in prose, and, finally, other forms of fiction.

In both his published and unpublished work the romantic influence on Djilas is unmistakable; it even survives the increasing realism and naturalism of his mature literary period. Djilas ponders deeply about nature, about his own emotional life and his feelings towards others; he admires some aspects of the Middle Ages (in his "Jail Diary"); and he identifies Satan as the revolutionary hero of Milton's *Paradise Lost* (which he translated into Serbo-Croatian). Romantic portrayals of nature and revolutionaries in his two autobiographical works, *Land Without Justice* and *Memoir of a Revolutionary,* as well as his great preoccupation with Njegoš, one of the greatest Slavic poets of the Romantic era, confirm the romantic tendency in Djilas. But Djilas is not only a romantic revolutionary; he is unique among Communist revolutionaries.

An idealistic revolutionary who became a committed Partisan, he rose to the top levels of government leadership. But, frustrated by the failure of the new society to attain equality and justice, he became a critic of the system. He was purged. But there his path shifted from that of many other disillusioned revolutionaries: his fate was jail, rather than execution or forced exile.

In prison he had time to reflect upon his ideals and on where the revolution had gone astray. When his sentence ended he was able to return to a reasonably normal life in his own country and to write. Thus, the course his life followed gave him a unique opportunity, for there were no others who could write about the revolution and about Communism from his perspective. To study this complex man, therefore, may yield fresh insights, not only into his character, but also into the nature of the revolution itself.

Born in 1911 on a lonely farm located majestically on a plateau above the little village of Podbišće, near Mojkovac, where some of the bloodiest battles for Montenegrin independence had been fought and where their memory still lives, Milovan Djilas became a living example of the spirit of Montenegro: the fierce independence that enabled the Montenegrins, alone of all the south and west Slavic peoples, to retain their independence from foreign empires; the idealism and toughness necessary to survive the hardships of a rugged and hostile land; the profound sense of active kinship that linked men and enabled them to withstand their enemies, both natural and human.

Like all Montenegrins, the Djilas family valued learning. In order to continue beyond elementary school, Milovan left his village and moved to Berane (today's Ivangrad), where he discovered both literature and Communism. Like all young intellectuals, he was beset by moral dilemmas: his personal desire to write was in conflict with what he felt to be a moral obligation to work for a better society, a society with justice and equality. It was while he was still a high-school student that he resolved the conflict between personal desire and social duty, in favor of his obligation to change society. Wherever these two should become incompatible, he would sacrifice his writing. His first decade of adult life, however, did not force him to this point. In 1929, at the age of eighteen, he went to Belgrade to study literature at the university. There he found other students with ideas and experiences similar to his own. In 1932, he joined the clandestine Communist party. He was soon arrested for his revolutionary activities, and on April 23, 1933 he was sentenced to a three-year jail term. This interrupted his studies[1] and his political

---

1. Djilas was in the last semester of his studies in literature. However, he never wrote his thesis and never received a university degree. After the revolution, he turned down a law degree offered to him, on the ground that he had not earned it.

activity, although not his writing. His prison experience only served to strengthen his commitment to revolution, and following his release from prison, in 1936, he was an active member of the Yugoslav Communist party. Despite his deep political involvement, he continued writing— often under pseudonyms—up to the start of World War II.

When the Germans invaded Yugoslavia in 1941, Djilas became a Partisan. The Partisan struggle against foreign invaders now consumed all of his energy. Until 1956, with the exception of the short piece "The Dead Village," written during the war, he wrote solely for political purposes. He saw the German occupation of Yugoslavia and the ensuing Communist revolution (1941–1945) and, later, the Soviet threat to Yugoslavia's independent existence, expressed in the Cominform Resolution of 1948, as forces compelling him to put aside his literary career. His need to submit to these external forces inspired him to immerse himself in the revolution, and, in the process, he became one of Tito's most devoted collaborators. The same need made him write, just before the crucial Battle of Sutjeska with the Germans in 1943, a farewell message to Tito. Convinced that the chances of his personal survival were slight, he wrote affirming that no sacrifice was too great for the cause of victory.

Their guerrilla efforts against the enemy, their undoubted bravery, and their support of a unified Yugoslavia transcending nationality differences soon made the Partisans the center of the Yugoslav resistance movement. From this foundation, the Communists were able to launch a revolution without Russian assistance. When the war ended in 1945, Yugoslavia was a Communist state and Djilas one of its top leaders.

He was formally in charge of education, but he was also charged with responsibilities in the ideological sphere. During the entire period he held official position, until January 1954, his writings were almost exclusively concerned with political and ideological questions. His services as an ideologist were invaluable to Yugoslavia during the critical period following the Cominform Resolution of 1948 which isolated Yugoslavia from the socialist camp. The Soviet Union accused Yugoslavia of "revisionism," of failure to be sufficiently socialist. Over a period of months, Djilas, with Moša Pijade and Edvard Kardelj, responded to the Soviet attack. Firmly believing that Yugoslavia was socialist, they concluded that the Soviet Union was not. In the Soviet Union the bureaucracy had become dominant; hence the Soviet Union was not socialist, but state capitalist. If Yugoslavia was to avoid the dangers of state capitalism, it would have to develop a nonbureaucratic form of government. The task was to build a new model of socialism. Djilas was one of the originators of the idea of introducing management by the workers as a return to original Marxist doctrines and to avoid the danger of subordination to the bureaucracy.

A dedicated revolutionary, whose task was to transform society, Djilas carried out his ideological tasks with typical Montenegrin zeal. One of his Montenegrin Marxist compatriots, discussing the "cult of personality" surrounding Djilas during those years, said, "One could think freely, talk freely and write freely—as long as one agreed with Djilas. But anyone who disagreed with Djilas had to watch out!" Isidora Sekulić is a case in point. She wrote about Njegoš, the famous Montenegrin poet, prince, and bishop (and inevitably one of the literary subjects closest to Djilas's harshly in the press.[2] Although no physical harm came to her and she was heart). In 1952, Djilas disagreed with her analysis and attacked her not confined, as might have happened in Stalin's Russia, she did cease publishing almost completely. Djilas wrote later that at the time he had believed that his criticism of her work was just like the criticism of any author by any critic. Subsequently, he admitted that because of his rank and the implication of criticism coming from him, this was an illusion.[3]

As early as January 1950, at about the same time that he was developing his ideas on the threat of bureaucracy in the Soviet Union, Djilas was beginning to develop more liberal ideas on ideological diversity. He began to argue that the Communist party, having successfully completed the revolution and having overcome the counterrevolutionary threat, had now to abandon its ideological monopoly and permit diversity. This was necessary to avoid becoming bureaucratic. His concern with the stultifying effects of ideological and political monopoly continued to grow, and became a major theme of his attack on the Communist bureaucracy.

Djilas, one of the four top ranking Yugoslavs, was perhaps Tito's heir apparent; Tito had always looked upon him with favor. But while at the height of his power, and cognizant of the possibly dire consequences, this rebellious Montenegrin felt compelled to speak out. At first enthusiastic about the possibilities for producing a just and equitable society, he had gradually been frustrated by the realities of a totalitarian one-party system. Hopeful of bringing about change within the party through developing opposing factions that would enable the party to fulfill its revolutionary ideals, he wrote a series of articles, published in *Borba* between October 11, 1953 and January 7, 1954, critical of the growth of the bureaucracy and especially of its preoccupation with privileges and its abandonment of many revolutionary dreams. As a consequence of these "heretical" articles,[4] an extraordinary plenum of the Central Com-

---

2. *Legenda o Njegošu* (Belgrade: Kultura, 1952).

3. See Chapter 4, "Notes," April 6, 1959.

4. "Djilasism," if it exists (Tito attacked it by this name in 1954, 1968 and 1972–1973), is not an ideology. Djilas himself rejects the notion of prescribing new dogmas to replace bankrupt old ones. That is why he stresses the "unperfect" nature of society. When fellow party members Krsto Crvenkovski and Veljko Vlahović became enthusiastic supporters of Djilasism in 1953 (for which they were censured in 1954), their sup-

mittee of the League of Communists was convened on January 17–18, 1954 to "resolve" the Djilas affair. Following his party trial, he was removed from all party and governmental positions. In the subsequent weeks, deeply troubled, he questioned his past devotion and present relationship to the party. On March 4, 1954, he turned his party card, bearing the number 4, in to his local party organization, with the following statement: "As of today I do not consider myself a party member and I am resigning from the organization by my own free will."[5] In January 1955 he faced a state trial on charges of violations of Article 118 of the Yugoslav Criminal Code—specifically, engaging in hostile anti-Yugoslav propaganda through having interviews with Westerners and the Western press, especially with *New York Times* correspondent Jack Raymond. The trial was held in the District Court of Belgrade on January 25, 1955. Djilas was found guilty of seeking to "undermine the people's authority, defense and economic power," and sentenced to jail for a term of one and a half to three years. He appealed the sentence, which was then made conditional.

Isolated and alone, Djilas clung stubbornly to his convictions. Not only did he refuse to recant, but also he continued to develop his nascent ideas about the bureaucracy, ideas that were published in his most famous book, *The New Class*. On November 19, 1956, his article "The Storm in Eastern Europe" was published in *The New Leader*. It supported the Hungarian revolution and voiced skepticism about the sincerity of the Soviet desire to improve Soviet-Yugoslav relations following the visit to Yugoslavia in May 1955 of Bulganin and Khrushchev—the first attempt to normalize relations between the two countries since the break in 1948. He was tried a second time, in secret, before the same district court, on November 27, 1956. On December 12, he was sentenced to three years of "strict confinement" and sent to Sremska Mitrovica Prison, where he had already served the greater part of his three-year sentence as a Communist in Royal Yugoslavia between April 1933 and April 1936.

When *The New Class* was published, in August 1957, a third trial was held, at the District Court of Sremska Mitrovica, and Djilas was found guilty of a deliberate attempt to "compromise socialism as an idea and the international workers' movement." He was sentenced to an additional six years, making a total of nine.

---

port was probably typical of that of many honest Communists anxious to rejuvenate their system through sincere criticism. They wanted to strengthen the party by decreasing social inequalities and by gaining the genuine support of the masses without the need for undue application of political or economic pressure. In that sense Djilasism does exist. It is not an ideology so much as it is the advocacy of continuing critical appraisal of the social system, of freedom for the individual to participate, to agree and to disagree.

5. *NIN* (Belgrade), May 8, 1973.

After serving four years, two months, and twenty days, of which twenty months were spent in solitary confinement, Djilas was released from jail on January 20, 1961. It was a conditional release, based on the results of several negotiating sessions between Djilas and S. Penezić, who represented the government and the party position. Djilas promised to abstain from any hostile, antistate activity or political writing.

Still the recalcitrant Montenegrin, he then wrote *Conversations with Stalin* (finished by November 1961 and published in May 1962), which not only violated the conditions of his release, but also allegedly revealed state secrets.[6]

Djilas was charged with violation of Article 320 of the Criminal Code, which forbid revelation of state secrets by any person who had held public office. He was arrested on April 7, 1962, a fourth trial was held, and on May 14, 1962, he was sentenced, in accord with Article 320, to a term of five years, to which was added the three years and eight months he had remaining to serve from the previous sentence. After serving four years and nine months, he was released, on December 31, 1966.

Despite a five-year ban on publication, which ran until the end of 1971, Djilas fearlessly continued to write, and to publish, though outside Yugoslavia, both fiction and political essays. After *The New Class* (1957), he published eleven books: *Land Without Justice* (1958), *Conversations with Stalin* (1962), *Montenegro* (1963), *The Leper and Other Stories* (1964), *Njegoš* (1966), *The Unperfect Society* (1969), *Under the Colors* (1971), *The Stone and the Violets* (1972), *Memoir of a Revolutionary* (1973), and a translation into Serbian of Milton's *Paradise Lost* (1969), as well as numerous articles in major Western newspapers. At the end of 1973, none of his work had been published in

6. Vladimir Dedijer had earlier written about many of the same matters in his book *Tito*, considered an official biography. His version of the Tito-Stalin split is basically the same as the story in Djilas's book. It is more likely that Djilas was jailed again not because he revealed state secrets, but to placate the Russians, with whom Tito was trying, in 1962, to establish closer ties. This view was confirmed by the long series of articles on Djilas that appeared in the Belgrade weekly *NIN* between June 17 and August 12, 1973. These articles, the first officially sanctioned discussion of Djilas since his fall from power in 1954, point specifically to his derogatory remarks about Khrushchev, as well to as his comments about the position of the Yugoslav party on the Albanian question, as reasons for his rearrest. In fact, whenever Yugoslav-Soviet relations are worst, Djilas is treated best. On the eve of the Soviet invasion of Czechoslovakia in 1968, Yugoslav authorities issued Djilas a passport to travel to Western Europe and America. Although the government could have punished him for violation of his parole conditions, Tito was content to reprimand him for sharp criticism of the Soviet Union. But in early May of 1970, with the danger of Soviet invasion past, Djilas's passport was withdrawn, a few days before his scheduled departure for a trip to Western Europe, Scandinavia, and the United States. In the summer of 1973, when Soviet-Yugoslav relations were warmer than at any time since the early postwar days, Djilas was attacked extensively in the press.

Yugoslavia since 1954. In the summer of 1972, the plans of the Belgrade literary periodical *Savremenik* to publish in Serbian his short story "The Leper" (published in English in 1964) were canceled, after open party pressure because of his "hostile position against the socialist community." An offer to publish his monumental literary-historical study *Njegoš* was also mysteriously withdrawn in the summer of 1972.

To understand Djilas, we must understand his basic dualism. One form this dualism assumes is art versus politics. Literature (art) represents the personal, and is where his desires lie, while revolution (politics) stands for the social, and he conceived it as having a prior claim over everything else. Although he decided in favor of duty to society at an early age, in fact it was a number of years before he had to make a real choice. He remained torn, and at times his response appeared to be dictated by neither desire nor duty, but by what was most beautiful.[7] One day, before the war, he has said, while he was supposed to be performing some task for the party, the day was so beautiful that he went fishing instead. In this instance beauty lay on the side of personal desire. But when he had to choose between literature and revolution, he did so not only out of a sense of duty, but also because now beauty was to be found on the side of the revolution. "It was more important and even more beautiful to 'make' the revolution than to 'describe it.' "[8] Later in his life the conflict appeared as personal integrity versus personal security. The duty to be honest, to oneself and to others, was more important than life itself. He was so committed to the principle of duty that he no longer felt that he even had a choice. Regardless of the consequences, for himself and for those he loved, he was compelled to speak up and to confront the party.

The continuing conflict between the satisfaction of personal desire (writing) and collective responsibility (revolution) suggests that Djilas should be viewed in each of these dimensions separately as well as in their interrelations. Viewing him as a revolutionary, which in fact he was for most of his adult life, it is possible to trace various stages of his intellectual and spiritual metamorphosis. Viewing him as a writer, it is possible to demarcate different periods or phases where first literature, then politics, dominates; in his later life he shifts readily back and forth between the two.

Seven periods of creativity in Djilas's writing can be identified, and both the continuity and the change in his thought and in his writing can be traced. Within each period can be seen both themes and their forms of

7. The role of beauty in Djilas's choice is one of the central themes in J. W. McDonald's "Political Themes in the Thought of Milovan Djilas" (Ph.D. diss., Columbia University, 1971).
8. *Legenda o Njegošu.*

expression: literary (in the sense of belles-lettres), political, philosophical, and autobiographical writing. The presence or absence of certain forms in a particular period is indicative of changes in interests and commitments.

1. During his first five years of literary activity (1928–1933) Djilas traversed the road from the romanticism of lyrical poetry and love stories to social criticism. He published forty-nine poems and short stories and thirty-one reviews and literary essays.

2. While in a prison near Belgrade and later at Sremska Mitrovica and Lepoglava during his first jail term, from April 1933 to April 1936, he wrote ten stories (nine of them about imprisoned Communist revolutionaries; the other, "The Tribe") and a novelette, "Black Hills." All of these were confiscated by the police or prison authorities and were subsequently lost during the war.

3. Between 1936 and January 1941 Djilas gradually gave up writing poetry and literature altogether, in favor of revolutionary activism and political writing. He wrote his last poem in 1937. It appears that his purely literary impulse was subjugated to his duty as a party member in the field of poetic creativity. He believed that poetry must be "felt" to be true, and when, after one attempt, he concluded that the party-approved style of "socialist realism" (as found in the poems of the Russian Myakovsky) did not fit his poetic personality, he ceased writing poetry. However, he continued active involvement in the revolutionary struggle through his political essays, and while a full-time revolutionary activist he supported himself by translating Gorki's works from Russian, among them *The Life of Klim Samgin*. His short stories "Dead Fish" and "Rajac" written in August of 1938 were, with one exception, to be his last works of that genre for twenty years. His total commitment to the revolution now proved incompatible with his writing, and he abandoned literature for the revolution.

4. From July 1941 to 1954 he was fighting, first for the revolution and later to consolidate the revolutionary gains. When he wrote, it was, for the most part, in the service of the revolution. He wrote only one story, "The Dead Village" (1942), in a style reminiscent of early Camus. He wrote a few literary essays, the most significant being "The Legend of Njegoš," a doctrinaire Marxist analysis. The rest of his writing was political, ideological, and journalistic.

5. From 1954 to 1961 (which included his first jail term under the Communists), Djilas was absorbed in settling accounts with himself. This was his most introspective period; he was "wrapped up in himself." This is most clearly seen in his essay "Nordic Dream," written immediately following his trial by the party in January 1954. It was the first of many attempts at self-examination. Another autobiographical reflection is his lengthy unpublished essay "The Omniscience of Folly," which deals in

detail with the workings of the inner party leadership. The idea for this article first came to Djilas in December 1953, in the midst of the rising political storms that were to carry him out of political office. Under the title "Modestness and Revolutionaryness," it was being prepared for *Nova Misao,* the same periodical that had published his "Anatomy of a Moral," and it appears to be a sequel to it. The article was rejected, and Djilas revised it extensively in the summer of 1954 and again in the summer of 1955. He also kept a "Diary of Thoughts" (1953–1954), which contains both personal reflections and his views on the changes in Communism and in the world at large. As his extensive "Jail Diary" from the first term reveals, he continued to reflect on his past, but he also made observations about politics, ideology, philosophy, and the prison environment. Some of his autobiographical reflections from this period appear in *Land Without Justice* and in some stories in *The Leper and Other Stories* and *The Stone and the Violets. Conversations with Stalin* is also in part autobiographical. As the years in jail slowly passed, Djilas completed the settling of accounts with himself and began to turn more to literature and to topics not directly autobiographical. Much of the work on *Njegoš* and *Montenegro* was done in prison.

6. During his second jail term (April 7, 1962–December 31, 1966), Djilas continued to write, mainly nonautobiographical literature, although parts of *The Unperfect Society* are autobiographical. *Under the Colors,* written in this period, is a historical novel about the complex relations between Moslem and Christian, between Albanian, Montenegrin, and Turk at the end of the nineteenth century. He also wrote short stories, translated Milton's *Paradise Lost* into Serbian, and started work on another large novel, "Worlds and Bridges," about the conflicts at the turn of the century. It is the first volume of a projected trilogy. His relatively brief "Jail Diary" from the second prison term consists mainly of notes on his literary progress.

7. From about 1968 on, Djilas turned his attention again to politics. Despite being drawn to literature, he apparently cannot avoid involvement in politics, this time as a democratic socialist engaged in an unceasing search for a better world. He now moves back and forth between politics and literature and autobiography. In the sphere of politics he writes about the Soviet Union, the state of the Communist movement today, and about the unperfectability of society and its implications. He continues his autobiography. Where *Land Without Justice* relates his childhood years in Montenegro, *Memoir of a Revolutionary* covers the years from 1928, when he went to Belgrade to attend the university, until the beginning of World War II. It describes his years as a student, his jail term in royal Yugoslavia, and his life as a professional revolutionary. In literature he continues to work on his trilogy.

The stages of Djilas's revolutionary metamorphosis do not correspond precisely to the specific periods in his writing. The desire for a just society made him a revolutionary, but with time his opinions about how best to achieve that goal underwent profound change. He is not unique in this respect. It is not uncommon for those who are most strongly committed to the ideals of equality and justice, and who believed they had found in the Communist revolution the means to attain them, to become disillusioned with the Communist new society.

The metamorphosis of the idealistic revolutionary can be seen from Djilas's experience, and also from the experience of others, to consist of a number of stages. (True revolutionaries are not to be confused with opportunists. The latter, never having been truly committed to revolutionary ideals, and often joining the ranks after the period of hardship is over, do not even question whether the ideals are being attained.)

In the first stage of change the revolutionary experiences a growing awareness of society's inequities and a gradual crystallization of an intellectual and spiritual commitment to revolution as the means to attain a better society.

The second stage consists of his decision to commit himself to the struggle to destroy the existing social order. This is done with great zeal. If it serves the desired end, no sacrifice, personal or collective, is too great, no act too brutal. At this stage, in the total struggle to seize power, the revolutionary is the least sentimental, for sentimentality is weakness and interferes with attaining the goals of the revolution.

In the third stage, following the triumph of the revolution, he works doggedly to build his perfect society according to some preconceived plan. But gradually his frustration mounts as he perceives that the construction of his new society is not an easy task. During the destruction of the old system, he accepted the concomitant brutality unquestioningly; but now he becomes sensitive to the continuing abuses of human dignity.

In the fourth stage, increasingly aware of the deficiencies of the society that he and his comrades are creating, he seeks to improve it. He spends long hours analyzing what is going wrong and seeks to persuade his comrades to adopt reforms.

The fifth stage is characterized by the recognition that the new society is as unjust as the old one and equally resistant to change. This realization evokes a deep sense of guilt for having destroyed the previous system at such a high cost in order to establish a new one that is not demonstrably better. All that suffering, often inflicted at the revolutionary's own orders, appears to have been in vain.

In the sixth stage, with the party, in the name of the revolution, continuing its unchallenged reign, reality forces the idealistic revolutionary to settle accounts within his conscience and to determine a new course of action.

The seventh stage sees the open settling of accounts. It usually ends with a complete break with the regime that had betrayed the ideals of the revolution, a break very painful because of the long association with comrades and the long dedication to Communism as the means to attain social goals. The break is also dangerous, because the consequences of the action cannot be foreseen.

The eighth stage involves bearing the consequences, whatever they may be. There is usually expulsion from the party, exile, political and social isolation, and frequently jail or death by execution or suicide. The former revolutionary becomes a social outcast, a seeming nonentity. The suddenness with which this change comes about and its totality cause a grave shock. But should he survive the immediate consequences, there follows the opportunity for long and deep reflection.[9]

The ninth stage sees the resumption of the quest for social change, for an improvement in the social order, but from a new perspective. Having settled accounts with himself and his past, having resumed a normal life, the idealist continues to struggle for change, but now with vastly more experience and having shed his previous illusions about the nature and perfectability of society.

Djilas appears to be unique among Communist revolutionaries in having passed through all these stages and in having recorded his thoughts fairly completely. Some revolutionaries become disappointed in the revolution at an early stage and abandon it. Others are disturbed but compromise their principles for privilege, comfort, family, or sheer survival. But for the true revolutionary, commitment to his goals makes silence impossible. Some who have undergone the metamorphosis from romantic revolutionary to critic have been prevented by external factors from writing about their experiences. Imre Nagy was perhaps one such person, but he did not survive the Soviet occupation of Hungary.[10] The Czechoslovak leaders Dubček, Smrkovsky, and Svoboda have all been silenced, at least temporarily. Trotsky, in exile and bitter, was a similar figure. Though one of the most perceptive critics of Stalin's Russia, his personal rivalry with Stalin prevented him from being an altogether objective analyst. Djilas, on the other hand, remained amazingly and unusually without rancor toward his former comrades who removed him from power and sent him to jail. This is especially visible in *The Unperfect Society, Memoir of a Revolutionary,* and "Jail Diary."

9. In "Jail Diary" Djilas suggests, only partly in jest, that statesmen should be forced to spend a year or two, but no longer, in solitude to reflect. Jail provides one such opportunity for total isolation from the outside world. (A monk's cell would seem to be out of the question for atheist revolutionaries.) Such solitude helps one to review one's life and to clarify complex issues.

10. The Soviet occupying authorities assured him safe passage from the Yugoslav embassy, where he had sought asylum. But when he left the embassy he was arrested, taken to Rumania, and later summarily shot.

Other critics, including Arthur Koestler, Ignazio Silone and, more recently, Roger Garaudy and Leszek Kolakowsky, have written about this metamorphosis, but their perspective is different from that of Djilas because they neither made revolution nor built a new society; they were theoreticians and observers only. Thus Djilas is unique in having undergone this metamorphosis and in having described it. *The New Class* and *The Unperfect Society* present his political analysis; *Land Without Justice* and *Memoir of a Revolutionary*, his personal experiences; his collections of short stories, *The Leper and Other Stories* and *The Stone and the Violets*, depict the revolution in literary form. It is not that others might not have chosen to follow the same course; but virtually no one else had the option.

Through the different periods and different forms in which Djilas has written one can find elements of both continuity and change. Among the most prominent continuous features is his dualism, his view of life as a struggle between two principles. It may appear in the form of a conflict between his desire to write and his commitment to the revolution. First he sacrificed literature to politics, and then, after a long introspective and autobiographical period, returned again to literature. In recent years, as in his first years in Belgrade, the conflict is not acute, and thus he is able to combine all three—literature, politics, and autobiography. But when political events press upon him, he puts away his other work and takes up his pen in the struggle for a better world. This dualism, present in his autobiographical works, is also found in his fascination with the Montenegrin legend of Tsar Dukljan and in his decision to translate *Paradise Lost*. Another form it assumes is in the way he sets duty to one's kin against duty to society, as seen in two of the short stories included here, "War" and "The Collapse of Hell."

Another element of continuity is Djilas's optimism and his belief in life. Although an avowed atheist, he does not suffer from existential angst, or despair over the futility of man's efforts. He identifies intellectual or artistic creativity as being that which is alive in man, that part which makes man human. For him, to be alive is to create; to create is to make something beautiful; and through beauty the creator lives forever.

There are other continuities. He remains concerned, in all that he writes, with social justice. He is a keen observer of the social order and its injustices, whether Communist society in the fifties or Montenegro at the turn of the century. Closely related is his use of settings that he knows intimately. The familiar detail and the known locale in his description of time and place is an essential element of his style. In both autobiography and fiction, he writes of his native Montenegro, of Serbia, of Belgrade.

Continuous, too, is the lyrical quality of his writing. Though his early lyricism gave way to the flat measures of Marxist political prose, his later narratives resume a certain musical quality.

There is also change in Djilas. He has shifted from external subjects to introspection, and when he returned to external subjects his writing was stronger because of the incorporation of autobiographical elements. He moved from shorter works to longer, more complex forms. And, like many an author, poetry was a product only of his youth. But when viewed over the span of his writing to date, the elements of continuity appear the more important, even though he has, of course, matured in both style of expression and depth of experience.

The political, revolutionary Djilas is not a person apart from the literary, creative Djilas. This is clearly seen in the conflict throughout his life between politics and literature. Beyond that, there is no obvious correlation between his evolution as a social thinker and his development as a creative artist. In some respects, from the vantage point of the present, the twenty-year hiatus in literary work appears as a momentary halt; and yet, had he not taken that detour, he would be neither the man nor the writer he is.

In composing this volume, the editors have tried to present Djilas as he was at each stage of his revolutionary and literary development—the young and the mature Djilas—and his metamorphosis from romantic revolutionary to advocate of evolutionary social change.[11] The book is divided into six parts, which do not adhere to any rigid chronological scheme, though within each of the sixteen chapters his ideas are, on the whole, presented chronologically.

The primary purpose was to illustrate the development of Djilas's thought on political organization. This is of interest not only in itself, but also because the revolution was his principle activity for more than twenty years. The man today cannot be understood without understanding the metamorphosis of his thought on the crucial issue of social change and the perfectability of man.

Each of this book's parts corresponds to a major segment or interest of his life. It is not Djilas the political man alone who interests us, but Djilas the whole man. Thus there have been included, not only items

11. In Marx and in the works of some other Communist revolutionaries it is often possible to distinguish between the romanticism and idealism of their "youthful" writings and the pragmatic commitment to more specific, realistic goals in their "mature" period. Their goals are tempered by the realities of the world and human imperfections. In Djilas's case, romanticism and realism are often interwoven. In the young Djilas there is an important component of the romantic revolutionary, and though his romanticism is pushed into the background during his years of high office following the victory of the revolution, romanticism re-emerges even stronger in the years following his fall from power and his imprisonment. In fact, it may even be argued that without romanticism he could hardly have retained his sanity or survived nine years in jail, especially his twenty months in solitary confinement.

from all periods of his political career, but also examples of all forms of expression (poems, stories, diaries) from all periods of his literary life.

Over one-third of the book consists of items previously unpublished. These include "Nordic Dream" (an essay written just after his party trial), an early draft of *The New Class*, extensive excerpts from his "Jail Diary," a few brief excerpts from "Diary of Thoughts," a short story ("The Collapse of Hell"), a "final" assessment of Stalin, and several articles of a political nature written since 1968.

Another third consists of items previously published in Serbo-Croatian between 1928 and 1954. (None of his work has been published in his own country since January 1954.) Many of these are from prewar and wartime publications and are not readily accessible even to the scholar.

The remainder of the book consists of items that have appeared before in English. Fourteen of these—the articles that brought about his downfall—originally appeared in *Anatomy of a Moral* (1959), currently out of print. They are included here, with some cuts, and with the addition of one major article in the sequence—"Objective Forces"—which was omitted from *Anatomy of a Moral*. Another eighteen selections appeared, mainly following Djilas's release from jail at the end of 1966 in widely scattered European and American newspapers and magazines. Many of these articles have subsequently been revised by Djilas, and the most recent versions have been given.

Except for the first part, where the materials are mainly drawn from certain of Djilas's books, because that is where he discusses his roots and values most extensively, relatively little has been included from his important books available in English. Thus, this volume will serve to supplement those books.

In selecting the excerpts to be included, the editors were acutely aware that they could not satisfy all potential users. In particular it was necessary to make some compromise between the interests of the general reader and those of the East European political specialist. The interests of the latter would best be met by complete translations of entire articles; while most general readers would find the long-windedness of Marxist political analysis tedious. The editors attempted to resolve this dilemma by cutting passages from certain long articles so that portions that contribute to the understanding of the development of Djilas's thought could be included. This is especially true of the political writings, and particularly those contained in the third part. It was necessary, therefore, to provide titles for the excerpts selected. In general, in such instances, phrases from the text have been used as titles.

For quite different reasons—namely, the loose and disjointed character of the "Diary of Thoughts" and "Jail Diary"—extensive cuts have been made in the excerpts included from those sources. "Diary of Thoughts' (brief notes from 1954 to 1955) and "Jail Diary" (an extended diary of the years 1958–1966) —unusual documents, with a wide range of reflections of a philosophical and personal nature—come to 1,500 manuscript pages. All cuts are indicated by ellipses in brackets. It should be noted that Djilas himself uses the device of ellipsis extensively in his writings; ellipses *not* in brackets were present in the original texts. Footnotes appearing in Djilas's original texts are indicated by numbers. Notes added by the editors are signified by asterisks.

It is, of course, always difficult to excerpt and edit material in this manner. Despite every effort, there is the inevitable danger of distorting the author's meaning. Except for the third part, cuts have been minor.

It is for his concept of a new class that Djilas is best known. As the selections in this volume abundantly illustrate, this is not a notion that came to him suddenly, but one that evolved over a long period of time and that finally, when he was under extreme pressure, exploded into the book of that name.

Although he first wrote about the bureaucracy as early as his 1932 story "Wheat, Wheat, Wheat . . . ," he was aware of the rich tradition of antibureaucratic satire in Russian literature. The themes of the personal limitations of petty bureaucrats, the needless red tape, the inexorableness of the bureaucratic machinery, and the suffering endured by the common man as a result are to be found in many of the Russian works Djilas read in his youth, including the social satire of Nikolai Gogol. His antipathy to the bureaucracy also appears in his "Letters of Comrade Veljko to the Montenegrin Partisans," his call to arms in 1941. Of course at that time it was the old bourgeois bureaucracy that Djilas feared could creep into the new "people's committees" of the national liberation forces. After the victory of the revolution, however, the same criticisms were found to apply to the more complex Communist bureaucracy, too. In fact, soon after the war of national liberation had been won, Djilas had his first inkling that all was not well in his new, socialist world. At home, he found that even Communists were behaving like bureaucrats. Abroad, the Soviet Union, the complete bureaucracy, threatened Yugoslavia's very existence. Thus the subject of bureaucracy rarely left Djilas's mind. He proceeded along two tracks. One part of his mind was evolving his analysis of the nature and consequences of the bureaucracy in the Soviet Union.[12] The other part was perturbed that socialism was not develop-

12. His criticism of Soviet Communism has, to be sure, influenced Soviet views of Djilas. His unorthodox ideas about the development of socialism in Yugoslavia aroused Stalin's ire as early as 1944, and on the eve of the Soviet-Yugoslav split in 1948, Stalin and Molotov, in letters addressed to Tito and Kardelj singled out Djilas as a deviationist to be removed from the Yugoslav leadership. Djilas, ever the loyal Communist, offered to resign to prevent a split. Tito rejected the idea and kept him on.

ing its full potential in Yugoslavia. Gradually the two tracks converged, and he came to see that socialism failed to develop in his own country because of the party bureaucracy. He attempted to prevent that bureaucracy from solidifying its position, as had happened long before in the Soviet Union, but his efforts were quickly brought to an end by the entrenched party.

How shall we appraise this man? Djilas is a political figure, an author, and a man of ideas. Though he has dedicated his life to no single realm, he contains within himself qualities found in some of the great Russians.

Like Alexander Herzen, the Russian revolutionary of the nineteenth century, Djilas did not hesitate to change his views, even at the cost of losing the allegiance of his friends and supporters. Although Herzen and Djilas arrived at the same conclusion—that revolutionary violence might be less effective than gradual reform in improving the lot of the common man—they reached it by different routes: Herzen through theorizing and revolutionary journalism of a high order; Djilas through revolutionary activity that led to his becoming part of the ruling elite. Both Herzen and Djilas were viciously attacked by their former comrades, who, in order to defend their own theories were ready to make man submit to the revolution even if it brought in its wake suffering, inequality, and tyranny, the very things it was supposed to have eliminated. Unlike Herzen, Djilas chose to remain in his own country and to fight for his ideas there rather than seek a safe haven abroad.

Like Leon Trotsky, Djilas sensed that the greatest danger for Communist revolutions would be the bureaucratization of the party and the consequent emergence of, as Djilas put it, "a new class of owners and exploiters." (Djilas notes that, like a good Communist, he did not read the works of the heretic Trotsky until much later in his life, well after he had completed his own analysis in *The New Class.*) The conclusions he drew were different, however, from Trotsky's; and unlike Trotsky, he

---

Following the break with Russia, Djilas was one of the major defenders of the Yugoslav path to socialism. After *The New Class* was published, Soviet propaganda singled him out as one of the most dangerous enemies of the Soviet Union, and following his writings on the Soviet invasion of Czechoslovakia in 1968 and publication of *The Unperfect Society* the next year, *Pravda, Izvestiia, Literaturnaia Gazeta,* and the Soviet radio labeled him "the king of anti-Communism," a "puppet" of American ruling circles cast in the role of the "ideological teacher for American youth," and a "rekindler of the cold war." Sergei Trapeznikov, in *Na Krutyh Povorotah Istorii* (1971), a Soviet book on Marxist revisionism, ranks Djilas among the six most important contemporary revisionists in the third era of Marxism since 1956. (The others are Herbert Marcuse, Ernest Fisher, Roger Garaudy, Ota Sik, and E. Goldstuker.) Possession of Djilas's works, especially *The New Class,* in Russia, is said to bring a jail sentence of three years and exile to Siberia. Ukrainian dissident Danylo Shumuk received a fifteen-year sentence in the fall of 1972 for circulating *The New Class.*

was not exiled and hounded by secret agents, nor did he feel resentment (disappointment, perhaps, but not resentment) toward his former comrades.

The greatest literary influence on the young Djilas, and the one that was to continue throughout his life, was Fedor Dostoevski—the writer who so movingly described the tragedy of prerevolutionary Russia, the personal sufferings and psychological torments of both the common man and the intelligentsia. While in solitary confinement for twenty months in 1956–58, Djilas rediscovered Dostoevski, as he reread his works and found in them a deeper significance. Perhaps his admiration for, and to some extent identification with, Dostoevski can be traced to their similar experiences. Both, from their early childhood, had observed the misery of the common man and the financial crises of their bourgeois families. Both became interested in social protest; Dostoevski read utopian socialist literature, Djilas read Communist literature. Both were arrested and sentenced to prison for so-called revolutionary activities by their autocratic governments, tsarist Russia and royal Yugoslavia, respectively. Both understood the tragedies that befell their countries because of the inability of autocratic systems to resolve social ills. In response to these unresolved problems, both began to search for solutions: Dostoevski through his writings, in which men and women of all social strata sought to resolve their conflicts by physical or psychological means; Djilas by abandoning the literary road and embracing, as his hero, the man of action, Lenin. After twenty-five years, while in jail, Djilas in essence abandoned Lenin and returned to many Dostoevskian ideas. Whether it is Dostoevski defending tsarism and the Russian Orthodox faith in his mature years or Djilas criticizing and rejecting the totalitarian aspects of the system he helped erect, their underlying motivation is the same: the search for truth, faith in the common man, belief in progress, defense of humanism, and the realization that no social order can be perfect.

But perhaps the closest resemblance between Djilas and a living person is to be found in the writer Alexander Solzhenitsyn. Like him, Djilas is deeply imbued with the Slavic tradition. Their work and its impact has been different, but there are certain similarities in their subjects. It is not for nothing that they have the same enemies. Both are concerned with the sufferings of the common man under tyranny, whether the tyranny of war or of pre- or post-revolutionary regimes. Both are men of unshakable principle. While in quite different positions at the time of their confrontation with those in power (Djilas a top-ranking politician, Solzhenitsyn a Nobel laureate in literature), they both chose to oppose, rather than succumb to party dictates and remain silent or tell lies about the system in which they lived. They have used similar arguments to defend the freedom of artistic creativity, and they both have faith that the forces of good (truth, beauty) cannot be permanently overcome by the forces of evil (totalitarian governments). Though Solzhenitsyn was forced into exile, both believe it is best to remain in their own countries, for they believe that their creativity would wither if they were utterly cut off from the nourishment of their native lands.

Djilas is unique in that there are few statesmen who are also men of letters. He has been both, and consequently combines the qualities of a humanist-writer and a pragmatist-statesman.

This is Djilas, the rare revolutionary who wanted his utopia to work but who, when he realized that it would not, had the courage to admit it and to seek new answers; and who, having lost faith in the perfectability of man and human institutions, was still compelled by some humane inner imperative to continue the struggle to improve man's lot. This is Djilas, the creative artist who wanted to be free to write in peace and thus to learn what man is, because to him it is the creative in man that is truly human. This is Djilas, the humanist, whose roots lie in Slavic soil but whose concerns are universal, devoted to man's humane potential and dedicated to establishing conditions for its fuller realization.

I
ROOTS

It was misery that led many to take up the Communist path[. . . .]

It was neither Marxist literature nor the Communist movement which revealed to me the path of Communism[. . . .] It was classical and humanistic literature that drew me to Communism.

Land Without Justice, 1958
(Trans. Anon.)

1
Family and Nation

A man can abandon everything—home, country, land—but he cannot abandon himself, that by which he lives and by virtue of which he is what he is. [. . .]

There are times when an idea, a faith, in the face of all possibilities, achieves the impossible. [. . .]

Every man has something to regret before he dies; but a man would not be a man, he could not survive, if he were to sacrifice his ideals to mere existence. It is hard to be a Serb, but nice. A fine death is greater, less burdensome than life. [. . .]

I am a Serb, a Montenegrin. [. . .]

We are small, we are weak. Worse and stronger enemies have trampled on us, but we have never given them our soul, nor have we ever surrendered the Serb Idea.

Small and weak. But everything is not numbers and force. . . .

Montenegro, 1962
(Trans. Kenneth Johnstone)

The Men of Katuni

Being a Njeguš, from the first glimmer of consciousness Njegoš belonged not only to a proud and militant clan, but also to that bastion of Montenegro and its freedom—the Nahi of Katuni.

The Nahi* of Katuni was for Montenegro the same beacon that Šumadija was for Serbia and the Piedmont was for Italy. But it was also quite different from these. The Piedmont was a state, while Šumadija was a formation of free and nationalist peasants and merchants. The Nahi of Katuni was a collection of clans united solely by the struggle against the Turks, and then only somewhere from the seventeenth century on.

* *Nahi* is the Turkish word for an administrative district.

25

The clans of Katuni were certainly among the first to refuse, or, better to say, to persist in refusing, to submit to the Turks. What alone is certain is that they were the first to achieve a position in which they could finally offer resistance to the Turks. Other clans followed suit, mostly out of self-interest, in the struggle that the men of Katuni had already begun. Clan after clan had broken away before, then reverted to the Turks, and rebelled again. Just how and when this took place is not known about many of them. However, once the men of Katuni broke away from the Turks—at the end of the seventeenth century—they were never to return to their sway. [. . .]

They nurtured an inner spiritual implacability toward the Turks. They did not clash with the Turks solely for transient causes—high taxes or acts of violence. They were a different, opposite world—another conception of the world and of life. In their craggy heights, bleached by sun and storm and bereft of everything that a body needs, ceaseless struggle with the Turks was not only a way of life, but a cult. They not only believed in the myths of their religion and nationality; they lived by them.

One could cite, and we shall, a whole array of reasons why it was precisely the clans of Katuni which first finally broke away from the Turks, why it was among them that the myth crystallized into ideas and realities—into a program of action. [. . .]

The great myths—a doomed Serbia, the flight of its nobility into the Montenegrin mountains after the fall of the empire at Kosovo, the duty to avenge Kosovo, Miloš Obilić's sacrifice, the irreconcilable struggle between Cross and Crescent, the Turks as an absolute evil pervading the entire Serbian nation—all these myths took on their sharpest and most implacable aspects here, among the men of Katuni. Here these sentiments went beyond and above all others. Obilić and Kosovo were not something that happened some time ago and far away, but they were here—in daily thoughts and feelings and life and struggle with the Turks. It was a struggle against extermination—for the survival of the clan—one in which faith and nationality, the Cross and freedom, were more perfectly merged than in any other province and anywhere else in the Balkans.

The men of Katuni and the Montenegrins of those times lived peculiarly in their myths. These were not only beliefs, but national history—its continuity, daily life. It is not important that their history was not like that, not actually so. What mattered was that they completely believed it to be such, and acted accordingly.

The men of Katuni, Montenegrins, were sharply defined in all things, and with finality.

Those were the beginnings, and they were always decisive.

But it was not only the myths, the ideas, that came to their highest expression there. Most of the folk epics—at least those Njegoš first heard and later collected—came from the Nahi of Katuni. Nothing reveals as clearly as they do the mentality of his immediate homeland. They string together events and thoughts, one after another—all very much alike—without embellishment, without color, stark and almost crude in their brittle monotony. It is not really poetry at all, just as the men of Katuni are ethnically neither a nation nor the kernel of a nation. But there is the basis for an imperceptible poetry, spare of fantasy and movements, a bare recounting, the carving out of vital and mythical truths, better to say, of vitally mythical truths. [. . .]

It was among the men of Katuni, more than anywhere else, that heroism was bound to become the highest virtue. Njegoš's cult of heroism was not fabricated, but borrowed—as was practically everything else of his—though refined and idealized. It is of a special kind—not only bravery in battle, but also humaneness and resistance to all evil; especially humaneness: to kill without torture, to raise weapons only against those who bear weapons, to take but not to steal, to forgive but never to ask for mercy. Marko Miljanov called it *manliness*—and that is the most exact expression for it—but Gesemann, being unable to translate it, called it *humanitas heroica*. It is a contradiction: to kill and to be humane, to do evil while fighting evil. In Montenegro, in the Nahi of Katuni—and is it only there?—this was both logical and commonplace, reasonable and just: the struggle for survival, but based on ethical principles.

As a ruler a Montenegrin, by heritage a Serb, in ideology a Yugoslav, and in his ethics a universal man, Njegoš was to remain to the end a man of Katuni in his personal character, and especially in the finality and implacability of the truths that he uttered and that set him afire. His language, though interwoven with strands of other Montenegrin dialects, was that of the Katuni clans. So was his manner of expression, however personal. He, too, did not expend more words than he had to, and he recounted only what he could not resist telling.

The men of Katuni swear by God and their *gusles,** but they are not given to long prayers and chants. Nor can they be. Storytelling is like fighting. They tell tales aplenty, but these tales are also realities—"balm for the soul," with little of the imaginary. That is how they are in other things, too: reserved and withdrawn in their personal lives, poor in land and cattle, but not stingy, intolerant, or intemperate, rather, given to great ideas and to the struggle for their unrealizable realization.

The land is one of destitution and forlorn silence. Its billowing crags engulf all that is alive and all that human hand has built and cultivated.

---

* A *gusle* is a traditional south Slavic one-stringed instrument which is played to accompany ballads.

Every sound is dashed against the jagged rocks, and every ray of light is ground into gravel.

The stranger is deceived by the aspect of the land. The Russian Captain Egor Kovalevsky, who came at Njegoš's request to look for precious metals, while his government sent him to collect intelligence on the side, made a note on the view from Lovćen: a sea of stone, and then, not without bitterness, he added, "For the Montenegrins the road is everywhere," for there is really no road at all. Thus have said the English and others, down to this very day. For Pierre Loti this was a desert, a terrifying scene from the moon. In speaking of his region of the Kuči, Marko Miljanov blurted out just the right expression: *a crucified wilderness.* That is Montenegro, that is the Nahi of Katuni: a wilderness and a sea of stone, but one lifted high upon a confusion of peaks, gashed by canyons and gorges, and gouged by gaping precipices burrowing into stone cracked by heat and frost.

It lacks the serenity of the desert or the spaciousness of the sea. It has some of both—but the silence is stony and the spaciousness is overhead in the endless heavens.

It is plains and vales, terraced fields and stone huts—even more cramped and lost here than in the rest of the Karst. The trees are gnarled, stunted, choked in thickets, cut by man, exposed on bare limestone—neither oak, nor hornbeam, nor beech, but only dry grass, brittle, hardly green at all—a fantastic dream world. A painter of that region, Petar Lubarda, turned that stone into great art. And he found stone in everything—in the human form and beneath it, in that sky which is snagged on the crags and crests, and in the air charged with a violent storm waiting in ambush behind the clouds. Even here man has penetrated with his roads, fields, whitewashed walls. But all this, along with himself, soon gets lost. All is stone. Even all that is human is of stone. Man himself is made of it—without an ounce of fat, honed down by it all and with his sharp edge turned outward on the whole world. Every evil assails him, and he uses evil to ward off evil, on soil where even the wild beast has no lair.

Once, perhaps not so very long ago—some two hundred or three hundred years past—the rock was covered by forest. It was certainly because of this forest that the whole region—and later the country as a whole—got the name of Montenegro, or Black Mountain, first recorded in the year 1435 in the treaty between the Despot Djuradj Branković and Venice: "The Katuni of Montenegro." Jovan Erdeljanović has shown through traditions and place names that the region once also had water. Humid groves lined the silver of the streams: across the plain of Cetinje there meandered the river that gave it its name; deer and mountain goats roamed the clearings and the heights. But the men multiplied. And the evils multiplied. In fighting the Turkish bane the clans also destroyed the forests and the meadows. Those same powers of sun, wind, and rain which once brought their bounties to the land now helped to bring it destruction. There remained the gashed, the ever-wounded stone, and handfuls of rubble on the hillsides in choked abysses. There remained the sand viper and the raven—and man, who survived in all this, sang new incantations and invented new charms, thought great thoughts, founded a state, and began to rally together a race which had been downtrodden and scattered over the Balkans.

How populated was the Nahi of Katuni when it inaugurated Montenegrin, Serbian, freedom? It is reckoned that in Njegoš's time Montenegro—all four nahis plus the numerous Piperi and Bjelopavlići clans—contained something over one hundred thousand souls, and that it was capable of sending twenty thousand soldiers into battle, inasmuch as everyone fought who could lift a rifle. The Nahi of Katuni could hardly have had over some twenty thousand souls—unlettered, without a municipal and administrative center, scattered over a space of barely one county, and isolated by the lack of roads, by ravines, clan hatred, superstition and misery, lawlessness and anarchy. This is where our national myth was crystallized, this is where our national history began.

As we said, the men of Katuni were not the first to rise up against the Turks. The clans of the Brda, the Highlands—the Nikšići, the Kuči, and others—were more warlike in the sixteenth and seventeenth centuries, and their irrepressible rebellions even splashed over into Old Serbia and the region of Užice. But the men of Katuni were the first to maintain their victory and to make the contest a final one. They were certainly always at odds with the Turks, or else they would not have declared the idea of final liberation and a war to the death. The ideas were few and the passion one, but everything about them was tough, keen, final. It was they who stamped the Montenegrin state and Montenegrin entity. Though Serbian to the core, the Nahi of Katuni alone was not to accept unification with Serbia in 1918 until the very end. It had made history too long by itself to permit others to make history for it.

History does not choose the easy way.

In the time of Njegoš, the Nahi of Katuni had not a single town, and not even a horse trail along which a caravan might travel without difficulty. It was Bishop Rade himself who was to lay such a road—from Cetinje to the Crnojevići River—and also establish the first hostel—at Krstac—to receive the traveler en route from the gentle coast to the skyward cliffs, into a state whose capital consisted of one monastery and three or four buildings, and whose government consisted of a monk and several shepherd chieftains. [. . .]

The houses were divided by a lattice—one half for the cattle, the other half for humans. [. . .] The Senate building in Cetinje, the "Little Zion," which Bishop Petar had constructed, was partitioned by a wall, so that the senators, the government, entered on one side, while the horned cattle entered on the other. Njegoš was angry at the irrepressible Vuk Karadžić for recording this. [. . .] When Vuk Karadžić came to Montenegro, at the beginning of Njegoš's reign, there were no pans, and what bread there was was baked in ashes. There were no trades. [. . .]

How could there have been any wealth when in many parts of Montenegro all trade was by barter? A little land and cattle, a bit better food—that was wealth.

Everything was meager and sparse, from day to day. There was honor and glory in fair measure—and nothing else. [. . .]

When the Turks came to Montenegro, they encountered tribes [. . .] in Montenegro as well as in Northern Albania. And it was these tribal collectives that came into conflict with the Turks. [. . .] Circumstances and the strength of the tribe dictated whether it was capable of taking further steps toward independence or whether the Turks would be successful in imposing serf relations upon it, thus destroying it as an entity.

The tribes of Montenegro, especially of Katuni, had that strength—all the more so since they were of a different faith and tongue and way of life from the Turks, and because they had someone on whom to lean for support—on Venice—in an epoch of ever greater wars and other troubles which assailed the Turkish Empire. [. . .]

It was in the tribe, too, that the national consciousness developed and grew stronger, thanks primarily to the Church—the only surviving guardian of the tradition of the medieval Serbian state. It is important, perhaps even decisive, that this church had been autocephalous from the time of Saint Sava. [. . .] Only as such could it become the bearer of national consciousness and a state tradition. [. . .] The resistance to exorbitant taxes and to serfdom was transformed into a religious and national movement. [. . .]

The only thing that could destroy the Montenegrin tribes was extermination or internal dissolution. The Montenegrin tribes, or at least the majority of them, were not yet ripe for the latter at the time of the Turkish invasion. The tribe in Montenegro contained within itself, in its blood ties, inexhaustible powers and vital forces which one not nurtured by them can hardly suspect. In addition to these forces, here and there in little remote and isolated monasteries, there flickered the memory of the medieval Serbian state, feudal, but our own, which the inchoate and disintegrated feudal masses transformed into a myth and epic of ancient glory and hope.

It was a prefeudal form, the Montenegrin tribe that encountered and survived the Turks. Its primeval strength and power, now inspired by a myth which emanated from the people and a concept of statehood propagated by the Church, expanded in ever greater circles to include individuals and movements beyond itself: the First and Second Insurrections in Serbia, Karadjordje, Hajduk Veljko, and Vuk Karadžić as well. This amalgam of tribal strength, the concept of the state, and the myth was greatest where the tribe had been best preserved, and where other conditions were also favorable—in Montenegro, among the tribes of Katuni, in Njeguši.

As was so often the case with Serbian states, the tribe of Njeguši found itself on the crossroads between two worlds—West and East. As ever the Serbian people, so, too, the Njeguši found their own way. They made secure their way of life and molded our history. They were situated on a likely spot for this; besides, they were themselves resourceful and resolute. History favors the bold and the wise. It also seeks the line of last resistance. It only breaks through the weakest, most rickety gates. Here, around Lovćen, was the Turkish Empire's point of least resistance. The Njeguši found their own way—through strengthening the bishopric and inaugurating the governorship—in order to cut into a festering tumor. This was the doing of all the men of Katuni. They were fighting only for survival, but they began a new epoch in Serbian history.

True, there is no evidence that the Njeguši tribe excelled in any way over neighboring tribes. Yet they certainly enjoyed an advantage. For one thing, they were the closest to the Venetian towns on the Bay of Kotor—only some four or five hours away—and they were the farthest and the most remote from the centers of Turkish rule. It may thus be concluded that they were in the best position to break away, to get out into the world and to look farther. It was across their lands that trade and goods from the sea went into the interior of Montenegro, and with them gold and Venetian influence and the stream of a more civilized life. [. . .]

The Njeguši were themselves aware of their significance. Had they not ensured for themselves a continued succession to the bishopric and to the governorship? [. . .] They were like all the other tribes in that they plundered others, defending their own, and avenged their dead. But they differed in keeping for themselves the two most important posts of joint rule. Vuk Karadžić has recorded that within each tribe as well the chieftaincy became hereditary, and that the elections were more in the nature of confirmations, inasmuch as the most powerful clan always stood behind the chieftain. But the bishop and the governor were not tribal chieftains. The bishop and the governor were elected at an assembly of Montenegrin chieftains. And it was the Njeguši who first succeeded in having these joint rulers always come from their midst, thus making both positions quasi-hereditary. Though a tribe like any other, the Njeguši, primarily out of their own tribal interests, to be sure, became the strong hub of inter-tribal interests as well. Consequently nowhere was the idea of a common struggle for the liberation of the Serbs more determined. [. . .]

It was from the Njeguši tribe—from the commingling of tribal emotion and Serbian consciousness, from a feeling for myth and the mythical past as immediate reality—that Njegoš's poetry grew, just as his state was a link between the tribal order and the idea of the medieval state that the Church had nurtured and kept alive. When Njegoš called all the Serbs "a tribe, my tribe" he did this with a completeness of feeling that left no room for anything else, that knew of no other community but this blood kinship. It was this idea, plus folk poetry and state necessity, that elevated this tribal feeling into a passion and spread it throughout the entire nation.

Njegoš was a Serb, but a tribesman. It would be most exact to say that he was from the Nahi of Katuni, of the Njeguši, a Serb of the Petrović brotherhood—and especially this last.

For though a Njeguš by tradition, and to a degree in feeling, he could not, he was not able to, belong entirely to his tribe. Tribal willfulness and exclusiveness had already become a hindrance to the further struggle against the Turks and to the establishment of a central government. [. . .]

All who ever visited Montenegro in the time of Bishop Rade have confirmed the great piety of the Montenegrins. But hardly any of these visitors noted that this godliness did not have much to do with Christian dogma or even with church ritual. There was little of worship, and even less of dogma. [. . .]

Njegoš was generally uncongenial to dogma, while the Montenegrins were too primitive and too infected in earlier epochs not to be superstitious. Not only their superstitions, but even their Christian beliefs had the quality of magic. As for Njegoš, his lack of dogmatism, however personal, also reflected his milieu. So it was even with his uncle, Bishop Petar, a great ascetic and later a saint, but in whose numerous epistles one can hardly find any mention, and then only parenthetically, of Christ, the Mother of God, or a saint.

Yet Bishop Petar and Bishop Rade and the Montenegrins all had constantly on their lips the name of God—the one God, the Almighty and the Creator, who is in and acts on all things, the power and the law above all. Otherwise, the two bishops were rationalists—religious rationalists. They wished to introduce civil order into the land, and they were hindered by "old wives' tales," belief in magic and superstition. In his epistles to the Montenegrins Bishop Petar instructed and entreated them not to believe in such nonsense, while Bishop Rade poked fun at it in his works. Petar's understanding of God emanated from his faith and the Church, while Rade's was philosophical and poetic. But with both of them that understanding was, so to say, Montenegrin.

Alongside their belief in magic and superstition, the Montenegrins did believe in one God. They even expressed familiarity with him, in the thought that God's power was limitless, but it was here, in us. Lacking bells, some Montenegrins signaled the beginning of church services by firing rifles: Let our God hear us, one way or another. This magic and at the same time rational conception of God—magic in feeling and practice, and rational in consciousness—was very strong and shows profoundly and more completely than anything else the piety of the Montenegrins, and of the two bishops, Petar and Rade. Only, with them, and especially with the latter, this magical intimate relation with God became rational— more of a conception than a belief.

However, as soon as it was translated into practical life, especially in the struggle with the Turks, the Montenegrin faith showed to what degree there was something basically un-Christian, something even contrary to Christianity, in it. Anything that might impede this struggle disappeared from the Montenegrin religion, if indeed it was ever there. There is not a trace of nonresistance to evil. The Montenegrin can understand and can do everything except turn the other cheek. Montenegrins are the only Christians who not only act out of revenge, but also believe in revenge as if it were the most consummate joy and the highest justice. Revenge is one's pride before men—a mystical dedication. One Montenegrin has said for them all: "Christianity was born in blood." It is a saying among them: "What we have not fought for we have not earned."

The Montenegrin God is a God of vengeance—not just that, but that above all else.

The fasts are strictly kept for the good of the soul, and the feasts are observed—especially the folk holidays, Christmas, the day of one's patron saint, and All Souls' Day. But there is little of prayers and processions, and what there is of these, the people do not put much store in. A Montenegrin once crossed himself while passing a garrison in Kotor, thinking that it was a church, and when this was pointed out to him, he replied calmly, "Well, the Devil has taken so many of my prayers, let him take this one, too!" Another Montenegrin, on buying an icon, did not wish to buy the one of his patron saint, Luke, because he was portrayed as barefoot and unimposing, and he preferred Saint George: "Give me that hero over there; and my Saint Luke forgive me as best he can!"

That faith and that God were also among the inherited obligations of the boy Rade—toward the cosmos and toward man. Having grown up quickly, he understood them all the sooner. And he was to join together all of these obligations toward his land, his people, and the brotherhood, through song, thought, and deed.

A handful of men stood fast in Katuni, and the blood of the Petrovići boiled—on a bare crag surrounded on all sides by a Montenegrin and Serbian world that was suppressed, divided, and bloody.

Only Lovćen stood above the darkness.

Lovćen's peak was close and unforbidding. On its gentle slopes the herds grazed mornings and evenings. From its heights one could see what the Njeguši could only feel: mingling of the sea breezes with the mountain air, the gentle and the sharp, the clash of two worlds. Here colors met and blended into one another like realities and hopes. The rock and the sea. Evil and good.

The sea that lapped one side of Montenegro was in the hands of the Latins, while the rock that melted into the Plain of Zeta was in the hands of the Turks. Between them rose the rough green-tinged wilderness of the Nahi of Katuni and the rest of Montenegro—embattled tribes and tributaries; all thinking the same thought, speaking the same word, and feeling the same pain in their breasts. Beyond Katuni, which lay at the foot of Lovćen, the chieftains of all the tribes had gone to the Turks and even now were flying their banners and taking their bribes to wage war on their own brethren and to fetter them in alien bonds. Everywhere darkness; only Lovćen blazed. Karadjordje had been driven from Serbia, while Njegoš's uncle Bishop Petar had been driven from the Littoral. The Serbian lands spread sight unseen, but even the skies above them were crowded with their misfortunes.

It was this land—Montenegro—small and troubled, across which Turkish and Latin cannon called out to one another, which bore the pledges of the whole Serbian race and universal greatness in its midst. It was a bad land, but a heroic one, accursed, but ours.

So it was. Such was life. This is what was handed down from one's ancestors—from the first to the last.

Njegoš, 1966
(Trans. Michael B. Petrovich)

The Radenović and Djilas Families

Mother's father, Gavro Radenović, had come from Plav, from the village of Meteh; his people were called Metešani. My father would say in anger that the Radenovići-Metešani were Albanians, but this was not true. The Radenovići were Serbs from time immemorial. [. . .] Despite all migrations and massacres, they flourished; they have maintained their homestead to this very day. The Radenovići became blood brothers with surrounding clans, which had become Turkish. Only their perseverance and heroism, and the protection of the Šabanagići, renowned begs of Gusinje and Plav, whose tenants they were, kept them alive. Gavro fled to Podbišće with his brother after killing some Luković Moslems. He had settled in Podbišće long before my father. It was there that my father met my mother's brothers and my mother, whom he came to marry at the beginning of the century.

Mother's kin differed in everything from the Montenegrins. [. . .]

In contrast to the Montenegrins, or the highlanders, the Metešani were a proud people, but unostentatious. They were loath to take up quarrels over words, but they were prepared to devote inexhaustible effort and invincible heroism to any issue involving something real or intolerable. They, more than the villagers, thought and lived in a world of reality. Such, too, were their dress and speech—rough and without much color. They had neither the *gusle* nor heroic songs. And their women were different. They lived more at home and were withdrawn. They never scolded, unlike the Montenegrin women, all dangerous shrews who, once they begin to abuse others, can never stop. The Metešani did not beat their wives, or at least they did so only rarely. With them a man did not regard it as shameful to take a woman's place in any task. [. . .]

Mother, too, was different from the Montenegrin women. She was cleaner, more industrious, more domestic. She closely resembled her father and brothers—tall, big-boned and fair. Unlike her husband, she was taciturn and unimaginative. Only when she boiled over with anger did she utter a sharp word, and then never a vulgar one. Yet she always made her point. She never quarreled with anyone in the village or with her in-laws.

My father, on the other hand, was a tireless talker with a boundless imagination. Talking was his great and inexhaustible delight, and he could not live without imagination. He found it easy to get into a quarrel. It was obvious that, especially for his environment, he was a man of great and remarkable intelligence and capability. He was not acquisitive, one of those who always talk of making money and never do, nor was he a spendthrift. He spent money only in moments of great decision or sudden opportunity. But his ventures all proved to be unrealistic and profitless. He had irrigation ditches dug, with crushing effort, but the water would not flow. He built and planted where seeds would not grow. He would buy a new property only to sell it all one day in senseless anger and bitterness.

Father was sick with the love he bore his children, especially his first-born son. Though he never beat his children, he would talk and talk to them, giving advice or cursing in anger. Mother beat the children whenever they became too much for her, but without cursing or scolding. Her brief and wrathless beatings were easier to take than Father's endless counsels and curses. Mother's love was barely noticeable. She loved and did things without either offering or seeking love and gratitude. Her wisdom was simple, unobtrusive, but real and somehow instinctively infallible whenever it appeared.

The roots from which a human creature arises are many and entangled. And while his growth is unfolding, a man does not even notice how and whence comes the wholeness of his personality. The component parts become lost in it. He is derived from various strands, but he also forms himself—rearranging impressions from the outside world, inherited traits, and accepted habits, and thus himself having an effect on life about him.

But who can comprehend it all?

Man does not leave behind the world he found. Though he rose from it, he himself has changed it, while also becoming changed within it. Man's world is one of becoming. [. . .]

My father shared something with both his brothers. He was garrulous like the older brother, and quarrelsome like the younger. But he was more garrulous than the former, and less quarrelsome than the latter. In everything else he was different.

He belonged to that first generation of Montenegrin officers who had any sort of education. But education or not, they remained peasants in their way of life, in their speech and behavior. They all lived in villages, in houses that were somewhat more handsome; they dressed in fancier clothes, and ate better, but they, too busied themselves with their cattle and land like all the peasants, hiring help only for the heaviest tasks— plowing, digging, and mowing. All of these half-educated officers, teachers, priests were easily identifiable in Montenegrin hamlets before the last war. On market days they talked about politics in the coffee- houses, sipped brandy and disputed endlessly about Russia and England, the Croats and Belgrade. They still voted as tribes, always discontented, and dressed half in national costumes and half in city clothes, a new shirt under their gold-covered tunics, or a coat. [. . .]

Who is there to say from which of these strands I sprung? It was from an environment of peasant civil servants, more peasant than anything else, like so many Montenegrin intellectuals of my generation.

Our household was completely peasant, but it lived a better, a more civilized life—if one can use that term—than the average peasant family. There was always coffee and brandy in the house for Father and guests; there were unmatched plates, but nevertheless plates, and coverlets of down and blankets, and even comforters. There were always fleas, and frequently even lice, though Mother waged ceaseless war on them. In winter the cattle were kept in a manger on the first floor, and during warmer days the laden air of the manger was overpowering. I did not wear any underpants until I entered high school, not because of poverty, but because of custom and our way of life. It was a long time before I could get used to their slippery softness.

Though we engaged hired hands and sharecroppers, Father himself always worked on the land, and Mother labored like other peasant women—even more, for the increased demands of her educated children all fell on her shoulders. She was illiterate to her sixtieth year, until the last war, when the death and revolutionary activity of her children impelled her to learn what was becoming of her family and her country.

During my father's border service the so-called Kolašin affair erupted. Some officers were condemned for plotting the violent overthrow of the Prince's absolutism. My father, too, took part in the arrests and the search of the houses of the accused, but he pretended not to see one bomb he found. There were executions and horrible deaths in the Kolašin affair. But the most horrible memory was the whipping of the arrested men with wet ropes. People condemned this even more than the executions. Until that time no one had ever beaten Montenegrins during an investigation, except for robbers in their own country and then only by their own authorities. Their human dignity had never been affronted by beatings. They have now become accustomed to others trampling on their human pride, but they have not changed their opinion about those who do so.

The War of 1912 found Father on the border, charged with the duty of inciting border clashes that might serve as an excuse for war. One dawn he led his villagers in an attack at Pržišta, which dominated the approaches to Mojkovac. The struggle with the border guards was a very bloody one. My father leaned a ladder against the sentry house, climbed up, and threw a flaming shirt on the roof. Some forty sentries were shot to death or burned, without a man giving himself up alive. In their enthusiasm, our side had underestimated the bravery and resistance of the Turks. There were many dead and wounded on our side, too—all young men, who died eager for war and blood and greedy for glory. There were among them children of fourteen, who had run to battle while their elders watched. [. . .]

There is much evil and sorrow in a national tragedy. If Father had not returned soon, it would have seemed as though there was nothing beautiful or tender in life. Only then was I able to get a clear picture of Father, though I long knew about him and had felt his constant presence despite the war and the distance that separated us. He arrived on a high and slender mare, himself slender in his gray uniform, all trim, in boots and with a revolver in his belt, the one he boasted the Austrians did not touch, though they met him along the way. Father was thin and gray and gaunt, like a wolf which runs and runs through the mountains. That slimness and lightness made him handsomer and more tender toward us. He yearned for his children and home with a desire that could never burn itself out.

He had spent the war in Albania, actually in occupied Metohija, constantly fighting rebel Albanians and, toward the end, the Austrians, who had arrived in pursuit of the exhausted Serbian army. In the struggle with the rebels, slyness and skill were needed as much as courage; in battles with the Austrians, which did not actually last long, one needed perseverance, for their artillery pounded away at our troops, rather poorly armed for battle against such an opponent. [. . .]

It was spring and a sunny morning in 1916.

Father was busy at something in his room. My uncle's son Peter, already a lad, flew in and shouted that the Schwabe* were coming. Father grabbed a revolver and threw it out the open window into a thick potato patch to conceal it. Then Father stepped out in front of the house to meet the Austrians. There were three of them. One was as orange as a fox and had a long fox's snout. He told Father that he was under orders to escort him to the command post in Kolašin, supposedly to give some information. All of us at home already suspected, knew, that Father would not return. But nobody cried. Our pain was cold and full of hatred and scorn.

Father got ready quickly, as though he were in a hurry to escape the tension that reigned about him. Perhaps he was thinking of acting as Vešović had done, rather than surrender. Maybe he was afraid of bursting into tears. He kissed us all, lifting us, kissed his mother's hand and waved to his wife, and then jumped on his horse. Peter, our first cousin, went with him a part of the way.

Neither of them returned. The Austrians kept even the gelding. The house was left empty, without Father, and we felt like orphans. Father was good, and handsome. We could not mourn him enough.

My older brother, Aleksa, whom Father had captivated by his constant attentions, wept inconsolably long after. Even at night he sobbed uncontrollably in his sleep, powerless to calm down even on awakening. I would find him under the ash trees in back of the house, sitting alone on a rock, wiping his cheeks with thin bony fingers, while the tears ran and ran inexhaustibly from his large, bleary, nearsighted eyes. His big, transparent, and cold ears were so sad then. I, too, wept, not so much over Father as over my brother. Father soon became a shadow—a substantial and real shadow because he was talked about at home—but one without warmth, whereas my brother's tears were tangible and inconsolable, somehow a part of himself. Our younger brother would join our weeping, even though he did not know what it was all about. He wept noisily,

* Montenegrin term for German-speaking people, in this case the Austrians who were occupying Montenegro.

bawling, but with just as much sorrow, even more sorrowfully, for he wept only out of grief for his brothers.

Now that Father had been led away to a distant foreign land, he became even more real and closer through his rare letters, written in a legible hand, and the little packages Mother would send him after saving up rendered lard for months. Now he was someone whose coming we awaited, and thus he became dearer and more precious. His picture was placed on the wall, only his, and it reflected both our sorrow and our hope. He was as though real in that picture, sometimes stern, at other times engaged in amusing conversation, all cleverness, or tawny and hunched up like a jackal in a forest glade. [. . .]

Then Father returned, even more spare and gaunt and graying than when he was taken away. He was still nimble, like an old wolf, from afar, hungry and tired. He brought with him the snow, thick and cold. The unexpected joy petrified us. My brother could not move his head from Father's breast, where he had buried it. And Mother, to hide her tears—for it was not becoming for a woman to show before others too much happiness at her husband's coming—ran out, into the woods. Only then did we realize that during all this long and tormenting time what we really loved in Father was unattainable happiness. He had been a marvelous dream. Now he was here. We loved him, but of the dream and happiness there was no more.

Father took joy in his sons and his house. But it was a worried joy. Had internment weakened and broken him? What happened to Father happened, in fact, to the majority of Montenegrin officers. He was an opponent of the unification, though he was hardly a fiery supporter of King Nikola. In the modern Serbian army he, a half-peasant, could not advance. He felt that his homeland was also thereby belittled. The sacred things of his youth were insulted—the Montenegrin past and name and arms. Some Serbians called the Montenegrins traitors and threw up into their faces that they, the Serbians, had liberated them. The Serbians sang mocking songs, one about how the wives of each greeted the Austrians—the Serbian women with bombs, and the Montenegrin women with breasts. All this gave offense and caused confusion. Those around King Nikola acted dishonorably in the time of tribulation, but the ordinary soldiers felt no guilt or shame. They died, suffered, and languished in prison camps.

Dissatisfied with the new state of affairs, Father nevertheless accepted service as gendarmery commandant in Kolašin. It did not help to think much about it; he found himself in the tormenting position of having to act against his thoughts and desires.

The course of history was changing, and one could not manage to warm himself at two fires at once. Choosing between conviction and a better life, most, including Father, decided in favor of the latter. Must it be so? Is this not a deliberate rejection of free thought, something that is peculiar to man alone, that which is most human in man? [. . .]

Somebody must have said something about it to Father. He hurried back home on horseback all alone, from Kolašin, arriving in the middle of the night. He immediately confronted Mother with the charge that she was in league with the rebels, all the while shouting and stomping about in his boots. Having gone back on his own convictions, with the blood of rebels already on his hands, Father now carried things to their extreme. Enraged, he drove Mother out of the house. We children joined her and found ourselves in the woods, out in the snow, wailing and in tears. After Father left, we all went back to the house as though nothing had happened. That is how it goes in quarrels between husbands and wives. The guerrillas continued to come, but more rarely and with greater secrecy. Now we kept this from Father, by tacit agreement.

Father did not convince even his own family, let alone his superiors and colleagues, that he had sincerely adopted the convictions his job imposed on him. He was transferred, then placed in the regular army, and finally pensioned. The same things happened to other Montenegrin officers. Their efforts on behalf of the new regime were rewarded, but they themselves had become superfluous. Like the others, Father returned all the more dissatisfied, not knowing what to do with his unexpended energy, as though he was no longer able to adjust to life.

So, too, old Montenegro was all out of joint. Her mountains and crags still stood, but she herself had fallen, sunken in hatred and blood, seeking but unable to find herself. [. . .]

Land Without Justice, 1958
(Trans. Anon.)

A Peasant Child

Even in a rich country in normal times the life of a peasant child is a hard one, spent in bitterness and even in peril. He frequently falls ill when there is none to heal him. He is constantly beaten by everyone, even at school, regardless of what kind of pupil he may be. Whenever I was switched across the hands, I observed how bony my fingers were and how lean my palms; my fists were like little birds.

The whole earth is engaged in a constant struggle, and the child is dragged into it from the time he first becomes conscious of himself. Men fight with one another, and the animals prey on each other. Poisonous snakes lie in wait behind every rock, behind every tuft of grass. The earth is sown with thorns and rocks. [. . .]

Aimless wandering through the mountains remains to me a memory of unspoiled beauty. The mountain draws a man to itself, to the sky, to man. There the struggle that reigns within everything and among all things is even more marked, but purer, unsullied by daily cares and wants. It is the struggle between light and darkness. Only there on the mountain are the nights so vast, so dark, and the mornings so gleaming. There is a struggle within everything and among all things. But above it there is a heavenly peace, something harmonious and immovable. The heavens impose the question: Who are we? From whence have we come? Where do we go? Where are the beginnings in time and space? No need to feel impatience or anger over the answer, no matter what it will be. Men on the mountain are an even greater mystery. And the stars are as near and familiar as men. The earth and sky and life become unfathomable, daily riddles that arise spontaneously, and that demand an answer. And so, forever, all must give reply. All, from the old man to the child. For the mountain is not for a tale, but a poem and for contemplation, and for purified emotion and naked passion. Life on the mountain is not easier or more comfortable, but it is loftier in everything. There are no barriers between man and the sky. Only the birds and the clouds soar by.

A summer outing in the mountains is for the young people, who yearn for the effort of a climb, to unleash their strength, and for the chill nights and mornings to bathe in freshness. On the mountain everything is rough and raw, but clean as in a song or a maiden's embroidery. Life seems to shift from man to nature. Even human life becomes all enveloped by the sun, by the verdure and the blue, drenched by them, less ashamed of its passions, less withdrawn, like a herd of horses galloping freely across endless pastures in a time when they had not yet been subdued by man.

One goes to the mountain also for a holiday, to rest the body and to give free rein to the mind, to play and thus to melt into nature and the universe. The beauty of the mountain is not merely in the clean air and diamond-cold water, which cleanse the body within. Nor is it in the easy life. Its beauty lies in that ceaseless and all-pervading effort and exertion, which are not really oppressive. Stern in appearance, the cleanliness of its waters and air overpowering and yet invigorating, the mountain nevertheless dances in luster and color, and forces all creatures, above all man, into dances of spirit and body that are guileless with all their boldness and abandon.

On the mountain there is something for everyone—for the young, brightness and play; for their elders, sternness and constraint. Sorrows are more sorrowful there, and joys more joyous, thoughts are deeper, and follies more innocent. The cattle immediately come to life there, as though fattened by the freshness; they become playful in the fenceless spaces. Like a river or a city, each mountain has its own life and own beauty. Mount Bjelašica was special because its streams and grass reached to its uppermost heights of wide and rolling meadows. She was warm in her coldness and gentle in her steepness. Her air was as chill as on the heights of a glacier, yet the sun shone as hot there as on the villages in the valleys. In her pastures one found a bower and a haven.

Every clear evening in the middle of the pasture a huge fire is lighted; around it dancing and singing surge up. The fire is not lighted because of the cold, but to radiate joy and light, to enliven the mountainsides and peaks, and to join the youths and maidens in their mad gay dance. In these camp meetings, in their dances and songs, there is something irrepressibly savage, something just barely and invisibly kept from tearing loose from human bonds and from reverting to a primeval wanton and joyous madness such as man had never known. When the fire and the dancing subside, shrieking and laughter break out on all sides, and then begins a wild chase and commotion. Impassioned youths dart after the maidens, pinch and embrace them. The maidens grow even more resilient and elusive than in the dance, as though the darkness has jerked them up short into a life of strict rules which decree that they can dance and joke in public but must be virtuous and unapproachable in private. The widows, who sit before their huts listening all aquiver to the dance and who lose themselves gazing at the frenzied motions of the shadows against an endless sky, creep into their beds beside their children, crushed by an onslaught of emptiness and bitterness. All seems to die, in a twinkling, but constrained hearts still beat loud on the hard bedding, bright and sinless thoughts sprout and spread, while murky desires burn out and smother one another. A little longer—and then the morn. The first cock brings peace and the dawn and daily cares and tasks.

Even without the mountain the village boys and girls learned much about love life from coarse and unabashed jokes or by watching the pairing of animals, especially cattle. Whenever cows were coupled, the girls or young women who brought them retired, while the lads made a point of bringing the bulls while the girls were still there, making rude jests the whole time. There were games that were even ruder, such as jumping on little girls and on heifers, games of which the boys and girls were themselves later ashamed. The children began to play them while still quite young, but these were games. The mountain, however, seemed to evoke in children a foretaste of the passions that were much later to flare up.

I was ten years old. I had already completed elementary school and was preparing, inside myself, to go to the city. It was as though I had reached an understanding with my childhood to end it there in joyous exertion. That summer I spent in the mountain, with the cattle, I had to get up early to drive the animals to pasture. The mornings were oppressively bright, but the fresh heat and quiet of the day was welcome, and so was the deep slumber and oblivion of the night.

Kosa was a hired hand, a strong and sturdy mountain girl with a rough face but gentle yellow eyes. She was good-natured, gay, and tireless in her antics with the boys at camp meetings. I watched over the cattle, while she did everything else. She was one of those busy bees who managed to do everything and yet have a good time. We slept together, in a cramped lean-to next to my aunt's large hut. Even before then I liked Kosa, who was always gay and good at everything. But it was on the mountain, that summer, that I fell in love with the enticing warmth and softness of her body. Each time she would return from the campfire, still in a sweat, she would lie down beside me, nestle up against me, and place my hand in her bosom, glad that she could uncover herself next to a boy. The moonlight cut through the beams like flashing swords. I lay there aroused, unable to fall asleep again. I felt a secret delight—I did not myself know why—spring from Kosa's body, which now seemed like a part of my own. Never before had I felt such a sensation. But, neither the mountain nor Kosa helped. With that delight and knowledge of her body came also shame, and so, roused out of my sleep, I lay there taut and motionless. Yes, Kosa was impassioned; she was embracing the boy and getting the boy, instead of some older fellow, to caress her. Or maybe she was hugging me as she would a younger brother? And then again maybe . . . ? She, too, was awake and in motionless silence. And I could not, dared not, do anything but tremble inside and quiver, powerless to solve the riddle of her body and her desires.

Everything else, as well, is revealed on the mountain and becomes simpler and clearer.

Down below, in the villages, tribal and clan divisions were already beginning to fade. The mountain, however, had been divided from earliest times. It was known to whom every peak and spring belonged, as well as the pastures and meadows. The tribes no longer fought over their valleys, but the shepherds still fought over their grazing lands, made up mocking jests and howled derisive songs at other camp settlements. [. . .]

On the mountain one also felt still more the difference between the poor and the well to do. The poorest of the poor had no cattle whatever of their own, but hired themselves out to herd the cattle of others as sharecroppers. The huts of the poor were small, and their cattle always nestled against other people's cattle. They were thinner and weaker, as though they knew whose they were. Among the poor even heroism counts for less. They did justice to a heroic bull, but a man they were apt to forget. [. . .]

The mountain is not kind to such poor heroes, only to those who are strong in everything. She gives, but she also takes. Only those who are strong in everything can survive in her and even grow stronger. One always longs sadly for the mountain, for its strength and purity, for the endless beauty of its peaks, whose colors blend and die in one another until all sinks in a bluish mist. The mountain has aroused new perception and feeling, though perhaps she did not do this herself. As everything within man is first expressed as an experience and a picture of the world, so such emotions are bound with the mountain and remain in us, in me.

Land Without Justice, 1958
(Trans. Anon.)

2
Values

The outlawed revolutionaries and the broken remnants of the revolutionary organization were waiting for answers and decisions from me, and only me, while I, in man and tree, in pool and stone, in the sky and in the grass, was searching for the childhood and youth preserved in my memory. [. . .]

That reality, that link between me and the world, was one facet of my being, my thoughts of Spain the other. I could not and did not want to deny this. [. . .] I knew that there is no other world but this, but my world and my dream of it and my memories were real to me and equally necessary to my life. I would do my duty; I would not forget Spain or the men fighting in the forest. [. . .]

My sole intention was to do my duty toward the outlaws, and my sole desire was to rejoice in the lake. At any moment I could have moved away up the mountainside toward my duty, but I did not want to leave the woods and waters before I must.

"Woods and Waters," *The Leper and Other Stories*, 1964
(Trans. Lovett F. Edwards)

Two Faiths

The Proof of God's Existence

In this land one believed more in fairies, witches, and vampires than in any idealized and inscrutable Christian or any other god. God was only a phantom who was good to the good and bad to the bad. [. . .]

In the third grade we had to learn, quite thoroughly, the entire church service, as though we were being trained for the priesthood. Father Jagoš Simonović [. . .] could not stand having his subject only superficially learned; on the other hand, neither did he want to give failing grades in a subject such as catechism. [. . .]

Once, before the entire class, I engaged in a discussion with Simonović on this very point—that it was not important whether or not one goes to church and prays, but whether one believed. I stubbornly stuck by my opinion. The rest expressed their agreement. Because I knew his subject but poorly, I drove Simonović's patience and made him angry. I felt that he hated me. This was not true, of course. But I caught him in his weak point—impatience. I wanted to take revenge on him. The revenge came spontaneously, all by itself.

A good student in everything else, I had a failing grade in his subject. It was generally known that in this subject no one ever received a failing grade on the second try at the examination. However, because I had publicly belittled the subject, it was obvious that the priest was going to flunk me unless I knew the material. In the course of three or four days I learned everything and applied for re-examination. The priest was quickly convinced that I knew the subject. He was obviously pleased, but he was offended because I did not look at him while answering. I found him distasteful, with all his feeble advice, imagined eloquence, and nervous fussiness, and so I made up my mind not to look at him. He caught me by the chin, lifted my head, but I would not look at him. I even shut my eyes. He began to shout, to scold, but all in vain. He even tweaked my ear. If God is inevitable, why was this servant of His so impatient and overbearing?

Simonović was, actually, only a typical Montenegrin priest—true, educated and sound in dogma, but accustomed to having the younger generation and his inferiors submit to his will and his conceptions. Both then and later, he was very active in the political arena. After the dictatorship he belonged to the party in power, and was even one of its local leaders. During the war, however, to everyone's amazement, he made common cause with the Communists and, though he had bad lungs and was sickly, he endured to the end through all the difficulties. True, his nationalist teaching, not his religious, proclaimed that one must always and unconditionally fight against the enemy forces that are occupying the homeland, and this he carried out. Just as Simonović consistently defended his religion, his vestments, prayers, and incense burners, so in war, he consistently defended his nationalist beliefs.

We grew, and so did the religious problem, for everyone in a different way, but ever more serious and complex for all.

If God exists, why are men so cruel to one another, so selfish and wicked? If God does not exist, is not all then permitted?

It would have been senseless to pose such questions to Simonović, even if they had been sufficiently formed in us. Whether unable to reply or, by chance, indisposed to discuss them, he simply silenced us.

Archpriest Bojović of Berane, whom we had from the seventh year of high school, was just the person for such discussions, not only because he taught us Christian dogma and ethics, but even more because of his

personality. Bojović was extremely reasonable and well read, and elo-
quent as well. Had that been a time for great church preachers and the
country receptive, his fame as an orator would surely have gone far
beyond the borders of his diocese. In speaking, he sought, and found,
vivid and memorable phrases. His speech flowed like a clear brook, or
like honey, as the folk saying goes. In addition, he had a pale and worn
face and was known as a completely chaste man and as one who never
intervened in local political squabbles and intrigues. Confidence and
warmth were inspired by his fine features, seemingly chiseled by inner
suffering, and his small trimmed beard.

Rare was the one among us who doubted the existence of a power that
exists in all things as a law. In other words, we believed in God. More
important for us were the proofs of the existence of that power, and for
these we searched everywhere. Archpriest Bojović was not angry or even
amazed when we demanded proofs of God's existence. He apparently
regarded it as quite natural, especially from young people. He answered
calmly and reasonably, his proofs, in the main, similar to those of
Dostoevski. Mercy, which inevitably exists in man, is proof of God's
existence. The argument was very moot, but convincing—for those who
wished to believe. Man himself feels what he can and what he cannot do;
there exist within him certain moral restraints. That is God. The proof of
God's existence must first be sought in man, in his inner ethical categories. The very existence of these categories proves that something
inscrutable and foreordained regulates man's destiny. These and similar
proofs offered nothing new; their strength lay more in the way they were
presented—in a beautiful and patient and, if one may say so, noble
exposition. [. . .]

Archpriest Bojović's explanations were completely in harmony with the
youthful disposition for justice and mercy. He could in no way have
directly influenced the trend in favor of Communism. Yet he inspired
great thoughts and feelings concerning justice and mercy, which, in
addition to other factors, of course, especially, insofar as I was concerned,
the surrounding reality, led toward Communism. That was strange, for
the Archpriest's arguments were designed to turn others away from Communism and every form of violence. But the desire for justice, equality,
and mercy gave rise to reflection and efforts to create a world in which
these would be a reality.

Later, I always felt within myself that I owed an unpaid, Communist
debt to Dostoevski and to Archpriest Bojović, a debt I did not dare
acknowledge even to myself. Were not the first impulses toward Communism those arising out of a desire to put an end to the world of force
and injustice and to realize a different world, one of justice, brotherhood,
and love among men?

Whereas Simonović demanded that we accept what he told us as a representative of the church, Archpriest Bojović never demanded anything, not even that we believe in God. He thought that men must believe in something, in any case, and he regarded it as his task, and the task of every man, to encourage others to be persistent in their faith, that is, in mercy and justice.

During the civil war Simonović found himself on the side of the Communists. This was unexpected for those who did not know him well, especially in view of his previous political affiliations. Actually, firm in his nationalist convictions, he was really being true to himself. Archpriest Bojović remained apart during the war, not actively helping one side or the other, and certainly must have wavered, like the rest. In keeping neutral, he, too, was being loyal to his own principles.

To be sure, life itself had a stronger influence than any preachers on those who were disposed to oppose brute force. [. . .]

If religion is unable to better human relations, nor are so many wars and rebellions able to do so, is it perhaps because nothing at all can be done? Still, men do work at this and succeed just the same, even if only a little. What will be the force that will bring about the great transformation?

Young people—each in his own way—pose questions and seek answers. It would appear that the solution lies in this constant search. But everyone wants to find nothing less than the final solution in his own time—especially those among young people who are dissatisfied with the state of affairs they find, and who are sufficiently strong and serious to look social reality straight in the eye.

Land Without Justice, 1958
(Trans. Anon.)

Communism—a New Idea

Every man, especially a youth, yearns after various paths in life, and frequently he is forced to take the very one he never quite felt to be his own.

I was the only one of my schoolmates who quite definitely regarded himself as a Communist, even in the eighth grade. But I wished to be a writer. Finding myself even then, and especially later, with the dilemma of choosing between my personal desire and those moral obligations that I felt I owed society, I always decided in favor of the latter. Of course, such a decision is a pleasant self-deception: every man wishes to portray his role in society in the best possible light and as the result of great personal sacrifice and inner dramas. Yet it is true, even where this is so, that a man who rejects self through a struggle nevertheless does only what he has to do, conditioned by the circumstances in which he finds himself and by his own personal traits.

It was neither Marxist literature nor the Communist movement which revealed to me the path of Communism, for neither the one nor the other existed in the backward and primitive environment of Berane.

There lived in town a Communist—the brother of a merchant, an agent for the Singer Company. They called him Singer, too. The very fact that he lived in eccentric solitude and read a lot was enough to draw suspicious attention to him, though he was not active in any way. When I tried to approach him, he seemed to become frightened, and though he promised to give me something to read, he never did. He was the town wonder, but dead and powerless, like a fountain without water. Later, when a Communist organization was formed in Berane, it ran afoul of the passivity and exaggerated caution of this man, who believed that it was wiser to do nothing illegal, and that it was sufficient to meet legally and to talk. He was, of course, an opportunist and a liquidator, and was rejected and crushed.

Ilija Marković, who came as an instructor in 1926, attracted me most of all, even though he was not an open Communist. He might have been between thirty-five and forty years old. He was gaunt, tall, with an unwholesomely flushed face, curled lips, and bad teeth, extremely large beautiful dark eyes, and a high, tranquil and thoughtful forehead. He was gentle and yielding with the girl pupils, he lectured well, though somewhat carelessly, and he conducted examinations in the same fashion. He engaged in few friendships, but read a good deal. He gave no sign whatever of any organized Communist activity. He did not engage in any. His whole activity consisted of intimate conversations. As a university student he had belonged to a Communist organization and had been active. He was one of that generation of Communists which replaced the first, postwar one, and which developed its own character, neither too militant nor quite conciliatory, in the semilegal circumstances of the dictatorship.

Neither Ilija Marković nor Singer influenced my own development in any decisive way. They did not even enter into conversations about Communism with me. I was too young and too inexperienced for them, and perhaps they were afraid to engage in such dangerous conversations at a time when the royal dictatorship held sway with a severity that found less reason in popular resistance than in its own lack of self-confidence, from which arose its determination to establish itself firmly and to frighten its powerful opponents from the very beginning. [. . .]

With me, at first and also later, the dictatorship only intensified my somber state of mind and discontent. It was the cause both of my spiritual wanderings and of my dissatisfaction with social conditions. It seems to me that it was precisely these repressed dark moods, this psychologizing, that provided the base for a political and social discontent which was all the more profound because it was moot and unconscious—out of the very fabric of the soul, out of every pore of one's inner life. Later, in Belgrade, when I became acquainted with my fellow students at the university, I noticed that they, too, each in his own way, to be sure, had traveled the same path—the same literature à la Dostoevski and Krleža,[1] the same inner crises and somber moods, dark discontent and bitterness over cruelty and injustice among men and in society generally. Hence also a certain contrived, concocted attitude, rather pretentious and no less disheveled, unstrung, and rebellious.

It was classical and humanistic literature that drew me to Communism. True, it did not lead directly to Communism, but taught more humane and just relations among men. Existing society, and particularly the political movements within it, were incapable even of promising this.

At that time I was reading Chernyshevsky.[2] He and his clumsy novel could not make any particular impression on me certainly because it was so completely unconvincing and shallow as a literary work. He might have been able to rear a series of revolutionary generations in Russia, and to have a significant influence even in our country until modern times, but for the generation under the dictatorship he was without any significance. Such utopian musings, sentimental stories, and the like left no lasting traces. *Uncle Tom's Cabin* and Hugo's *Les Miserables* caused only a temporary impress, albeit a very strong one, which was forgotten when the book was laid aside. Marxist or socialist literature of any kind did not exist at all in Berane at the time, nor was it to be had. The only thing that could exert any influence, and indeed did, was great literature, particularly the Russian classics. Its influence was indirect, but more lasting. Awakening noble thoughts, it confronted the reader with the cruelties and injustices of the existing order.

Yet it was the state of society itself that provided the prime and most powerful impulse. If anyone wished to change it—and these are always men with such irresistible desires—he could do so only in a movement that promised something of the kind and was said to have succeeded once through a great revolution. The guardians of the *status quo* only made something like this attractive to a young man by their stories about the Communist specter and by their panicky preservation of old forms and relations.

This was a desire for a better and happier life, for change, which is

1. Krleža Miroslav, a Croat, was a novelist and Marxist writer who had a great influence on young Yugoslav intellectuals between the two World Wars and oriented many of them toward Communism.
2. Chernyshevsky was a Russian revolutionary who died in exile in Siberia in 1889, and whose work *What Is to Be Done* (1863) was accounted a classic by later Russian radicals.

inborn in every creature, and which in certain concrete conditions could not take on any but the Communist form. Communism was a new idea. It offered youth enthusiasm, a desire for endeavor and sacrifice to achieve the happiness of the human race.

Ilija Marković knew that I felt drawn to Communism, and that I was in love with a girl toward whom he had more serious intentions than those of a high-school student. I could tell by the kind and considerate way he treated me. This would have been gratifying, for it showed his generosity, had it not struck me as being a contrived pity, which I had never asked from anyone.

I was beset by questions that shook all of my previous moral, emotional, and intellectual conceptions. Was it honest for an older man, moreover a sick man, to entice—even with intentions of marriage—a girl of sixteen or seventeen years? And his pupil at that! True, there had already been marriages between instructors and pupils in the school. But such things were not done by the bearers of such great ideas as Communism, which was supposed to bring not only justice and an end to misery, but a new morality among men.

And what was I to do, if that is how it was? Was I to love or to hate this man? Was I to hold him in contempt or to admire him as a contender for the same ideal? The posing of these and similar questions did not at all affect actual relationships, but had vast importance for my inner life and further development. On the answer depended the growth of my inner moral personality. Of course, I answered straight away: There is no real reason to hate him; this would be selfish and unmanly on my part. Yet from this answer to a corresponding reality within myself there was a very long and painful path full of mental twists and turns and visions that could only excite moral repugnance and even jealousy. Feeling that I hated this man, I suppressed the hate.

I succeeded even in liking him, though without warmth, even more than was required by our tie, either personal or ideological. Through this I got over my love. That inner metamorphosis, which ended in my stifling within myself both jealousy and love, quickened my vague progress toward Communism and conscious turning to literature.

It was as though my adherence to Communism, too, depended on my success in mastering myself in this personal morality play. This was my first great sacrifice, in the name of nobility, even a pretended one.

My last year in high school was full of painful and complex inner conflicts. This was followed, finally, by a certain clarity, at least in the form of the question to write or to fight. Even then, future lines and tendencies made their appearance and left their mark in the midst of troubled psychological conflicts, social discontent, and an overtaxing nostalgia. From this moral and emotional crisis I emerged strengthened, with some bitterness inside myself, but with an ethical principle—that one should not hate men for personal reasons, and that one should not mix personal needs and problems with one's ideology.

At the end of the school year, on St. Vitus's Day, the majority of my schoolmates appeared with canes and tie. These were considered the signs of maturity of the graduating students. It all seemed to me too common and formalistic. I also put on a tie, but a different kind—a red one. I thought about it a long time before I did it, for a tie of that color was the badge of a Communist, and none dared to wear it. If I am a Communist, I thought, and I am, then I must be publicly true to that conviction. There was childish bravado in this, but also defiance at a time and in a place where no one was defiant.

There existed—and perhaps still exists—a picture of myself just after graduation, in a Russian-style peasant shirt and a sash, with my arm hanging over the back of a chair. I had recalled even before sitting in front of the camera, that Tolstoy held his arm in the same way in a certain picture and that he, too, wore a peasant shirt. I was consciously imitating him. The shirt—its cut and everything—was designed by me in imitation of Tolstoy, of the Russians. Later it caught my fancy, both for its originality and practicality, and I wore it as a university student. Despite such imitations of every kind, which I carried to an extreme, there was then, and after, and in these very imitations, a dark inner turbulence, a profound dissatisfaction with the existing state of affairs and with the limitations they placed on human and social potentialities. A vague inner spiritual and intellectual torment beset me even then and would not let me go.

Marković came up to me after the diplomas were presented, obviously as man to man because of Dušanka, and as comrade to comrade because of Communism. He walked with me from the school to town, telling me, sagely and gently, how in Belgrade, at the university, everything would be nicer and better: many new friends, a life of greater ease, a more progressive and developed environment. But there was no need either to console or to encourage me. I had already made my peace with many things—with sentimental love and with helping the world through charity. Things and human relations presented themselves in ever harder and harsher forms. It was still a land without justice.

I spent the summer in Bijelo Polje, where my family had already resettled. Bijelo Polje was similar to Berane in many ways, except that the Moslem population in and around it was more numerous. Its way of life was still patriarchal, its houses poorer, and the uncleanliness even greater. There was not even a dirt road to connect it with any other town except Plevlje. Here was a remote region, rich in fruit that rotted away unused, godless, filled with the halt and the blind. The rebellious and overweening Vasojević tribe had poured into the Lim plain and had taken over both it and the little town of Berane. Here, however, the

Montenegrins were interlopers who had forced their way into a town that was not theirs. The former Turkish landlords of Berane were hardly noticed, but here their adversity filled every little corner of life—their songs and stories, evening gatherings under the old pear trees, and the desperate nightly carousing.

But this did not concern me then. I was preparing myself for a new world, with my eyes already opened to comprehend it and with a troubled soul, fearful of becoming lost in it.

Land Without Justice, 1958
(Trans. Anon.)

The Lessons of the Past

Šudikova

Ours is only one of the ways of life that have been and that will be, that they who came before us knew and those who come after us will know. To reopen that way anew each time is to live, to create one's own world. Thence comes the irresistible charm of digging up the past and dreaming of the future.

I was young, had only just begun to know the world, when I first discovered Šudikova. Today I rediscover it, as a grown man, in prison, about to leave the world. Šudikova has been with me all that time, perhaps from all time, and will always be within me.

The ruins of the little medieval Serbian church of Šudikova are on a shelf of the River Lim about an hour's walk downstream from present-day Ivangrad (once Berane), at the very beginning of the Tifranska Gorge. No road leads to it, as if there could be no path between us and the past except that of the spirit. But the inquisitive traveler will easily find it if he keeps to the right bank of the Lim as far as the confluence of the little Budimka River and then clambers for about a hundred, perhaps two hundred, yards up the cliff above the Lim. He cannot make a mistake, for there is no other access to the Tifranksa Gorge. Like everything built by man, the little church nestles in a spot accessible to men.

Nothing, or almost nothing, of Šudikova remains, even in the inexhaustible peasant memory, except the fact that the Turks, no one knows when or why, razed the altar lamps of the Serbian faith, which in that remote niche must at one time have threatened their overlordship. Nothing, or almost nothing, remains to remind one of the life of the priests and monks and the gatherings of the pious. There remain only the foundations and the floor of the little church, made of the gray and easily hewn stone that abounds in the neighborhood and for whose working not much labor is needed. No one knows when the church was built. As far as one can judge, it must have been in the early years of the Serbian state, in the twelfth or thirteenth century, if not before, and the worn ornamentation on some of the stones shows that on that spot, for thereabouts, there was some sort of pre-Slav building. The shelf on which it is built is not much more than three hundred yards long, and only about half of that if one excepts the wide and gentle slope from the Tifranska cliffs to the river. Overgrown with thickets and brambles, it seems even smaller, powerless against the plants whose invasion heralds the hour when even the last patch of grass as well as the ruins themselves will be swallowed up, so that the men of the distant future will never discover it unless someone comes to its aid in time. The mighty oaks and elms and lindens under which men gathered still stand there; the Turks did not cut them down, for they could not take them away, and they remain the sole living symbol of the little church's spiritual existence.

In Turkish times the builders of Balkan churches and monasteries sought out hidden and out-of-the-way sites, suitable for solitary meditation, yet accessible to believers and open to the skies and watercourses. Šudikova—it is not even known what the name means—faces a ravine honeycombed with countless caves for hermits; below, is the chill green river, and beyond, the parish valley, which stretches away as far as the Koma Mountains on the horizon. It was not so much the builders' aim that the little church should catch the eye, as to ensure peace and freshness for its servants and those who came to visit it.

Sheltered by a wooded ridge, it is a nest that men, profiting by the natural conditions and their own skill, adapted to their compelling need for a world different from that of every day, a yearning for the eternal and the unchanging. Its only wealth is rest for the eye and for the soul.

Djurdevi Stupovi, the monastery an hour's walk away upstream on the farther bank of the Lim, was built to dominate the plain, so that the eyes and ears of the faithful could easily find it. Its prominence and size confirm the faith and power that lay behind it, but Šudikova, on the contrary, is withdrawn into isolation and deafness, as if men were not necessary to it and still less to its faith. Out of the way, small, and of impermanent material, it is in no way especially striking; its beauty is not in itself, but in the link between man's work and nature, and in the skill by which men found and built a retreat for their thoughts of eternity.

Man never knows in advance why or how some place or object means so much to him. As man becomes wise only after the event, so only later does he fall in love with certain spots, finding in them affinities that at first sight he has not noticed and even discovering in them ideas that by their very nature cannot exist. Man subsequently confirms the presentiments that first attracted him by something that only later he grows fond of and that will only then become significant to him. It is the old story of the lover who falls in love at first sight as soon as he has heard the beloved's name. [. . .]

The truth is this: years passed, five, ten, twenty, thirty, when I never even thought of Šudikova. But I did not forget it. Every time I passed along the road on the far side of the river, and over those years this happened many times, I looked eagerly for it till I could discern, on the harsh enormous cliff, its little green nesting place, and from time to time pictures from my youth burst forth mingled with musings about the inevitability and power of men to find spots suitable for their spiritual, bodily, and every other form of life. Therefore, Šudikova appears to me today as an experience and a vision, a picture and a thought, with fresh and unexpended force—and that is what I want to express.

But why, why should it have remained thus concealed within me? Surely it was the hidden and lurking sense of my destiny, my dream and my awakening? Surely somewhere in the vast expanse that I have seen in the course of fifty years there must have been something that could replace it? [. . .]

It is known that human life existed in the Lim Valley long before the coming of the Slavs, who began to arrive in the Balkans from about the sixth century A.D., and from the tenth century onward it was a cradle, though certainly not the only one, of the Serbian state and church. Tradition has it that the palaces of King Milutin were in the nearby village of Budimli—the King must have been glad to pass the summers there—and other villages in the neighborhood also have links with that famous ruler or with others of the Nemanja dynasty. Šudikova, small and out of the way as it is, must have been one of the oldest and certainly one of the more important centers of that early Serbian state. Since Turkish rule lasted from the end of the fourteenth century almost up to our own day, the church, razed but not forgotten, links and expresses the continuity of the Serbian people over almost a whole millennium. The similarity, indeed, is only apparent, and it is still vainer to expect its present aspect to reveal a picture of the downfall of the medieval Serbian state. [. . .]

Directly opposite Šudikova rises a harsh, black cliff on which is a fortress—Jerinin Grad—such as powerful men always build on the highways of human life, that in the name of their ultimate ideals they may maintain the lordship of their time and give a form to their society. Šudikova and Jerinin Grad are opposites, both in appearance and in position; on the one side asceticism and psalms, on the other armed men and force, both keeping watch over human existence. [. . .]

Church and fortress, as is well known, served in different ways a common end. They are two forms, two aspects, of the same society. But how great are the differences between them! Šudikova stands amid the rocky precipices for what it is—small, simple, fragile, something outside and beyond its mission in time. It is the expression of the inescapable and inextinguishable human longing to reveal the reasons for its own and man's existence, that by the linking of its transience with the unchanging and unattainable laws—with God as he was defined in medieval times— man should find consolation and tranquillity in this world of change and struggle. By its form and place Šudikova could only be an expression of its times. Just because it was that in all its heart and soul, it also expressed through its transience the inevitability of man's instinctive search for the eternal; it sums up in a single moment that linking of man's transience with the unchanging, that beauty which is outside time. [. . .]

The fortress, too, is petrified human existence, the same as the little church, but differently expressed. It, too, is beautiful—a single structure of stone and mortar on the crest of the sullen rock. Its beauty, too, is in the directness and obviousness of its intention; though its walls have now fallen, it seems as if it still lives to keep watch over men and their deeds. Faced with it, man feels his powerlessness, and it rises on the cliff displaying its onetime power over men.

Šudikova is spiritual life, as pure as it can ever be.

Every man must create for himself some way of life by the very fact that he is alive. And every man lives by it, trying to justify both it and himself and trying to link it with eternal law. Šudikova is an expression of that human inevitability, though certainly for a specific era. Its building was modest in every way, and the sound of its bells, lost in the tumult of the cataracts, was not often heard afar. But they summoned no one, only reminded those who lived there and the hermits in the caves around once again to examine their consciences, their actions toward men. Had they not indeed withdrawn from the laws to which men are subjected and which can only be attained by living and respecting the conditions of human life?

Every man must live in the spirit; no man can escape eternity—is not that the message of Šudikova? [. . .]

Šudikova is still a beloved and living survival of the people of this land. Unyielding and indestructible because true to itself, the small and disunited Serbian people stood fast against the invasion that flowed over three continents and reached the shores of two oceans, devastating lands and laying waste civilizations. And when everything had fallen, the Serbs still survived, isolated in their ideal, in the belief that the people and social groups, even individuals, were indestructible as long as they held fast to their spiritual heritage, which in the final analysis was identical with their choice of eternity and their sacrifice for the good of men.

Šudikova passionately and consistently held that view even before the Turkish invasion. Was it not for just that reason that the Serbs have survived despite the fire and stake of an alien faith and rule?

Nothing is repeated, least of all history, and it is not true that civilization inherits from civilization. Every civilization must begin with the essential needs of a specific human community and must disappear when it is rotten-ripe for destruction. Šudikova is the purest form of the early Serbian spiritual feudal way of life, which cannot be repeated and cannot be renewed. Nonetheless there is in it—and this is what makes one catch one's breath and clouds one's reason—some undifferentiated human continuance, human existence as such.

[. . .] What it shows to the greatest extent and which alone it believes to be true, to be the universal and revealed law, is in fact the purest and most cogent essence of its time and place and that the most consistent unselfish sacrifice is the guarantee of existence beyond its own times. Šudikova may also be the inspiration of an atheist who will find and build his own Šudikova. [. . .]

The rivers will disappear. How much more Šudikova? The stars will move from their courses. How much more human ideals? But man will always have to confirm and conquer his own life by renunciation. How else could Šudikova be beautiful with the beauty of a star imprisoned in the rock, and how could it resist those who by its destruction wished to assure their temporal power and lordship?

To its beauty, as to all beauty, there is neither end nor beginning. [. . .]

But there was something that linked these two worlds. The universal spiritual life of Šudikova, its withdrawal into its own soul, into the human conscience, and finally its renunciation of reality, seemed to open the floodgates to life and give a warning that in just this way are opened the sluices against oppression, exploitation, and stupidity. The human yearning of Šudikova for eternity, for the reconciliation of human relationships with the immutable laws of human life and human nature, was a summons to freedom and to surrounding nature, to the flower to burst into purpose and orange, to the earth to give it nourishment, to the river to seek new shores, and to the animals to increase and multiply without thought for the morrow. [. . .]

The Leper and Other Stories, 1964
(Trans. Lovett F. Edwards)

II
POETRY
AND REBELLION

All through my life I have wanted to study literature or, more precisely, to write novels. And whenever (and that was frequently) I had to choose between the tasks assigned to me by the Central Committee and the party and the attempt to realize that desire to write, I "denied" that urge. Such were the times; conditions never "normalized," and I hope they never will, for that would mean that the tasks of our party had ceased, the tasks in which we should seek and must seek happiness, meaning, joy and beauty in our lives. And thus, had I abandoned my comrades who fought for the creation of the party before the war, I would have been shirking my duty, in their eyes and in mine. Then the war came and the question did not arise at all. And after the war there were too many petty details. And then, above all, it was necessary to overcome the terrible danger that threatened the fruits of the revolution itself. It seems that only after the campaign by the leadership of the Communist party of the Soviet Union against our country and against our socialism did the most beautiful and most magnificent revolutionary era begin. For in these times it was more important and even more beautiful to "make" the revolution than to "describe" it.

Legenda o Njegošu, 1952

3
Tales in Prose and Verse

[. . .]
Man is a thing among things, the greatest lie among lies,
and he hunts vilely from day to day for a speck of wretched
　　　happiness and sun.
He lives only to deceive himself; and he deceives himself
　　　consciously in order to go on living.
[. . .] To die, to die, and finally to forget that you are the
　　　vilest thing among things;
and to know no longer that there is no bloodier irony for
　　　man than to be man.

[. . .]
My beloved, my trampled-down worms, my countrymen who along the
　　　dug-out city streets sing with your sledges,
　　　spades and hoes,
you will never know how much I, wasted, loved you at this
　　　pre-death hour,
nor how much your bloodthirsty song opened bottomless crevices
　　　in me.
Nor would you believe, I know, that despite the passionate hatred
　　　of man and all that he touched, even
　　　in his dream,
I would gladly die at the stake, with a curse and a song, for your
petrified hopes and for your palms and for your eyes in which,
　　　instead of life and heaven shines hunger.
Now sing, shout, dig, and rebel in the name of the only truth:
that man must not be a slave, not to God nor to man; not to the
　　　machine nor to gold; nor even to himself.

[. . .]
Sahara, Sahara, within four naked walls of a cramped little room
　　　in the attic of Cemetery Street Number 4 . . .

I do not see, I do not know, I do not hear anything,
only when by chance I lift my eyes
in the bloodstained half-darkness of the evening that burns behind
        the city, from bare walls quietly shine
two visions, two deaths, two skulls, two vampires upon this world,
two dark, malevolent, inexplicable grins from the figures
of Dostoevsky and Lenin.

"Sahara u meni," Misao, Vol. XIV, No. 5–6, 1932

Poetry

Tifran*

Eternity has rested on your shoulders. Time has touched you with its chisel. And there you are still, tall, powerful and proud. . . . You are as mighty as the Lord himself—sharp and rough like petrified pain. You are washed by the tears of entire generations. From a distance you look like a wounded white swan because your spotted autumn growth resembles drops of blood.

You give me new energy; energy not to lose heart, to keep silence, to conceal everything; energy to die—but never to beg at a stranger's door. Hey, is it true that you neither had anything nor wanted anything? . . . You forgot everything—and you became happy. Mother Nature rocked you away and left you to yourself.

As I stroll slowly every spring through dirty streets, hey, old man, I sell my heart, polluted with life. . . . Oh, give me your chest, broad and strong, yet quiet like the evening shadow! Give it to me! . . . It seems to me that then my soul would never again tremble with pain, I would live again a new, more beautiful life, and my heart would be joyous, full of radiance and happiness.

The River Lim, deep and green, washes your granite pedestal. Unable to kiss your peak, the river throws against you foam that blooms like a white poppy in the sun. Here and there you are painted with pines and shrubs, smiling patches of brown and green. . . . The pines murmur some forgotten, perhaps never-sung song; the shrubs, like an azure flame, lick your icy heart.

In the morning you bathe in the purple radiance of the fog. From afar the frozen dew glitters on your chest like a golden vest of days past. You drift, like a shipwrecked boat on a milky sea, on the wave of mist which

* A mountain in Montenegro near Djilas's birthplace.

sleeps in the valley. On your stony forehead the sun places a crown, golden and large as an evening cloud. . . . And thus you are dreaming, dreaming endlessly. My thoughts wander there: craving your dignity and your height, your sun and your heavenly expanse, deep and blue like a first love. I bathe my soul in the misty sea and return cheerful and clean like the first beam of the moon's light. . . .

The moon covers you at night with a dress of blue silk. You lose your roughness, sharpness and coldness as you wrap yourself in something soft and warm. Your old man's wrinkles vanish and the face of a child appears in their place. Then my soul is opened wide, soft and blue like your sky. I am happy when I can look upon your strength and the happiness of others.

I know that you are not aware how much I love you then, old man. . . .

Venac, Vol. XIV, No. 4–5, 1928–29

Day Laborers

To my teacher Mr. Ilija Popović

I. Morning

There are still many thin, dark threads of the night. The sun is far away, behind the hill. At the bottom of the sky, like the happiness at the bottom of the heart, dawn is spreading. The sky is pale, cold, dead. . . .

They had gotten up before dawn. Stiff, without enough sleep, silent, they sway like reeds at the edge of the marsh. Each man carries a hoe on his shoulders the way he would carry a son in his arms. They begin to dig. The soil steams, releasing a heavy, rotten smell. They are plowing the corn stubble under. And with it, day after day, they are plowing under their own days, too. . . .

The sun is nowhere to be seen. Only at the bottom of the sky, like the hopes at the bottom of their hearts, dawn is spreading. . . .

II. Noon

The sky is empty, desolate: no clouds, no birds, no butterflies. As if nailed, the sun peers down from the smooth, cloudless day. It scorches without mercy. . . .

Their shirts are all torn at the shoulder. Their shoulders, sunburned, redden like the dawn. Thirst . . . water is too far and time as dear as the master's gold. Their sweat drips into the fine, dry soil. And with it their strength, their hopes. . . .

The sky is without birds, butterflies or clouds. Desolate and empty souls without a smile. . . .

III. Evening

An incomplete moon, arched like ripe wheat, weeps over the meadows. The cold, damp night presses down upon the fields. . . .

. . . They already turn from their work. . . . They leave behind the soil upturned under a scorching sky to rest upon the hard floor under another's roof. Working, they awaited the moon, but the longed-for rest and peace will not await them. . . . Their hopes are as pale as moonlight reflected in pools of water.

The moon, like the unfinished smile in a young girl's face, glides across the sky. The night, like the sorrow that covers their heads, spreads over the fields.

Venac, Vol. XV, No. 1, 1929

A Child's Dream

Whose slim canoe is that, Mother,
　　　　　　　　　　floating down our river? . . .
I want to get into it
and float away somewhere:
far, into eternal peace, to the end of the earth . . .
—That is the young moon, my son,
that dives into the water
to charm the fish with its smile.

—For a long time I am dreaming about that slim canoe, Mother,
floating down our river.
Whose is it, and when, pray, will it carry me
to my heavenly dream,
to happiness and eternity?
—That is the young moon, my son;
it is stealing a kiss
from the daughter of the old fisherman.

—Isn't this, Mother of mine, the canoe from my childhood dreams
that is floating slowly down the river?
Return it back to me, so that I can get into it

and dive into happiness,
light, peace and glory.
—That is the young moon, my son,
come to take away
your sunny childhood dream . . .

Venac, Vol. XV, No. 6, 1930

Three Plants That Sprouted from My Dark Insides Under the Spring Sun

[*A supplement to the social poem "At the Estuary of the Sava into the Danube"*]

I. My father reads aloud from the newspaper a story of his son
Slowly, word by word, line by line, sound by sound,
the whole story fell firmly into place in the old man's mind.

Oh, that story, as painful and torn as a spring sky!
. . . How his son is in love with a sickly working woman from just
          outside the town
and wanders dreamily through the streets and cafés from dusk till dawn.
And then the words spilled warm and bright like rays of sun:
"She had an enormous, friendly heart under her coarse blouse,
and her hand, shriveled up from sickness and work,
a small gentle hand, like an apple branch just blooming, broken."
And she wrote long letters to the son, letters drenched with tenderness
          and quiet,
like a plain, well showered by waters, spring and sun:
"My beloved, are your hardened eyes still angry at the world?
And did you begin to believe in God and the crucified Christ? . . ."
And he wrote to her: "Maiden of mine, frail plant that grows in
          darkened depths,
not showered with sun, tender care or sleep,
I never believed in anything completely.
I am without color, without sounds or desires, forever a cursed dreamer.
I do nothing; thought long ago dried up in me.
I drag myself, not quite finished off, through the streets; or I go outside
          the town and lie upon the grass,
and shadows of clouds, sailing by, flood my misted eyes."
Later the girl died. She lay upon her modest bier smiling
as only those dead who loved during their lifetimes can smile:
loved God, and man, birds, clouds, poor people, and things.

And the son cried. And, drop by drop, with his tears, he died inside
   himself.

"My own son, my betrayed hope,
why is it thus?
I dreamt how you would bring home a rich girl,
ample, robust, ripe like a sheaf of wheat;
and how you would come here and I would roast a whole ram for dinner.
Your father was a brave man, he carried a rifle and a blade,
and slaughtered dreams, and lambs and men.
He believed in God, the Devil and Man—and you believe in nothing.
Your father dreamt no further than the plow and dagger.
And you? and you? Full of pain, dead, and soft, you walk along the
   streets,
and you have a delicate heart like the faint scent of basil and incense.
My own son, my faded hope . . ."

And the old man is sitting down to write many harsh words to his son,
to shower him with energy, faith, memories and strength.
He rubs his broken glasses on which had fallen a bright mist.
But all in vain, for the mist is still there, covering the unseen bottom of
   his soul,
and instead of words a single tear wrenches itself from the depths of his
   being.

2. And despite all that: the father wrote the letter to his son
I read in the newspaper a story about the death of my son.
That news touched my heart like the tip of a frozen knife.
Don't be a fool! Do you know what the peasants see in you?
You shall be their leader, their hope and salvation.
Every day they ask me when you will return to tell them about the world,
   about life and labor,
and I grow proud, I stand taller and I swell. My chest blows up like a
   mountain,
my hands, like the tops of spruces, thrust their fingers into the sunny
   sky.
Meadows and wheat fields are rippled by wind and fullness.
And the horse in the meadow whinnies wildly, waiting to be mounted by
   the youthful leg.
Come this summer, my son. Don't anger your father.
We shall go to the mountain and fell the slim, smooth trees,
and your young muscles will be tested by the sway of the scythe.
Leave your dreams for the children of rich people to soak their days in
   them;

you study, work and save. And grow robust, strong and powerful as a
          forest.
A descendant of those who lopped off heads, beat their women and defied
          death,
it is a sin and a shame that you get sick over a woman.
Over a woman . . .

3. And the son, late at night, mumbled over his father's letter
The city has sucked all the sap from me, oh my father;
the city sucked into its darkness my bloody shriek and my sunny cry.
The city wove into my dark soul countless roads and ties.
You don't know that here men breathe and think like objects,
they behave like houses, trams, streets, cafés and numbers.
Each one goes into his corner and neither Man nor God can persuade
          him to come out.
No one can persuade him: your smile, joy, sickness, sin;
you can die for the palest human dream but he will pass you by, selfish
          and grim.

. . . despite the fields covered by grass
and the paths tracing like a silken thread;
the mighty fall of the trees and the wide, green trace of the scythe in the
          fields
and the spirited stallion with wild bursting energy—
I shall be dead for all . . . Then why all this?
Don't you know, father, that I died long ago
and that your vigorous blood is frozen in me?
Where shall I go? The peasants will say that I am the shadow of death;
and you shall suffer because of it. Listen, father, leave me alone to melt
          into the silence,
into the smoke of the cigar, the fog above the city
or into some misty bluish night that flows with the Sava River into
          emptiness and purposelessness.

As for the girl, that was more or less only a story
(a weak literary piece, banal and short) ;
I loved in her the budding being that was wounded by sickness, work and
          softness.
You know, father, what it means to love the knife,
the honest word, brandy and money; wild horses, ripe bundles of wheat,
          and women,
but you never loved a dying plant . . .
This spring not a single tender-blooded spurt gushed over my heart.

Nothing exulted me and nothing made me weep,
not even that letter of yours, spelled out slowly,
stroke by stroke, from your heart, drop by drop, sound by sound;
Bless you, father, if, from the emptiness within me,
you could extract, if nothing else, a stream of suppressed tears!

Outside the late night moans; along the sky, wires, roofs—in my dreams
in the flood of darkness, emptiness and deception press upon my torn
    heart.
I do not even have dead dreams any more. The sky is without stars,
    clouds or birds:
only the night, without the day, without the drop of hope and light.
I move into it. It beckons me! It already draws me into its depths!
(I hear the Sava River, through the night, softly whispering in the
    distance.)
Forgive me, father. Forget! Don't wait any longer for me.

Only one thing: Don't cry too loud, don't wake in vain the mountain
which, huge above you, ruptures and bleeds the evening sky with its
    peak.

                                        Misao, Vol. XIII, No. 5–8, 1931

Montenegro

Land of my birth,
dark, evil, painful,
we are still thirsting for hate and love.

You are not a woman with strong hips and breasts,
nor a lamenting mother in the rainy dusk, mourning
her only son, fallen on faraway battlefields.
You are not a wild animal that secretly in darkness searches
with its eye for a helpless victim;
nor a café in which outlaws come to spend the night on
the breasts of women;
nor are you a plain, soaked by water and baked by the sun.
You do not pray earnestly to God in the evening
or joyously wake the sun or give life to the dawn.
Born, we are alone—don't you know?—on a hot stone
from whose crevices instead of plants spring love and hate,
faith and life and—somewhere—a man.

Along our roads eternally travel the same days and nights,
wagoneers and outlaws, who sleep in the forest with wolves
and in caves with snakes.
Our only headrest eternal stone and pain and red-hot sky,
we did not have time to nurse from the mother's breast.
Blessed be our simple women: who milk cows, give birth to children,
suffer, love, and are beaten by their husbands.
And our men, harder than tempered steel, more austere and proud
than cliffs that rend the sky.

We do not know faith without doubt or sky without clouds,
or song without lamentation.
Cursed, afflicted land of mine,
no one will tell our enormous sadness,
not even the vibration of the maple gusle,
nor the angry sound of the knife-edge;
People will pass without seeing us; they will cover their eyes,
so that the soul is not scored by the sharp stone and faces of men
and women.
who bear in their loads of wood the hard life of the mountain people.
We suffer from hate and love and false dreams,
and are thirsty for life and silence in our mountain wilderness;
we seek only fresh green grass and a span of sky over us—
in order to release our soul.

Montenegro, insatiable! You drain me, instead of the drop of rain,
dreams, sun.
You breathe with me, suffer, wander, write in misty suburbs.
You are in me: with pains, cliffs, blood, sin . . .
And if it is destined according to your grace, and God's,
I will carry the cross and will become a poet in the faraway world,
instead of an outlaw in your canyons,
thirsty land of my birth!

Misao, Vol. XVIII, No. 1–2, 1932

A Tale

Men are sitting in the darkness and talking . . .
Old comrade Franjo repeats the same story:
We, the sailors, took over the ships in 1917,
arrested the officers,
replaced the captains,

removed the black and yellow flags from the masts
and hoisted the new ones,
large and bright like a bloody sun
which rose above the waves,
above the masts,
above the confused dreams of soldiers,
fluttering in aroused life
like the morning bird
shaking from its wings the midnight darkness and the last drops of dew.

Yet they deceived us with white flags
and shot many . . .

Great days. A great, beautiful story.
An old story, a little story,
always the same story—
(today new battles are being fought) .
Year after year crumbles,
dampness and semidarkness,
pale faces and eyes that spout embers.
The day looks like day,
the day looks like night,
the night seems like day.
The same heartbeats ring constantly like hammers tempering steel,
always the same circle, the same dream,
keys bark and bite like dogs,
keys beat on men's backs and awaken them
through the dim light and peace
through night and day.
Men sit in the darkness and tell the old stories
knowing full well.
that new lamps are not being lit,
that trains thunder,
that new flags burn like the sun,
that the earth gives way
under the trampling of millions.

Men heard that in Spain
men are fighting for life and death.
Men gasp, men think,
skulls are cracked:
thoughts, like moving columns, follow one another
in green lines across battlefields, thunder,
green uniforms are burning in the sun,

bayonets glisten.
Men are silent.
Men do not hear blows and curses.
Men think,
move, sigh and fight,
men see
how this dead house
of steel and concrete
trembles and crumbles;
bars are melting;
keys warp as if of wax.

Men are moving, tightening their fists,
flexing their muscles and expanding their chests,
getting up . . .
In the light of morning a flock of pigeons circles and swings in the sunny
    shower.

Men see and know
that the dawn is coming,
that they are not alone,
and that the fences that separate them from millions of others
are only fences of steel and concrete . . .

Published under the pseudonym Milo Nikolić
Naš Život, No. 5, 1937

Short Stories

Two Loves

I

—Will you have a good harvest, Tanjo? Is the house going to be filled
with wheat? . . .
—Thanks to the Lord, Stamena, it will be full.

Tanjo's soul is calm and serene. Only he is a little uncomfortable
because his shirt has split open at the seams on his shoulders and he has
to turn away a little when she approaches. He is not ashamed; she knows
that he is a poor man and what it means to be poor; but still, he doesn't
want her to see it. And she likes to stop by, to look at him, to laugh and
to continue on her way.

Tanasije now lifts his flail high, powerfully, as if to reach the sun. The
golden grains tumble in the straw, like tiny scattering stars. As each

kernel grew it ripened him in his strength and his heart. And thus, the falling grain whispers his happiness and weaves for him a fine, sunny day. . . . Poor and alone, he brought to life an entire world, bound to the soil, conceived in it. The soil brings deep satisfaction and devastating pain, each in its time. He knows that, and yet he believes that to leave the land, accursed traitor, would be like being deprived of a hand or an eye.

Tanasije (called by the nickname Tanjo because of its brevity, not out of fondness) loves that parcel of land in front of his hut as if his heart were spread upon it. It is small but luxuriant. It was given by the peasants in his commune because he was poor and alone. Tanasije curled up in it as if it were a soft warm bed. For a long time he had worked as a day laborer, and now it was about time to have a roof over his head and somewhere to rest. . . . This coming winter he will have enough food and meat for two persons. And enough hay for two, the cow and the calf that would spend all summer grazing in the shade. Only it is empty without a wife. He can't stand being without a wife. He sings about her, yearns for her. He is twenty-seven years old! He is ripe for her. It is not that he ought to get married, but he *must* marry. As a young boy he did not even dare think about it; he had no house then. But now he has a house, land, a cow, a calf. Can all that be left without a wife? Tanasije asks himself. Perhaps I can find some poor girl. It could even be Stamena. No, I can't ask her; she comes from a rich house. Her family thrashes wheat with two horses while I do it with my own strength—that won't fit together. After all, if there is no wife, he will devote himself to the land. That passion that sought a wife he will turn to the land—as much as he can. The rest he must suppress in himself. . . .

She is carrying water. She stops and looks at him softly for a moment, as if she wants to fix him, so strong and hard-working, in her memory forever. Joy fills her soul as she admires his powerful chest and sunburned face. A tenderness swells in him like the rushing of a mountain brook.

—Aren't you tired, hey? . . .

—No, I tire very slowly. . . .

—It must be difficult for you, all alone—and she looks up at him shyly. Her eyes show the beginnings of a deep love for him.

And suddenly Tanasije wants that tenderness and warmth to engulf him forever.

That too will pass, like everything else. . . . And Tanasije looks at her happily. He gives a big grin and almost bursts into song.

Tanasije feels now that the gap between them can be bridged. So what if she is rich and I am not? That cannot keep her from becoming my wife if she desires me. But he is made uneasy by the thought that she might scorn him.

—Would you come back later?

—What for? Her face turns crimson.

—I want to tell you something—and doubt flickers in his eyes, like a dull pain.

She looks at him just as she had before, and that pain vanishes. They understand each other. They divine the nearness of love: there will be happiness, there will be joy, there will be . . .

II

Dusk colors the sky. The sound of bells and the lowing of cattle echo through the valley. Tanasije trembles with anxiety and with desire.

He meets her along a narrow path. The magic of the dusk foretells something. . . .

—I wanted to ask you—Tanasije says quickly and awkwardly—would you be my wife?

Her face softens. Her neck, pale as young cheese, is glowing in the darkness. That throat entices Tanasije. . . . Oh, that lovely throat that shines in the darkness.

—Well, say it. . . . So that I know . . .

She says nothing, only lowers her head awkwardly. Tanasije suddenly feels strong. He lifts her head and murmurs warmly:

—Oh, my dearest, my strength . . .

The straw rustles beneath them in the fragrant night. It mingles, golden, in her raven-black hair. Tanasije does not know whether the scent comes from the straw or Stamena or both together. Nor which one gives off the more beautiful or the stronger scent.

He thrashes the wheat, contented and powerful. By fall, when the grain is harvested, she will be his. His life will gain another love, he will be fulfilled. He will at last, within himself, unite the life and the soil, and thus glorify his efforts. . . .

He continues to thrash the wheat, powerful and mighty, as tireless as God Himself.

Venac, Vol. XV, No. 8, 1930

Mile, the Student Milkman

Every morning he got up so early that the streetlights were still burning. The crooked streets on the outskirts of town were dirty and full of potholes, and the air was misty in the early-morning fog. The night was waning, and the sky above the city, above the roofs and the towers, was beginning to glow with a bluish tint. The cold crept into his bones. The fingers on the hand that held the milk can began to stiffen, to ache and turn blue. Frozen and tired, he dragged himself from street to street, from door to door, from yard to yard. Toothless and shriveled old women came out, yawning and blinking, and held out containers into which he poured the milk. Serving girls, rosy-cheeked with the dawn and with their youth, came out quietly and waited patiently. A little farther on, in the apartment at the corner, a sickly couple quarreled for a while over who should go out for the milk. At first Mile found himself laughing at them, as they wriggled and quarreled in muffled voices under the quilt in their dark, tiny room. Stubbornly the husband argued that no other husband in the world gets up for the milkman. The wife, speaking in a sharp, hissing voice like a typewriter, complained of her anemia and his lack of sensitivity. Finally, she added, as far as she was concerned, she could do without the milk. Then the husband got up, stuck his sleepy head through the window and held out a green cup in his hairy hand.

"Pour half a liter," he said huskily, yawning.

"Jova, Jova, half a liter for me also," the wife's voice was heard calling.

But the husband took only half a liter and went back to bed. Then she jumped out of bed, shouting and cursing. But when she finally appeared at the window she was dignified, for she wished to appear well bred in front of the milkman. After all, he was a university student, and not some coarse peasant with a fur cap.

"Half a liter, please . . ."

Mile left that dismal street where he had sold only five or six liters. "What awful people: They squirm under the quilt while I shiver like a dog, frozen to the bone." And he shivered from the cold, and from resentment. . . . He was constantly beaten down by the struggle for bread. The worst part was humiliating himself in front of people who thought only about themselves, niggardly people whose only concern was whether he would pour one drop more or less of milk. Because he saw such people each morning at dawn, before they had had time to disguise themselves, he could not help knowing their worst side. But there was no way out of this kind of life. His father was heavily in debt and his brother was mentally deranged. Letters from home always made him weep, because he knew that he could not help them. Back in the village they think he has grown up, he has power, he will not forget them. They believe in him, they wait for his help to restore the once prominent household. But Mile was not one of those hardy people who can work half the day at heavy physical labor and spend the other half preparing exams and writing. Exhaustion crept along his bones, each day more unmercifully. Early rising, little sleep and much work over his books slowly drained him of all his strength. . . .

"We all have to make a living, don't we, my friend? I have six children," a stout, swarthy peasant in a fur cap said to him. "You students,
you have it easy. You teach the children of city people. You write a few
petitions for people, and your family at home remembers you too. . . .
But I, we, we have only our milk. . . ."

"What are you complaining about? You sell 200 liters of milk every
day, and then you complain that I am taking away your bread by selling
20 liters. . . . You should be thrashed!" Mile said angrily and started to
go. The thought of his work, his humiliation, overcame him. He had to
let off steam. "And look at me," he wanted to cry to this man, a complete
stranger and a rival for bread. "Look at me! I am young, healthy and full
of energy. I should be living, yes, really living. But, instead, I drag myself
down these streets, into unhealthy apartments and flooded courtyards.
While I struggle to get enough to eat, my life and my youth are flowing
by." His eyes filled with tears at the thought that his youth was being
spent barrenly, without purpose. But he held them back and thought, I
must hurry. It's almost six o'clock. . . . I must finish delivering the milk
by seven. Mrs. Ilić, Mrs. . . ." He began to repeat the names of his
customers. Mile had already forgotten about the peasant, when he
shouted "Good-bye."

"So long . . . So long, comrade!"

The peasant looked at him in amazement, a worried expression on his
face.

"What's the matter with you, young man? By God, you're either sick or
going mad," the peasant said.

The concern in his voice moved Mile deeply.

"So long, so long!" and he ran down the street. He was pained to think
that he had found a human being who was concerned for his well-being,
and he had treated him rudely, maybe even hated him.

The first customer in the next street was a Mrs. Lazić, the wife of the
tubercular streetcar conductor. He had to leave for his job early, well
before dawn.

Mile entered their apartment, poured milk into the cup on the table
and turned to leave. The young, dark-haired woman was still in bed. Her
plump white arms lay on top of the covers.

"Sit down a minute and get warm," she said, smiling agreeably at
him.

He had been attracted to her for a long time. Whenever he left the
apartment, it was as if something had made him drunk—his head spin-
ning, his vision and his conscience blurred. He took with him the scent of
her fresh body and of passion. That scent drove him crazy, making his
blood burn. Well, I am young, the devil help me. . . . But what can I
do? I have no time; I must deliver the milk, and later . . . when the
husband comes . . . he thought to himself.

"Please, why don't you sit down," the woman insisted. . . .

"My milk can is outside, and . . ."

"Oh, don't worry. No one will take it." As she propped herself up on the pillow the quilt slipped and exposed her firm white breasts. She pulled the covers up quickly and smiled coyly. "How's business? A handsome young milkman like you must sell a lot of milk to the girls, eh?"

"Oh, I don't have time for that. . . ." And he started to complain about his hard life, about his difficulties at home. It was nice to be able to talk to someone about his problems. But the woman obviously was not interested. Finally, he got up to go. "I am late. It is already quarter after six, and before seven I must . . ."

She grabbed his arm and pulled him toward the bed. Her dark fiery eyes implored him. There was something pathetic and sick in them—passion and youth, dried up in the desert of her life, cried out for water.

"Stay, please; you have time," she whispered with trembling lips. "Please stay," she pressed him, pulling his arm toward her more firmly.

. . . The milk had to be delivered by seven o'clock. If he didn't finish by then he would lose his customers, and then he would be out on the street. He would have to go home without having passed his exams. He was his father's last hope; the old man could not survive without it. And his shy little sisters and his two brothers who had just started high school would not be able to depend on him. And the peasants would laugh, nudging each other and saying how the son of Jovan Marković who had studied for so many years was worse off than a peasant, since he couldn't even earn a living.

"I'm sorry, please let me go, I must leave," and he tried to free himself.

"Stay, please, I beg of you . . ." and crazily she pulled him closer to her. "Stay! . . ."

His resolve weakened. The lithe body that held him writhed and implored him, suffering visibly. His anxiety about delivering the milk on time hung over him like a raised dagger. But finally everything was blotted out. He felt himself crushing her, her breasts, her lips, her hair. She—this stranger—began to tremble in his arms. He was overwhelmed by oblivion.

Suddenly he remembered. He pushed the body away.

"No, no, I do not dare. I don't have time."

And he ran toward the door, flustered.

The woman sat up in bed, crushed and exposed. And then, dropping her plump arms despairingly onto the quilt, she stared in anguish at the door which had just slammed shut. . . .

He grabbed his milk can and raced down the street, still trembling with passion. Sorrow welled up within him and, in a daze, he delivered his milk. . . . His brief encounter with this strange woman made all the more intense his yearnings for a woman, for life. There was no relief. His soul consumed by passion, and unable to change the reality of his life, he was overcome by despair.

Cold and merciless, the world outside waited.

Smena, Oct.–Nov., 1931

Wheat, Wheat, Wheat . . .

The crowd of peasants blocked the entrance to the low gray building. It was as solid as a prison, with its narrow barred windows and its ironclad doors. Arms had once been stored in this house; today it houses sacks of wheat to be distributed to the famine-struck peasants. A mass of heads, hands, and sacks waited at the entrance. Vacant eyes stared into the depths of the building where the stored wheat could be dimly seen and whence burst the irritated voices of those who distributed it.

"Are you people or are you livestock? Wait your turn! Even livestock know some kind of order!"

"There's no order when you're starving, sir. . . ."

"Starving? And if you were stuffed full you would grunt like pigs. I know you people, this is not my first day on this job. . . ."

Usually one got ten to fifteen kilograms. Wheat was given "to be worked off," and each peasant was debited for it. It was owed to the state. As every peasant knows, it is a heavy burden to be in debt to the state, the priest, or the merchant. How much work was owed per kilogram nobody knew. Furthermore, nobody had bothered to figure it out. Let them charge us as much as they want, just give us something so our children can have a spoonful of gruel tonight.

Mile Kušovac, a sallow peasant with a quick tongue, griped to the peasants gathered round him. His mouth was parched; the skin on his cheeks was sagging; his green eyes glowed dimly, exhaustedly, like steel that has only partially cooled.

"I've already been waiting for six days and they haven't given me anything yet. First they told me that I needed a 'slip.' And later they told me that my village had been scheduled earlier and that I'd missed my turn. I'm just a simple peasant, what do I know about slips and schedules? Nothing. I only know that my youngest child is nearly dead; his ribs show through his skin. My young wife, still nursing the child, has had so much trouble already."

"The worst are the children. If only we hadn't brought them into this world."

Like a single man, the crowd swayed in the hot dust, undefeated. They weren't thinking about the sun or the dust. Or about the hot street stinking with manure. Their nerves were as tight as stretched wires: each thinking, When will they call *me?* *Me!* Each thinking about his own sufferings, about hunger and sickness at home, about his own cow, his own wife, and his own son. And all those thoughts melted into one enormous pain which tormented the mass of heads, hands, and eyes. Hundreds of peasants had but one thought: Hunger. Why? For what reason? When will it end?

Muslims, in their shallow white caps, like mushrooms after the rain, mixed in with the others in that cramped space before the door. Under the heavy weight of hunger their caps lost that centuries-old form that separates them from the Montenegrin caps, now greasy and torn.

The peasants from the village of Ravnorečka did not get any wheat. Their mayor had ordered them to come that day. But his schedule was not the same as that of the clerk who gave out the wheat. Someone had made a clerical error. Yes, an ordinary little clerical error.

"All 150 of us will lose a day's wages, as if we had time to be lazy. We're already ruined. We planted too little because we didn't have enough seed or enough oxen. And now while we're waiting here for nothing the sun will burn all our crops. And what will we eat in the winter and the spring? . . ."

But gradually they calmed down. Somebody came out and explained everything: an unintentional error; they could come again tomorrow. Tomorrow? For one more day their children's stomachs will growl with hunger; 150 scythes will wait in vain for someone to sharpen them on the stone, and the sun will dry out the grass and untilled corn. But who thinks about that? They are only peasants; what the hell, there are so many that there's never enough for them. It is sufficient to give them a handful of wheat so that they don't starve to death. What more do they want? The hell with them; each peasant would like an entire sack.

Noon was approaching. The officials who distributed the wheat went out for lunch. The peasants made room for them to pass. The secretary locked the door and passed, huge and perspiring, between two walls of ragged, dirty people. The peasants followed them with their eyes until they had reached the corner, and then sat down in the street to wait for three hours. The sun scorched, reflecting off the roofs onto their heads.

"The wheat they're giving us now is what they bought from us last fall. We had to sell it to pay the taxes, to support the community, to give to the church, to celebrate the patron saint, to pay for illnesses. What choice did we have? Who among us knew, brothers, that the situation would be so bad? We are peasants, what do we know?"

"Yes, we sold wheat for one dinar a kilogram, and now, they say, they're charging us two and a half dinars. Somebody made some money there. They'll earn even more because we'll have to build roads without pay to pay for the wheat."

"They knew it would be like this. They knew that there would be a crisis, so they bought the wheat from us. Marko, do you have any tobacco for a cigarette?"

"How can I, a poor man like me?"

"And what happened to your cow, Mustafa?"

"It died. It almost starved last winter. It was only skin and bones. And when it began to eat too much spring grass it got sick. I was as sorry as if a person had died. If it were alive it would lift our spirits during this broiling-hot summer. Many others lost their cows. . . ."

An automobile approached, bright and shiny. People got up from the street to make way for it. The car covered them with a cloud of dust and fumes. When it had passed, people sat down again. A mother, a large bony woman, dark with gaunt black eyes, nursed a child. Her husband was sick and she had carried the child for five hours in this heat to get a sack of wheat, as dear to her as the child itself. She had come early to get a good place, but they turned her away, saying that her village was not scheduled for delivery yet. And will it be today? Who knows? She will have to wait, since there is nothing else she can do. A half-crazed man on crutches moaned constantly. Driven by hunger, he had traveled for four hours.

A tall, sallow Muslim, still young, towered above the sitting crowd. He never sat down. He was trying to slip in closer to the door, but the others began to hit at him and to grab at his legs.

"Where do you think you're going? Wait! Why didn't you get up earlier this morning? Do you want us to . . ." Numerous hands grabbed him, and he fell sprawling. He fell across the mother with the child. Screams and curses . . .

Worries raced through the minds of the peasants, searing like live coals, cutting like icy edges. Why famine, when last year there was a good harvest? They had had to sell their wheat, hoping that the harvest would be good this season and that work would be continued on the Adriatic railway. But there was no harvest. They sold off their livestock for practically nothing: sheep for 100, lambs for 20, cows for 250 dinars! The peasants weren't responsible for the low prices. Wheat was expensive; so was salt, kerosene, a doctor's examination. Two dinars each. Like a kilogram of meat. One merchant bought up a lot last fall and sold it secretly at a high price. That kind of trading was forbidden by law. But everybody except the authorities knew that such trading went on. The authorities were always the last to learn about such things, just as the husband is the last to learn about his unfaithful wife. Having sold their livestock this year, next year there will be even less; next year they won't have anything to sell; their unfertilized fields will grow scrawny corn, the grass in the meadows will be tall and thin. What kind of a year will that be?

Three o'clock came. Work began again, but it lasted only as long as the regular working hours. Again, pushing and muttering.

"How much did you get, Ismail?"

"Ten kilos. Nothing. If we weren't starving, who would give up two days' wages for that?"

The woman with the child had not been called, but she managed to push her way through and get inside.

"What do you want? Where is your slip? Is your village scheduled for now?"

"I don't know, but I do know that last night we had nothing to eat. . . ."

"You don't know? Out! Your village is scheduled for tomorrow."

"Scheduled? What kind of a schedule do you have when you're dying of starvation? Give me at least . . ."

"Out!"

And the woman left. Tall, as thin as a shadow, she walked slowly down the street, carrying the child on her left arm. Where should she go now? It's a five-hour journey to her village. Night will overtake her on the road. But still she went, tired and hungry. Tomorrow, if she can, she'll come again. But she was not sure herself as she walked along the narrow mountain path that she would have the strength to walk another ten hours tomorrow with a child in her arms.

At six o'clock work stopped. Not even half the peasants had gotten their wheat.

"Come tomorrow. The office is closing now. It is not possible to work outside of regular hours."

"How could we wait twelve hours in this ungodly heat and get nothing?"

"Do you know what a day's pay means to a peasant right now?"

"You aren't hungry. If you were hungry, you wouldn't be so worried about regular hours."

The key turned in the lock. The peasants began to disperse. They didn't give any wheat to Mile Kušovac again today. His village was scheduled for today but they didn't get as far as his name. "Regular hours" prevented that. He was born unlucky.

"Where should I go tonight? I won't find them alive. And how will they live through the night without wheat? There aren't any more nettles. What are left are too old, hard as wood, inedible."

They gave them a fistful of wheat so they would not die. They pacified their hunger so they would not go wild and start attacking somewhere. Hungry people are dangerous; hungry people don't think; hungry people may even sense the truth, and then . . . That's why you give them some wheat; a little wheat, just enough so they don't die from hunger. In this way, by dispensing charity, the system preserved itself.

Injustices happened here as everywhere else. The mayor, the secretary, everybody gave wheat to their relatives in the village even when the relatives had some at home. Bad systems have bad servants. Inhuman. This inhumanity is only a special form of selfishness: I, mine, for me. That selfishness was most vividly seen by all the peasants when Milija Matović, the uncle of the secretary, took 40 kilograms of wheat with him. For those 40 kilograms he sold himself for as long as he lives: to think the way his honorable nephew thinks. And the secretary managed to kill two birds with one stone: he has fulfilled his duty as a nephew toward his uncle, and at the same time has established control over his uncle's life.

The peasants were leaving noisily, in groups. Moslems and Christians mixed together. In 1918, after the Austrian retreat, they had slaughtered each other in this same street. Rifles shot from behind every corner, lurked in every yard. They were killing each other because of their beliefs. But now they had come to the conclusion that they were all the same; that their hunger was the same and that their struggle was the same. And their beliefs? You pay the priest for the christening and the ulema for the *sunet*. And if there were no christenings or circumcisions, if there was no tax, who knows if they would exist? Anyway, hungry as they were now, they didn't have time to think about God. God surely is not hungry. Let Him think about those who have plenty to eat, and let those who have plenty to eat think about Him.

"The wheat is not ripe yet. It is young when you bite it, soft and milky. We won't be able to wait for it. And you'll see, as soon as it is ripe, it will be much cheaper on the market. We have to sell it regardless of the price, and then in the spring there won't be enough wheat left again. Who is responsible for all this?"

"Who?"

The peasants did not know the truth: that the price of wheat falls the moment they harvest their wheat and rises the moment they sell it, since when the peasants have it there is more than enough for everyone who wants to buy it, and the price is low; and when they don't have it, you sell it to them at a high price, because they need it to live. Money was made by such speculation. And the so-called obligations—to the school, the community, the church—all had to be met.

The day was drawing to a close. Peasants from the village of Selište moved away through the forest in the dusk.

Mile Kušovac, the last one, dragged his feet.

"And even when you get the wheat, when they finally give it to you, they make a triple profit on us. You will work it off on a long summer day. They like a long day better than a short one. . . . Just when you most need to work in your own fields and meadows so the sun won't get them."

"Yes, they robbed us that way; the merchants rob us on the market; it's no good wherever you turn."

"No good . . ."

When they emerged from the forest a dog barked down in the village.

"Where can we go with nothing? Not only did we lose a day's pay, but on top of everything we are wandering around in the dark. We are very late."

"We wait until six o'clock and not a single grain. As if anybody cares that darkness overtakes us."

"That's what should concern us most of all. They all make a living from our work. Each grain, even when we sow it, is not even half ours. Yes, they make a living off of us, from trading with our wheat, our livestock, our lard; from our taxes and our draft labor."

That was Mile Kušovac speaking, banging his cane along the road. For the seventh straight day he was returning home without wheat. He wondered whether he'd find them alive, and what his wife would say when he threw down the empty bag. And what his son would say.

And the child in the crib?

Razvršje, Vol. I, No. 3, 1932

The Motorcycle in the Provincial Town

The motorcycle roared into town raising a cloud of dust. The children spotted it first and chased it through the streets. They finally surrounded it in front of the small hotel at the marketplace. The motorcyclist stood tall and slender in his sports outfit. He talked for a long time, with cool measured movements and a calm voice. The children listened intently, their eyes and their mouths open.

"This is called a motorcycle. You ride it this way. . . . When you want to start it . . . Here's how you accelerate . . . shift gears . . . put on the brakes . . ." he explained.

A crowd gathered slowly. The motorcyclist continued to use the same measured words and movements, as if he were still talking to children. He talked as if he were troubled by something deep within him. Or within that accursed machine on two wheels, which shook crazily, spitting out acrid blue smoke.

"Where do you come from?" asked a short older man with a Montenegrin cap pushed far back on his head.

"I am from Srem," the newcomer said. "I am a traveling salesman."

"I know you people," said the Montenegrin. "Too many of those traveling salesmen"—he underlined the words—"have multiplied these days. As for your claim that you are from Srem—you are not. People there are fat and do not ride upon such machines. I was there . . ." and he walked away across the marketplace, erect, dignified, carrying his cane.

"Did you people see that?" He approached the first person he met. "If he had come here fifty years ago everybody would have thought he was the Devil, or else a Turkish spy!"

The traveler entertained the cluster of people. Another smaller, obviously elite group gathered around Mato Vodokapić, the innkeeper, a wealthy but aloof host. He had spent three years in America and returned home poorer than when he left, but out in the world he had learned how to make money. A large man, he was wearing the Montenegrin dress, with wide blue trousers, white socks up to his knees, a gun at his belt, and a new Montenegrin cap set back on his head. He looked as solid as a piece of granite. He twirled his mustache, pushed his cap back, and waved his arms around to clear more space around him. The people listening to him were Montenegrins, the permanent patrons of his café. They were stubborn skeptics who didn't want to be taken in by some city slicker telling them lies. At the same time they were secretly dying to find out what the machine was made of and whether it could be of any use to a brave honest man.

"This is nothing new for me, brothers. I had three of them at one time when I was in America. This motorcycle is nothing compared to the ones I had. Everybody has a motorcycle in America. Even the black gypsies. . . . To tell the truth, I wanted to bring two or three back from America to give to my best friend and to my *kums** (everybody who was not a *kum* of Mato imagined that he was the best friend) so that we would have all the latest things here. . . ."

At that moment the stout old Montenegrin who had ridiculed the traveling salesman from Srem approached Mato. He caught him by the sleeve and, speaking as sharply as the edge of a knife, said:

"I know, Mato, my *kum,* that there is no Montenegrin who is closer to you than I and that if you had brought anyone even a knife from America to put in his belt you would not have forgotten me. But I would not take that . . ." and he motioned toward the motorcycle with his cane. "I would sooner become a Turk! Where, pray tell, can one of our men, in this dress and bearing arms as befits a Montenegrin, fly on one of these machines? Give us a horse, a lively colt, one that, when you whip him on the plains, races so fast that only things that fly can catch you. . . ."

"Jovan, you are old-fashioned. You should give up the old way of life and start to live like the rest of the educated world. I would have one of

* *Kum* is the term applied to both the godparent of one's child and to the best man at one's wedding.

those motorcycles that you're going on about now if I'd been able to buy it in our country. You don't have to exercise it or feed it. And when you ride it you feel as if you're flying. . . ."

"Mister," interrupted the traveling salesman, "if that's so, I shall sell you the motorcycle. As far as I'm concerned . . ." but Mato continued to bombard the crowd with a long story about himself, the motorcycle, America, Belgrade, about everything. "Here, ride it, go ahead, it's not hard . . . this way . . . We'll settle on a price later. . . ."

Mato realized that he was trapped. It was true that he had ridden on a motorcycle in America, several times, in fact. But always on the back, while a Czech friend from the factory drove the motorcycle. . . . Immediately after his return from America, Mato Vodokapić had opened his café in this little town that the Montenegrins had liberated from the Turks in 1912. Clever and adaptable, he lured people to him. And those Montenegrins who maintained a somewhat patronizing attitude toward the older residents of the town gathered in his café to avoid mixing with the "common people." His business thrived and he married a girl from a better, more prominent house. . . . After so many years of living out in the world and in this little town he managed to stand out a bit from his fellow-townsmen because of his knowledge and his ability in business. And he was a Montenegrin—a hero and a peasant—and also a gentleman from the city, soft-spoken and well mannered. He always said that one should accept what the world has to offer and live from it, and that America (which he mainly saw in his factory and out of the window of his cheap rooming house), with its trains and its machines, should be emulated; while at home he screamed at his wife and hung his knife and his gusle next to the icon of St. Luke. . . .

He tried to wriggle out of it.

"You know, young man, I sold it a long time ago and I've forgotten how. . . ."

"Don't worry, you can't forget. You just try it; it's a superb machine. . . . I'll start it for you. And when you want to turn it off, just push here and—that's it."

The crowd started to mutter. Everybody knew that Mato was lying and that this was the first time he'd ever seen a motorcycle.

"Perhaps American motorcycles were different, Mato," one of the men teased him.

That insulted Mato. He realized that he was trapped; either he would remain a liar or . . . He mentally crossed himself three times and called upon St. Vasily of Ostrog, St. Peter of Cetinje, and St. Luke (his family patron saint), and . . . he sat astride the motorcycle. . . .

"Don't ride it, my *kum* Mato," Jovan begged. "As I tell you, and God and St. John too, you will be disgraced in front of all Montenegrins."

The motorcycle roared and drowned out Jovan's words. Mato gripped

the handles as strongly as one holds a plow or a knife and started
weaving down the street. . . .

First he felt the powerful whipping of the wind on his face. And when
he lost his cap he made an instinctive move to catch it and almost turned
over in the ditch. . . . I'll turn it off, he thought, retrieve my cap and go
back on foot. It's still not too late. . . . But when he looked for the
handle to turn it off, amidst all that speed, he couldn't find it and he
pulled the handle that increased the speed instead. The motorcycle raced
like lightning. Now he couldn't turn it off. It was a wonder that he stayed
on, scared, startled, crouched over the seat. He maneuvered it around
corners, wobbling along the road, often coming to the edge of the ditch,
scattering travelers along the roadside.

Finally he flew off the road and continued across the fields and bushes
and over fences. Nowhere did the machine stop, and he did not dare
(nor had he the time to think of it) to save himself by jumping off. . . .
An old peasant swore after him as his sheep were scattered in all
directions.

"Just you wait, you nobody, you cursed alien faith . . ." and a rock
flew past Mato. The peasant continued to swear and shout until he
suddenly spotted Mato's wide blue trousers and his Montenegrin silk
sash. Not believing what he saw, he raised his hand over his eyes thinking
that his old eyes were betraying him. What befell you, O Montenegro, a
curse on you and may you be burned to ashes. At least if I could have
caught him I could have seen who it was that shamed the Montenegrin
dress and the Montenegrin name. . . . These days any scoundrel can
wear the Montenegrin dress. Eh, what times we live in . . . he thought
to himself.

Mato drove into a group of women who were setting up their looms.
The yarn caught in the motorcycle's wheels and began to drag a woman
whose hands were wrapped in it. She started to scream and the other
women screamed too. Fortunately the yarn broke and let her go in the
middle of the meadow.

People ran out of their houses shouting and making noises while Mato
continued to race in crazy circles through the fields. They ran after him,
trying to catch the person who was wantonly trampling their fields.
Women and children, men and dogs, all shouted and chased after him.

After a while Mato figured out how to control the machine and finally
put the motorcycle back on the road and turned toward town. . . .

People were still in the streets. When he appeared, they exclaimed in
disbelief. Mato burst into the crowd, flew past and disappeared around a
corner. Then, before they had time to catch their breath, he shot out of
another street, buzzed through them again and vanished around another
corner. He was riding very well, he turned the corners nicely, and he sat

astride the motorcycle as if he knew what he was doing. But he didn't
know how to turn it off. . . .

He was trying to figure out what to do. . . .

In the meantime the entire town came to its feet. People gathered in
the streets and crowded in front of his café. Mato spotted his wife, her
hands dripping with dough. She had been brought to the gate by the
banging and the noise. She shouted at him, cursed and groaned. Next to
her stood his *kum* Jovan, also shouting and motioning with his hands.

"He's gone mad, brothers! Get off the streets! Stop, Mato my *kum*, in
the name of God! . . ."

People fled to the windows and the stairways. The town echoed with
the voices of men and the shrieks of women. Mato flew through the
streets, disheveled and bareheaded, a cloud of dust behind him. The roar
of the motorcycle drowned out the voices. . . . The streets were empty
except for two constables, who strolled with measured steps, twirling
their truncheons. Spasenija, Mato's wife, stood in front of the gate, her
mouth open and her hands on her hips. . . .

"Woman, open the ga-a-a-te," shouted Mato at her as he flew by,
already disappearing around the corner.

Before she comprehended what he had said, he reappeared from a side
street. His large body and his baggy trousers covered the entire motorcycle.

"Open the gate, you nobody's daughter!" he shouted clearly at the top
of his lungs as he almost hit the corner.

Spasenija only now heard what he wanted and opened the gate wide,
standing in the middle of it with open arms, hanging on to both gate-
posts. In the meantime Mato had made another circle through the side
street and appeared again. . . .

"Open! . . . Get out of the way!" Rounding the corner again Mato
thought angrily, It is better to be dead than to have a crazy wife.

He appeared for the last time and drove at full speed through the gate.
He heard something rip behind him. His wide trousers had caught on a
nail sticking out of the post. The torn piece was hanging on the nail,
gently waving in the wind, as blue as a piece of sky torn from above. A
flock of hens scattered through the yard as if a bird of prey had suddenly
appeared among them. Mato could no longer hear or see. There was only
one thought in his mind: to save himself at any cost whatsoever, to stop
this disgrace. He flew under the apple tree, and its branches lashed him
across the face. But he did not even feel the pain. One thought only filled
his mind. For the last time he turned the handlebars of the motorcycle to
the left, holding them firmly, and he drove into a large haystack. . . . He
went in quite deep and was barely able to pull himself out before a
crowd started gathering. He was covered with straw. Instinctively he

touched his sash—his revolver had fallen out. With both hands he hid the place in his sash where his weapon was kept—to hide at least that loss from the staring eyes behind the fence. . . . Torn, dirty, his face scratched, he ran into the house, shouting at anything who stood in his way.

"And where is that city slicker? I want to kill him! . . ."

But the traveling salesman had vanished without a trace.

Mato went to bed early that evening to rest from all the racing and to remove himself from curious eyes. His joints ached, his muscles quivered as if they had spent the entire day with a scythe under the August sun. In the middle of the night he jumped up, half asleep, and grabbed his rifle from the wall. The motorcycle was roaring under the windows, and the entire house was shaking. The foreigner had stolen it from the yard where it had been leaning against the apple tree and had turned it on. Mato rushed across the room—and tripped over the crib. He fell flat on his face together with his rifle. The child woke up and began to scream, and Spasenija also woke up screaming.

"Mato, what's the matter with you tonight? . . ."

He got up and searched for the rifle, groping in the dark. But the motorcycle had disappeared into the darkness; he could hear it chugging in the distance. . . . Mato shoved his wife angrily, swearing:

"You are responsible for it all! What kind of a wife are you, planting the crib in the middle of the house? . . ."

So if by any chance you should stray into that little town, be sure not to arrive on a motorcycle. Because if you do, a tall man, now wearing a city suit but still with a revolver in his belt, will take a long look at you. And he just might see in you someone else, and then . . .

Politika, July 31, 1932

Dead Fish

It was summer, and the scent of hawthorne filled the air. We were hiding in the bushes, playing, and despite our hunger we were excited. Whenever we spotted the Austrian patrol, we retreated deeper into the bush and crowded together, peering through the branches. That's how the Komite* used to wait for the enemy. And then the stories about the Komite would begin. We all knew that Ilija, the son of the poor miller, Toma, had seen the Komite many times. But nobody wanted to ask him

* The *Komite* were irregular military units of Serbs that fought first against the Turkish and later the Austrian (*Schwabe*) troops occupying Serbia.

about it—perhaps fearing that one of us was a spy. Still, we wanted to
know all about them, we wanted him to tell us about them.

The Komite slept in the woods with the wolves. Everybody wanted to
see them, but no one knew where or when they would appear. To those
in green uniforms they were merciless. But to us they brought comfort—a
reassuring pat on the head, flour or zwiebach stolen from the enemy. . . .
We all knew that they used to come to see Toma, but nobody mentioned
it. There are many things in the world that we know but musn't talk
about, much as we would like to—especially we children.

"I saw them," said Trajko. "I even saw Todor, their leader. I almost
died of fright. A mustache as big as a shrub, arms as big around as that
beech tree over there, even larger, and his teeth . . ."

We all knew that he was lying. We began to laugh and make fun of
him. Only skinny Ilija—we were all stronger than he—remained gravely
silent.

"Is he lying, Ilija?" asked Jovo Zlatanin.

Ilija got up from the ground and began to fiddle with a twig. "I don't
know. He must be lying. Where could such a giant hide?"

He walked away quickly through the brush. We all glared at Jovo for
asking such a stupid question, especially for asking Ilija.

"Ilija, come back. We'll play Schwabe and Komite," Branko shouted
after him. He returned, but we couldn't play. Nobody wanted to be a
Schwabe, not even Trajko, even though we all agreed that he should.
Until now Ilija had always played the Schwabe—we bullied him into it.
But now . . . No, Ilija should be the leader of the Komite, because he
knew the most about them. Finally Trajko and Jovo started fighting
about it, and we barely succeeded in separating them.

"The Komite do not fight among themselves; they fight only against
the Schwabe. Since there is no Schwabe among us . . ." said my elder
brother, the largest and strongest of us, keeping Trajko and Jovo apart,
"we are going to go fishing under the rocks."

The sun was warm and it was pleasant to walk with bare feet on the
hot stones. On the hill above us, where the road twisted through the
dense brush, we saw a group of Schwabe.

"They'll take somebody away again," said my brother. He swore, and
threw a large rock angrily into the whirlpool.

Toma's house is near ours, behind the hill. In fact, it is not really a
house, but a hut. It leans against the mill, whose grinding can be heard
all along the valley. Covered by birches and willows, the stream emerges
from time to time like the glistening back of a snake winding through
the rocks. Moving downstream as we fished, we were coming closer to the
mill. Then, when we could see its roof, we turned back without saying
anything. We were silent and strangely melancholy: perhaps somewhere

out there we would meet the Komite, we would see them, and then maybe one of us would give them away. But who? This one, or that one? . . . You can't trust anybody but yourself.

Branko took out a small blade and began to clean the little trout. My older brother lit the fire. He liked to look important—that's why he carried his tinder box around wherever he went, and why he smoked corn silk. But lighting a fire isn't such a big deal—I could do that too if he let me. But he never did—he said I was too young. And when I once stole the tinder box from him while he was asleep, I wouldn't let my younger brother use it either. . . . The trout were so little that we didn't bother to bone them. No, we all said, there is nothing sweeter in the world than trout—all of us were sick of eating cooked nettles, bran, ground corncobs and wild onions. This is the meat and the fat of our dinner—the only things missing were salt and bread.

"I have eaten something sweeter than this," said my brother. "When I visited the priest, his wife gave me bacon with fried eggs—this much, a full plate, and a big piece of bread. That's the best thing in the world. And it fills you up. Fish is like water; before you know it you're hungry again, but you can't find any more. There are plenty of frogs, but they say nobody wants to eat frogs. . . ."

Jovo Zlatanin saved one of the two fish that were his share for his mother. The rest of us couldn't bear that. Each of us will give him a little piece to make up for it, or, even better, each of us should take one fish home.

"Where's Ilija?" asked Branko.

His fish, tied to a thin willow branch, were lying on the sand, but Ilija was not there. From downstream, from Jova's woods, from the mill, a strange clamor reached us. We fell silent with foreboding. All of a sudden a terrible scream rent the air. And then silence again, both there and here, among us. Branko crunched a fish head in his mouth, and we all glared at him angrily.

The padding of bare feet on the rocks and the rustling of the willow trees strained our attention even more. Ilija, breathing heavily, suddenly appeared. Blood spurted from the big toe on his left foot, yes, it was his left foot, as he stumbled against a rock. Frightened, confused, we stared at him, and he looked from one to another of us with agitated eyes.

"Schwabe! They are taking Father and Mother away! Father told me— don't tell this to anybody—that the Komite are either on Gradac or Šumatovac, and that I should run and tell them. The password is to bark like a dog. . . . I am going to Šumatovac . . . and you . . . since the two hills are far apart and Gradac is larger . . . you run there and tell them to run away, that they have set ambushes around the village, and tell them that it was Miro who betrayed my father. . . ."

He ran across the stream. Branko ran after him with the little fish.

"Take your fish; you might be able to use them, Ilija! That's your share. . . ."

Ilija stopped for a moment, motioned no with his hand, but took the fish anyway.

One after another we dashed through the fields and groves until we came to the foot of the hill Gradac. We sat down to rest. Suddenly, far downstream toward the village, we heard a shot, another, a third, and then an entire salvo. We looked at each other with alarm. Finally my brother got up, pushed his cap back and clapped his hands.

"Get up! There's no time to rest. Don't all start barking at once, but let's distribute ourselves, ten steps apart. First you bark, Branko, and then you. . . . We don't all have to go; those two should turn back," he said, pointing at Jovo and me.

We looked at him with such disappointment that he said no more, and when he made the assignments he put me on his left side and Jovo on his right. I was still scared, but I did not want to turn back. I was remembering all the good things my brother had done for me, forgetting all those beatings he'd given me—at that moment even they seemed trivial in comparison to our deep love for one another.

We ran for a long time through the damp, dark woods, hungry, almost dropping from exhaustion. All day long we wandered from valley to valley, but we found no one, and no one answered us from the depths of the woods. When the sun was already setting behind the hills, we ran into Jovan Sjecigora. We smelled the wild onions he was carrying before we saw the old man. The Komite used to come to Jovan; everybody knew that he knew them. So we decided to tell him everything. Without a smile, without a motion, he mumbled something like, "Who knows where the Devil is hiding" and told us not to be foolish, to turn back. . . . He mumbled something like that, or something else, only the Devil knows for sure, but we turned back.

The sun was going down when we reached the village road. Our legs felt as if they were about to fall off, our stomachs were empty, and the air was heavy with foreboding. When we came to the knoll we saw a small crowd of peasants and men in uniform down at the clearing near Toma's mill.

"Wait," said Branko. "We must make up a story about where we've been in case the Schwabe ask us. . . . I think we should say we were picking strawberries. . . ."

Carefully we descended the path and pushed our way into the crowd. There was the village chief, and the sergeant, and Miro, and many others. In the middle lay Ilija, his right cheek on the ground. Blood was clotted on his face, on his calves, between his toes, and across his hand, which was still tightly closed around the willow branch with the limp fish. Miro, a pock-marked man with shifty eyes, took the fish from Ilija's fingers and offered them to me. I shuddered and looked away. No one in the village would look him in the eye. He was trying to do something nice, but nobody wanted him to. He wanted to give us Ilija's little fish, he wanted us to eat the fish that Ilija would have eaten so gladly. "Ilija, Ilija, you take them, you eat them, they're yours, we've eaten ours already. Don't look at us, just take them, Ilija," we all wanted to say, but he just lay there, pale, even skinnier than he was in life. The flies were swarming around his blood, and the fish which we all refused lay on the ground almost next to his mouth. They had killed him when he crossed the clearing. A few more steps and he would have disappeared into the dense brush. They did not notice at first that he had escaped, probably to alert the Komite—that's what the grownups were saying among themselves. Only when they took his father and his mother out of the house did they start looking for him. They ran after him and called to him to stop, but he bounded through the bushes like a young buck. But when he tried to cross the clearing they felled him. He got up, but fell again, this time his limbs thin and twisted, his eyes empty and frozen—eyes that only this morning had been tender and green like new leaves.

It was already dark when more Schwabe arrived with a doctor and when they chased away all the peasants except the chief, Miro, and the priest. My brother and I set out for home. The scent of hawthorne filled the starry night. We reached out for each other; we grasped hands firmly. Only this morning we had been playing with him right here. . . . When we came to the stream, all at once we realized something was wrong.

"Listen, the mill is silent. Toma and his wife have been taken away, and Ilija. . . . Everything is dead here now."

Yes, we were used to the noise of the mill grinding or of the water falling from the wheel. This new silence was painful for us, and we grasped hands more firmly to weep bitterly in that silence. . . .

Published under the pseudonym M. Nikolić
Politika, August 29, 1938

4
On Literature

The question is primarily about social-democratic culture. Let no one take this amiss: we are not separating cultural work from its practical application in social life. On the contrary, all work must have—and does have—a social function, regardless of the direction in which it moves. Everything that is created is created, consciously or unconsciously, to serve some purpose, some propaganda. The only question is which particular purpose the creator is working for.

The arts are a special weapon of the class struggle. [. . .]

We know that literature is a part of the class struggle. It must follow that line which is required of it by the correct course of the class.

" 'Socijalna Misao' ili Falsifikat
Istorijskog Materijalizma,"
Slobodna Misao, Vol. XI, 1932

Thought is the most creative force. It uncovers what is new. Men can neither live nor produce if they do not think or contemplate. Even though they may deny it, Communists are forced to accept this fact in practice. Thus they make it impossible for any thought other than theirs to prevail.

Man may renounce much. But he must think and he has a deep need to express his thoughts. It is profoundly sickening to be compelled to remain silent when there is need for expression. It is tyranny at its worst to compel men not to think as they do, to compel men to express thoughts that are not their own.

The limitation of freedom of thought is not only an attack on specific political and social rights, but an attack on the human being as such. Man's imperishable aspirations for freedom of thought always emerge in concrete form. If they have not yet become apparent in Communist systems, this does not mean that they do not exist. Today they lie in the dark and apathetic resistance, and in unshaped hopes of the people. It is as if totality of oppression were erasing differences in national strata, uniting all peoples in the demand for freedom of thought and for freedom in general.

History will pardon Communists for much, establishing that they were forced into many brutal acts because of circumstances and the need to defend their existence. But the stifling of every divergent thought, the exclusive monopoly over thinking for the purpose of defending their personal interests, will nail the Communists to a cross of shame in history.

The New Class, 1957
(Trans. Anon.)

As Marxist Critic

[Two examples of Djilas's literary criticism ("Review" and "Uncultured History") are included to correct the mistaken impression that Djilas was always critical of Miroslav Krleža. Stanko Lasić, in his interesting book *Sukob na književnoj ljevici, 1928–1952* (Zagreb, 1970), intentionally or unintentionally presented only the most dogmatic Djilas, in articles severely critical of Krleža. He listed only seven of Djilas's articles written between 1936 and 1952. He omitted twenty-three major pieces of literary criticism of that period, most of which were much less dogmatic than the ones cited. Further, since Lasić's book ended with 1952, six additional articles from the more libertarian 1953–1954 period were omitted. Thus Lasić, by his selective omissions, incorrectly characterized Djilas, one of the major adversaries of Krleža, as a narrow and unimaginative critic.]

Reviews

Ivo Andrić's book [*Pripovetke*] consists of six tales. [. . .]

Somewhere within Andrić is located a milieu, special and alive. With his artistic nerve he engraves into that specific, distinct environment various types and characters and, what is more, real persons. Andrić's man is our man; but still, a man. Narrowly ethnic, according to one interpretation, alongside of that specificity Andrić is characterized by the special mark of a European writer, by historic epic realism. Each type that Andrić portrays bears above all the stamp of an individual, solitary and vivid. These individuals stand out from the sharply and precisely drawn environment chiefly in their passions and their raptures. Thus, when Andrić delineates, the individual is outside of and above the collective, yet he still has distant, invisible roots in it. This is not to be interpreted to mean that Andrić is outside his milieu and its totality. Not one of his characters is the bearer of an ideology; nor does any character cast light with his personality upon any strata, class or movement. Andrić is not some modern ideological writer. He is a historian, above all, of men and events; and of a dark, savage milieu crisscrossed with nationalisms, religions and classes. . . . Complaint could still be lodged against Andrić with respect to his heroes. They act from traditions, instincts, religious unrest and passions, dark and measureless. Women submit because of inexplicable secret urges, because of our Slavic tendency to submit, crazily and without purpose. Because of a passive need, perhaps, to be tortured. One lives, works, suffers, burns out, thinks—all without thinking. Andrić is outside his characters; with his pen, his chisel or his scalpel he bends over them intellectually. He does not sink intimately and deeply into them. (For example, we are more interested in why city loiterers rape a girl, what is going on inside them, than in a document stating that such people exist and such actions take place.) Andrić sees his characters, understands them, but does not feel in them the mysterious, the subconscious, the primitive. Yet he is less guilty of this, which we find a defect, than a score of our other writers. (To cite their names without detailed criticisms would be unwarranted.) Our writers see men, they carve them masterfully, on paper, but do not carry the men deeply inside themselves. They see things as they are and, moreover, as they should be—but that still does not mean that they live among their characters, in them; and that the characters live in the writer. Andrić, more by some inborn trait, occasionally probes deeper and "draws blood."

Moderation in expression and a certain artiness, modern and dry—these qualities are welcome (if artiness is welcome anywhere) to balance his violent themes. If Andrić roared along, his history would not come to life. And that remains his greatest strength. He is our only writer, for the moment, who in a real epic (and not an epic from the national poetry) can bring to life people and events from the past. Andrić is skilled in composition, methodical in his historical narrative style, and savage, primitive and moody in his internal expression. The surface, formalistic expression of Andrić is cold, intellectually artistic.

It has always seemed to us that Andrić, along with Bora Stanković, is the most Balkan of all the authors on this peninsula. He is a coldly calculating realist without the passionate and the painful lyricism of Stanković; in his epic expanse and in his comprehension of complex motives the balance is almost in Andrić's favor over all of them. With the zeal of a gold miner Stanković penetrated farther into the deep, the hidden and the dark. Andrić, without that passion for the unknown, would lose more than Stanković without his intellectualized posing of things, people and emotions in "their milieu."

All in all, along with Vasić and Krleža, Ivo Andrić stands as one of our most powerful and most profound prose authors. [. . .]

Milan Grol's criticism of the theater has long been needed. Our literature on the theater is generally poor, and Grol's book [*Pozorišne Kritike*] fills a major gap. [. . .]

Grol has prepared a pleasant surprise for us. A superb stylist, vivid in his expression, clear and concise in his evaluations, erudite, with the nerve of a literary critic, he is not, as is commonly supposed, merely an expert on the theater. His assessments of authors, plays and acting, theatrically and artistically, rank him as our best theater critic and as one of our best general critics. [. . .]

Grol never succumbs to rapture, exultation or inebriation in the face of important persons, works or events. He rises above all that and, with the calipers in his hands, looks penetratingly and objectively. Grol has absorbed culture, has a keenness of observation, an unwillingness to compromise and a brilliant turn of words, sentences, thoughts and emotions. And, above all, conciseness, principled and expressive. [. . .]

Grol does not have an intellectually defined position toward the theater or toward the arts in general. Such a position in his case would be both psychologically and theoretically impossible. [. . .]

What is most positive and most admirable in Grol's book is not only the theater critic's encounters and assessments, but also his literary and artistic achievements. [. . .]

The play, "In Agony," by Miroslav Krleža [. . .] is vibrant, internally dynamic, tense and painfully, bloodily agonizing. [. . .]

The entire action is internal, beneath the words and movements; subterranean, roaring, anxious and painful. Problems emerge spontaneously from the depths and, cut up with determination and without compromise, bring forth the fruits of artistic ideas. [. . .] Krleža's rushing thoughts thrash about; he destroys the ideas, the spirit and the soul of all that comes under the sharpness of his pen and his heart. He stands at the crossroads of two eras, of two discontents; and while he is prophesying the coming of the one, he is bloodily settling accounts with the other. His words are as heavy, gory, hard and merciless as his thought. And that shows not only courage but also strength—elusive, incapable of being forced into a mold, blazing like a flame. For this reason it is impossible to look at Krleža from an academic standpoint, according to some disjointed theories of art. [. . .] He is vitally alive, contemporary, collective and militant, and yet he preserves the hue, uniquely his, of something eternal that existed in the deepness even before it was born in him; and also the silence of Slavic tenderness and humaneness (above all, humaneness) .

Whenever we think of Krleža, one image always emerges; a machine
with countless screws, wires and springs (but still, a machine with a soul)
blundering along toward sharp jutting cliffs; and we are overwhelmed by
silent, intense fascination and anxiety: Will the machine smash the rocks
or will it crash itself into a thousand pieces? . . . What Krleža brings to
our literature is new in its ideas, in its desire and in its internal expression more than in its form or its verbal virtuosity. That is both good and
necessary. It casts a sharp shadow on our entire era, like a mark; that
there were people who were able to think and to feel without compromise.

Krleža denotes not only a movement but also a new epoch in our
spiritual and social creativity and orientation.

Zapisi, Vol. VIII, No. 6, 1931

The Development of Proletarian Art

[. . .]
Let us now return to the question of artistic technique.

With the development of proletarian art, which was contingent upon
the development of the proletarian class and its historical requirements,
proletarian artists are liberating themselves from the very technical
means that they accepted from bourgeois art. Forms, configurations and
stylistic expression now are more and more shaped by the class itself. The
style becomes the class, configurations receive ever more a class hue, and
the form is that through which the proletariat experiences events. And
here, with insulting obviousness, the class duplicity of bourgeois intellectuals is evident when they demand "form" from proletarian writers and
when they dispute their stylistic attainments. Doubtless, proletarian art
forms are not yet as perfected as those of bourgeois art; further, such
perfection is not a goal of proletarian art but only a concrete means. And
because proletarian art is still young, although it has already provided a
few classic examples, in its probably brief period of existence perhaps it
will never attain the bourgeois level. These bourgeois intellectuals
demand only their own form, just as they demand "ideological neutrality" from all art while in reality demanding exclusively the ideology
of their own art. Among intellectuals of the dying class prime importance
is often attached to the question of form. The question of form is
important for bourgeois art for two reasons: as bourgeois art dies out, at a
certain stage it transforms itself into "artism" (the relating of banal, stale
events and thoughts by nonbanal, novel means) ; and the class interests of
bourgeois art express themselves in matters of form as well as of content.
[. . .]

With the exception of the Symbolists, who have their own specific nuances, bourgeois art, having a premonition of the mortal danger to its class, with all possible means now espouses the concept of art without "ideological intent" or "revolutionary accent." Such art corresponds most completely to the interests of the ruling class. Hiding behind the test of "neutrality," art should be relieved of its revolutionary class concept; art should be covered with a mask of disinterest in the class struggle; its cutting edge should be turned into the fog, into stupor, where it will not deliver a potent militant blow to existing social conditions.

As Plekhanov says, "The source of artistic weakness is not, as may appear at first glance, in its ideology, but in the opposite, in the insufficiency of its ideology." [. . .]

National struggles are inseparable from the class interests of the ruling classes. The war for markets is the basis of all national conflicts. In the phase of imperialistic (monopolistic) capitalism the war for markets found its most widespread and profound expression. Thus the ruling class, under the iron pressure of that process, conscious of its interests, emphasizes and underlines the necessity of national prestige (Mussolini, Hitler, Gajda, etc.), which in reality means its class prestige in relation to the ruling classes of other nations. And besides drawing millions into war to realize its plundering intentions, it also draws the entire cultural apparatus of its class (different "scientific" theories about nations: biological, racist, empirical, and others; "patriotic" poetry, painting, music, etc.). [. . .]

The ruling class, nations of usurers which caused the World War, condemn war as a terrible social ill in their "peacemaking" League of Nations tirades. But at the same time they promote conflicts and encourage fascism, conscious that only in that way can they realize their imperialist aims. Responsibility for the war is borne neither by the Kaiser personally, nor by Franz Josef, nor by the Anglo-French Alliance, nor by Nicholas II, and even less by Serbia, Montenegro or the Sarajevo assassination. It is the system that is guilty, and they are only cogs in the system, political marionettes, bayonets which are to plunder booty for gluttonous appetites. For this reason every kind of religious-humanitarian opposition to war as a phenomenon isolated from the system that produces it is not only an ineffective weapon against the danger of war but, on the contrary, a special form of war propaganda. [. . .)

The World War was a staggering revelation for the broad masses of society. With the force of great historical events it unmasked all the hypocrisy of bourgeois ideals, all the lies of Kaiser-republican patriotism. All the old values were shaken to the foundations, and after the war the ordinary man—the soldier from the front—was appalled by the full exposure of realities. Reflecting that situation in postwar art there are three new responses:

1. Most artists found their previous convictions shaken to the foundations. For them war remains an incomprehensible phenomenon, since
they lack the skills for the proper examination of its causes and they see
in war only its evil consequences. Their convictions shattered, they fall
into a deep and gloomy psychological-intellectual depression. Unable to
cling to their old convictions, they have neither the will nor the strength
for new ones. In their works, the anguished flash of war illuminates
spiritual disorder, confusion and disillusionment; their condition is a
consequence of the war, and as such is elaborated in many different
tones; while the war itself, as the motif and the agent, is comprehended
only in fragments.

2. Another group of artists present documents of the war (atrocities
of senseless slaughter, the psychology of the front, assaults and trench
warfare and—less often—the psychology of the rear). They describe the
war the way a camera would have captured it, without explanation or
exposure of either causes or consequences. This is almost a role intended
for a photographic plate and not for committed artists.

3. Here we find the smallest number of artists, those for whom war is
only a manifestation of a system. Besides exposing the causes, they
present disturbing documents of war conditions themselves. War for
them is not a mystery but the inevitable consequence of existing social
relations. Hence those artists, and authors, following the logic of their
valid analysis, condemn war and struggle against it not for "humanistic"
or "humanitarian" reasons but because of their understanding of the
system that produces it. War is a consequence; the only effective struggle
against war is that which is directed against the conditions that created
it. For these artists and authors the World War served as the principal
theme in their militant struggle against existing social conditions. [. . .]

Slučaj Dušana Vasiljeva, 1933

Unnecessary Concessions to Surrealism

[. . .]
The dialectic serves as a guide to practical and concrete action. By the
application of the dialectic it is possible to discover what is positive and
will prevail and what should be completely rejected. Oskar Davičo himself illustrated the correct application of the dialectic very well in
unmasking overt and hidden neopositivism (see *Znanost i Život,* No. 1).
In that way he rescued the dialectic from those who idealize it, distort its
materialistic content, and remove its lethal bullets and replace them with
blanks.

Far from being a complete study of surrealism, the present article will offer a more precise interpretation of some of the points Davičo touched upon. The question of whether surrealism has positive aspects depends on the historical role of surrealism and on its place in the development of culture.

Surrealism sprang up in the jungle of postwar literary movements. While the working class was opening the way to new (socialist) realism, intellectuals of the ruling class were moving even farther away from reality and into even deeper individualism. The earlier problems, more or less clear to everyone, gave way to obscurity of form, personal dreams and automatic texts as the negation of any art. In this process of negation surrealism behaved quite destructively and anarchistically. [. . .] Understood in this manner by surrealists themselves and by the rest of the normal world, surrealism is not even a pure literary movement. One could perhaps better say that surrealism is a movement for the annihilation of art, for the annihilation of literature. In this respect there is also no doubt that surrealism passed through a certain evolution, evolving into the ultimate form of disintegration of bourgeois art. However, it would be a mistake to forget that it is at the same time one of the forms through which the financial bourgeoisie, fearing genuine artistic works, seeks to save itself and the unfortunate world from ultimate "destruction." To give an artistic work to the masses today is to arm those masses with the lethal weapons of knowledge and fervor. The financial magnates are afraid of art today. They would be much happier if it had never existed and if their own ruling class had not committed "original sin" by creating monumental works of art in its own past. It is interesting to note that even the Parisian surrealist Breton laments that he is read only by the grand bourgeoisie.

In any event, art and artistic creation further the struggle for social progress. The question, it is true, is not that simple. Dostoevsky existed ideologically at the far extreme of tsarist and clerical reaction; but in art he was a realist. And although his ideological position stood in the way of progress, in his art he cleared the path for new forms of expression, new realistic literary forms. [. . .] New realism is far from defending Dostoevsky's ideology or the darkness of tsarist dungeons. But new realism does not neglect the skill and the power with which he described the tragic realities of Russian society. Obviously, a truly artistic work signifies progress, whether in the sense of form or of content. New realism wants both the one and the other in contemporary social life. It is in this sense that every genuine artistic work furthers the development of culture and the progress of society.

[. . .] In the development of literature, surrealism did not further the struggle for new social content. It was new realism, the most progressive cultural movement, that carried on the struggle for new content. Thus it is ridiculous to tie these two movements together, to seek their kinship or mutual complementaries. Surrealism, however, attempted to do so because it was too weak to stand alone on its own foundations. But to bind them together would mean ideological revision of the Marxist conception of art, which, despite the good intentions of some surrealists, would doubtless be detrimental to Marxism.

In the matter of form, new realism introduced new possibilities of expression. Through the experience of the progressive movement before it, new realism grew richer in form and in content. In contrast, surrealism turns in a senseless circle, negating every form. Thus there is no kinship to be found between surrealism and new realism here, either. New realism is the only wholesome cultural movement, a movement that does not place the role of consciousness in opposition to art itself or the artistic work.

In the name of new realism it is necessary at this point to distinguish it from a certain vulgarization of new realism made by surrealists both in our country and abroad. New realism is sometimes denied artistic significance because of its emphasis on the role of consciousness in the creation of artistic works. They argue that a work does not become artistic merely because it propagates a certain ideology. That is true. But new realism never made such a claim. A work that is not artistic in form does not belong to new realism. New realism is nothing else but the recognition, on the basis of the experience of artistic and scientific development, that a genuine artistic work not only does not negate the ideology of the proletariat but also confirms it in its entirety; stated differently, it is "consciousness brought to the level of passion."

Things have gone so far that it is evident even without the burning of books that fascism is not capable of creating artistic works. This is so because to create the content of an artistic work means to establish social truths, which fascism does not desire; and to create the form of an artistic work is to clear the path toward new forms of culture, which fascism, as an anticultural movement, cannot do. The ever more consistent, ever more profound falsification of life makes it impossible for fascism to create artistic works; while the ever more direct penetration of the artist into life itself arms the artist with the capacity to recognize ever more certainly and enthusiastically the form and the content of genuine artistic works.

From the foregoing it is clear that an author need not be a Marxist to create an artistic work; but it is also clear that he must not be a fascist. It will, furthermore, be detrimental to the author and to his work as a whole if, viewing things realistically as an artist, he does not at the same time recognize all the consequences of that realism. Despite their ideological waverings, we would not challenge the literary importance of Desanka Maksimović, Gustav Krklec and Rastko Petrović, Ivo Andrić, Veljko Petrović and Dragiša Vasić. But experience has shown that the once intelligent and gifted author Crnjanski, in moving over to fascism, not only sealed up his art and his gift but also his intelligence, becoming a common "thug with a pen," a writer of shallow novels and commentaries for obscure papers. Authors, both mentioned and unnamed, should bear this in mind.

How does surrealism come out in the entire complex of these problems? In a marvelous, unselfish way Aragon was proud of the fact that abandoning surrealism made it possible for him to create artistic works. Aragon did not renounce the role of the so-called subconscious elements in his creations, elements upon which surrealism especially insists. To these subconscious elements, elements of experience and inspiration, he gave an active social function. Taken by themselves, these subconscious elements negate both the form and the content of art today. Surrealism thus does not signify the progress of art but its regress, a profound and critical decadence. Tearing down forms and not creating new ones (unless the lumping of words is some kind of a form), muddy in its content, surrealism does not signify forward movement but rotting and stagnation, even the chopping off of further development of art. [. . .] Thus it is not permissible in the name of new realism to take surrealism under its wing; nor can it be acknowledged that surrealism and related movements can contribute even "elements of genuine poetic creation."

The truth is that surrealism is a document of our times, an epoch of the most wonderful truths and the most hideous lies known to history. But to be a document does not make something an artistic work. Whatever else it may be, surrealism is also a document of the inability of a culture in disintegration to create artistic works.

The social role of surrealism is thus to interrupt the continuity of cultural development. Neither Marxism nor new realism wants such an interruption in the development of culture, and they will defend it against any interruption. That does not mean that followers of new realism cannot find some points of agreement with the surrealists in defense of culture. Several talents have been consumed in our country and abroad in that senseless and endless dizziness. A whole series of surrealists, some with more determination and some more cautiously, shifted to the position of new realism. The honest personal inclinations of surrealists must be distinguished from their ideological fuzziness which is quite contrary to their own subjective intentions. [. . .] Exactly because of the subjective intentions of these surrealists it is possible to find that some of them share common ground with new realism in defending culture, peace and social progress. But that is far from saying that in the name of new realism concessions should be made to surrealism or that positive aspects which will prevail should be discovered in it. For this reason, it is not warranted to look favorably on certain remnants of surrealism in Davičo's poetry; but it is warranted to give him support so that his poetry may become completely and utterly a new, genuine contribution to the poetry of new realism. On the basis of his poetry, the hope appears justified that he will himself succeed in over-coming his insufficiencies.

Znanost i Život, No. 5–6, 1937

Uncultured History

The author of these lines belongs among those who in the past have had very sharp public clashes with Miroslav Krleža. However, I see no reason either to be ashamed of them or to renounce them. Life is life and struggle is struggle, and it belongs to history to pronounce its judgment. [. . .] At the same time, I have *never* ceased admiring the brilliance of Krleža's intellect; and least of all today, when this truly great man and author, whose peers in Europe are hard to find, is being attacked by both the left and the right. Just now, on what calls itself the left, many of our cultural, political and governmental official and unofficial centers treat him like the carcass of a dog—it seems to me in the spirit of culture and good taste to do so just at the moment when we are celebrating the fortieth anniversary of his great and in every respect fruitful literary and dramatic works—and it is necessary exactly now to pour upon his head the kettle of past sins and mistakes and to stamp on him forever the seal of shame. And on the real right (for example, certain academicians, certain professors, and *Pogled,* the official organ of University ideologues, which emphasizes as a specific sign of its democraticness that it is not the organ of the "official ideologues") , they find it necessary to fire a salvo of poison and curses upon him since, in the final analysis, what place does that renegade, atheist, anti-Croat and anti-Serb, capitulator and rebel, Trotskyite and anarcho-individualist have in our civilized, Serbian Royal Academic and Yugoslav Franco-academic, not to mention socialist midst. . . .

And so it happened that in Agram [Zagreb] they organized a celebra-tion of Miroslav Krleža. Of course, for that initiative no official circles were responsible. It is said that no one from the government political leadership of the National Socialist Republic of Croatia participated, as one would expect at such an occasion honoring a revisionist and a blasphemer. The official boxes and first rows were desolate and empty, offering a melancholic picture of the emptiness and wasteland of many things in our contemporary socialist and bureaucratic reality. [. . .] But if it was thus in Agram, in Belgrade it was finer and nicer and it was not uncultured or publicly insulting, for the simple reason that nothing at all was done. (More precisely, something was done. Each of the three Belgrade theaters included a Krleža play in their repertory.)

Thus passed not only the fortieth anniversary of his literary work but also, if not worse, the sixtieth anniversary of his birth. Thus our socialist example showed that power on the one hand and culture and knowledge on the other do not in all cases go hand in hand. And as a rule, even less so in such cases. [. . .]

And just who is this Miroslav Krleža, who wrung out of his mind and his heart about forty volumes of not so mediocre prose and poetry, in a country where the authors of even two small volumes enter into the history of literature? This Krleža, who gave to the Serbo-Croatian language a new grace which had begun to be lost after the decline of folk epics and the first original works, and who in that way brought it from a gusle-pastoral and provincial way of expression to an expressive means of modern literature . . . That Krleža is resented on all sides . . . by the "Serbs" because of the generals, and by the "Croats" because of the priests. . . .

Although neither invited nor qualified to evaluate Krleža's literary value, as I said, I have always admired and drunk up the unrestrained and luxurious rhythms of Krleža's magic language, the concreteness of his imposing historical scenes, and that deep, tragic and painful tie to the soil and the peoples from whom he sprung and with whom he remained buried up to the shoulders despite all the contradictions and tragic searches and losses, despite the most subtle events, novel thoughts and forms, or perhaps because of all of them. [. . .]

Miroslav Krleža is in fact the greatest progressive ideological figure of Yugoslavia between the two wars, and especially in the first half of that period. With song and drama, essay and novel, travelogue and short story, pamphlet and criticism, with live words and the pen, he destroyed and consciously made ridiculous the bourgeois and feudal culture and cultural policy and in good part the very policy of Croatia and to some extent of Serbia, and thereby in fact, more than anyone else, prepared the ground for the revolutionary practice and the activity of newer, younger and fresher forces. How much significance history will attach to this side of Krleža's work and how much—of course more enduring—to the other, artistic, side, is known only by those who pretend that they can twirl history like a chain around their finger. But that today, when from a practical viewpoint we are still struggling against provincialism [. . .] the first side of his activity should be emphasized as most important can be doubted by no one who is really thinking culturally and politically, and least of all by those who sputter that their thought is progressive and democratic and socialist. Krleža is not someone who needs honor and praise, because he is what he is, even if the entire world tries painfully and loudly to deny that. Praise or scorn are today for Krleža like spitting on or trying to perfume the elephant: for with it or without it, the giant remains a giant, who creates a place for himself wherever he appears in our sweet and careful socialist gardens. But just because he was and is someone and something, not to say for socialism—in order that no one say that I have become a Krležaist at a time when even Krleža is not—but because it contributes to the progress of this country in the broadest sense of the word, I believe that by showing cultural recognition (without which he can go on, even if we did not dare to do it) to this magnificent Yugoslav figure we fight for progress and for socialism. [. . .]

Cultural history, that is, culture, is one unbroken continuity where generation is tied to generation, even if one generation is opposed to the other in its beliefs and creations. And in our case it seems that they think that they can sever this continuity as if culture and history began just with us. But what and where would we be today, in a cultural sense, without Miroslav Krleža? What would be our style and our language? And our spiritual progress in general? From where would we begin? From Matoš and Skerlić in the best case.

But be it as it may, all that demonstrates and proves how complex a struggle must be waged by democratic socialist forces for culture and for Yugoslavia and against puffed-up and self-satisfied bureaucratic-bourgeois provincialism and its mentality and its representations and understandings. And if these lines are even a document of this time and this struggle, isn't that something—a modest, unpretentious and disinterested recognition and acknowledgment of his work, and a joy to him also?

Nova Misao, No. 1, January 1954

Notes

Random Thoughts on Writers and Writing

["Jail Diary," from which these excerpts were taken, offers a view of prison life through the eyes of a political prisoner who spent a period of nine years in jail, 1958–1961, 1962–1966 (interrupted by a span of four-teen months in 1961 and 1962), and who spent twenty months in solitary confinement. Djilas was subject to various forms of harassment, ranging from confiscation of his letters to withdrawal of all privileges, including the right to have any writing paper for almost two years. (It was at this point that he resorted to writing on toilet paper and thus was able to continue writing—the only activity that enabled him to keep his sanity.)

Djilas writes about the little joys and sorrows of prison life, he reflects on crime and punishment as well as on prison reform, and, based on the limited information available to him, he writes about the prospects for war and peace. With "Nordic Dream" the jail diary constitutes an unusual political-literary document.]

February 19, 1958

These days I often think about Trotsky. I have finally decided that he is a very important figure and one who will grow more significant with time; indeed, this is already the case. All of his theories, evaluations and forecasts are utter nonsense. But despite his revolutionary utopianism he was the first to criticize the system. He did not understand the system but he did observe the moral depravity of its representative (Stalin). One can only learn today from Trotsky's negative example: that his course was incorrect, and that it was absurd for him to be astonished at the immorality of his opponent. But his service is that he first began to criticize from within, which only confirms that he is a great revolutionary. Of course, he was always that.

I have never been in any way a Trotskyite, and Trotsky as a figure never attracted me, nor does he even now. But history inexorably will give him his due and already has, in part. He will ultimately take his place as one of the great heretic martyrs; and that is still something.

And so it goes. Little by little worms are born and eat away at the hardest core. One today, another tomorrow.

An interesting observation: whenever I enter a thought in my notebook, it leaves me immediately and I feel a sudden release. So it is with Lev Davidovich. I have said all this about him once before, in *The New Class,* but it came back to me and now it has gone away again.

Moral considerations played an important part in my own rebellion, especially in the beginning. And particularly in this form: moral responsibility need not be borne for that with which one fundamentally no longer agrees. But even now I am "plagued" by moral questions.

February 20, 1958

I am reading Proust. A man of genius. The finest psychological-poetic analysis. Probably he is the greatest poet of the twentieth century. Engaging, although too voluminous, even as a philosophy. [. . .]

During the past few days I read *Across the River and into the Trees* and some other stories. Hemingway has a special talent that I have never observed in any other writer: he reproduces such details and nuances, most often through dialogue, that the most vivid sensation of life is created. Everything in his works appears casual, reporterlike and unobtrusive. But beneath the surface details are deep, intimated thoughts, entire philosophies—not articulated in the mind but compressed from experience. Perhaps Faulkner is deeper as a writer, but direct poetic force, that ability to re-create reality, is Hemingway's special gift among all writers. Only Tolstoy had it in larger measure, but only he. Hemingway speaks for the disillusioned post-WWI generation. But only in a thematic way as he re-creates the psychology and life of those men. In fact, he really portrayed something deeper and timeless—human instinct in action, the subconscious motive realized. He has a fresh vision of life. Really, a great—more precisely, a direct—poet of our time. What Hemingway does through ordinary details—he achieves the breath of life itself—is surely a special gift that cannot be learned or imitated. He goes about it with such ease, as if toying with things. And really, he is not a recorder of details. He selects only those details that reveal, those details that serve to conduct deep currents of life.[. . .]

April 10, 1958

Last night as soon as I realized that I must remain in prison for a long time, I drafted a writing plan to cover several years. It lists those themes on which I have already worked—perhaps I have thought about them more than worked on them—and on which I have gathered some material. I would not write on these themes if I were able to do something else. Of course, my plan will be realized only during the warm months. I don't intend to write polished manuscripts, but only to jot down on paper some thoughts. Polishing is sometimes a longer and more painful job, but once one has a text, then one can start. I intend, therefore, if I keep my health, to polish them when I am out of jail.

The plan is as follows:

1958: 1) Messages from Jail. Three parts (to my sister, my son, my wife). This will be reflective writing about the past, the present, and the future.

2) Montenegro—a novel-essay. Three parts (The Battle; The Foreigner; The End). An attempt to describe the "essence" of Montenegro, why her people fight and what they live for. I had some notes about it in my apartment, but since Štefica and Goša cannot bring them to me, I must rely on my memory and use in some ways Ćetković's book *Unifiers of Montenegro and Serbia.*

1959: 1) The Legend of Tsar Dukljan. An essay about good and evil beginning with the theme of the legend of Tsar Dukljan.

2) The end of the Turkish empire. A novel-essay about Berane (my landlady from my high-school days) and my Aunt Marta (the sister of my mother). I made some outlines about it but only very roughly.

1960: 1) Against the Death Penalty. An essay.

2) Autumn in the Lim Valley. A novel-essay with a theme from my school years around 1929, or exactly 1929 (the dictatorship era).

1961:   1) The Old Man and the Girl. A short story-essay on the theme of man's instinct for perpetuation of himself and his species.
2) Umbilical Cords, Hawks' Nests, that is, a story about relatives. [. . .]
1962:   1) The Life and Death of Vuk Lopušina. Short story-legend about the Montenegrin hero according to the folk song, with the theme of manliness and bravery, but in a new light.
2) Stevan Ljugonja. A humorous short story according to folk tales, with a theme of the common life and the common man in great heroic times.
1963: 1) *The Offensive*. A novel-essay with a motif from the Fifth Offensive and the theme of man struggling for a meager existence. This is only an idea in my head and I haven't written anything about it yet.

Of course, this is only my plan, which I will not adhere to rigidly, but will carry out according to the conditions of my life in jail and the length of my jail term.

The plan is for six years. As for those two years that remain, I have enough time to think until then. [. . .]

May 18, 1958

I was told that *Land Without Justice* was well received. This gives me courage, even if I discount some of the praise because it is by a politician and has some political motives. I must finish Montenegro, and I am convinced that after revisions it will be better than *Land Without Justice,* deeper, richer, with the glow of internal reflections. But only under the condition of solid revisions. *Land Without Justice* was also three times revised (the second revision was the major one). The first draft was unusable. [. . .]

May 19, 1958

I feel so pleasant, almost as if I were not in jail. There are two reasons for it—what I heard about *Land Without Justice* gave me some perspective on myself, as a writer: it linked me to the reality of the outside world. Second, I am writing, I am working, and I am reaching out towards a new horizon. Today I wrote six pages—very bad, very poor (the second chapter of Part II) —but I wrote them. I freed myself from one topic and that enabled me to make the transition to new things. [. . .]

May 27, 1958

Since yesterday I've been reflecting on my situation here. Very inhuman: total isolation, without foreign books, uninformed about what is happening in philosophy, literature and politics. They haven't returned Njegoš yet—perhaps all will have been for nought, a destroyed work. A similar fate probably awaits Montenegro. Not too many things remain to be taken away from me—save for books and paper. Perhaps the day will come even for that. And, what is most interesting, that does not bother me. Moreover, this life seems to me bearable, even good. Unable to make a deal with evil, how man can adapt himself to it. [. . .]

May 30, 1958

It is a completely unfounded thesis that most authors favor freedom and progress. Many do. But not all, often not the greatest ones. Like other citizens, authors also have certain orientations. Convention, comfort, conformity shape authors just as they shape other people. Therefore, one's artistic work must be viewed separately from one's political ideas, even though such ideas are interwoven with that work.

And even nature is in fact such. Political views and ideas are temporal. Artistic work is eternal. Because of that, it seems to me that one should not scorn too much an author if he often takes some conformist position. One cannot deny, however, that his responsibility is greater than that of other people because his influence is greater. His sense of moral responsibility must be a burden at the moment when he writes out of selfishness or fear, not out of conviction, that is, when he lies knowingly. At that moment he is not an ordinary citizen. When the ordinary citizen lies, he is saving only himself. But the author misleads others.

I talk primarily about authors, although my comments apply to all public workers; literature is not completely separable from ideologies, or from everyday politics. What is artistic can be isolated, but it emerges in a context of contemporaneity (ideas, atmosphere, etc.). Art is the living word and directly influences the conscience, and because of that the responsibility of the author is greater than that of other artists. [. . .]

June 2, 1958

There is one interesting difference between the way one thinks when one is walking about and when one is lying down. This I have observed only now while sunning myself. When I am strolling, my thoughts are scattered and persistent, pressing hard for an answer, even if they are circling around the same topic. When one is lying down, thoughts are lighter and effortless. Lying down seems to be a more natural condition for thinking. [. . .]

June 14, 1958

It is very dangerous for an author to be in love with his writing. I observed that in the case of M. Krleža and O. Davičo. They always add words, and they like a lot of words. It took me a long time before I learned to sacrifice entire pages. What I didn't throw away from *The New Class!* And added. But especially threw away. His own words, clever images, and rhetorical skills fascinate the author, but often they are empty.

The greatest virtue—to cut, to the barest measure. Of course, one must not lose clarity. [. . .]

June 28, 1958

I am reading Dostoevski's *Idiot*. I began reading this excellent work three or four times in my life, but something always interrupted me.

Probably this is the darkest of Dostoevski's books. But it is very, very deep! And I would even say, underestimated. No wonder, when measured beside *The Brothers Karamazov* and *Crime and Punishment*.

I maintain that Dostoevski is to be ranked with Shakespeare, Dante, and Sophocles. In his own manner he is the greatest writer of all. And the one who, in my youth, and even now, attracted me the most. He and Shakespeare are the supreme poets.

Dostoevski's method is very simple, although uniquely his own. His people act and speak the way that they think intimately. Hence a deeper reality than reality itself. To this correspond the language, style and composition. A long time ago it was observed that he was not a master of style and composition. However, this is an incorrect judgment. He is not an *artiste;* that is, he does not polish and overrefine. If he did, then that world, whose pictures and visions he creates, would disappear. In that simplicity, that "ordinariness" he is unsurpassed. In this composition of reality—its dynamism of action and its internal logical force—he is unsurpassed. He does not appear to me now as such a political reactionary as he really was. In any case—it is unimportant.

Is he more of an artist, or a thinker? He is an artist-thinker. [. . .]

July 30, 1958

Yesterday they returned Njegoš. Now I can see that I have invested enough work and effort in it. [. . .]

September 5, 1958

With Njegoš I will finish all that I have to say about Montenegro—almost all. There remain some small things: of great things—there is nothing. One should make a transition—when? when? when?—to important contemporary themes. The moment I leave jail. And up to that time—I will write some more small things.

Even without my intending it to be so, Montenegro, *Land Without Justice* and Njegoš constitute a whole. Montenegro—an epic novel; Njegoš—a poetic history; and *Land Without Justice*—a personal-lyric-epic story. [. . .]

September 19, 1958

I read Dostoevski's *The Double*. I had completely forgotten its story. But it was a good thing that I read it again, since only now did I understand its depth. Each man reproduces himself, is reproduced in others, and all the evils of others are also his own. I am surprised the *The Double* does not still belong among his famous works, although it is not far behind the greatest ones. When did he write it? His mastery in creating atmosphere is sensed just as it is in *Karamazov*.

Art, if it is not entirely human and if it does not penetrate into "eternal themes"—is not really art. That which is on the surface is art's inevitable clothing—form, the manner of telling the story. And art cannot be without it. There is no matter without form, nor does natural law reveal itself outside of matter, that is, outside its forms. The forms are infinite and changing which appear as motifs in art. The rest is lasting and indestructible.

Dostoevski belongs with Shakespeare and Sophocles. He is completely new in his own way. He is not only an author of genius and a thinker, but he also creates a new spiritual world. It may be that he is even a new civilization. Its prophet! And Lenin only the beginning. They are contradictions. But that does not alter the essence. Each is only a different spiritual form of the emerging civilization.

Roughly speaking, my theme also applies to Shakespeare and Sophocles. Parallels could also be found in the politics and philosophies of their epochs (Cromwell, English empiricism; Pericles, Aristotle). But those are only forms. And they speak about the truths of men and man's humanness. [. . .]

October 23, 1958

Man is the only being who is oriented toward eternity, and this is expressed most fully and most clearly by the fact that he creates artistic works as final, absolute values—fragments of eternity. No other being creates such works. With science man uncovers laws. But science is more oriented toward life; that is, science uncovers the unchangeable law for the sake of improving man's existence. Art does not make life easier. It beautifies: it ennobles. It links man with eternity, with his own eternal nature and creation. Without art, man would not differ much from the animals, just as without science he would not easily wrench himself from the animal kingdom. [. . .]

October 27, 1958

The Pasternak affair. Our press scarcely mentions it and the radio—just a few words. However, what is magnificent is the bearing—revealed in Pasternak's statements—of a spirit who has lived through all phases of the Soviet system and has neither yielded to it nor accommodated himself to it. Pasternak's statements are those of a free and a courageous man. Of course, the conservative Swedish Academy of Sciences could hardly wait to bestow their honor upon one of the opposition writers in the USSR. But even if he had not won their prize, Pasternak would remain a superb poet. He really brought something new to poetry—I don't know him well, but I know that much. The error of the Soviet leadership, as far as one can tell, is that they overreacted to his receiving the prize. But this is not so much an error as an inevitability. For what would happen if they had not reacted that way? The spirit of the opposition would slowly be legitimized, if only through the export of literature from the USSR. That is worrisome, and they fear it more than is necessary. Even in the USSR there are few writers who could export such good pieces as Pasternak. For me, here, Pasternak is a symbol of the unbending human spirit. Even were he not a good poet, he is no ordinary man. [. . .]

October 29, 1958

Yesterday the radio announced that Pasternak had been thrown out of the Union of Soviet Writers as a counterrevolutionary. Poor old man! How in this strange game between worlds everything has to break just on his back, and his subtle poetry.

Thinking about Pasternak, who is, of course, a man of the old generation, I am convinced that the spirit of a new and free Russia has awakened. His work affirms that the spirit of freedom is indestructible as is everything else that is human. [. . .]

November 5, 1958

Politics is, in fact, the creation of a new reality, as is art, but politics is all in reality, unlike art. But only in reality. Artists are not good politicians, and politicians are not good artists either. And I have been torn all my life between art and politics, as if I had two natures in me. I recall that conflict between desire and duty, and it seems to me that I am simply made that way. In fact, this is a fluctuation between the tendency to create and the wish to apply creation to reality. [. . .]

November 8, 1958

Every morning I am working on *Njegoš* and it is going well. [. . .] I think that *Njegoš* will be a good book if it ever sees the light of day. I compare it with Isidora Sekulić's book—today I can view her objectively. Her book is more beautiful in a literary sense, but mine will be more thoroughly documented and—more authentic. Even that is something. I work on it with love, I am paying Njegoš a debt—since from him, that is, from folk poetry, I benefited immensely. Even more than from Dostoevski and Marx. Much more, because all that he writes is our own and original. I want my book to be some kind of monument to him. All our past is expressed in him, and, it seems to me, quite a lot of the future—really, one can find here the promise of new life. [. . .]

November 19, 1958

When I wrote that art is creation, I did not mean that it was the creation of some realistic world, but that it was the artist's vision of the world. The fact that the real world serves as an inspiration to modern painting only underscores the truth that realism in art is imagined. Even when the artist tries to render a realistic picture of the world, he must improve it and purify it. His creation is a picture of that imagined reality and, as such, must be comprehensible to the public, even that public of the future. In the final analysis, in art everything is realistic and the expression of human realities—of the artist as a human being and of his time—that leave their stamp on the work that emerges. [. . .]

November 26, 1958

A personal observation. I began with literature, continued in politics, and ended with philosophy. Now I have cast all that aside, or, more correctly, all is synthesized in what I now write, in my life activity, even if that is serving time in jail. [. . .]

March 7, 1959

In man there exist irresistible and indestructible strivings for creation. They are none other than expressions of man's struggle against death. In line with that struggle, I understand man's tendency to produce new conditions of life for the young. When this striving is expressed in an emotive manner, through feeling, it is art; when it is realized in a material way—it is production; and if it is expressed in discovering laws—it is science. All that is in accord with the theses about the expanding and perfection of production as the most essential human characteristic. Still another thought: striving to create, man attempts to give shape to his world through dream, reality, impression, thought, rhythm, and the form of life (spiritual and other) —and that is art. [. . .]

The problem is simply this: Like any other creature, man lives and defends himself against death, but in his own peculiarly human way—with thought which is capable of uncovering laws and beauties, and with hands which are skillful at producing. [. . .]

March 26, 1959

The philosopher Bertrand Russell impressed me with his stand against hydrogen weapons. At the very least it represents the attempt of a human spirit to define his philosophical position, even though I am not familiar with his view in detail. In any case, of all the many contemporaries whom I have managed to become at least acquainted with (only in these last few years have I glanced at them, since, until recently, I relied upon Hegel and Marx), Russell takes a position that is far from being the closest to my own. Sometimes it seems to me that my intuitive and occasional attraction to Russell is not accidental. It is more an inborn kinship than a conscious agreeing. I remember also how amazed I was when I came across my own thoughts in Camus' *The Myth of Sisyphus*. But even apart from that, Camus was attractive to me as a writer—he has a simple deepness. I began to like Russell a long time ago, even when I was in power. And now I see that he has an appealing political position, although it seems that many things are not clear to him. "It seems" because of the meager information in our newspapers. It seems to me, however, that he views hydrogen weapons from somewhere outside our contemporary time when in fact they are its by-product and its reflection. But be that as it may, the voice of his profound, indestructible humaneness— so rare today—resounds here within this prison cell in my heart, and I, in my own way, join him on this dismal day that bears no resemblance to spring with its cold, steady rain. [. . .]

April 3, 1959

There is something incomparably beautiful in my imprisonment—in this internal peace, these reflections over my own conscience, my past, and the laws of human destiny. It all started much earlier, before jail— perhaps even in my early youth—but only here did it mature and finally assume its ultimate form. Sometimes I regret that I am not younger so that after many years, everything would crystallize and sort itself out. I could give it a literary-reflective form.

I did not anticipate that I would endure this imprisonment with such internal peace and determination. [. . .]

April 6, 1959

Isidora Sekulić died last night. I read it in *Politika* this morning. I cannot say that I am sorry; those are not my real feelings. But I am not indifferent, because I owed her something. I had attacked her too sharply and unjustifiably. She was a good writer, and her study of Njegoš, although in some respects arbitrary, is a magnificent work of literature. And now I cannot make amends. My sin is even greater because I was in power. Under those circumstances, although I did not permit any discrimination against her or her works, she was in an unequal position. I myself was under the illusion that our positions were equal; such was not the case, nor could it have been, nor was I able to see that it was not.

She will remain a great name in our culture as one of the most brilliant essayists and essayist-novelists, a keenly intelligent mind, an unsurpassed master of language and style. And I? In literature, nothing, or only a little, very little. In politics, something of a dreamer, a corrector of injustices and a seeker of absolute justice. No, let's leave aside those "guilty consciences" and "self-accusations." Isidora was, and remains, a remarkable spirit in her intellectual labors, in her dedication to her works, and in bringing light and knowledge to the darkness of the Balkan town. [. . .]

April 10, 1959

I read for the first time Dostoevski's *Notes from the Underground*. I am surprised that I missed it up to now. This is one of the deepest works—but what of his is not the deepest?

I read also Kafka's *Metamorphosis*—it is beautiful and deep. Before my jailing I read *The Trial*. I understood Kafka as an author who uncovers the conflict between man and absolute laws and who reveals man's impotence in the face of them. It seems to me that this is fundamental and new, and because of that, I consider him really an original talent of the most horrible and most essential beauty.

Without great thoughts, truths, and other ideas, there is no great art.

By the way, I am surprised at the kinship between some of my ideas and those of Dostoevski, especially ideas about the senselessness of change and progress among men. I became convinced a long time ago that Dostoevski was not a reactionary in politics, although he was conservative when it came to dealing with everyday problems; he intimated and saw many truths. In him, I think, began a new civilization, and especially new forms of art that embody truth about man before and above all else. Russia needs now to discover him and itself in him.

April 11, 1959

Dostoevski claims—and I believe him—that neither pressure, nor prison, nor the death sentence itself could force him to alter his revolutionary and socialist beliefs; rather, he was changed by contact with the Russian people, especially with the lowest stratum—those in prison. He was also influenced by memories from childhood—his father had often read the Bible to him and educated him in the national spirit. As for me, although I do not wish to compare myself with this great, this greatest man, during my period of change in view, the basic thing was the conflict of reality with my moral principles. And as far as my stay here is concerned, contact with the prisoners has convinced me of the reality of that conflict. Humiliations have only confirmed it, although one cannot say that there is real contact with people here. I sense this conflict and also find it in contact with the individuals and in the specific opinions and speeches of these unfortunates, and that tells me that I have at least a presentiment of the truth. [. . .]

May 5, 1959

Njegoš and Miljanov lie for a long time unread. [. . .] "The Legend of Tsar Dukljan" is boiling within me—I am reaching the point where I simply want to write a novel that will embrace the problem of evil as I have already understood it in principle. Let it boil! [. . .]

Thus, in this manner—jumping from subject to subject today—I have a tendency to write with joy and with ease. [. . .] And I feel behind each word and line how I become more cheerful within myself—what a magic power the expressed word has! To unburden oneself—isn't that creation, telling, freeing? Isn't each freeing a kind of creation? Not only artistic, but any kind of creation?

Everything nice is creation. [. . .]

And I would like to create—to write and write until I put everything down—but I can't put everything down. Because here the conditions are not the best, really. On the one hand, everything stifles and presses upon me, but on the other hand, I have to create. Creation is capable of overcoming all difficulties, including anger, and to find inspiration in them instead. Only in the evil of prison does man really find himself and his humanness. Glory to man and to prison—hail man and prisons!

May 6, 1959

Goethe somewhere said that the greatest evils for him were hope and fear. They usually go together, sometimes in reciprocal relations. But it seems to me that the best thing for a failed man, especially one who has suffered defeats like mine, is for him to destroy hope. With it then he would destroy fear. Although fear never bothered me much, hope does. [. . .]

Therefore, destroy hope—chase it from Pandora's box. Let everything be evil to the end! [. . .]

I have known—and I know today more than ever before—that in politics there is no mercy toward the weak, and that History nails only a lead tablet of oblivion over the defeated as over unpleasant episodes. But I never expected mercy, and when forced to do that in which I could not believe, I chose defeat. There are some of us who are also born from Mother Earth. Not even now would I choose another road, even though people consider me stupid, and all think that I am no politician. As I once stated, "It is better to be an honest man than a Minister." [. . .]

A little here, a little there, a little to the right, a little to the left—nothing in this world of ours, in fact, changes very much, not even I—I would not consent to change, even if I could change the world. Is that rigidity, conceit, dogmatism? No, for even if he wants to, man cannot change; he must act in accord with possibilities, which are created almost independently of his will.

Only through words can I recognize people—their characters, weaknesses, their little deceits and virtues, their belief in their own good intentions, and their need to lie and flatter. The style is the man. I would say that man is speech; further, he is the intonation of what he speaks, the distribution of works in his own sentence, even the construction of his speech. [. . .]

May 15, 1959

Sometimes, especially when I write, I feel very strongly that I have emerged from an enormous and passionate revolutionary upheaval. Moreover, I have emerged from Communism. Without the experiences I acquired there, I could not have today's present views or write the literature I now write. [. . .]

The philosophy which holds that in today's world the struggle is between good and evil among men is enormously simple, but it is not completely incorrect. I too wanted to say something like that, but I did not have time to work the philosophical problem out to the end and to free myself from simple-mindedness; I therefore kept quiet about it.

I always wanted to be on the side of the good. [. . .]

May 26, 1959

It seems to me that the longer my imprisonment lasts and as a leaden-like forgiveness falls over me, the more the truth will receive clear, radiant forms.

Nothing good and pure can remain so if it does not pass through humiliation and human suffering. [. . .]

May 30, 1959

Yesterday I remembered a motif which I wrote down under the title "Sister." In 1952 I saw at Biogradsko Lake a young, pretty girl—as such she did not interest me, although one could not deny her attractiveness. I gave her and another woman a lift in my car to the bridge on the River Tara. Goga, the secret policeman who accompanied me, sat in angry silence. Afterwards I asked him, "What is the matter?" He told me that the pretty girl was a "bandit," that he knew her, and that she also knew him from an interrogation. They abused her in all possible ways to make her tell them where her brothers, Četniks, were hiding. But they got nowhere. The only thing they did was to sentence her to a long prison term; later she was granted amnesty.

The literary motif remained with me, although I was sorry that I had given a lift to such a woman—it was simple courtesy on my part; even more, a gesture of good will because I was in my own birthplace, and as a

Minister I did not want to appear conceited or arrogant. But whatever was the case, the motif remained with me. Later, in the summer of 1953, I mentioned that motif to Kardelj, during a discussion about humanness and democracy. Who is right? The patriarchal sister who protects the counterrevolutionary brothers, or the secret police who defend the revolution and the national struggle? Kardelj agreed with me that from the humane viewpoint the sister is right, but that does not mean she should not be punished. Of course, I also leaned toward that view. But then I posed the questions: How would you treat this situation in a short story? Would you defend the right of the sister to remain a sister? He strenuously maintained that something like that should not be written about, regardless of what is right and what is not, while I stubbornly argued that it is absolutely necessary to write about these motifs and problems. Such writing, which holds nothing as an absolute, aids democratic development by uncovering new kinds of reality.

But what is most interesting, I did not even notice at the time the similarity between that motif and Sophocles' *Antigone;* the drama was translated into our concrete conditions and relations. I thought of that only after I was removed from power, and again here in jail. The thought killed in me the attractiveness of the theme, since I would not be so original if I worked on it; but it revealed a deeper thought: Great truths and artistic motifs repeat themselves, always in a new manner, and with them human destiny also seems to repeat itself.

I don't know whether I will ever write about that theme, but I am noting down its history as characteristic of myself and my time. And the theme itself as characteristic of people and human relations.

May 31, 1959

The story about Mališa Damjanović and his wife [. . .] I decided to call "Tudjinka" ("The Foreigner") because it deals with a woman who failed to adjust to anything Montenegrin or revolutionary.

I don't know where these tendencies to uncover in literature and in my own writings truth about people and human destinies will lead me, but it seems to me—and sometimes I fear it is so—that they are separating me from politics and from confronting myself with politics as such. But politics forces itself upon me and I must face reality directly. More and more I turn myself toward enduring motifs and toward the condemnation of tyranny and war as such; but this does not mean that I do not see also their inevitability. [. . .] It is not by chance that I wrote no literature while I was actively engaged in politics for more than twenty years. In that connection it is interesting to note that when I am writing novels and other literary works, I tend to evade ideas and ideology; but this is not altogether possible for me—obviously there is within me no artistic flexibility without reflective clarity, without meaning, without ideas.

All this narrows down to the fact that formulating something definitive is impossible and harmful because reality changes—one should strive for politics in which tyranny is reduced to the smallest possible measure, since tyranny cannot be totally excluded. That means that tyranny would be justified only in the case of defense of the nation, of the movement (our own or others). But what is defense? It does not exist independently of attack. Tyranny is justified only against tyranny, but this does not mean that lack of freedom is unfreedom. Tyranny which is unfreedom, regardless of whether or not it is against tyranny, can hardly justify itself. It is not only a question of moral justification, but a historical question as well: tyranny that is unfreedom finally undermines and destroys itself because it creates forces that remove it.

Yes, all this is still unclear in my mind, and too new. In politics, there is abstract sense that becomes clear only when it is seen concretely. What is theoretical is less important than what is possible; all abstract theories are senseless and therefore unnecessary.

There remains a problem: to harmonize the artistic with other points of view. But does one have to resolve it? Can I count on an eventual solution? On development of artistic works and ideas as they come, so that everything finally molds itself into a whole? This too is a creative method, but not one that instantly strives to resolve an issue or problem the moment it emerges. Isn't gradual development another way of accomplishing the same thing? Is it not even more characteristic of life itself?

Prisoners' chatter and ways of wasting time!

Sit down and write: [. . .]

July 13, 1959

I am pleased with Andrić's success in the United States. This is the beginning of the spread of an unknown culture and its people into world culture. Now it seems to me that making the rest of the world know Njegoš—through my book, if it proves of value, or through someone else's work—would be of great importance; it would link our epic and individual history with world culture. [. . .] Revolution introduced us into the world arena and everything that is humane will be exposed to the world? That is correct. Long enough have we been the orphans of history. [. . .]

Andrić is our greatest writer of prose and one whom we will not duplicate for a long time. Let us hope that in secret he is preparing some even more significant works. [. . .]

October 2, 1959

I dreamt that I was being strangled at dawn. I was winding my way through the dense brush atop a rock cliff over a river—the detail of the river and cliff reminds me of the real cliff by the River Una. But at the moment nothing is strangling me. I am thinking that my temporary inaction in writing is the consequence of a lack of ideas. Whenever I wanted to write something even if I had a subject, I could not begin to work on it if I did not have an idea about it, that is, if I did not know, even in vaguest outline, what I was trying to say. [. . .] The rough matter of the motif only becomes controllable and receives a form when an idea is added to it. Artistic work has no precise goal or sense, but it cannot grow without meaning, without an idea that leads the artist. The work emerges in our eyes as the creation of an idea, although it is not in reality so, since the idea only helped to create a form out of chaos, to shape a new world, a new matter, and that was all. [. . .]

December 18, 1959

Spontaneously I came to the conclusion, mostly through the writing of my literary works over the last years, that I in fact returned in my views to the classic Greek and Roman literary examples. It seems to me that the authors of those periods when art began to separate from popular melos, and human thought from religion, succeeded in the fullest, most simple and measurable way in expressing what they believed they must say. They didn't have any pure poetry or any kind of pure form; their art was always mixed with philosophy, or at least with meditation, with ethics and history, and Plato as a philosopher is, at the same time, a poet of myths and master of philosophical dialogue. Even Aristotle's works are not without poetry; in any case, they are not solely philosophy, but contain the history of Greek thought about society and human thought. In that sense the Greek dramatists, who are unusually great poets and thinkers, are most characteristic; so too are the Roman philosopher-historians, who are also the poets of the past and of their own time. Plutarch would not be so endearing a classical author if he were not an observant, lively painter of people, customs, and times. [. . .]

In that way any great author, or thinker, is at the same time a great moralist, but not in the sense that he preaches a specific moral. Art is indifferent toward morality; it does not pay much attention to morals since they burden art as an alien and artificial element. But art concerns itself with uncovering human destiny, that is, with the inevitable ways and conditions of human existence.

The return to the ancients does not mean for me adopting either their forms or their thoughts—that would be useless, senseless and fruitless—but realizing that the most important thing is that an idea be expressed in an adequate manner, that is, in a new form. This form can be either a novel or a short story, a memoir or an essay, or anything else, depending upon the material that needs to be expressed or the thought itself that simplifies and elaborates that material. [. . .]

December 23, 1959

An idea just struck me for a work that I will probably never realize: a Marxist critique. By that I do not mean criticism of the historical meaning of his thought or of the movement that came after it—on the contrary, one should praise Marxism in that respect—but I mean a criticism of that which has been surpassed, of that which is today scientifically incorrect and socially reactionary. It seems to me that my ideas are completely ripe for such a task. Today Marxism is identical with the reality of bureaucratic despotism, regardless of the slogans behind which it hides or the forms in which it emerges in response to the conditions in which it can exist. With this critique I would finally define also my philosophical, materalistic and social positions. *The New Class* was a Marxist book; the one that I am imagining would be only a materialistic book. But I don't believe, as I said, that I will ever write it. I note all this as a movement in my thought and as an indication of my mood. Yet, thinking about it, I came to the conclusion that that theme should not be separated and specially treated but should be made a component part of a book I have in mind called The Unperfect Society. Of course, for such an undertaking one needs to make an enormous scholarly effort it would, besides allowing me to write, serve me as relaxation from my purely literary works. Perhaps it is the opposite case—the literary works would relax me from ideology and politics.

It is getting colder. In the morning the cold bothers my hands while I write. This morning I will not even go out for my first recreation walk. I must note that I have regained again internal balance although my illness is not completely over. I think that this signifies a new phase in my thinking and other activities and also in my relations with the authorities; it is now definite that I am resolved to remain in jail. Now I not only accept this, but I accept it as an inevitability even more than that, as a circumstance that will not have solely negative consequences for me. Obviously, I as a public personality do not lose anything by it, and even more obviously, as a moral person, I must do nothing to free myself from it. [. . .]

January 4, 1960, 8 P.M.

The radio just reported that Albert Camus died in an automobile accident. Is it possible? A superb writer—all pure thought and pure conscience. How much he brought that was new, and now—at the height of his powers! When I read *The Myth of Sisyphus* in 1954 I felt as if I were reading my own words. He was one of those rare spirits who made one feel glad to live when he lived. As far as I know modern French literature, he was its deepest and most creative spirit. I really feel as if someone very dear and close to me had died; moreover, someone in the

shadow of whose thoughts I feel more peaceful and more productive.
[. . .]

March 1, 1960 (in the morning)

I am now reading the Bible. I never had time to read it before and I was always sorry that I did not have time to plow through this magnificent epic of the Jewish destiny. Now the opportunity is good and it fits into my plan for studying St. Basil of Ostrog. I began with the story of Job and will browse through the rest. Above all, these stories have a pacifying effect, with their archaic language and wisdom; they reconfirm that true wisdom does not grow old and that real artistic work is ageless. Strange, in the first chapters about Job I am finding some views identical to mine—about good and evil and about the inevitability of human destinies. I sense that the Bible, along with *Mountain Wreath* and Marko Miljanov, will remain with me as long as I am in jail (not, of course, because of the religion but because of its wisdom expressed in purest poetry, which also serves to warn people about the catastrophes that might befall them) . [. . .]

May 5, 1960

I see that everything I am now writing has the mark of jail and isolation upon it. I don't know whether this is good or bad, but for a future reader, if my work is going to survive, it could create a special charm. Where does one see the mark of prison in my writing? In all those memories, in the fact that they are just that, remembrances, and from them most frequently springs forth a vision particularly different from the conditions and atmosphere of the prison: lovely pictures and colors of childhood and youth, passionate and beautiful faces of men and women, happenings full of the life force, and direct contact with Nature. Essentially, all creation is like that. Each artist draws from his memory, if not all, a large part of his work. For me, here, this is characteristic. The role of memory is felt in everything, and in each picture there is a shadow of melancholy and of painful life experiences. Whether or not that quality is a threat to my art, I cannot say. It seems to me, rather, that exactly that brings a certain charm, even a value, to my present works. And then again, couldn't the jail itself and its isolation work the effect of purifying or cleansing me from the unnecessary and the nonessential? Perhaps my circumstances simplify and bring nearer to truth both my thought and its representation. I say "truth" and not "realism" although I have been a realist for some time. But there is no danger that my memory will run dry. I say memory, though one really means creative power—the maturing and combining of new motifs from within. The fact is that still—for the second year—I am playing around with small things like the Turkish Autumn; this proves nothing else but that I am not yet ripe for bigger

things. Secretly I am postponing those bigger things, because I am hoping
that the authorities will let me go. I know that my release will not come
about easily, but when it does, in the atmosphere of my family I can work
on those larger things at my own pace. In addition to that hope, there is
something more curious. All new and smaller motifs that appear in my
mind compel me to work on them, but they also offer me the convenience
of escaping from bigger and more complex works. I succumb very easily
and gladly to this spontaneous tendency, but at the same time, in the
back of my mind, I am not quite satisfied with it, and I prepare myself
for more serious and complex themes. [. . .]

The sky is covered with even clouds and it is very cold for this time of
year. [. . .]

May 10, 1960

I read that Sartre is coming to Yugoslavia. I don't know him much as
an author, and I did not read his most important philosophical work
(*L'Etre et Le Néant*), but I admire him highly as an innovator of ideas.
La Nausée is a good book—original in manner and in its view of reality.
I have read only two of his plays, and they are too paperlike; it is not
ordinary paper, but very firm and waterproof. Insofar as I understand his
political views, they don't seem to me very realistic or farsighted. But all
in all, he is one of the most significant personalities of our time, and if I
had known him when I had the opportunity to do so, I would have
learned more from him—today it is too late because I may never have the
chance to obtain his work, and also because I am already too much my
own self. [. . .]

May 14, 1960

It is interesting that even the lucid Sartre is incapable of breaking free
from his own milieu—from his times and surroundings and his own
ideas. At a meeting with [Yugoslav] authors he said that he is mostly
interested in the problem of how an author works and behaves in socialist society where the function of literature is no longer (!) criticism
and negation. He overlooks the simple truth that what is important for
art under Freud (capitalism) is equally important under socialism: there
is no true and great art if it is not also critical art (not exclusively critical
of political structures, but of all existing forms, including social forms).
The ideal society, that is, the one the artist should work towards (it is
questionable whether he must in every period) exists, indeed can only
exist, in the minds of philosophers, and also in the mind of Mr. Sartre.
An author like Sartre, from France, with her bourgeois civilization,
would be powerless, nay impossible, in a Communist state. Sartre himself
would soon find that out if in France there were no democracy, even De
Gaulle's variety of it. He, in fact, dreams up a problem where there is no

problem, instead of recognizing facts and seeing that real problems exist outside of his philosophy and the sphere of his own involvement. [. . .]

October 12, 1960

Yesterday I thought that *The Unperfect Society,* at least indirectly, had to be a philosophical book—something about human destiny, about conditions, about the inevitability of human existence. [. . .]

November 7, 1960

Somewhere I have written that I hold Russell in very high regard as a philosopher and that in one area at least (logical analysis) —although I don't know him well enough—I consider myself one of his followers. But today I must say (and it seems to me that I have already said it) that his struggle against atomic weapons for Britain, despite all its humane intent, appears to me not only unrealistic but also a sign of the disorientation and despair of old age. The same is true of the position of one segment of the Labour party. In reality, many of the English are so weighed down by magnificent humanistic and pacifistic (in part, socialistic?) traditions that they are incapable of grasping the real nature of the enemy and of contemporary events. Like everything else, both the noble and the humane must be created anew each time. Traditions are good only insofar as they foster that creation. [. . .]

September 19, 1963

The artist inevitably has ideology; artistic work must not. That is, if an artistic work embodies ideology, it has to that measure less art.

I do not mean, however, that artistic work can exist without ideas. On the contrary, without great ideas (thoughts, truths) there is no great art. An artist necessarily has ideology (that is, political-philosophical identity) for the simple reason that he cannot escape living in a particular period and in particular human relationships. [. . .]

November 21, 1963

The earlier conceived trilogy The Storm should be called The Millstone. I also thought of new titles for the three parts (different from the earlier parts). 1) In the primeval forest; 2) In the kettle; 3) In a vacuum.

Titles for me are always essential and even a precondition for work. (Of course, while I am in jail, I am not even thinking about writing The Millstone; there is no material, and I have other things to do anyway.) [. . .]

August 28, 1964

Today I got permission to buy writing paper and to receive a pen from home. Also Nescafé but no permission to boil it, which I would not do anyway. I don't know why, but since I have been under strict discipline for two years, it doesn't matter. It is good enough that everything is now more normal. For heat in the winter I have no definitive solution yet. I was told to inquire at the beginning of October. [. . .]

September 13, 1964

I have finished writing page 3000 on the toilet paper. I have finished more than half of *Worlds and Bridges*. There is still much to be done, and I don't know exactly what it will be—one should not push, something will come of it. I have noted this only as an indication of how far I have reached on this project. If I have some heat this winter, I shall be able to finish the first draft by late spring. [. . .]

September 24, 1964

Finally I received writing paper—I bought it in the prison store. I finished the ninth chapter of the third part of the second book [of *Paradise Lost*] on page 3126 of toilet paper. I have no idea how many pages that will be when typed. Besides the sufferings I underwent while writing on toilet paper, I will now have some idea about the volume of the text. However, my working notes, as well as the prose (first) translation of Milton will be written on toilet paper again in order to conserve writing paper, which is quite expensive. [. . .] I have been writing for several days on real paper, and it is much more pleasant and easier. [. . .]

October 9, 1964

Artistic work is, in fact, the creation of a complete and final world unlike this real one we are not capable of understanding and explaining as a whole. In that connection, if there is any sense in talking about God, then God should be man, and man an artist. Even great reformers are creators—it is not accidental, the connection between art and politics, that is, ideas! But the reformers create a world which in its nature is incomplete, that is, which must be continued and changed. [. . .]

October 27, 1964

It is strange how many things in creative work turn out differently from their initial conception. What I mean is *that work develops in the course of its creation: the work imposes its own logic, sense and form.* Of course, the initial ideas are important, even crucial, because one must start somewhere, but without continuous creation, they would not mean very much. [. . .]

November 22, 1964

There exists an essential difference between artistic work and the real world, that is—any other world (for example, the world of imagination).

Artistic work is a complete, even closed world—not in the sense that the artist cannot uncover new ideas and values, but in the sense that nothing can be either added to or taken away from the finished work—each addition or subtraction means the destruction of its balance and its value as a whole. The real world—social and cosmic, and even the personality with its visions—is, in fact, an incomplete world, a world in creation. Man's conflict with the real world, therefore, is inevitable—it is a world impossible to overcome or to comprehend mainly because it does not have any boundaries measurable by human standards and powers. It is in a state of continuous flux and change. Between man and artistic work, however, there are neither barriers nor conflicts except those that are temporarily erected by prejudice, ignorance and habit. Artistic work is, in fact, the only world that man can understand. No wonder then that he created it!

I have implied that artistic work is a synthesis of many elements and times. There is no artistic work that is not a synthesis—first of ideas and emotions, and, after that, of many other things. [. . .]

January 15, 1965

I'm not doing anything. That is, I'm not writing, and I feel a gnawing pain because of it. I am reading Mary McCarthy's *The Group*. I like it very much, although it is not my kind of literature.

I prefer social literature, which should be nurtured and supported. After all, any real literature is also social. [. . .]

January 20, 1965

I am near the end of *The Group*. Really good book. As far as I can see, it does excel in the genre of good social literature. Still, those are *human destinies in specific times*. The book has simple, warm-blooded poetry in it and beautifully absurd dark humor. The intellectual level and refinement of analysis are very high. The sensibility is exceptional—very feminine.

How every real author represents something new, something original! And besides that, such a book could have been written only by a woman! [. . .]

January 23, 1965

Mary McCarthy's *The Group:* an excellent book, fresh-spirited and poetic. It is good social realism! Intellectual. [. . .]

February 17, 1966

The weather is still warm. I'm not working on anything except reading Günter Grass's *The Tin Drum*. It appeals to me. It is bitter, inventive and gifted. [. . .]

November 15, 1966

I am reading a little of Sartre's *Road to Freedom* and I don't care for it very much, despite some nice ideas and details. The most significant thing is his thoughtfulness, his insight into humanity, although cold and rigid. I don't hold him in very high esteem either as a writer or as a personality (because of instability, that is, his temporary stability), although I consider him one of the most significant figures, if not the most significant, of our time in the sense of awakening and fostering new ideas and forms. He is, in fact, a heavy dogmatist. I am myself such a person, and thus it is natural that his rigidity repulsed me. [. . .]

November 17, 1966

My external conditions have improved. Relatively speaking, the difficulties are few. But my head, as always, suffers from internal pressures, throbbings and pains. In spite of it, I hope that today or tomorrow I will continue with the work on *Worlds and Bridges.* [. . .]

November 25, 1966

I am reading Dedijer's *The Road to Sarajevo,* an excellent, scholarly and profound book, although at times it suffers slightly from schematism, historical materialism, and an excessively strong patriotism. But those are inessentials. [. . .]

December 12, 1966

Each day I have attacks of migraine. Otherwise, everything is normal. A few days ago they gave me an electric heater for my room.* [. . .] Today I finished Dedijer's *The Road to Sarajevo.* A good book taken as a whole. Dedijer inherited two characteristic traits from the two best Serbian historians. From Stojan Novaković, a thoroughness in studying sources and in organizing material, and from Slobodan Jovanović, a lively prose style and an interest in detail. [. . .]

"Jail Diary" (unpublished)

---

* The electric heater was not, however, of much use. Within the month, on December 31, Djilas was released, after serving almost nine years in jail.

III

DOGMA AND HOPE

Marx and Lenin [. . .] foresaw that the victorious working class and socialism would be endangered by the defeated bourgeoisie on the one hand and by its own bureaucracy on the other. It is not by coincidence that Marx demanded that officials be elected for a specific period of time, and afterward be sent into production work. Engels and Lenin emphasized on many occasions that the change in economic relations, that is, the liquidation of private capitalist ownership of the means of production, is not followed immediately and automatically by a given change in political relationships. Rather, the dictatorship of the proletariat can develop in one of two ways: it can wither away as socialism becomes strengthened; or its bureaucracy can grow stronger, becoming transformed into a privileged class which lives at the expense of society as a whole, even though the bureaucracy is no longer necessary at that specific level of development of productive forces, either to fight capitalist remnants—since they are extinct or insignificant—or to organize production, since the free association of producers already can manage the process of production alone.

"Pre-election Speech to the Students and Professors of Belgrade University,"
                                        Borba, March 19, 1950

5
War

At Mojkovac the Montenegrins fought their last battle, fought to decide whether they could preserve at least some memory of themselves and of their name. [. . .]

Montenegro was defending itself against the conqueror. But Montenegro was at odds with itself, rent and torn. Before it ever burst into the round of blood and fire on the heights of Mojkovac, war had reopened all its wounds, the frantic feuds and insensate hatreds among the Montenegrins themselves. [. . .]

They were fighting for the legend by which they lived. They knew they could not win the war; but they knew, too, that they were bound to defend, perhaps even save, the legend of heroism and individuality by their lives and by their death. [. . .]

A desperate fight, a senseless fight, the last fight! But then, do men fight because it is wise to fight? Why do they fight, for what? Will they save or aid what they want—the Montenegrin state? No. Well then, is it for honor or glory? For ideals? The only realities at this moment. But does reason rule the world? Fighting is senseless. One might fight for one's life perhaps. And perhaps for ideals among mankind. Is man's mind given him to plan senseless conflicts? Have not all Serbian battles been battles of despair, forced upon us? All for the pure ideal.

Montenegro, 1962
(Trans. Kenneth Johnstone)

The Comintern View

In the New Year

Many have been taken in by the stories of London and Paris that the Soviet Union, by signing a treaty of nonaggression with Germany, if it did not cause the war, at least hastened its beginning. Nothing could be further from the truth. At the moment that the pact was signed there were only two choices: initiation of a war against the Soviet Union or initiation of a clash between British imperialism and its challenger (Germany). The Soviet Union had no reason to seek to evade the former. Moreover, it is erroneous to equate the Soviet policy of coexistence with bourgeois pacifism, for the latter is merely a mask for covert participation in imperialist wars. The peoples of the Soviet Union will always rise in armed struggle for a just cause, for a cause that makes possible the strengthening of the forces that fight against imperialist wars and imperialism. The difference between the Soviet policy and the reformist policy is like the difference between night and day. The Soviet Union is not willing to forgo small victories, but neither is it willing to sacrifice ultimate goals for minor gains. More concretely, if the Soviet Union were to become involved in this war on the side of either bloc or in favor of any bloc in order to achieve some small gains (for example, in Rumania), this would hinder the attainment of the ulitmate objectives posed before the state of workers and peasants. At the same time, such involvement would provide a convenient opportunity for the imperialists to postpone the settling of their accounts while they "resolved" the basic contradictions of present society by attacking the Soviet Union.

The Finnish war confirms this analysis. It shows with unusual precision the specific, unique course of imperialist wars. It confirms that exactly the same forces that were active before the war continued to operate after its inception, only under altered circumstances. While officially the English and French governments occupied themselves with anti-Soviet plans and attempted to find the weak point in Finland's Mannerheim Line, German heavy artillery was being covered with frost on the Siegfried Line. On the face of it this is an absurd and ridiculous situation, but in essence it is completely logical and understandable. England and France, although at war with Germany, were fighting, not Germany, but a neutral state—the Soviet Union. For its part, Germany failed to act against the two states with whom it was at war. The Soviet Union has observed these imperialist tendencies. The Red Army's thrust through the Mannerheim Line delivered a serious blow to the imperialists. It was a difficult war, battled in the cold at temperatures of −40° to −75° F. It is not accidental that the Finnish war occurred exactly at the moment it did. It was necessary that the Soviet Union face an increasing number of dangerous political provocations. Neither the English nor the French nor any other army was militarily capable of fighting under such climatic conditions and, especially, of fighting against the Red Army. The Finnish war revealed the true, "noble" intentions of the imperialists: to maintain peace among themselves by starting a war against the Soviet Union. When it became obvious after the signing of the peace treaty with Finland that this plan had failed, a vast military confrontation took place within the imperialist camp, which ended only when the German army had reached the English Channel and France had capitulated.

During that entire period the Soviet-German pact survived all efforts to undermine it. It passed many tests, and today it still sets the tone for international relations. In my view, the Soviet-German treaty is founded on the following irrefutable facts: a) England's onetime position in Europe was demolished in such a manner that the opponent did not win a total victory, but, rather, the contradictions increased; b) a speedy end to the war is impossible because of the invincibility of the German army and the equal invincibility of the British navy; c) relations among the imperialists (America, Japan) will inevitably further complicate matters; d) from all of this it follows that the war will be a long one, in which internal contradictions will increase among the warring nations, especially in Europe. National and social contradictions will multiply after the Germans attempt to construct a "new Europe" on the same kind of foundation as the "old Europe" created by Versailles. Furthermore, the elimination of British influence in Europe will make it impossible for the English to intervene in the event of more profound changes within Europe. As a consequence, the effective strength of the German army is increased and it becomes a threat to the goals established by the Soviet Union. However, the Soviet Union has always been friendly to the efforts of the German people in their struggle to break the imperialist chains of Versailles. Thus, should there be deep internal changes of an anti-imperialist nature within Germany that would point to ending the war, the Soviet Union would be willing to offer determined support to the German people in the struggle to prevent the emergence of any new Versailles.

Therefore it is possible to say, as Molotov did, that the Soviet-German treaty is of far-reaching historical significance. Unless the German leaders revert to the Munich route, from which they retreated when they signed the Soviet-German treaty, until the moment Germany achieves superiority in the imperialist world, the treaty will survive all attempts to wreck it. At that moment Germany will become the center for anti-Soviet plans. Even should Germany return to the Munich route, the realistic outlook for success is dimmer to the extent that the accumulated national and social contradictions within Europe are greater and to the extent that the German army succeeds in destroying its present opponents, who were precisely the supporters of the anti-Soviet campaign in the Finnish war. However, the more probable outcome is that the Soviet-German treaty will become an auxiliary instrument for the creation of sincere Soviet-German friendship in the struggle against the instigators of this war, in the struggle against all imperialisms and against all efforts to establish peace on an imperialist basis, and in the struggle for the establishment of a genuine peace. Unless German relations vis-à-vis Russia should shift to an imperialist basis, which would necessarily result in an anti-Soviet campaign, Soviet-German relations will not be altered by changes in some aspects of their relations, as some critics incorrectly allege. Small nations, and particularly the Balkan nations, should bear this in mind if they wish to avoid being caught up in the machinations of war going on around them today. Maneuvering, no matter how skillful, in the end always brings suffering to the masses of any nation. To secure genuine neutrality in this war, as well as to preserve national freedom and independence, it is necessary to lean firmly and without reservation upon the principal anti-imperialist power and to become a component part of its united anti-imperialist front.

This interpretation of the Soviet-German treaty is reinforced if we examine the treaty from the point of view of internal relations. The treaty generated deep changes not only in international relations, but also in the internal relations of all nations. It enabled the entire world to see the duplicity of bourgeois democracy, social democracy and imperialist pacifists of all hues. It became clear that those "democracies" professed "love" for the Soviet Union, for progressive forces and for a genuine peace policy only as long as the Soviet Union was willing to pull chestnuts bare-handed out of the fire for them to help them preserve their imperialist positions. The anti-Soviet slogans of the "socialists" who had captured some strata of the middle classes lost much of their force. The so-called democrats tried to represent the treaty as a deal between two dictatorships, as an equating of two dictatorships. But the treaty quickly revealed that the real identity in social-political views was between the two kinds of imperialist regimes who, because they failed to make a deal at the expense of a third party (the USSR), finally had to settle accounts among themselves by resorting to arms.

The so-called democracies, by their "friendship" toward the Soviet Union, their "freedom-loving spirit" and "progressiveness," and their reformism, succeeded in capturing the masses. This entire shoddy gimmick fell apart when the democratic countries came out openly against the Soviet Union in the Finnish war. All of this means that the military power of democratic countries is not absolute, but relative, and that it will vary from situation to situation. This is best demonstrated by the French example. Until yesterday, thanks to the policy of the ruling circles, it was one of the greatest military powers; today, it is worth nothing. [. . .]

The paramount problem for the so-called democracies in the first phase of the war, the phase of preparation for war against the Soviet Union, was the strengthening of the internal front. In the second, present phase of the war, after the German victories in the West that meant the destruction of the old order based on Versailles and the beginning of the creation of a new imperialist order, the entire conflict was reduced to an open struggle for colonies, sources of raw materials and markets. In this phase the internal front of necessity attains decisive importance for the warring sides. It becomes indispensable to link the masses to the military goals of the war leaders. The internal front becomes progressively more important as the prospects for a rapid, easy and successful conclusion of the war become ever more uncertain. In the Soviet Union the situation is just the opposite. Its military power remains absolute in all situations. This is so because, unlike the Western countries, there is no internal front in the Soviet Union, and because any war in which the Soviet Union fights would be a genuine struggle for peace, a struggle against the imperialists to remove the causes of imperialist wars, a struggle to defend the Soviet State, and not a struggle to seize foreign territory. [. . .]

From all this we can deduce that 1941 will witness the further sharpening and spreading of this war, the further disclosure of the true character of this war, further terrible suffering on the part of the masses, and the further strengthening of the position of the Soviet Union. All of this will inevitably reinforce the contradictions of contemporary society. This is the year in which European peoples especially will understand more and more clearly the senselessness of a war whose end is not in sight because imperialism cannot resolve the contradictions of contemporary society by either the stroke of the pen or the swath of the sword. No action can succeed as long as there are basic contradictions in contemporary society. The imperialists' attempt to "resolve" those basic contradictions will result in the loss of even the narrow mass support remaining, through the manipulation of which they have been able to conduct the present war. [. . .]

This year can become the decisive year of transformation, from an imperialist war to a genuine peace, which does not ravage and plunder foreign territories, to a peace among equal and free peoples.

Published under pseudonym V. Zatarac
Izraz, Vol. I, 1941

The War of National Liberation

The Dead Village

I walked along a simple village road on a summer morning that was clearer than usual because of the previous night's shower. I was sick at heart and wanted to weep. I could not put out of my mind the faces of

comrades who had died the day before fighting the Ustaši* here, somewhere around me, in the fertile fields and meadows. Yet the horror of
what I saw that morning—even though I had already heard about it,
heard about it so many times and had believed that I understood it—
shocked me so that it obliterated the grief I felt for my comrades. . . .
Yes, coming face to face with real life is very different from reading about
it. . . .

First, near the road, under the broad expanse of a large pear tree, we
found two peasants. They lay there in the trampled grass in the shade—
the same shade where the harvesters sometimes relax—shot through the
back of the head. The bullets had come out under their right ears,
opening such gaping wounds that their brains had oozed through them
and spilled onto the ground. Six other peasants had been shot here
earlier; trails of black, sticky blood on the dew-covered grass were the
painful reminders of their last breaths. Those six were gone now. One of
the few survivors must have removed their bodies.

We continued down the road. On both sides there were hedges and
ferns. And then, suddenly, in the middle of the road, ten or twelve
corpses—I can't remember exactly how many. It seemed to me that only
two of them were grown men. The others were women, girls, boys, children. Three or four paces away from the pile of carnage was an empty
cradle—without swaddling clothes, without child, its straw stiffened
from a child's urine. The straw in the cradle seemed to be still warm
from the child's body. But the child lay amidst the pile of corpses. Its
head was smashed in; it had no forehead; there was not a drop of blood
in the hollow, rain-washed skull. A brain—perhaps the child's?—a mere
handful of dense white *kasha* with fragments of flesh lay beside the head.
How was this child killed? By a bullet? By the butt of a rifle? A knife? Or
was the child's head soft enough for the spikes of the Ustaši boot? The
child lay on its left side, its face turned up toward heaven, its shirt soiled
with blood, its bloated little belly peering out. A puny face, its features
frozen in a scowl. The back of the skull was missing. . . . It was a girl.
One day, perhaps on just such a cloudless day as this, when the sky, the
earth, the fields, the meadows and the forests were lavishly colored—she
would have enjoyed life, love, youth. . . . But I did not think such
thoughts then. I thought of nothing. I only stared, feeling cold, wonder-
ing to myself, Why don't I feel anything? Why don't I cry or feel
anguish?

The other bodies were also mutilated. The face of a ten-year-old
showed stab wounds on the forehead and cheeks. One boy with a hollow
skull like the other child lay curled up beneath a shrub at the roadside,
his slender hands and bare feet twisted. As the body had cooled, its skin

* The Croatian fascists of World War II.

had shrunk, exposing the white bones of the temples. If the child were not so mutilated one might think that he had fallen asleep in the shade by the road, safely hidden from view so that his family would not scold him for sleeping instead of watching the herds. . . .

I moved on. At the crossroads, on the crest of the hill at the approach to the town, I saw twenty-five or thirty bodies. A pile of men's, women's and children's trunks, limbs and heads. A dark female braid tied with a scarlet ribbon mingled with the sadly drooping mustache of an older peasant.

The road is quite wide there, as it should be at the crest of a hill facing the town: the peasants can sit here at dusk, relax and look at the town. But at the edge of the road next to the fence there were only corpses, crowded together as if piled up by a storm.

There were two mothers with their children, not yet weaned. If in the first group you could not tell whose the children were, here it was different. One mother, young and dark, had been holding her child in her arms when she fell on her face, almost covering the child with her body, as if to protect it. The child's hands were crossed at her breasts. The other mother had not been holding her child as firmly. She lay on her back and her child, who had fallen nearby, was curled up in a heap, its shirt rolled up over its chest. The first mother, with her black lashes and eyebrows, was reminiscent of a romantic painting of a slaughtered mother with child. But this was not a painting. This was a real mother killed with her child, frozen while still holding the unweaned baby at her breast.

As I turned back toward the village I met two peasants. One, a fifty-year-old man without a cap, pointing at his bloody swollen jaw, said to me:

"We were in the house, hiding from the shooting. They came in and herded us all together—all, even the children. They asked us: 'Were there Partisans here?' Yes, they were here. 'Why didn't you shoot them?' How can we, when we Serbs have no rifles? I said. They began to beat me. I saw trouble coming and ran away into the brush. They fired at me but they missed, and I am here now. As for my wife and my children, I don't know. . . ."

The other peasant, with a fur cap and white hair, said:

"We ran into the barn to hide from the shooting. Two families. They threw a bomb inside, but before it went off I ran into the meadow behind the house. They threw a second bomb inside, and after that I heard a rifle. Two sons and a daughter-in-law—I wonder where they are. They killed my old woman. . . ."

A little storage building with stone walls. Whitewashed walls and

blood. Bloodstains high on the wall. And there in the semidarkness, a
pile of torn bodies, broken limbs, heads, and such huge wounds—larger
than the width of a hand. . . .

"Come over here and look!" a peasant called to me.

I entered the house. A seventy-year-old man wandered amidst the overturned furniture and broken dishes. He seemed to be constantly doing
something, searching for something to pass the time, and he wandered
aimlessly through the devastated home. In one room two of his sons and
his wife lay dead—his old peasant woman dead, huddled against a chest.
The young blond son with his red mustache lay in the middle of the
room, his brains spilled out, his legs spread, his hands contorted in the
air—huge peasant hands, their dirty nails still full of earth from working
in the fields. The older son had managed to crawl at least halfway under
the bed. A small room, but filled with blood. There was a footprint in
the blood. The old man, wandering aimlessly, must have stepped in the
blood of his sons.

In the next house everything was overturned, too. The door was
riddled with bullets. A peasant woman lay near the fireplace with her
throat slit, her white larynx protruding through the wound. This was a
young woman, around thirty years old. Blood was smeared on her chin
and face and over her hands. With arms and legs extended, she was lying
peacefully and gracefully in her deserted home. Her plump little hands
peered out at us from wide flaxen sleeves, which were not quite clean.
Her hands were greasy, the way hands usually are after milking cows.

Each house was the same.

No one was alive to bury the dead.

Two or three peasants wandered about. They were not crying; their
faces were glassy-eyed, hard and expressionless. They may have lost
everyone—not all the bodies had been found yet; they were scattered
throughout the woods and meadows.

The abandoned cattle lowed as they wandered across the fields. In the
meadow near the road, two peasant women tended a herd of sheep. I
shouted at them but they stood still, as if they did not hear my call. I
suddenly remembered! I was wearing a black cap and a black shirt; they
must have thought I was an Ustaši. Then why weren't they running
away?

"Don't worry. I am a Partisan!"

They came toward me—one a gaunt old peasant woman, the other
young and plump. She had recently married someone in a neighboring
village and had come back to visit her family—but there was no family.
She was searching for them. She was afraid to be alone and begged me to
come along with her. We wandered through the battlefields. In the
meadow near the road we found two more young men. Near the tin

tobacco shed we saw a wallet, greasy, open . . . empty. Looking at one of them the young woman said:

"He was from my house . . . oh, terrible wound . . . beloved . . ."

But she did not cry. Nothing. She spoke in the same tone she would use when talking about everyday matters. Finally, after we had visited many houses full of dead people, in front of the large pile of corpses at the crossroads, she turned her numb glance upon me. Looking at me from under her heavy lids, clenching her hands, she said:

"What has happened, brother?"

I felt nothing . . . not even sorrow for my comrades who fell in that village. It seemed to me that dying would be easy, devoid of emotion. . . . Even if I knew it was coming I might not try to hide from the bullet. No feeling—no identity, nothing. Look, the peasant women did not run; no one cried.

And yet man is capable of cold-blooded revenge.

In truth, only one emotion dominated my heart and my entire being, and surely the hearts of others: As long as such acts continue, to live in this world is meaningless.

There is no choice; it is either we—or they. . . .

Članci, 1941–1946, 1947

Reflections on the "Soul" of the War Criminal

Men of traditional thought cannot understand the war criminal: what goes on inside his "soul," his psychology, the "mechanism" that controls his thoughts and emotions. This inability to comprehend is understandable, since men of traditional thought (one could say men educated in the spirit of bourgeois liberalism or influenced in their thinking by bourgeois liberalism) tend to think of the present war as resembling all previous wars or at least as resembling the War of 1914–1918. But the present war differs from all previous wars, and in the same manner the crimes committed in this war differ from those committed in all previous wars. [. . .]

Despite their confusion, men of traditional thought offer several explanations of the phenomenon of war crimes. These explanations are of four types.

1. German war crimes assumed massive proportions in this war. [. . .] On that basis many conclude that there is something abnormal about the German people, some extreme brutality peculiar to them. [. . .] Now, there is no doubt that German invaders have always been distinguished

by cruelty. [. . .] But even the most cursory examination reveals on the one hand that this is not a unique German trait and on the other that the war crimes committed by the Germans during this war cannot be compared with their crimes in previous wars, either in their organization, their planning, their character, or in the mass participation of the soldiers. If those who see war crimes as a specifically German invention examined their own homes, they would immediately see the same weeds growing in their own yards. Indeed, in many yards not only have the weeds not been cleared out, but the weeding has not even started. [. . .]

It may nevertheless be argued that the German efforts were incomparable in magnitude and that no one else ever planned war crimes so carefully, no one else ever constructed "death factories," no one else ever made an industry out of war crimes. In a certain sense that is true. The Četniks and the Ustaši killed people "simply"—they burned them, butchered them, shot them, threw them into the fire, buried them in ditches, beat them to death with hammers. The Germans, however, conducted "scientific" experiments on thousands of people. Shaved the victims in order to use their hair as fibers, burned people and used their ashes for fertilizer. But there is still no essential difference; it is just that some mastered their craft better than others. [. . .]

2. As for the theory about the subconscious desire to destroy which is found in each individual and in each people and which exists in greater measure the more the individual and the people are underdeveloped, this theory is not only incorrect, but it serves to cover up and to justify war crimes. [. . .]

3. The third theory argues that contemporary war criminals are just common criminals who have seized the helm of the ship of state. This theory is also incorrect, despite the fact that among war criminals, both at the top and below, there are to be found large numbers of common criminals and despite the fact that the crimes of the war criminal are in many instances also common crimes. It has been established that Hitler was an hysteric and a madman, and that Goering spent a long time in a mental institution. Among the Nazi leaders there were many swindlers and common thieves whose orderlies, following closely behind the troops, collected art objects, rare books, jewelry, anything of value they could put their hands on. The leaders themselves carried out murders, they ordered others to murder for them, they toured concentration camps and wrote reports about the "executioners." They cheated, stole, plotted and stabbed each other in the back. The leaders of war crimes—who were also the leaders of the state, the armed forces and the movement—constructed an entire system to carry out their plans of conquest. But this system inevitably brought criminals to the surface, loosed the "dark instincts of unruly mobs" and organized the mobs to carry out crimes. To accomplish this, the system had to create an appropriate "ideology" of crime, an

ideology of "animal nationalism," an ideology to justify the destruction of other peoples.

But criminality and criminals are not what is fundamental in that system, regardless of how much the entire system was criminal in a certain respect. What is fundamental is the system itself. And the entire system is nothing else but the power of monopolists, the open dictatorship of the monopolists. The Nazis fought a classic war for plunder, to plunder other countries and to decimate and enslave other peoples. But this plundering was carried out as a means of establishing the rule of the German plutocracy—the bankers, the industrialists, the barons. [. . .] Individual imperialist states or their ruling circles, in order to realize their imperialist goals, come into conflict not only with similar ruling classes in other countries, but also with the entire peoples of those countries. Contemporary war crimes are a social consequence of such conflict. [. . .]

The war criminal is not a common criminal. All those Nazis, fascists, or whatever else they were called, are "normal" men. Many of them have studied at universities, many have read extensively, many appreciate art and literature. [. . .] But although in ordinary bourgeois life they live like beasts—they seek only to attain wealth and position, they deceive their wives, they marry for advantage, they like decadent art, they treat their children not like human beings but with the extreme selfishness of animals, plundering from their children for themselves while at the same time for their own children and their own homes they would destroy millions of other children and millions of other homes—they do not usually come into contact with the criminal police. Business machinations, selfishness, deceiving wives, a predatory relationship with family, nation, peoples, neighbors, these are really normal forms of behavior in capitalism, which atomizes individuals and families, alienates man from man. In war criminals this behavior is merely carried to the extreme. [. . .] They are in reality people who find themselves in some specific position in a system that they created and maintained and that in turn made of them inhuman monsters who shrink from nothing, for whom it is "normal," "natural," "understandable," "logical" to destroy thousands of men, women and children, entire peoples, entire cultures. For the common criminal such things are neither "normal" nor "logical." The common criminal commits a crime against an individual for his own personal gain. The war criminal commits crimes against peoples, against certain strata of the population, not for personal gain, although there is often something in it for himself, but for the preservation of the system, for the movement, for the power of monopolies, to conquer markets, to acquire sources of raw materials. [. . .]

4. As for the theory that every war has its war crimes, and thus also this war, albeit in much greater measure, this theory neglects the fact that this

war differs from all previous wars. Furthermore, this theory fails to distinguish between the aggressor, who destroys the population, the independence and the culture of other countries, and those who defend these countries from destruction and who punish the aggressor.

Let us look at the mass annihilation of populations in some typical victorious invasions. For example, the Mongol conquest is taken as an example of such destruction, and Hitler's hordes are usually compared to those of the Mongols. No doubt the Mongol invasions are a good example of the mass annihilation of populations and the destruction of entire cultures. But those invasions cannot in any way, not even in the magnitude of destruction, be compared to the present, Hitlerite imperialist invasions. To compare them would be to compare the mill on the stream with the modern power mill, the bow and the arrow with the airplane, the contemporary banker with the barbarian prince. [. . .]

If we follow the trials of the war criminals, regardless of where they take place or who is tried, we can observe some similarities in the behavior of the accused. These similarities, in my opinion, are essential for the understanding of the psychology of the war criminal.

What is most obvious is that to their perpetrators all those monstrous crimes appear "understandable," "logical," and "natural." [. . .] If their crimes cannot be hidden, they offer "logical" explanations. In Nuremberg they claim that it was war—they didn't plan it to be so—that annihilated the populations of entire regions, annihilated peoples, and not the actions of individual commanders; and that the orders—to annihilate, to shoot, to liquidate, to stop at nothing—in reality arose from the need to secure the unhindered operation of the troops, and that if the Russians, the Serbs, the peasants of this or that village had been peaceful, those things would not have happened.

This "logic" of war crimes arises from the fact that the war criminals themselves are the product of their system and that their consciences and their behavior are molded by a system that for them is the only possible system, the only logical system, the only natural system (in reality—it is the system of enslavement of the working classes and of other peoples). Accordingly, all acts that this system commits in the course of war are logical and natural. The perpetrators of these acts look upon themselves as thoroughly modern individuals who completely comprehend the spirit of the "new" era (in reality—the spirit of appropriation and enslavement by means never before seen in history). "Their" logic in reality is the logic of a specific movement in crisis—imperialism—a movement that to preserve itself inevitably defends itself with monsters that appall men of common decency. [. . .]

Not only was the absurd "ideology" of the war criminals (fascism, racism) "logical," but so also was the behavior of all those who failed to resist war crimes, who tried to explain (that is, to justify) the war crime and the war criminal by the inevitability of certain situations, by objective circumstances, by the logic of war, etc. Such people fall into a panic when confronted with fascism and with imperialism, and seek an excuse to avoid taking a stand in this bloody war "between fascism and Communism." They pretend that the choice is between fascism and Communism, even though in reality the choice is not that at all but whether to participate in the struggle on the side of slavery or on the side of freedom. But by the very manner in which they pose the question they have already made their decision: to be the obedient servants of fascism or imperialism, regardless of whose imperialism it is. They regarded the occupation as a "natural" situation (because the enemy—against whom they didn't want to fight anyway—was stronger), and one could only make the best of it, and adjust to it. [. . .]

For the Germans it was "natural" that only they could carry weapons. According to their beliefs, no other peoples had that right: the honor of conducting war, of bearing arms, of being a soldier, was a privilege accorded only to them. [. . .] Accordingly, Hitler's troops considered it "natural" that war should be "total" when they conducted it, but they began immediately to cry "in the name of civilization" when bombs began to fall and destroy Berlin, Nuremberg and "their" other cities, to destroy "their" cultural monuments, to kill "their" women and children. The German soldiers also considered that they had a "natural" right in a foreign country to do things forbidden to them in theirs: to plunder, to rape, to kill, to burn. [. . .]

It is interesting that the crimes were not carried out according to some established pattern. Each war criminal introduced his own "fantasies" into his crimes. Some of them shot people only in the "usual" way, covering the eyes of the victims or turning their backs to the firing squad; others killed only with machine guns or automatic rifles; others shot only into the base of the skull, or the heart, or the forehead. Some slaughtered rapidly, some slowly; some dug eyes out; some used to shoot with cannon shells; then there was poison gas, throwing people into common graves, burning them in gigantic furnaces, and listening to concerts of classical music before executions. Introducing something of one's own, something individual into the manner of carrying out the crime, ultimately enabled each criminal or group of criminals to acquire a pattern, to become a "specialist" for one or another way of killing. Over a period of time these "specialists" learned their craft, their individual ways of killing "perfectly." All of this shows that the war criminal thinks while he prepares and carries out his crime. As a rule he did not suffer from some undiagnosed insanity. After he finished his "work," he went home, ate his dinner, listened to a concert or climbed into bed with his wife. By day he killed thousands of persons and at night he slept peacefully, awaking the next morning refreshed and ready for "new" tasks, "new" jobs. [. . .]

What was going on inside the "souls" of the war criminals while they committed their monstrous deeds? And later, did any of them have a bad conscience, did something human in them at any time remind them that children, paintings and parks are blameless? No, nothing was happening inside them. Their "souls" were absolutely serene, their consciences did not bother them, for they were "modern" men, men who understood the "spirit" of the "new" era. The average soldier did what he did because "it had to be so," because "it was natural," "understandable," and because "those above" knew best. [. . .]

Naša Književnost, No. 8, July 1946

The Inhumanity of War

War

Running from east to west, the great river flowed into a still-greater river. It always has been and always will be that a lesser river flows into a greater. Around these rivers, as around all rivers, there have always been battles and wars and frontiers, for life follows rivers, and they divide or link together men as chance may have it, according to time and circumstance.

For three months the battle had been raging about this great river. But because the opponents had equal forces, neither was able to drive back the other, especially in winter, which had now set in, for winter demands more men and material for an offensive. Along the banks and between the rivers, the armies dug in, mustering their forces, so that in spring, when it thawed and the green leaves began to appear, they could destroy one another. The front intersected the great river—but to all rivers, and to this one, too, it matters not a jot if a front intersects them. Thence the front ran to the south and the southeast, where it joined the other, still-larger, river and flowed with it—it is all one to any river whether there are battles along its banks. The front was torn with trenches, dugouts, and every sort of excavation, a belt of land scarcely thirty miles wide, which embraced the two rivers, the great and the greater. To the land, too, it was all one if the front crossed it or did not cross it. It was all one to the meadows and the vineyards, to the villages and the towns.

But it was not all one to the people who lived along the riverbanks, though they were not to blame for the war. The soil and the sun were good for man, and men lived there. War means oppression or lordship over men and their lives and cannot but disorganize human life wherever it may be; it would disorganize the lives of these men even if they did not live there, as soon as it reached them.

Because in war there must always be two opposing armies—for without them there would be no war—each will do its best to destroy everything that might be of value to the other. In war there is nothing human or created by human intelligence or craftsmanship that would not strengthen an opponent, so the most certain way to weaken the opponent is to destroy everything that might be of benefit to him. War has no understanding, nor can it choose what could be or could not be at any given moment of advantage to the opposing side. Therefore in war the most sensible thing is to destroy everything—houses and fields, cattle and roads, bridges and museums, and, naturally, first and most important of all, human beings and the manner of their lives.

In its withdrawal westward the enemy had broken down all the bridges over the rivers and destroyed all the boats, even those so small and insignificant that lovers could hardly find space in them—and because they are in love, they want to hold one another close and save one another. Nowhere near the front or even very far away from the front—for the front may be here today and there tomorrow—was there a bridge, a ferry, or a raft. Worse still, even those boats and wherries the fishermen had hidden from the advancing army had been requisitioned by the retreating army, not so much that they might be of use to it, as that they might be of value to the enemy for transporting spies and agitators, or if, by any chance, they might advance again.

But men must go on living even in war and despite war, and so, behind the front, they renewed the river crossings. They had no materials and, because they were sensible men, they knew that every new boat or ferry would be requisitioned. Therefore all their comings and goings were by the military motor ferries, for an army must have, and did have, means of crossing the river. An army exists in order to have everything that its adversary has and has not and even what it might have.

The soldiers on the ferry were good fellows—all soldiers are good fellows when they are not being soldiers, and even when they are soldiers but are not at war—and they transported the people, their beasts, and everything else free on their ferry. They were the more considerate because they, too, belonged to the people of the country over which the war was being waged. They did so only at the times when the ferry was not working for the army, or for the war—which was quite natural, for they were there and did what they did and were what they were only because of the war.

The enemy planes preferred to fly by day, so the ferry worked for the army at night and for the people usually by day. But the people, even though they were not in the army, soon became aware of this and avoided the hours of daylight. For the most part they crowded to the crossing points in the evening, when the enemy planes no longer flew and the home army had not begun its transport, or in the early morning, when the enemy had not yet begun his flights and the home army was no longer crossing.

All that morning, as dull and chilly and damp as many a winter morning, especially in wartime, a lament could be heard from the left bank of the river where the front was. The soldiers and the three officers on the bank—a major of the counterespionage service, his assistant, a captain, and a lieutenant who controlled the ferry and the crossings— knew that it was one of the peasants. Only the peasants wailed so incessantly, loudly, and senselessly when they brought back from the front a corpse of a brother or a father, and even more were it a son or a husband. The officers had been willing to come and help the unfortunates to cross even before twilight, but they had to hide the ferry in the willows because the enemy reconnaissance planes emerged out of the clouds all day, and at all times of the day, as if they took pleasure in watching the river, which was neither blue nor silvery, but muddy-colored, and the willow clumps, drowned in gloomy, rotting marsh, merged into a gloomy leaden sky.

The grunting ferry had been dragged from the marsh earlier. The dark lowering clouds came right down to the water's edge, and the twilight had begun to gather, so the officers decided that there was no further danger from the planes.

The keening, which had ceased, suddenly began again, as if waiting for the motor to fall silent and the ferry to nuzzle the bank. A crowd of peasants, men and women, with their beasts, crowded onto the ferry, and among them an elderly bearded peasant who urged his mettlesome horses with mutterings to get on the ferry. He used the sort of phrases he used at home, but more tenderly and more sadly, for there was an unpainted pine coffin on the cart, upon which a peasant woman, also elderly, and muffled to the mouth and eyes in a kerchief, laid a bony hand, fearing lest she be separated from it.

"Come, my grief, bear my sorrow to my lonely house," mumbled the peasant, twitching at the reins, while the peasant woman, with laments and even more grief-stricken words, put her other hand on the coffin, embracing it.

The captain, fair, emaciated, and thickset—he could have looked quite different, for he was only important because he was a captain—shouted almost angrily at those who were already on the ferry to make room for the cart, and even jumped to the bank, seized the reins, and pulled the horses forcefully onto the ferry. "Leave it to me, uncle. I grew up with horses. You there! Make room!"

The horses recognized the strong and masterful hand and followed the captain, champing and testing with their hoofs the solidity of the planks and the depth below them. The peasant thanked the captain, calling down blessings on him and on the whole army. So, too, did the peasant woman, with more subdued and even more sorrowful keenings. The captain seemed embarrassed by so much gratitude. Rubbing his hands as if to brush dirt off them—the reins had in fact been muddy and greasy— he unobtrusively and modestly rejected it. "It's nothing! It's nothing, uncle. It is our duty to help the people. That is why we are here. But who have you got there, in that coffin?"

"Who?" the peasant wondered sorrowfully. "It's an ill day for me. It is my son, my only son. I have given two already, and now it is his turn. That is who."

The captain clearly wanted to say something consoling that at the same time showed understanding, something like "Yes, freedom costs very dear!" but he could not find the right words, or else it seemed to him they would be superficial in face of the peasant's grief. She was obviously the mother of the dead man. So he remained silent and only sighed. But in his place the lieutenant, at the tiller, spoke. He, too, was fair, but tall and with mustaches so sparse and blond that they only served to draw attention to his baldness; he, too, might have looked different, for he was important just because he was a lieutenant. "What will you? War is war. Men die every day. Sometimes we carry more dead than living."

A tall, thin, elderly, and wrinkled peasant turned to the father with the question: "Are you bringing your son back from the front?"

The peasant told him that he had gone to visit his son at the front and had brought him clean clothes and food—he, too, had fought in a war and knew very well what soldiers needed. At dawn the day before yesterday the enemy had attacked and, as ill luck would have it, his young, green son, who was not yet twenty, had been killed by a shell. "All his guts had been blown out, and neither his father nor his mother was in time to hear his last wishes," he added as if he were talking to himself and his wife, but all the more despairingly.

And the mother ended her death-wail with: "What can we tell you? It is our burial. Our line is over forever."

The thin peasant, playing with the Adam's apple in his scraggy throat, went on as if he had not heard the father and mother. "Mine, too, was killed, a month ago, but I did not bring him back. Let him lie with his comrades. But you, how did you find a coffin at the front? There is no wood there and no carpenters—nothing!"

The father turned aside, as if he had not heard the last question. "And I don't even know where we shall take him. It is just our peasant foolishness to find consolation only in the grave."

The captain said that others, too, had brought back their dear ones, though certainly without coffins. "The Command of the People's Army respects our customs, though it would indeed be right for a soldier to lie among soldiers."

The ferry nudged the bank, the horses shook themselves, and the captain again seized the reins and led the horses, who now went gladly, their hoofs eager for firm earth beneath them.

A path led along the river dike, and the army had made and graveled a road from the landing place through the mud and the stagnant puddles. Along that short, narrow road, flanked on both sides by thin mud churned up by the wheels, the travelers began to line up, one behind the other, ready to show their papers to the major, who had not yet appeared from the little hut alongside the road. The captain led the horses onward without paying any heed to his place in the queue. The people stepped aside into the mud unwillingly, but without protest, for this was a dead man and, what was more, was being escorted by an officer. But the thin peasant—he whose son had been killed a month before—pushed his way through, waving the stick in his right hand as if it were helping him to move more quickly, and hurried toward the hut, paying no attention to anyone. Furthermore, when the lieutenant warned him to keep in line, he only turned and, still hurrying onward, waved his arm impatiently and pointed with his stick to the hut, shouting: "I've urgent business up there!"

After that—silence; only the cart creaked over the sand and feet sloshed in the mud. Everyone realized that the thin peasant had something important to tell the major in the hut.

For his part, he did not conceal the fact, and when the cart reached the dike, the major was waiting for it and gave a sign that it should move aside. The peasant stood behind him, watching him, grinning knowingly and cunningly and shifting from one leg to the other. "I heard, I got to know today," he bragged, "that there is something in that coffin. And you, Captain, you mustn't be offended that I said nothing to you. I was afraid lest they tip the coffin into the river. I waited till they got across, and there is a higher authority. And you mustn't be angry either," he said, turning to the parents. "It is our duty to speak up if we notice anything suspicious. War is war."

The father and mother had stopped, confused, dumfounded. The mother was the first to come to her senses and she began to curse the peasant's malice and lies, and to implore the major. "Have pity, leave us with our sorrow for a day."

Emboldened and aroused by her support, the father stood at ease in front of the major and also began to plead with him; his attitude was firm and soldierly as much as imploring. "Be understanding, Comrade Major. We are parents. This is our son. Our village is far away."

The major was dark, youthful in appearance, and very alert, with an expression more inquisitive than cold—and he, too, might have looked different had he not been a major. He replied to the peasant as though he were not speaking to the man standing there before him but to someone who was not there, to whom it was laid down in regulations that he must be amiable. "We must inspect everything, according to orders. You needn't worry."

Then he went over to the cart and, tapping with his fingers on the coffin, ordered it to be opened.

The soldiers quickly obeyed, and without much difficulty took the coffin off the cart. The mother lay on it, moaning softly: "My empty home! My empty home!"

But the soldiers had nothing to raise the lid with, and that encouraged the father to implore the major once more. "Don't lay sin on your soul. Have understanding."

It seemed that the major was not listening, nor could he have been, for he was examining the travelers' papers. Nonetheless, he said to the father, and perhaps to the travelers, too: "All right, all right, everything will be all right."

A truck came, and the major stopped it with a wave of a hand full of someone's papers. The captain knew what he had to do, and asked the driver for a hammer and a pair of pliers. He gently removed the mother from the coffin, but she stayed nearby, crouched and withdrawn, with fists clenched to her face and moaning even more despairingly about her empty home and her black fate.

The soldiers at once pried open the lid, and the major, who had by now finished examining the papers, gave a sign for it to be raised. Inside, there was a clean-shaven, brown-haired youth in peasant dress. He rolled his eyes, made a movement to rise, then smiled shamefacedly and remained lying there.

"Is that your son?" asked the major.

"My son," the peasant answered. "Two of my sons have already been killed."

"A deserter?" the major asked next.

"No. I wanted to save him, to keep my line alive. What do land and house and state mean to me if all my family is extinguished?" answered the peasant unemotionally.

The travelers had stopped in curiosity, but the major ordered the soldiers to move them on, and they quickly and raggedly retreated before the rifles. The driver, too, went away as soon as he got his tools back; clearly all this did not interest him, or perhaps he had more important things to do, or troubles of his own. Only the thin peasant remained. No one drove him away, and he remained standing there as if he had some special right to do so. He spoke, almost to himself. "And I thought it was a spy or something of the sort. I didn't mean any harm, may God help me! May God help me!"

Crouching by the coffin, the mother began to smooth the youth's hair away from his brow, damp with sweat, consoling him. "Don't be afraid, my soul. He is a good man, a good man—he is one of ours, the people's."

Enheartened, the youth sat up in the coffin, but the major made a sign to him to lie down again. As at a command, he lay down tensely.

"Captain, do your duty!" ordered the major.

The captain quickly drew his pistol and, as if he had been waiting for the order, cocked it. Without waiting for any order, the lieutenant took the mother by the shoulders and firmly, though not roughly, took her from her son, lifted her to her feet, and moved her a few paces away. A soldier pushed the father aside with his rifle and placed him beside the mother.

It seemed, too, that the young man realized it only when the bullet entered his heart. He cried out, his body arched, and his head and limbs beat strangely on the planks, and then he fell back like an empty sack.

The major said irritably: "Now take him away!" And at once added mildly: "We are doing, and will go on doing, our duty."

The parents did not hear him, but broke into wails and sobs, grieving for their son. The soldiers, by force, but not roughly, kept them away from the coffin, which they put carefully back on the cart, not forgetting to tie it down. They placed the lid on the coffin; they no longer had any tools, and the ferry had to leave again as soon as possible, for a line of military trucks was waiting on the road.

As soon as the soldiers had finished, the horses moved away of their own accord. The peasants followed the cart. And the thin peasant wondered to himself: How could I have known that?

Probably a knot had fallen out of the wood at the bottom of the coffin, for the blood flowed out, black and silent. The mother kept her hand on the coffin, wailing incomprehensible words, and the father, lamenting, walked beside the horses, forgetting to urge them on.

The lieutenant said: "Funny people, these peasants; they are wailing now just as they were before."

But no one listened to him, either. They were all far too busy looking after the traffic.

The Leper and Other Stories, 1964
(Trans. Lovett F. Edwards)

The Collapse of Hell

*To Matija Bećković**

It would have been better if I had never regained consciousness. Then their doctors could not prolong my sufferings, nor could Mićun, the unregenerate traitor to Christianity, gloat over me, waiting for the words that in my weakness would slip from my lips. . . .

I am deceiving myself. What plagues me, what worries me, is something else. . . .

It is dangerous even to faint in the presence of such an ungodly creature as Mićun. From time immemorial, ever since man and man's authority has been known, a prisoner's hallucinations have never been accorded credibility. Yet Mićun and his tainted kind pay the closest attention to the utterances of prisoners. No wonder. God gave man a mind. But Mićuns know nothing of God or of human beings. They thrive on mindlessness.

Lie in wait, lie in wait, Mićun. You succeeded in catching me . . . but you will not catch my words. . . .

Because I know—I'm not sure how or from where, but I know—that even in my unconsciousness my mind will not desert me. That has never happened to anyone in my family—and it won't happen to me either. God will preserve the mind he gave me. I will not betray my comrades. . . . Here I am calling my co-fighters comrades, using the same words that the Mićun-scum use among themselves. . . . They have profaned our beautiful language. . . . Oh, God, why don't I know some other language so I can at least talk to myself and not defile myself with words that come out of their slobbering mouths.

I should certainly like to tell that foul-mouthed devil: "All your trickeries and inhumanities are in vain. You only heal someone in order to extract his soul from him bit by bit and to subvert his mind."

But I'm just deceiving myself with all this. Something is boiling within me, something is tearing me apart, something worse than cowardice and betrayal.

I know something that I dare not believe, something that I don't want to know. . . .

Evil spirits have mastered the world. It's as if I am not in this world any more. But surely this is the same jail that I was in under the Serbs when I returned from the underground in 1921. Was it '21 or '20? It must have been '21, since my Nikola was born a year later. . . . Where was

---

* Matija Bećković is one of the most popular young poets and satirists in Yugoslavia. Following his public identification with Djilas, and official attacks on Djilas, Bećković was dismissed from the staffs of several publications and has been unable to get his works published. His best-known book is *Reče mi Jedan Čoek [As One Man Told Me]*. He is also a coauthor of *Che: A Permanent Tragedy* (1970).

your youth corrupted, my son? Those obsessed people lured you away. Your youth made you follow them when they were chased away to Bosnia, those accursed ones. Somewhere there in Bosnia you remain, without a grave and without a monument. Not even they know when and where you died, but they glorify you in order to humilate your father as a traitor. . . .

My mind is getting foggy. . . . Not because of that from which it cannot escape, but, rather, because of my effort to push it away. . . . Which me? Who am I? Where am I? Who is stronger than his own mind? Here I am wrestling with my mind in order that it not know what it already knows. . . .

And the world is more or less the same: the same jail as in '21, the same echoes through the corridors, the same stone arch over my head. Even the same Dr. Glomazić—only then he was young and a supporter of unification with Serbia, and the gendarmes and police clerks were fawning over him. And now he is a prisoner; he bows and scrapes before the shallow-brained militiamen, who can't even "baaa" like sheep. My doctor, how we used to quarrel about what is Serbian and what is Montenegrin. Then the Mićun bastards multiplied themselves and pressed us until they plunged us into the abyss. Now, my doctor, we could talk together like men, if they would allow it, and if I dared reveal my true self. . .

Everything seems to be the same as it was. . . . Only the uniforms of the guards are different. Yes, I even have a hospital bed. Those extractors of souls did not allow me to go to the hospital. They made some kind of a hospital room out of my cell. They know what they're doing. They aren't like the Serbian gendarmes, who knew only how to curse and to jab you with rifle butts. Instead, these are perpetually shoving in front of me everything that a wounded or sick man should have. But they hide me in this cell chiseled into a rock far from light and sound. . . .

But I am thinking and talking to myself about one thing while something else is eating me up, something worse than wounds, worse than the death of both my sons, worse than the collapse of Montenegro and the extinction of Serbness.

Someone is walking down the corridor . . . two of them. . . . They are saying something. . . . I can't understand what they're talking about, but I know that one is Mićun and the other is Dr. Glomazić. . . . They are standing before my door, whispering. Are they coming in? Why do they keep my cell locked when I can't even move? Regulations, I suppose. It seems the key does not turn in the lock, although the lock is the same that was here in the twenties—might even have been the same under the reign of the Prince. . . . Yes, even my Prince used to jail his enemies here. There have never been, nor will there be, rulers without jails. . . .

But the key is turning in the lock—once, twice. . . . I even wanted to convince myself that the key is turning in my head, not in the lock; the key is torturing my mind, twisting. . . .

Maybe I could deceive the doctor. . . . No, not deceive him but test him. That is difficult because doctors know so much. But if that one who looks like Glomazić really is Glomazić, perhaps there is something human in him that will help me discover, that will reveal to me, where I really am. . . .

I'll pretend that I'm not in command of my faculties. . . . Perhaps I'm not. Perhaps I'm just dreaming all this, and I'm already in the other world, in hell. . . . No matter, so long as it's not in Mićun's domain. The Devil transformed himself into Mićun and invented the doctor and the jail to torture me for my sins. I am sinful, I know that well. . . . I have killed, even if it was for Montenegro, even if it was for my dreams.

They can't be devils—their heels are not pointing forward. But that doesn't prove anything. If the Devil assumed Mićun's form, he would have retained his cunning and would have cast a spell on my sight.

Go on, doctor, poke me, listen to me as much as you wish! But you cannot hear or discover what is inside me. . . . This only I and Mićun know. I and Mićun . . . Oh, God, do I deserve such punishment that you have to entangle me with him in my life, in my death, and forever? . . .

I can hear the conversation between Dr. Glomazić and Mićun now, although I'm pretending that I hear nothing.

"Well, what do you say, doctor? Is he conscious?" asks Mićun, stretching himself, swarthy and huge, with his shoulder holster and boots.

"It is hard to say," answers Glomazić, wiping his glasses. The doctor is blond and a little plump, rosy like a baby but with a stubble. It seems he is slightly asthmatic, because he is always clearing his throat. He continues. "His reflexes are normal. But that does not mean that some of the vital centers are not damaged—speech, hearing. . . . Yes, speech . . . Vukota, do you hear me? I am Dr. Glomazić. You have known me for a long time. Why are you silent?"

I shall remain silent until I orient myself a little better. . . .

So Dr. Glomazić sold himself to them! Or maybe he did not sell himself, but . . . but subjected himself to them out of fear. Fear is a potent celestial force. It is not said in vain that the rod came out of paradise. I have never understood or acknowledged that force. Perhaps it would have been better if I had; I might not be where I am now, nor would my sons have been killed—Nikola as a Communist, and Danilo in my army—nor would my daughter, Miruša, have done that which is never done. . . . Miruša, my favorite, did you do it? No, I cannot believe it, I will not believe it, but I cannot die until I know for sure. . . . Now I don't understand what they are saying. I see nothing except fog and bloody rivers. I always used to dream about bloody rivers: wars and uprisings. On top of everything, an unbearable nausea is overwhelming me, as if I had eaten deadly nightshade. Or is this happening because of Mićun's presence? I know that he is here, although I no longer hear or see him. This poisonous creature managed to worm his way into my innards, into my blood. . . .

Suddenly I can hear and see them again. I hear better than I see. . . .

"That means," says Mićun, lighting his cigarette, "that he could recover. . . . And perhaps he is just faking. Doctor, why don't you stick a pin into his ears or his tongue to see whether he can hear and talk?". . .

"The centers of speech and hearing are not in the tongue and ear. Obviously he loses consciousness from time to time and ceases to react. The lower part of the body is totally paralyzed. The motor centers are seriously damaged. It is necessary to have further tests. . . ."

"Don't prolong it, doctor! You can't fool me, even though I don't understand your elaborate medical explanations very well. It is necessary for us—bear that in mind—it is necessary that he recover, that he regain consciousness!"

I see, Mićun, you want to torture me in order to find out about my collaborators. . . .

"He must go to trial!" says Mićun, becoming exasperated. "Public trial. He's not a nobody! People must see him and hear from his own lips how he collaborated with the occupation forces. Whether you can cure him or not is your business. And the rest is our business. But—and I underline this—our treatment of your case depends on your ability to make him well. Our goal is not to destroy you. With your knowledge—despite your serious crimes—you can still serve the people. . . ."

I was wrong again: Mićun wishes to humiliate me publicly. That's what he wants. He could have killed me the moment I fell into his trap. But he needs me alive. He's not interested in me, but in the people! He wants the people to see me as a coward and a penitent. He wants my arrangements with the Italians to be read publicly and witnesses to be questioned about my so-called betrayal of Montenegro. . . . But that would mean he's not the Devil and I am not in hell! Or is this, too, a trick of the ungodly one? To torture me through shame and through betrayal by my daughter Miruša. . . . All this is so painful and inextricable. . . . But I had better listen carefully to how the doctor will answer Mićun. Now he is coughing again. . . .

"I am doing everything that science and my long years of medical practice have taught me. Anyway, you know very well that I was always an opponent of Montenegrin separatism. You Communists are closer to me today: you preserved the state in whose creation I invested my youth and to whose preservation I dedicated my entire life. . . ."

"I know that, I know that. But I also know that you and they hate us equally. Why should I believe you? Prove it to me! I'm interested in action, not words."

"In this case," the doctor defends himself unconvincingly, "I'm only a doctor. . . ."

"That's the heart of it," shouts Mićun, "because you are not and cannot be merely a doctor. You are also a criminal, a very serious one. I took you rather than the doctor from the city hospital not only because I want this matter to remain secret, but also to offer you the opportunity to earn our forgiveness. Only a fool believes empty words. Action, action is what is needed, my doctor! Moreover, you now have a twofold opportunity to prove yourself unbiased as a doctor by curing your long-standing enemy and, at the same time, to convince us that you begin to see your errors and crimes against the people and their struggle. Can't you see we are offering you the opportunity to save yourself—that's not so important—and we are also offering you the opportunity to redeem yourself? This is very important for you as a man and for us, the humane people's authority."

"You put me into a very difficult, indeed impossible, position. What if I am not competent as a doctor, what if science doesn't know how? . . ."

2.

I don't know how much time elapsed after the visit of that werewolf Mićun with Dr. Glomazić. And how could I know? I fainted, and perhaps fell into a deep sleep. Here there is no day or night, since the light bulb burns constantly, and nothing happens that would tell me what time of day it is or how much time has passed.

I feel much more rested after my unconsciousness or deep, dreamless sleep.

Something strange is happening to me: my entire life passes before my eyes. . . .

My childhood, when I tended goats in the karst. When I fought and loved with my four brothers—two were taken by the Spanish fever and two left their bones behind at the battle for Skadar. My childhood merges with my youth. . . . I attended the noncommissioned officers' school in Cetinje. . . . Then came marriage to Stana and life with her. . . . Warring against Turkey and Austria . . . going underground during the Austrian occupation, and again after the unification with Serbia in 1918 . . . Chased by the gendarmes and by advocates of unification, I was forced to escape, first to Albania and, from there, to Italy—to the town of Gaeta. I hoped that I would see my old king there, my Master. Instead, I was confronted with shame and troubles—the Italians put us into barracks, dressed us in their uniforms, and trained us as their army. Helen, the Master's daughter, was the wife of their king. I had hoped that we would be treated as citizens of a country related by royal marriage; instead, they made us into their Balkan reconnaissance unit. And when the old Master died, they made peace with Belgrade, squeezed us dry and left us. We disbanded then, like dogs without a master, turning beggars, servants and vagabonds, just to preserve our bare existence. Finally we fell so low that we had to accept the mercy of Belgrade and return to our homes, sick at heart, our hopes dashed. I managed to build a house again and to walk proudly around it. I thirsted for Montenegrin independence. Then the war came, and Serbian power and its state, Yugoslavia, fell like a rotten log toppled by the bull sharpening his horns. The Italians gave power to us, the opponents of union with Serbia. They even offered us a state. It was a sad and bitter state, but it was still called Montenegro. I believed that if the Montenegrin state were restored, in time we would be able to escape the Italian embrace. . . . But our youth was corrupted by the Serbs and by the Communists. The moment we proclaimed a Montenegrin state, the uprising burst out in Montenegro. The Italians were surprised by the uprising, and they were also bitter toward us; but we had deceived ourselves too, and believed that Montenegro was not that which it was—the Montenegro that even today is burning out and dying in me. Where could I go? Where could the real Montenegrins go except to the Italian soup lines behind their front? I hunted Communists hiding in caves, just as they hunted me until yesterday, but they are even worse animals than I used to be. I did not have the chance to wash my hands in their blood. Soon the Communists and the advocates of a Greater Serbia began to slaughter each other. The Italians now reversed themselves and began to help those who sought union with Serbia. And so it was that our hopes failed to materialize. For one side, we were lackeys of the occupation forces; for the other side, we were betrayers of the Serbian cause. Yet all the time I remained true to my faith—Montenegrinness itself! I was longing for a Montenegro that would be more Serbian than Serbia, the Montenegro where Serbness was begotten! Then Italy collapsed. The Germans came, and for them Montenegro was only a pile of rocks protecting a wicked and venomous people who shot at them. I survived under the Germans as if I were in a trance, until they collapsed and the Communists began their reign. . . . Everyone had someone on whom to lean and somewhere to run to, but I—I fled into the night—into the caves. My fate was worse than the wolf—the wolf at least has a cave with a she-wolf and cubs. The springs and shrubs were transformed into spies and ambushers. . . . The truth is my witness: I met a wolf carrying a slaughtered lamb, and I snatched his booty from him. . . . Only when I thought the Communists had lost my trail and had forgotten me did I approach unobserved the house of my daughter, Miruša. I found nearby a deep cave which could be reached only by someone who knows the terrain well, and then only by crawling

through brambles and crevices in the limestone. Not even Miruša knew of
that crevice. Not even she, although, God forbid, I never planned to hide
from my own daughter. She knew nothing except the place where she
gave me food at night and the steep path by which I came. . . . And yet,
they caught me while I was stealing along the precipice above the abyss
toward Miruša. I am an old mountain wolf and nothing escapes my ear
and eye. . . .

I am conjecturing: they knew the direction from which I came to meet
Miruša, and they set the trap for me there. . . . I knew that someday they
would kill me, but to catch me alive—I was convinced I would never
give them that pleasure. I always kept my weapon ready and cocked,
and I moved only along jagged rocks so that they could not seize
me. It was the same this time: it appeared to me that trees and brush fell
upon me, so successful were they in hiding and becoming part of the
terrain and darkness. But I responded with all my strength—I still had
strength, although in my sixty-odd years I had seen more evil than good,
and I rolled over the cliff taking two of them with me. . . . I don't know
what happened afterward. I regained consciousness again in a truck
somewhere . . . or was that the other world—hell? . . . The truck
bounced as if we weren't driving on a road—perhaps that made me
regain consciousness. Next to me I heard the moaning of the two I took
down with me. My head felt as if it didn't belong to me—it was bursting
in a hundred directions, and I could not put it together again. Someone
was smoking, and I observed grim faces and weapons on the benches. I
kept losing consciousness in the painful jolting of the truck, and kept
regaining it even more painfully. Finally we reached a level road and I
blacked out. . . . And then, when they carried me out, I came to my
senses again and heard Mićun—yes, I'm sure it was Mićun, because I have
known him since his childhood; he grew up on my lap—I heard him
saying to someone, "It must be explained to her that her father is responsible for his plunge down the cliff and his injuries. It should be explained
to her, because we did promise to catch him unharmed and to spare his
life. Anyway, she knows that his life is not important to us, but what we
want is his unmasking before the people." That, or something like that,
Mićun said to someone in the darkness, thinking I was still unconscious
. . . Mićun, or perhaps the Devil himself. . . .

That, or something like that, Mićun or the Devil . . .

Miruša, my beloved, my only, daughter, she betrayed me! This is the
reason I escaped into memories—and the reason I am trying to escape
from this world, or from hell. . . . Perhaps my mind deceives me because
the ungodly ones are tormenting me with your betrayal . . . because
something like this was never heard of, not even outside Montenegro! For
what reason would she do that? What could compel her to do such a
thing? There is no reason: her husband remained abroad as a prisoner of

war—they can't harm him; the children are small—they don't bother children. She has no more brothers for whom to make a sacrifice. She is faithful to her husband and honest, like all the young brides in my clan. She didn't even play around with anyone. She refused to accept their bastardly faith, which does not know or recognize either sin or virtue. Is it possible that such a despicable being can come into existence in God's creation?

How can I endure this? How can I accept it?

I will die—I know that. But I cannot even die before I know the answer. . . .

Perhaps the world is no more. Perhaps Mićun, knower of all evil, or his double from hell, the perpetrator of all evil, said this on purpose to torture me with insoluble torments. Perhaps I am not even alive and he is tempting my soul in hell. . . .

May it be true, merciful God, that this is happening in hell. . . .

3.

Mićun and Dr. Glomazić came in to test me and to prod and poke at me. Again they are contesting for my soul, for my life. . . .

Let them contest as much as they want—I know that which I dare not know. . . .

Their examination lasted for some time, perhaps even half an hour, until the guard called Mićun and he left in a hurry. The guard remained, leaning in the doorway chattering with some woman in the corridor—she must have been one of theirs, because she had cropped hair and was wearing trousers. Now I will test the doctor: If he is the Devil, he will assume his true form before the cross; and if he is what he is—there must be something human in him. But I must be clever and cautious. If he does not belong to the family of Satan, then the doctor is at the mercy of the merciless . . .

"Who are you, a man or the Devil?"

"Good. You've regained consciousness. Finally you have spoken. Don't you know me, Vukota? I am Dr. Glomazić. We used to know each other well many years ago."

"I knew a Dr. Glomazić and remember him well. A long time ago we dug trenches opposite each other. But I doubt that you are that doctor. I doubt that I am the person I used to be. Where am I? Who are you? Am I alive, or am I in the other world?"

"You are alive, Vukota! You hear, you see. . . ."

"I know that. But from my forefathers I know of a hell as well as of this world. Perhaps you have transformed yourself into the Devil, or the Devil transformed himself into you."

"I understand you. You were hiding in the woods for a long time, then you were wounded and fell unconscious. But it's not like you to fake. You used to be a serious man. I can prove to you that you are in this world and not in the other world. But why should I bother about it? Believe what you believe. You were always a little hardheaded!"

"Yes, I am. I trust that you will not try to change me now, doctor? But if you are the man you were when you were my enemy—tell me what happened to me and where I am."

"That is not for me to tell—because I cannot explain it to you. My job is to care for you and, I hope, to make you well. Which part of your head hurts? Aha, that part! Is your vision blurred? Sometimes? And do the edges of objects waver? Good. Do you feel anything, Vukota, when I touch the soles of your feet? No. Motor nerve centers . . ."

"I don't care about that any more than I care about last year's snow! What I want to know, and I beg you for the sake of my torments and yours . . ."

"Do not plead with me, Vukota! You can find out for yourself where you are. Do you drink water? You do. Do they give you food? They give you food. Can the soul, even in hell, partake of material food? And why would the accursed ones try to make you well? What good would it do them? Look at me, I am crossing myself. Could one of the accursed do such a thing? Chief Mićun will not make the sign of the cross because he is an atheist. But I can, because I am a Christian like you, although I don't care that much for churches and priests. And you too can cross yourself. That's the way. Well, now, did I disappear? Your mind is perfectly sound. Only two people in this room, you and I, know the answer to this question: Who was the jailer in 1920 when you were in this very jail?"

"Sergeant Popović—may the earth expel his bones."

Here our talk was interrupted because Mićun returned, sullen, gaunt and tense. But the conversation with the doctor convinced me that my thoughts are not confused. I had the feeling that I knew where I was and what had happened to me. I was only afraid that my dreams and my memories had gotten mixed up with each other. Thus it seems I lied to myself—hoping in vain that what had happened did not happen, and that I did not know what I do know. . . . I suspected that Miruša betrayed me, since she was the only one who knew when and from where I used to come. This thought struck me the moment they got their hooks on me. I denied it and kept trying to convince myself that it could not have been. Who could dare think such a thought? One's own daughter! Every age has its own evil. But this evil transcends time and is the evil of all evils. . . . The world still stands as it was. And men are as they always were.

If only I could at least take revenge upon her! I should be able to drink my own blood. But I don't have the strength for anything any

more: I am paralyzed, jailed, with a broken head and a broken mind.
. . . I should throw her into the abyss so that nothing identifiable
remains of her in the way that Montenegrins have always treated the
godless.

While I am thinking about it, in all this evil and in my downfall, a
tempting, secret thought comes into my mind—to bite off her nose and
thus mark her as the dishonorable have always been marked. As long as
she lives, let the world point a finger at her!

"Yes, his condition is improving visibly," the doctor hastened to explain
to Mićun. "Just a few moments ago we even talked."

"I heard you talking while I was coming. What did you talk about?"
asked Mićun, peering down at me.

"Oh, nothing in particular, really. I was testing his memory and his
judgment. We were trying to remember, for example, the war with
Austria. . . ."

"Okay, doctor. Why don't you leave us for a moment."

Now Mićun and I are alone. He starts pacing up and down the cell. He
lights a cigarette and offers it to me. But I refuse: broken as I am I could
easily burn my mustache and thus shame myself before him, and besides,
I don't want him to tame me as he enjoyed taming the others.

"As you like. If you want to smoke, smoke," replies Mićun with a grim
indifference. "I want to talk to you about something important. Don't
you see that we are not your enemies the way you think? We are trying to
cure you, we want to save you. . . ."

"May the merciful God save you in the same way!"

Mićun smiles bitterly at my simultaneous curse and blessing, and then
he continues:

"You think that I have forgotten—and I am ashamed that I have
not—you think that I've forgotten how you held me on your knee and
told me stories about heroes and how I rode behind you on your horse.
You were a second father to me, and your Nikola was like a brother to
me, both while we were students and later, during the war. My father
and you, from neighboring villages, were classmates in the academy. You
were good friends. I cannot deny that you were good friends, although
my father died from hunger in the concentration camp of the occupation
forces while you were persecuting your own people. You finally emerged
as an enemy of your people and the servant of the occupation. Yes, yes,
enemy and servant. And what else can the enemy be but a servant? What
can the servant be but an enemy? And because of that it is sweeter for me
to take revenge upon you than upon someone who is nothing to me. But
the party teaches us that our goal cannot be revenge, but the re-education
of man. You were born into an evil world, and you cannot be completely
responsible or guilty for that world. That world no longer exists—only

your guilt remains. Your understanding of your behavior governs the punishment that will be meted out to you."

He pauses, waiting for his words to take effect. But I have already thought out my response. I will try to make him believe that I am going along with him. . . .

"It became clear to me that the Italians didn't care about us, but only about themselves. I knew a long time ago that my Montenegro had collapsed. I didn't have any other choice but to run to the woods to save my head. But I cannot, broken as I am into bits and pieces, comprehend everything at once. . . ."

"Well, well, I see you have begun quite well. We will help you—but you must not try by yourself to pardon yourself. Everything is honorable and heroic if it is done for the people and for their struggle. Why don't you look at us Communists? We are harshest upon ourselves and our own. . . . Think for yourself—we don't want to force you. But everything depends on your behavior; not on your behavior here in jail toward us, but on your behavior before the people and for the people. Your world, as you yourself can see, is gone. And the people, new generations, your daughter and her children, the blood of your blood, must live. We'll hold you in jail as long as we must, and then we'll send you home. You can still have time to live comfortably. . . . Dr. Glomazić will pay you visits. His record isn't completely clean, but since he is a doctor one can always forgive him his political sins. And even I will come to see you. You can always invite me. We are not like those Yugoslav police—we take care of people and always have time if there is a need to show someone the right road. . . ."

"I have no right to anything! But I would like to ask you a favor. Can I see Miruša?"

"Miruša? Why?"

"Well, I don't have anyone but her, and I want to talk with her. I might even die, and I would like to make my peace with her. . . ."

"She is here. She has been begging to see you. But we have not allowed it so far. We very seldom allow visits to prisoners while they are under interrogation. Very, very seldom! Your case is a difficult one, but in view of the fact that she is not involved in anything, and in view of the fact that you yourself began to realize . . ."

Mićun has left, and I am waiting, waiting with an idea in my mind. . . .

Miruša comes—sooner than I expected, like a bitch held in waiting until needed. I am fearful when I see how unchanged she is: dark, green eyes, lithe. She remains expressionless and stone-faced. I can read from that what I already know.

"Come, my daughter," I say to her.

"Oh, Father, what have they done to you?" bursts out as she falls onto my chest, trembling without tears or sobs.

My left arm clamps her like a manacle and I whisper words that hiss like bullets from my mouth: "You betrayed me! You betrayed your father, cursed one!"

I am getting ready to do the one thing that I still can—to bite off her nose with my teeth. But she answers through sobs and whispers: "I did, my father! What could I do? They promised they would do nothing to you, and so . . . I thought, your time is past, and we must survive somehow. Forgive me, Father! Forgive me, the product of your own blood, forgive me for the memory of my brothers, for our family name, for the sake of my children. . . ."

Can one forgive treason and the betrayal of one's own father? Can any kind of penitence wash that away or make it less painful? There is nothing there to forgive: she is what she must be in a world in which there is no room for me. . . . I'll let her cry her tears out on my shoulder and in that way shield my other hand until I can take the dressings off. I'll plunge my nails into my crushed skull, into my brain. . . .

That's the way, that's the way. . . .

"Cry, my daughter, cry. And I . . ."

I touch the wound; the bone splinters are bypassing each other and cracking. Just a little more and I will force the small splinters and my nails into my own brain—into the mind, into remembrance, into life. . . . Pain and mist. How sweet is the feeling of unknowingness! It appears that they notice I am doing something to my head. Mićun screams, calling the guards, summoning the doctor. . . . Mićun is right—there is no hell. There exists only the world in which Mićun is the almighty—a horrible world without a hell and without Satan.

"Cry, cry, my daughter! Make it easier for yourself, my poor child! There is no hell, no demons, my daughter! There exists only this world, and people. And people . . ."

                                                        January, 1970 (unpublished)

6
The Revolution
Endangered

Yugoslav Communists, the working class, and all the peoples of Yugoslavia did double duty during the war: we fought for the liberation of our people and our country and at the same time we fought to help the Soviet Union, to help all the forces that fought fascism. In reality, that double duty was one—to fight to the death for our people. It cannot be otherwise. The liberation struggle and our current efforts are each but a part of that great struggle which humanity conducts against the forces of reaction. [. . .]

Our revolution was of extraordinary proportions. It changed not only old relations, but also the soul of our peoples. [. . .] The revolution not only overthrew the bourgeoisie and the monarchy. It placed power in the hands of the working people and at the same time gave new life to the nationalities and the peoples of Yugoslavia. [. . .]

The Soviet Union came into conflict with us because its leaders and its government sought to force Yugoslavia into a subordinate position. As events proved, our quarrel was not about whether or not we were building socialism, or whether we were consorting with imperialists; the question was whether our country should be subordinate, should be exploited, should cease its economic development. [. . .] The choice was simple: we could become subordinate and tolerate exploitation, thus abandoning the causes for which the revolution was fought and making meaningless the sacrifices of hundreds of thousands of Yugoslavs who fell in battle; or we could continue the revolution, by struggling for the speedy victory of socialism in Yugoslavia, for the transformation of our country into an equal with other states, and of the Yugoslav peoples into the equals of other peoples. As honest and faithful patriots and members of the working class we did not hesitate to choose this second road. It is not the easy one.

Speech at the Anniversary of the Montenegrin Uprising, Cetinje, July 13, 1949,
Borba, July 14, 1949

The Revolution Victorious

Perversion of the People's Power

The main question in every uprising, as history shows, is that of power. But the struggle for power in our uprising developed in a different manner and along different lines from the classic examples of uprising and revolution (for example, the great French Revolution or the Great October Socialist Revolution). [. . .]

The basic slogan of our party during the war was "Fight the enemy, drive him from our land." [. . .] An apparently curious contradiction developed in the struggle for power in our country: the people, led by the party, had as their main task the armed struggle against the invaders and against the spread of chauvinistic hatred and civil war; while re-actionaries of all descriptions had as their main task quelling the people's struggle through collaboration with the enemy and by fanning the flames of chauvinistic hatred and civil war. We resolved the question of power gradually, building up the people's power from scratch and strengthening it in the course of the struggle against the invaders and their allies; while the reactionaries treated the question of power as virtually the only question. And thus it happened that they who were fighting for power and only for power lost it; while the people, who were aware that a new order would come, that in the course of the struggle they would obtain power, but who considered their most important and most immediate task to be ridding the country of its enemies, acquired power. [. . .]

Thus [. . .] the main question, the question of power, was resolved. Power was acquired by the very same masses who had risen in revolt against the invaders with the very same weapons with which they had driven out and crushed the invaders and their servants.

The development of the struggle along these lines gave the new form of power certain unique features which we must examine carefully if we are to understand correctly the character of this power and prevent its perversion in the further social development of our country.

What are these unique features?

In the first place our power, considered as a whole, is fundamentally democratic. [. . .] However, because of the unique way in which this power was established, the struggle of the working masses for their own completely democratic power is a still uncompleted process, a fact that is reflected particularly at numerous lower levels. Although the lower organs of power—the people's committees—are consistently democratic in their electoral procedure and in their functioning, in many instances (particularly in places liberated in 1944–45) they are not consistently the organs of the democratic working masses in the struggle against remnants of reaction, but are, instead, the scene and object of bitter political struggle. Regardless of their consistently democratic form and their basically democratic and popular character, the people's committees have yet to acquire democratic content, and thus have yet to become the organs of the working masses in the struggle for a genuine democracy, in the struggle against the enemies of the people. [. . .]

In the second place, power in our country has a broad popular base. This is because not only the working masses—the proletariat and the poor and middle peasantry—but also numerous honest patriots and all persons who have a constructive attitude toward the new Yugoslavia (such as, for example, the vast majority of the intelligentsia) could easily see the treacherous, nonpopular character of the former authorities. Our power reflects the interests of the working people; it is the power of precisely these people—the workers and peasants—but at the same time it unites and represents all those progressive, patriotic forces that participated in the construction of the new Yugoslavia. Therein lies its strength. However, one must also take into account the fact that hostile elements are constantly penetrating this power. A continual struggle must be waged against them to insure that that power—particularly the lower committees—does not become a weapon directed against the people, against their authority, against their progress and their achievements. Our enemies are fond of exploiting democracy and the democratic forms of the committees for their own ends. It would be a mistake, though, to restrict these forms and to restrict democracy because of this. That is not the point. What is essential is that democracy not be merely formal. Such a democracy is weak, it is inconsistent, and it is not truly popular in character. Ours must have a democratic content, it must be truly (and not merely in form) a broad democracy, defending the interests of the masses who created it and upon whose support it rests. Otherwise, the democratic forms can be manipulated to serve the narrow interests of certain reactionaries or reactionary groups. [. . .]

The present people's committees are [often] viewed as an intermediary stage in the development of another, superior, form of authority—a soviet form of authority; or else as a perfected form of authority. Both views are incorrect. Comparisons such as the former ignore the fact that our committees are unique in their method of formation and in their way of functioning, while the assertion that the committees are a perfected form of authority disregards the fact that they have yet to become a fully popularly based form of power and that a serious struggle must still be fought within and for them. Furthermore, this assertion diverts the attention of the masses from the need to continue fighting for their power.

Our people's committees on the whole have a democratic structure and a democratic form, as do the soviets, but they nevertheless differ from the soviets and have certain unique features that follow from the general conditions of their development and from the present level of social relations in our country. The soviets are the revolutionary organs of the people (the proletariat and the poor peasantry) in their struggle against the enemies of Soviet power, while within our committees a bitter political struggle is still being waged. Therefore it could be said of our people's committees that they both are and are not a fully developed permanent form of authority: their structure will, in the main, remain unchanged; but their political content is continually changing in the struggle between progressive and reactionary forces. [. . .]

Nonetheless, extremely serious mistakes are being committed in practice in the countryside. [. . .]

What are the mistakes in practice that constitute the greatest obstacle to the proper functioning of the committees?

The most dangerous and most frequent mistake is the result of underestimating the significance of the committees. People are neglecting to wage the bitter struggle that is necessary to preserve the committees from their enemies—both within and without—who are undermining the work of the people's authority. This struggle is a complex one and it requires skill and patience. Nothing is achieved if by expelling a rascal from a committee one thereby alienates the masses from the party, from the front, and from the committee itself. It is essential therefore to work persistently among the masses, to make them take an active part in the struggle to improve the work of the committees, to purge the committees and to transfer them into the hands of the most honest, most capable representatives of the people. The full significance of this struggle can best be seen from the fact that numerous measures of the federal government and of the governments of the republics have been distorted or even not put into effect because many committees include persons who are foes of the people's power. [. . .]

Another serious mistake is isolating authority (the people's committees) from the masses. This may occur because of a callous bureaucratic attitude toward people or a lack of concern for the vital interests of the masses, or because of a policy whereby clerks assume the role of committee members and thus isolate both the committee and the committee members from the masses. [. . .]

A further serious mistake is the tendency to avoid the implementation of democracy, both in the internal affairs of the committee and in the work of the committee with the masses. Within the committee this usually takes the form of one or two committee members taking everything into their own hands and either ignoring the meetings and decisions of the whole committee (plenary meetings—the collective organ of the masses) or reducing such meetings to a mere formality. In work with the masses, it is reflected in their exclusion from decision-making and from criticism of the work of committees and committee members at general meetings of the electors. [. . .] Conspicuous examples of the violation of democratic principles are those instances where the higher authorities, fearing that enemies would seize power, have failed to hold elections for committees. [. . .]

Finally, attention should be drawn to the application of the two methods of governing: persuasion and coercion. It often happens that these two methods are confused, or that only one of them is applied. These two methods are in fact only two aspects of one and the same principle—democratic self-government of the masses, by the masses, and for the masses. Coercion should be avoided wherever possible, that is, wherever there is no flagrant violation of the law or brutal abuse of the interests of the people. Our authority should not be either impersonal or callous; it should not treat people like objects. It should be sympathetic to the problems of the masses, and help the masses, working together with them in seeking solutions; it should convince both the masses and individuals of the correctness of various measures, and make them familiar with the laws. However, this does not imply that, because it is democratic, our authority should be lax; on the contrary, for the very reason that it is democratic, that it derives from the masses and reflects their interests, it must be strict in enforcing the law and in protecting the people from their enemies. That is why, under the present conditions, the use of coercion is unavoidable in dealing with negative individuals. To reject the use of coercion would mean to turn over power to the enemy, just as to abandon persuasion would permit authority to degenerate into a callous bureaucratic instrument for ruling the masses. [. . .]

Komunist, No. 1, October 1946

Yugoslavia and the Soviet Union

The Fraternal Consultation of Communist Parties

The meeting of Communist parties held in Poland in the latter part of September is of great significance for the world-wide workers' struggle and the world-wide struggle for national liberation. The Communist parties gained valuable experience in their countries' struggles for freedom and independence, and emerged from the great war against fascism much strengthened. They demonstrated to the entire world that they are consistent fighters for democracy and the rights of the common workingman, and against imperialist efforts to turn their countries into colonies. [. . .]

The defeat of German, Italian and Japanese imperialism seems to have made little impression on imperialists in Washington and some other capitals. The sharks of Wall Street and their overseas accomplices see the defeat of Germany and her allies as the elimination of their competition, an opportunity for them to take the first step in realizing their own mastery of the world. Mouthing phrases about democracy and freedom while simultaneously adopting fascist methods of enslavement, they would dearly love to wipe out the gains made by freedom-loving people in the great antifascist war. In contrast to the peace-loving policies of the USSR and other democratic countries, the imperialists are trying to create warmongering blocs and to transform the United Nations into an instrument that serves their own policy of conquest. Whether in Indochina, China, Indonesia, Madagascar or Greece, either they interfere directly with armed might or their vassals and quislings fight for them. These barbarians would like to convert such highly cultured peoples as the French, Italians and even the English into their obedient slaves. They want to resurrect imperialist Germany and pit it once more against the freedom-loving peoples of Europe. And, oh yes, they envision a solution to the Trieste problem that would create an Adriatic nest of provocateurs and spies. No crime is too repugnant if it serves their goals.

To a large degree the American imperialists have already eliminated any real freedom of speech and of the press in their own country, and they have bought up a whole slew of newspapers in England, France and Italy. Slanders, lies, provocations—these are their basic tactics; blackmail and extortion their policies.

American expansionism has found an accomplice in Western countries in the socialists of the right. Under the guise of accepting "American aid," socialists of the right and democrats of the Bidault and de Gasperi type have slowly but surely dragged their countries down into the mire of American monopolies. At the instigation of the reactionary Labour party the socialists of the right have already held four international conferences whose accomplishments are cheered by the reactionary press—which is controlled, of course, by American imperialists and their accomplices.

Communist parties cannot sit idly by and watch these monstrous plans being put into action. We know that American imperialists and their lackeys are not happy at the sight of Communist parties co-operating on the basis of mutual understanding in the struggle against the enslavers and the provocateurs. News of this meeting of Communist parties, however, will inevitably give heart to all true patriots and democrats who—regardless of their party, religion, nationality or race—are struggling sincerely for the liberation of their countries from imperialism. This is particularly so because American imperialist domination is today a cruel reality, which must be fought not only by strong national efforts but also by world-wide co-operation. And Communists are the most persistent fighters for national independence. It is necessary to advance with determination and courage; and in our epoch it is the Communists who are the most courageous, and the most wise. Without Communists it would be impossible to organize successful resistance to these Wall Street provocateurs. They have carefully learned their fascist methods from Hitler, Himmler and Goebbels, and they—like their infamous predecessors—believe that other peoples inhabit this globe only to be their slaves. If the American blackmailers, for their part, have succeeded in frightening some people with their propaganda about the atomic bomb, then the fraternal consultation of Communist parties will embolden the patriots and democrats who are struggling for their countries' independence and for peace and democracy.

The fabricators of lies in the press will spare no pains to represent falsely the significance of this meeting. As usual, they will make a lot of noise about the Communist menace, about Moscow's attempts to enslave other countries and their Communist parties, about world revolution and the rejuvenation of the Comintern. No one should be confused or made afraid by this meeting. But if someone must be confused or afraid, then let fear and confusion lie with those who are preparing to enslave other peoples and whose criminal deeds have been unmasked by this historic consultation. [. . .]

American imperialists and their schemes are a major threat to humanity. While their so-called aid corrupts the ruling circles of a nation, they are in reality milking that country's wealth and thwarting its further development. And they try to conceal their aims behind propaganda about the danger of Communist and world revolution. But thirty years have passed since the creation of the first socialist state—the USSR—and throughout that period Moscow has demonstrated that it does not interfere in other countries' internal affairs and that it extends aid only to those who are struggling for national independence. It could not be otherwise. Only those who hope to gain something interfere. Moscow is the capital only of the workingman; the social structure of the Soviet Union does not permit the exploitation of another country or another people. Precisely because of that, Moscow radiates freedom and justice for all mankind. It defeated the German imperialists and their allies and brought freedom to the peoples of Europe—a freedom that American imperialists are now attempting to take away. Moscow—the fortress of freedom-loving mankind—pursues a policy of aid to liberation movements, to peoples struggling for independence, peace and democracy. As a result the imperialists malign Moscow as the one that meddles in the internal affairs of others. They wrote that the Communist International was only temporarily dissolved. Now, with reference to the fraternal consultation of Communist parties, they will repeat all the old lies cooked up in Goebbels's "anti-Comintern" kitchen.

The Communist International played an enormous role in the creation, and especially in the ideological strengthening, of the militant workers' movement. The recent meeting revealed how Communist parties, despite the different conditions under which they operate, are united by the indestructible bond of Marxism-Leninism. Their complete agreement about the international situation clearly demonstrates that the most progressive forces in contemporary society, the Communist parties, are conscious of the tasks that face them and the conditions under which they must conduct their struggle.

The strength of present-day progressive forces derives from their ideological-political unity and not—as foreign reactionaries would have us believe—from a world headquarters that directs the struggle against imperialism. The Cominform operates on the principle of mutual understanding among fraternal parties. Each country has so many unique features that it would be ridiculous for Communists, faithful patriots, to ignore them. The Communist movement in each country is the product of the specific conditions in that country. What binds Communists together irrevocably is their dedication to the teachings of Marx, Engels, Lenin and Stalin—which is identical with dedication to the cause of their own people, to the honor and dignity of their nation, to true democracy and peace among peoples. The task of all Communist parties must be the same: to stand at the head of all progressive forces, to consolidate the struggle against the provocateurs of war and reaction. Any other stand would abet the agents of would-be American "world mastery" in their intrigue against Communism.

The peoples of Yugoslavia can only be proud that Belgrade is the place where Communist parties will conduct their consultations in the future. The peoples of Yugoslavia can only be proud that their country will in this way assist the efforts of the most progressive forces in contemporary society for the well-being of laboring, peace-loving mankind and for the peoples who are struggling to liberate themselves from the imperialist yoke.

Borba, October 8, 1947

The Struggle for Socialism in Yugoslavia

[. . .] The Fifth Congress clearly outlined the route to socialism that our country will take and the rate at which it will develop. Our struggle for socialism can be easily summarized.

In the first place, our country is rapidly transforming itself from a relatively backward, primarily agricultural capitalist country into an industrial and agricultural socialist country. Because our economy is planned, we can say with certainty that our industrial development will be rapid and that socialism will be victorious in Yugoslavia. By the end of the first Five-Year Plan, at the end of 1951, our country will be so highly developed industrially that internal social conditions will be ripe for the liquidation of antagonistic classes and the establishment of a socialist social order. [. . .] But we must bear in mind that the transformation of the village to socialism must be brought about *voluntarily* by the working peasantry. [. . .] Administrative measures will only cause damage and delay in this process. [. . .]

In the struggle for the development of socialism in our country we are encountering problems we could not foresee. [. . .] The criticism that began in the letters of the Central Committee of the Communist party of the Soviet Union and the Cominform Resolution has become, in some countries, like Rumania, Hungary and Albania, a monstrous campaign of denunciation and a total boycott of the new Yugoslavia. [. . .]

Thus the second point to be made is that, because our struggle for the building of socialism has been misinterpreted by the leaders of some democratic countries, the official Communist movements are causing us difficulties instead of helping us. [. . .] No one can prove that we are not building socialism in our country; the test of such a claim cannot be a statement but must be reality. By the same token, the fact that our transition to socialism proceeds at a different rate and in a different manner from that envisioned by Marx, Engels, Lenin or Stalin does not mean that their laws about the construction of a socialist society are invalid. Revolutionary practice and the specific route to socialism may vary, but the general laws of development continue to be valid. [. . .]

This means that the building of socialism in our country faces the same difficulties that were encountered in the USSR. In our country, as there, we must contend not only with the open resistance of capitalist elements in the city and the countryside before the decisive battle for the final building of socialism, but also with those same elements within our ranks who offer resistance during the final stage of the struggle. But socialist construction is developing rapidly in our country. Indeed, only two years after the war, without a phase of war Communism and without a long period of construction we adopted the Five-Year Plan, which will lead this country directly to the threshold of a socialist society. Because of this, our internal political struggle is also developing rapidly. We can maintain this tempo because of our domestic economic structure, because of the high level of consciousness of our masses who are working for the party through the People's Front, because of the masses who are constantly joining us in our struggle, and because of the existence of the USSR and the other democratic socialist countries.

The third characteristic of our struggle is that our country is building socialism with its own resources. [. . .] It is said that we are trying to build socialism without the Soviet Union. [. . .] I can't say that we wanted it to be this way. [. . .] We are not doing this to avoid joining our resources with the socialist forces of other countries, but, rather, because we wish to develop our productive forces to the maximum. [. . .] Practice has taught us that if we really want to build socialism in our country, our productive forces must be developed as rapidly as possible, without waiting for foreign aid. [. . .]

Lenin often emphasized [. . .] that unification of socialist states must in any case be realized voluntarily. [. . .] He does not say that one country should wait with its socialist construction until complete unification with other socialist countries has been achieved. On the contrary, he points out that all countries should build socialism as thoroughly and as quickly as possible, to strengthen the position of socialism vis-à-vis capitalism, while at the same time seeking ways to realize unification. We do not contradict Lenin. According to Leninism all questions arising between socialist states should be resolved on the basis of open discussions, on the basis of mutual understanding. We have always favored this. We do not conclude from Leninism that the unification of socialist states should be accomplished through the invention of monstrous lies about another socialist state and about the Communist party and government of that state.

We consider such tactics incorrect and impermissible. They are left over from the previous era, and should not characterize relations among socialist states.

It is natural that the struggle for the unification of socialist countries be led by the strongest country, the country that has moved the farthest in the building of socialism. [. . .] Certainly we recognize the leading role of the USSR in the struggle for socialism in the world. That role could be denied only by someone who is unaware of the real relation of forces in the world. But such a leading role, as we understand Leninism, is not strengthened by belittling the struggle of other peoples. [. . .] It is very fashionable in the Communist press at the moment—under the guise of emphasizing the leading role of the USSR—to minimize or keep silent about the struggle of the Yugoslav peoples. And what does this mean? It is tantamount to telling our people that their forces and history are insignificant, that they are passive observers—and certainly they are not that—in the great struggle of humanity against capitalism. [. . .] Those who think that they can strengthen the leading role of the USSR by belittling the struggle of Yugoslavia or other nations are mistaken. They are helping only the imperialists, who accuse the USSR of placing too little value on the struggles and history of other peoples. The revolutionary struggle of each country is an integral part of the world struggle which was begun by the Russian proletariat and the Russian people in the October Revolution. The recognition of each struggle strengthens the leading position of the USSR. But that is not happening today. Careerists and men of dubious intentions are minimizing the role of the peoples of Yugoslavia in order to justify *their own* weaknesses (and not those of their peoples) in the great struggle between the USSR and fascism. [. . .]

Comrades, I shall now turn to another aspect of the building of socialism.

The struggle to build socialism in our country is a struggle to create a new man, a man whose consciousness and emotions will be different from those of the capitalist man.

That new man will be unselfish, sincere, brave and modest. He will hold the people's welfare and the people's property above all else. Already such men are emerging. The new man watches each gram and each penny of the national property, treats the national property with as much care as he would his own. He struggles courageously for the truth. He fights relentlessly against lies, denunciations and cheating. He is sincere and open, and trained to recognize the enemy. [. . .] He is fearless in the struggle for socialism, for the well-being of his people and his country. We already have heroes—even more than in the National Liberation War. Despite scarcities and enormous difficulties, our masses are building their country anew with untold sacrifice and courage. Their sweat washes each new factory and waters each acre of land. The hands that build our industry and our agriculture will certainly wield weapons to defend their efforts with equal skill and determination. Mass heroism is inevitably created in our conditions. The new man is also modest. He loves his people and his country, but he loves other countries and does not belittle them. He is confident of his own strength, but he does not belittle the strength and value of other peoples. He does not want to become a hero himself but strives for the victory of the common cause. He competes with untold determination, not for glory but to demonstrate what can be accomplished by human will, so that others may be inspired by his example. He wants to develop successfully in his job, not because he seeks recognition but because he knows that the duty of men is to work for the general welfare, to give their all so that the people can have a better life. To progress continuously, to learn and to develop in order to give to the community—this is the goal of the new man.

That new man developed in our country directly out of the struggle for socialism. But he did not develop effortlessly. The new man was created by work, by conscious efforts by sacrifice, and by the process of building socialism. But above all, he was created through the broad educational efforts of the party. Creation of the new man is a conscious process. Herein lies the great service of our party, but also its great task. Creation of the new man must not lag behind socialist construction. Our working man who already has some of the characteristics of that new man should be helped so that these characteristics take root, so that he becomes conscious of them, so that they become an integral part of his life. [. . .]

Borba, September 4, 1948

The True Nature of the Bureaucracy

The Brutality of the Bureaucracy

[. . .] Molotov's speech in Warsaw [. . .] shows the arrogance of the victor toward the vanquished. [. . .] He merely reiterated the standard theses, which are apparent in the real content and in the cowardly form of the speech: old Poland played on the contradictions between Hitler's Germany and the socialist USSR, and had to collapse (he does not go into the details of how and why) ; then Poland was liberated by the Soviet army and a new Poland was created; here he recognizes that the Poles, "with the assistance of the USSR," succeeded fairly well in constructing the "foundations of socialism" (a term unknown to Marxism, and unexplained and inexplicable) ; finally he emphasizes that the only hope for Poland is to remain in close friendship with the USSR, for there is no longer a Germany or any indication that Poland would be able to play on the contradictions between the USSR and any other power. [. . .]

This, then, was Molotov's entire speech. [. . .] Certainly in terms of style this speech could have been given by any member of one of our communal committees, although in terms of its content, its lack of beauty, it could have been prepared only by a Cominformist. [. . .] It does not show even a spark of kindness or appreciation for the sufferings of the Polish nation. On the contrary, everything in Molotov's speech shows an inhumane and antisocialist attitude, shows the mental and spiritual poverty of the Soviet bureaucratic leadership. [. . .]

Both bureaucratism as a system and the bureaucracy as a caste—the ruling stratum—are the sworn enemies of the working class, of the real intelligentsia and of all real thought. The bureaucracy secretly despises the working class because they are "backward." [. . .] It is waging a continuous, well-concealed war against them, and, by means of its own privileges, destroying the unity created by the objective process of production. The fate of the exploited is always the same: they are despised, even when they fervently believe the words of their masters and obey. [. . .]

The bureaucracy hates and fears real intellectuals and true intellectual activity because they cannot help but reveal the essence of the bureaucracy, its gluttonous, parasitic "spirit." [. . .] It attempts to break intellectuals, to bend their spines, and to "organize" their work and "direct" it toward trivial sycophantism and apologetics, and away from true knowledge, true art and real thought. [. . .]

The vast bureaucracy, made up of the semiliterate, semi-intelligentsia, is a remnant of the old social relations. Because ostensibly workers and peasants are backward, and know only how to give up their surplus labor for nothing, there was a "need" for someone to organize and manage the processes of production, that is, to live without working, from the work of others. Certainly someone must direct the work process (as someone must direct an orchestra); but this should be the engineers and technicians, the educators, medical personnel, and so forth, who are the live human component of the work process, and not outside it. (Similarly someone must work in the state administration, because the social plan must be managed to some extent and because the state is necessary to society and to the process of production itself.) But the bureaucracy is not composed of those necessary intellectuals who, by the nature of their work, are not bureaucrats (even though, in a bureaucratic system a large portion of them can become bureaucrats), but of those "intellectuals" from the party and elsewhere who are ostensibly "leading" the real intellectuals and the working mass, elevating them "ideologically," organizing them and keeping watch over them. Whatever the bureaucracy is doing, it is not performing a necessary function. And if productive forces continue to develop, inevitably clashing with existing social relationships and demanding their change, its work of "education," "persuasion," and "organization" becomes increasingly unnecessary (it was that as soon as private capitalists were abolished and their sabotage thwarted); and it becomes ever more arbitrary, overstaffed and corruptible in its attempt to justify its own existence.

It has already been stated by Kardelj that Soviet bureaucracy is the last bastion of the class society. [. . .] Failing to become a class, the bureaucracy contains the worst characteristics of all previous classes. It is ravenous and insatiable like the bourgeoisie, but without its spirit of enterprise and thrift. It is heedless of the value of human labor like the feudal lords and the slave owners of antiquity, but it lacks their spiritual culture. It is greedy and chauvinistic like the petty bourgeoisie, but without its industriousness and patriotism. It resembles those buildings that are a composite of all possible styles, but lack any internal harmony. [. . .]

The bureaucracy (I take the Soviet bureaucracy as an example, since it is the most developed and the most grotesque) cannot rest on old ideological foundations which, if only superficially, are Marxist-Leninist. Such ideology, even when only apparently accepted, comes more and more into conflict with the bureaucracy's real needs. [. . .] And no wonder. As long as the Soviet bureaucracy struggled against private ownership, even while it was realizing its own rule, it was able to refer to Marxism. But now it cannot do so, nor does it dare to do so. [. . .] It is necessary to create a new ideology. That is being done. But in the process the poverty and lack of principles that characterize the bureaucracy as a remnant of old social formations are exposed. [. . .]

Considering its historical and social nature then, it is no wonder that the Soviet "socialist" bureaucracy demonstrates untold brutality in all aspects of contemporary life. [. . .] This is a modern "iron heel"—ruthless and willing to commit the most terrible crimes "in the name of" the highest ideals. Democrats and socialists were unable to perceive this because of the intensity of their struggle against capitalism. But the democratic and socialist world, in the course of its development, will be forced to recognize this phenomenon, to conquer it and to remove it from its path.

Borba, September 6, 1951

Class or Caste?

Class or caste?

There are two essential elements that determine whether a given group of people constitutes a ruling class: first, its position in the process of production (that is, whether the people work or whether they live at the expense of someone else's work) ; and second, its relationship to the means of production (that is, whether they are or are not the owners). This is the crudest test, which is applicable to *all* ruling classes in history.

We can apply this most basic test to the bureaucracy in the Soviet Union.[1] This bureaucracy lives at the expense of someone else's labor. It has exclusive control over both production and distribution (the surplus of labor) ; the direct producers have no rights. The vast bureaucracy grabs the lion's share of the surplus of labor for itself, and distributes it according to rank. The role of the bureaucracy in the economic system reinforces its political (and police) monopoly, and so too the outward manifestations of rank, the despotism of the higher orders toward the lower ones, and the fear of the lower orders for their superiors, that are inevitable in such a system. Thus, in its role in the process of production

---

1. The term *bureaucracy* as used here does not mean officials of the state administration, courts, police, officers and the like, but the bureaucratic organs of management of the economy in industry, commerce and agriculture. These bureaucratic organs arise because in the transitional period organs for administration and enforcement in the economy are necessary; but in their own way these organs become a special force over society.

the bureaucracy in the USSR does not differ significantly from previous ruling classes.

But the bureaucracy does not own the means of production in the traditional sense, because ownership is collective rather than individual.[2] Thus this group differs from all earlier ruling classes. Obviously we have here a new phenomenon, something that appears to be a class but is not, or, rather, in some ways is and in other ways is not a class.

Another characteristic of all ruling classes is that they are self-perpetuating. Because the members of the class are private owners, because they manage and distribute property, they can pass their positions in the class on to successive generations. Is this true of the bureaucracy in the Soviet Union? Certainly there is some degree of self-perpetuation; statistics show that most of the students in the higher schools and universities are the children of officials. But the individual cannot pass his position on to his progeny, nor indeed is his unique set of privileges necessarily passed on to anyone. For the bureaucracy does not reproduce itself as a set of individuals, or as a set of positions. Rather, it perpetuates itself as a body, drawing its members both from its own ranks and from the peasantry and the proletariat. If we look at the bureaucracy in this light we can see that it is a new historical phenomenon. [. . .]

It is something transitional: being the remnant of the class society, class struggles and class relations, the bureaucracy embodies the negative remnants of all the old classes—the absoluteness of the feudal class, the insatiable greed of the bourgeois class, and the chauvinism of the petty bourgeoisie. The fact that it is transitional does not necessarily mean that its life will be short or that it will mellow. Its duration and character depend on subjective and objective international and domestic factors. (A very detailed analysis would be necessary to reach any conclusions.) However, because the bureaucracy embodies the most reactionary characteristics of former classes, and because it has achieved a lordship over all forms of social life that has never been achieved by any other class, we can conclude that it is prepared to perpetrate crime on a scale never attained by any class in history. But this still does not mean that it is a new class.

We can summarize all this: If the bureaucracy has class characteristics—and it really does have many—this still does not mean that it is a class. It must be something else, and that can only be a caste.[3] The

2. It is not difficult to see that this ownership is only a step away from the collective ownership of trusts and monopolies by individuals under capitalism.
3. While Trotsky spoke about the bureaucracy as a caste, his analysis and final conclusions are quite different from ours. His critique recognized only foreign characteristics and was basically non-Marxist, because it explained the objective process through the influence of personalities, rather than explaining those personalities by the process itself. A bureaucratic adventurist, instead of the victory of the bureaucracy

essential characteristic of a caste is that privileges of all kinds are accorded on the basis of functions performed, and not on the basis of ownership.

It is very important, both for us in Yugoslavia and for socialism in general, to be sure of the answer. If the bureaucracy were a new class, its victory could not be prevented; it would be inevitable because it is brought about by objective social processes. Thus, if we were dealing here with a class, a new class, and not a caste, the struggle against the bureaucracy would be futile and utopian, and we who fought would be comical reactionary figures. But since the bureaucracy is not a class, but a reactionary antisocialist tendency that appears in the transition from capitalism to Communism, the struggle against it is revolutionary and progressive. And it can succeed. The fact that bureaucratism is an inevitable danger of the transitional period—which was clearly foreseen by Marx, Engels and Stalin—does not mean, nor did they maintain, that the bureaucracy must win out over the socialist tendencies. Nor can one maintain that the victory of the bureaucracy is inevitable merely because it occurred in the first country that struggled to build socialism. On the contrary, if it had to happen there (I will not deal with the reasons), this does not mean that it must be the same in other countries, where objective and subjective conditions are different and so the socialist tendencies are stronger.

Misled by the fact that victory of the bureaucracy was possible in the Soviet Union, Stalin came to the conclusion that it was inevitable and that it is a general law of the development of society. (However, it is a general law only that bureaucratism appears as a danger; not that the bureaucracy will be victorious.) He presents its subjective victory, subject to the conditions specific to Russia, as an objective law, himself as the so-called (divine) embodiment of such an "objective" law. And so he believed that the "objective" process alone, the inevitable victory of the bureaucracy (as affirmed by the development of the Soviet Union) would overthrow the Yugoslav leadership and put matters "in order" in Yugoslavia. But it is only the tendency toward bureaucratism (toward the formation of a caste; it does not concern a class) and not the victory of the bureaucracy that is objectively conditioned. The outcome depends on the strength of the working class and the conscious forces of socialism in that objectively conditioned and inevitable struggle.

It is not difficult to see that the theory of the bureaucracy as a new class could serve only Stalinist, bureaucratic tendencies. It would sow con-

---

in *one* country, the USSR, he advocated the realization of Soviet bureaucracy (Soviet revolution) through the victory of the USSR over the outside world. It is not coincidental that Stalin's recent ideas—in his period of world conquest—resemble Trotsky's ideas more and more and that the differences between Trotskyites and Stalinists in essential questions becomes less and less. [. . .]

fusion in the ranks of the proletariat and all conscious fighters for socialism, and kill their faith in the glorious victory of socialist social relations.

Borba, April 6, 1952

The Further Development of Socialism in Yugoslavia

Educational Tasks in the Struggle for Socialism

After the war our country made significant progress in education. [. . .] The number of schools and of pupils increased enormously; entire new groups of institutions were founded in the fields of science and culture [. . .] and an even more significant transformation took place in the philosophy of teaching and in the ideological and political education of teachers.

Of course, we would be foolish to pretend that our educational system has changed completely and fundamentally. [. . .] Changes in teaching programs, in the number and kinds of schools and the number and types of teaching cadres can all be planned. But the change in human thought can be accomplished neither by administrative measures nor within a specified period of time. It is a continuing process which, in the final analysis, is achieved only through the resolution of the contradictions between productive forces and productive relations. [. . .] True, in the history of the socialist movement, that is, in the Soviet Union, plans were made to wipe out the remnants of old beliefs, to change human opinion within a specific period of time. But history proves that these methods did not produce the desired results: democracy did not develop; rather, the administrative apparatus maintained its ideological monopoly. [. . .]

As socialism progresses, administrative measures must be used less and less. Censorship and prohibitions of all kinds are measures for the proletariat to use against reaction and counterrevolution, and should be used only against them. [. . .] The administrative apparatus in socialism cannot possess an ideological monopoly without at the same time violating the principles of socialist democracy and paralyzing the initiative of the masses. This prevents the development of a healthy ideological struggle between that which is old and lifeless and that which is evolving with the development of productive forces and social relations. [. . .]

We have undoubtedly achieved a great deal in our struggle for the ideological and political transformation of the educational system. [. . .]

As our educational institutions struggle to apply dialectical and historical materialism correctly, our party and our country are strengthened in
their struggle against revisionism, and new resources are awakened,
creative energies released, in all fields. [. . .] But we still have serious
inadequacies to contend with. [. . .]

Thus, the question is, where should we start in deciding on the further
development of education? What is the objective historical foundation
from which we should determine our educational policy?

The objective historical realities are the revolution, the building of
socialism and our cultural and educational heritage. The people's revolution, as we know, altered the foundations of political and social relations in our country. [. . .] It succeeded because of the application of
the Marxist-Leninist theory of historical materialism. Marxism-Leninism
was the ideological foundation of our revolution. [. . .] And the principles of the revolution—socialist democracy, the building of a society
without exploitation, the political and genuine equality of peoples—
remain the lifeblood of our social, political and ideological development. [. . .]

The development of education must therefore start from the fact that
there is a socialist transformation in our country. [. . .] This will inevitably lead not only to the elimination of capitalist elements, but also to
the decrease of the role of the bureaucracy and the expansion of the role
of the masses. If the liquidation of capitalist relations was not followed
by the development and strengthening of self-management of the people,
the development of socialism could not continue. We must keep these
principles in mind when we talk about the tasks in education. Our
educational system must aim for a deeper and wider socialist democracy.
To determine the foundations of our educational policy we must first
determine what is unique to the people's revolution and to the construction of socialism in our country. Only those who are doctrinaire can
maintain that socialism has only one form; to conceive of socialism in all
countries as monolithic, of a single type, means to slow down the development of socialism throughout the entire world. [. . .] For the general
law of events is realized only through the individual, the particular and
the specific. To abolish the particular and the specific is to attempt to
halt the inevitable movement of the material world itself; in social relations this can at best succeed temporarily. And here lies the enormous
significance of uniqueness for the socialist movement. [. . .] While all
countries will ultimately develop socialism, their routes to socialism will
be determined by their unique historical conditions. Failure to recognize
this limits the possibilities of individual countries in the struggle for
socialism and thus slows down the world-wide struggle for socialism and
democracy. [. . .]

Finally, our educational development, if it is to progress, cannot ignore its heritage—the ideological inheritance from earlier struggles for democracy and the inherited specific forms of education and upbringing. [. . .] It would be erroneous to think that the entire educational system and the entire pedagogical method inherited from the past were invalid and should be thrown away. [. . .]

The principal question in formulating an educational policy is: what do we want to achieve, what kind of man do we seek to build? [. . .] One thing is certain: we should educate a free socialist man who thinks and works courageously and with determination, one who is broad-minded and not one whose mind is forced into a rigid mold. [. . .] He should be a man who loves his country and respects other peoples, a citizen of the new Yugoslavia. He should be spiritually rich, morally strong, and physically healthy.

Obviously there is no pat formula that we can apply; we must find our own forms and methods. [. . .] But this is not an easy task; we cannot simply ascertain what is appropriate once and for all and administer that formula from an office, regardless of how intelligent the people in the office are. [. . .]

What we want can only be achieved through the struggle against bureaucratic methods. We must make certain that the appropriate role of administrative bodies at all levels—that of general management—is maintained, and that it is we who ascertain what forms of free ideological discussion are mutually consistent with socialist democracy and the struggle against bourgeois decadence, on the one hand, and with the development of widespread individual initiative, on the other. If it is our duty to prevent, even by administrative measures, the dissemination of any propaganda that would tend to promote the exploitation of man or to destroy the equality of our peoples, then it is even more our duty to enable all those who honestly struggle for socialism, for the progress of science and culture and for the education of the socialist man, to prosper and to express themselves completely. For it is through the free exchange of ideas, the critical examination of certain of our methods, that we will find fruitful forms for further development. Nothing could be more detrimental to socialism than the destruction of initiative, than a bureaucratic monopoly over human thought.

We have always been and remain adamantly opposed to random experimentation in education. But if we prevent widespread initiative and the free exchange of practical experience and opinions about the struggle for socialism in our country [. . .] we shall ourselves be making a bad, if not disastrous, experiment of national proportions. [. . .]

The question is how, and when, pupils should receive a general ideological education which will enable them to formulate a correct view of the world.

Obviously the entire curriculum should be taught from the viewpoint of the struggle for the revolutionary change of society. The application of dialectical and historical materialism to all areas of science and culture—the search for concrete inevitabilities in science and culture as manifestations of the general inevitability in nature and society—will provide the general ideological background necessary for the formulation of a correct view of the world. Thus the treatment of Marxism-Leninism as a separate subject—which would separate dialectical and historical materialism from the whole of science and culture—would be incorrect.

This does not mean that a student should acquire his view of the world only from the incorporation of Marxism-Leninism into the study of science and culture. [. . .] In that case he would be unable to understand general laws, to formulate the entire picture of laws that operate in nature and in society. [. . .]

We think, therefore, that the study of the general principles of philosophy (including the foundation of logic and psychology and in a very abbreviated form the general history of philosophy) —that is, the general principles of dialectical and historical materialism—should be obligatory in the last two years of high school. These grades correspond to the age at which youths mature, a significant period in the formation of their understanding, their knowledge and their consciousness.

The study of historical materialism and Marxist sociology (the foundation of social sciences) should also be obligatory in all universities and higher schools—probably in a two-year sequence. Students will thus acquire a firmer grasp of the basic laws of the development of society and of the social sciences at a time when they are already mature and are actively entering into society.

And finally, in our opinion, in the last two years of high school the subject of the structure of the state (instead of the study of the constitution) should be introduced. Thus, the student will become familiar with the basic laws and principles upon which our revolution was built and upon which our socialist democracy is developing. [. . .]

The role of the party, people's authorities and mass organizations is crucial in the further development of our education. Without their work it is inconceivable that our struggle for a new socialist society and a new socialist man will succeed. [. . .] Party organization among students is generally satisfactory, but it seems that the relation between students and professors has not yet been satisfactorily resolved. In an attempt to achieve discipline there has been a tendency to ignore the fact that students are mature people, or at least in the process of maturing. Certainly students should honor their professors and respect their authority. But there is no justification for limiting free discussions between students and teachers, particularly in regard to specific issues in the social sciences and philosophy and theoretical problems in the natural sciences. Even before the war, in reactionary, capitalist, monarchist, centralist Yugoslavia students were able to express their opinions freely before many professors who [. . .] believed in the free struggle of ideas. And there is no reason why this should not be the case today. [. . .]

Borba, January 3, 4, 5, 1950

The Working Class—the Leading Force of Socialism

Marx and Engels maintained that the collapse of capitalism was inevitable. They reached that conclusion on the basis of a scientific analysis of society in general as well as of capitalism in particular. But they did not think that the collapse would occur by itself. They maintained that any social order, including capitalism, can only be changed by a force born within it, whose social (class) interests are in conflict with it. In capitalism only the working class can be such a social force. [. . .]

Marx and Engels also believed that the working class is the major force in the building of the new, socialist society. A hundred years ago they said, "It is the task of workers to liberate workers." This theme, apparent in all their works, was often taken only as a slogan, as a fighting phrase; very little attention was devoted to its real significance.

The question is simply this:

Is it the party, *i.e.,* the governmental authority of the proletariat (dictatorship of the proletariat), that is the chief force of socialism, or is it the working class?

It is very important, for us here in Yugoslavia and for socialism in general, to find the correct answer to this question, in order to gain a clear orientation in our struggle for socialism.

All official Soviet theoreticians since Lenin, led by Stalin, have maintained that the party, the state, is the chief force not only of socialism but also of Communist society.

Let us look more closely at this theory, which has prevailed for so long in the Soviet Union.

It starts from the premises that: 1) the party is the leading force of the working class, without which it could not carry out an organized and conscious struggle as a class; and 2) the working class cannot build a new society without the party's power, because force must be used against the class enemies. [. . .]

But from these valid premises, Soviet theory developed in an anti-Marxist and antisocialist direction into a complete theory that denied any role, either in theory or in practice, to the working class in the struggle for the new society. Since the party was the vanguard of the working class, since the party's power came from the struggle of the working class (the revolution), Soviet leaders erroneously maintained that they alone should make decisions concerning the building of socialism and the form of social relations to be developed. In practice that meant that the upper echelons in the party and the government would make the decisions, since parties cannot exist without leaders, or governments without executive bodies. Thus the power to make decisions concerning the nature of socialism and the manner of building it, at both the theoretical and practical levels, was transferred not just to the party, but to the party elite. This process, already familiar to us, transformed the governing authority of the proletariat into a force above the proletariat and therefore above the whole of society. [. . .]

But this does not explain the error of the "Soviet" theory about the party and its authority as the major force in the building of socialism. [. . .] Socialism cannot be victorious without power, that is, without the party of the proletariat; nor can it survive unless it develops its productive forces more extensively and more rapidly than capitalism does. Socialism is created, above all, through the physical labor of the working people, including the intellectual labor of engineers, teachers, doctors, technicians and scientists. It is the product of the *physical labor* of the working class. The party and the government as organizations do not create the material goods essential for the transition to a socialist society; they function merely to protect the building of socialism from the enemies of the working class, to mobilize the masses and to propagate the ideas of socialism and socialist social relations.

In a bureaucratic system such as the USSR's, the role of the party and the government is the same. On the other hand, in a democratic socialist system such as ours the roles of the party and the government have to be different. In one essential respect they are the same: both the party and the government are instruments of the *Class struggle* of the working class. But they operate differently: the government is the organ of power, while the party is the organized consciousness of the working class. It mobilizes and instructs the working class and it mobilizes the masses to criticize and to control the government itself, to assure that the government operates in accord with the interests of the working class.

Therefore the leading force of socialism is the working class. Its nature determines the character of the society in each stage of its struggle for socialism.

Two things follow from this. First, the basic task in the struggle for socialism is the liberation of the working class in production. The less these productive forces are obstructed, the better the working class can perform its historical mission—determined by its position in production—to build a new society. Second, the working class is not a pure class, immune to enemy influences, nor is society composed only of the working class; it also includes the petty bourgeoisie and remnants of the bourgeoisie. Therefore, not only organs of force (against the enemy) but also organs of consciousness (against the enemy and against his ideological and political influence) are necessary in the struggle for socialism. That is, both governmental authority and the party are necessary. The organization and function of these differ, both from country to country and from phase to phase of the struggle within a country. Nonetheless it is essential that the party and the government exist, in some form and with some function, as long as the working class leads the class struggle, until the final victory of socialism—Communism—is achieved.

In our country we are now at the stage where the working class is liberating its forces in production and exchange to become the leading force of socialism and where the government and the party are beginning to differentiate their roles. The party is becoming primarily an expression of socialist consciousness and the organizer of the political struggle, of the ideological and cultural enlightenment of the masses; while the government remains the primary organ of power in the struggle against the enemies of the working class and socialism, in the struggle against all those forces that, in one way or another, seek to prevent the development of socialist forces of production, and therefore of socialism. But it would be a mistake not to realize that the party retains some of the character of the organ of authority, just as the government retains something of the role of the party. They are striving for the same goal: the continual free development and operation of the major force of socialism—the working class. But each is an instrument of a different kind in the struggle.

Borba, May 1–3, 1952

The Asian Way

Eastern Sky

The dusky deserts of Africa and Arabia fell behind us. [. . .] Below us India appeared. [. . .] It seemed already that India would not be completely strange. [. . .] We had heard so much about India and, like many others, had long felt a vague love for it and had some dim preconceptions about it. In a sense we weren't wrong and when we confronted the reality, the ordinary Indian world and daily life were neither strange nor incomprehensible to us. [. . .] But this residual feeling, and the perception of it, although it proved to be correct, was still so superficial yet so accurate that only real contact could reveal to us that underneath the superficial similarity, underneath the fact that Indians suffer and struggle, even if in a different way, nonetheless like us, is a resemblance that despite all the differences is deeper and closer than we had ever imagined. Because we tried to prepare ourselves in advance to really experience Asia (India and Burma) we believed that we could comprehend it more deeply than the average Western traveler, like us part politician, part journalist, part something else. And for that reason from the moment the giant plane touched down rather clumsily on the Asian continent, our joy burst out, somewhat naïvely; somewhat childishly we Yugoslavs, small and backward, feel that we will understand Asia better and feel closer to it—although we really don't know Asia at all—than any others from the West. [. . .]

But our satisfaction and joy were only partially justified. Because we are also European in almost all respects. Even if we are backward, Asiatic Europe, we are still Europe.[1] [. . .]

That's all nonsense, of course, because such concepts as European and Asian, East and West, are only relative. The "civilized" Europe of Kaiser Wilhelm and of Stalin is not civilized, nor is the "backward" Asia of Gandhi and Sun Yat-sen backward! There is neither East nor West, because what at one moment is one thing, the next moment is something else. As Bacon wisely observed, East and West do not exist in a geographic sense; people invented them. [. . .]

The gigantic muddy rivers of humanity roll sluggishly but ceaselessly by, neither the beginning nor the end visible. With their ancient and their new philosophies and religions, with their peasant and bourgeois and proletarian leaders, with their countless languages and cultures, they are moving onward, not fearing death from starvation or from the technical might of the West, overflowing everything they meet, not worrying about obstacles, not quite conscious of their destination but convinced that they will reach a better life just as the waters of the river do not know that they will flow into the calm sea and yet, despite everything, they must flow into it sometime and somewhere. . . .

Perhaps because of that the mouth of the Ganges, although seen only from a plane—and perhaps its grandeur cannot be seen in any other way—evoked in me a vivid picture of the enormous masses who for thousands of years have been cutting a swath through history, moving backward, forward and still more forward. [. . .] Old men with biblical beards, deep-set fiery eyes, people wrapped in robes like ancient sculptures . . . Old men with carved heads, unbowed but bearing the marks of cruel times, they are our ancestors or wise old men from isolated villages and little towns. We are the barefooted children, the people who sleep in the streets, in huts and wooden houses, on the earthen floors or straw mats and boards. And one moves further and further back! That far away childhood still lives here, still exists, despite everything new and

1. I inderstand Europe to include the USSR except where explicitly mentioned to the contrary in the text.

even through that which is new. Even today Indian women, even those with European education or a European orientation, wear the ancient sari which is youthful in its ancient beauty. It is the same with men's clothing. It is the same with everything: these peoples are young, although with ancient cultures which were interrupted, changed, cross-bred, destroyed to give birth to new ones but which still endure and which enter—even in an indirect and incomprehensible way, perhaps through religions and beliefs—into the soul, the bearing, the feelings and the way of thinking, into the visions and words of even the simplest Indian peasant. Perhaps this inborn subtlety and imperceptible care in the way people behave toward one another is a residual, inherited and intuited, rather than being learned, and which until recently was visible—if not so highly developed—in our own patriarchal environment. [. . .] Here it is a natural quality of the common man. Humanity's past still lives on here among the people and within them, while in Europe it is sensed only through old buildings, books or classical works whose beauty cannot be eroded by time. [. . .]

Any person who ever felt in the slightest measure that eternal, uninterrupted humaneness of Asia [. . .] will always carry something of the radiance of its beauty as if he had found his true self, as if he had cleansed himself and returned to the wellsprings of human values. [. . .]

In this environment [. . .] unusual comparisons come to mind. I was in the United States, where man has made technology his servant but it is also his master. I admired much that was attained in the New World—the granite beauty of New York, the sweeping horizons opened by roads and bridges. But in that world life so quickly becomes clear and simple that man could be overwhelmed by the desire to live in that way. The watch is a magnificent invention and it is useful and pleasurable to have one. But only someone who was born in a technological society, who never saw or felt anything outside or beyond it, can live by the clock. I am not trying to say that the United States has too much technology. On the contrary, I can't imagine a country where there is too much. Technology as such does not enslave; it liberates. What enslaves are those same social relations that enslave technology itself. . . . Soulless capitalists weigh spiritual and moral values on a scale like a commodity. This is what makes man the slave of technology, makes him an animal and gives birth to animalistic cravings. Russia is somewhat different. There technology was desired as a weapon to rule the people. The ruling stratum transformed that technology into a gigantic animal cage inside of which, in the name of the highest moral and social virtues, baseness and crime are inevitably the natural way of life of millions of despots from the smallest all the way up to the supreme bureaucratic tsar. No one who understands the contemporary Russian system at all could crave it for any purpose except to illustrate the most horrible form of modern life, for the existing mechanism makes it impossible to come into contact with the sensitive, emotional and perhaps, because of long dismal slavery, cruel soul of the Russian people. But the craving for Asia never leaves those who have really felt the grace of its eternal human existence and the uninterrupted fabric of humane relations among people, even though they assume a cruel form. Such humane relations exist elsewhere of course—even in the United States and in Russia. Businessmen and bureaucrats are not the only people in those countries. But in Asia that humanism, uninterrupted since the beginning of mankind, is felt not more intensely but more directly than elsewhere. In ancient India, in young Burma . . . even recalling them revives youth, and not only youth, but also the first colors and sounds, the first steps and glances into the endless and changing beauty of nature and of men within it.[2] [. . .]

Death began with the birth of man and even before. And man, after his first cognition of the world around him, began to fight death with each thing he created, large or small, material or spiritual, but each endures in the existence and creation of mankind. Man disappears as a biological entity but becomes human, a part of mankind and its existence. This is the essence of the Asian feeling for life and death. We in Europe do not know these feelings any more, since abandoning traditional beliefs but not being able to attain materialism leaves us surprised and shocked by the inevitable transformation of our own matter from one form into another, from the form in which we are and through which we are conscious and through which we feel, into the form in which we are no longer, where consciousness and feeling no longer exist.

Asia imprints exactly those deep and lasting pictures of serenity: peace in the face of death, without heroism or pathos, and through life itself a direct picture of the endless continuity of humanity. Life is beautiful even if fraught with hardship; but to depart it is as natural, as strange and as inevitable as was our coming into this world. [. . .]

Exactly because Europe managed to cover in a few decades what it has taken Asia several centuries to attain, Europeans seem to have lost this living connection with the past, with the continuity of humanity, and

2. I do not wish to contrast Asian humanism to soulless Western technology. [. . .] I am speaking about the way in which the continuity of Asian development is itself preserved in the life of the masses, which has acquired lasting humanistic forms despite barbarous customs. Modern capitalist civilization, because of the need for further material development, has eliminated some barbarous systems (slave and feudal labor) and customs that still endure in Asia. The material, technical backwardness of Asia is what makes it live the way it does and what enables one to perceive the barbarous relations and customs. The shadow of those relations conceals the uninterrupted Asian humanism and the continuing creativity of the majority of the Asian people. [. . .] Just as Asia does not need technology merely to unwrap some forms of humanism and to remove the remnants of barbarous relations, the same technology is in itself not yet capable of abolishing the barbarous essence of contemporary Western society.

thus they fail to find the "Asian" internal peace in facing the future. Hence the European loses his faith when faced with the endless misery and backwardness of Asia. He sees the difference between "progressive" Europe and "backward" Asia widening perhaps as fast if not faster than that between Europe and the United States. He sees that Asia might need perhaps centuries until its hundreds of millions of people wrest themselves out of misery and catch up with Europe. . . . And when Asia reaches the point where Europe is now, Europe will be still farther ahead. And so on without end. The average European fails to see two things: that to the Asian masses, for Asian possibilities and habits, even centuries do not seem so desperately long; and, second, that the time is coming when the West will not be able to make progress so easily at the expense of Asia or to make progress leaving Asia behind. [. . .] The old classes and old relations are dying in Europe while in Asia new human relations are being born and from the death spasm of the old world emerge new and more just relations between Europe and Asia, and among peoples in general. [. . .]

My talk with Rada Khrishnon, Vice President of the Indian Republic and an idealist philosopher, was one of the most pleasant and rewarding experiences of my Asian trip. While we were at two different poles—the meeting of a Yugoslav socialist and materialist with an Indian "non-socialist" and "non-materialist"—we still found common views on a series of social and political questions. [. . .] And in India the idealism of Rada Khrishnon was incomparably more progressive than the vulgar and subjective idealistic materialism of the Cominform. [. . .] Vulgar materialism in contemporary Russia is also the ugliest form of subjective idealism and religious mysticism, just as, in practice, its "socialism" is worse than "democratic" exclusiveness and monopolism in the Western world.

Here in Asia, in India, all this is felt with unusual intensity, in sharp relief.

And thus it is not only sad that European socialist thought—Social Democratic as well as Comintern—over the course of four decades was unable to understand Gandhi and the Gandhian movement. There is also an important historical lesson here. The socialists did not understand Tolstoy, although they enjoyed his works as much as others did and poked fun at his ideas more than at the ideas of others. And yet that same Tolstoy was the mirror and the yeast of the Russian Revolution. He did not organize revolutionary cadres, because he could not do that, nor did he want to, but his heretical antichurch Christianity and his refusal to resist evil, his shallow but ethical philosophy and religion, corroded the religion and power of the ruling classes and uncovered the absurdity and inhumanity of existing human relations. Gandhi's ideas have much in common with those of Tolstoy. But only in that. Because that emaciated, tireless Hindu who had no fixed ideology but only immutable principles, armed only with his goat and his loom, operated at the conference table and sabotaged the war efforts, moving hundreds of millions of people speaking different languages and of different colors into the struggle against English imperialism and domestic feudalism, and created ripples amidst the largest human mass, which finally led to the national liberation of India and began its modern history. [. . .]

Gandhi found precisely those forms of the struggle and the ideas to gather the masses to liberate India. Each Indian—whether peasant, city-dweller, intellectual or even worker—could find in Gandhi's eclecticism an expression of his own thoughts and feelings. [. . .] Gandhi was brave, determined and faithful to his fundamental beliefs. He always believed in the uncontainable power of the people. [. . .] His ideal was the return to the old village community without the feudal lords and the imperialists. Although this vision was unrealistic and unrealizable, without it the Indian peasant—the major force—would not have been mobilized; with it, he was able to gather the masses to demand ancient rights. [. . .]

In this vast peasant country lacking arms and technology, Gandhian non-violence, that is, civil disobedience, was not only a possible form of the class struggle, but also the only form for drawing the masses in the millions into that struggle. It was far more militant and progressive than all the "strict revolutionary" slogans, which are only vulgar chattering when they fail to express the real objective revolutionary process and were only parroted alien phrases. The massiveness, the determination and the durability of the Gandhian movement forced the English to retreat. At least they knew how to leave before being thrown out. The once clever French bourgeoisie could not read the future [. . .] and thus France wasted so many resources and so many people in a senseless war in Indochina. The more traditional England more easily renounced the rich Indian empire than the modern French republic its distant and expensive colonies.

But if Europe and the West fear long wars, Asia does not. With its expanse and its masses it can exhaust any economy. Those who do not understand that are already learning a very difficult lesson. The policies of favoring and of pressuring Maoist China are equally absurd, because they do not treat this country as an objective fact. Only realistic relations are possible with the New China, and not the relations desired by certain groups. China will follow its own path regardless. In Asia even third-rate journalists know that, while in the rest of the world this is not understood by even the greatest statesmen. Vast staffs of politicians and soldiers study, plan and contemplate . . . but what happens will depend on the internal logic of the Chinese people and on international relations.

The same applies to India.

Gandhi, Nehru, the socialists, Burma, China, Indochina and Indonesia—all those are elements of the movement of Asiatic peoples toward a new life. If democracy wins anywhere it will not be of the classic bourgeois European type, if for no other reason than because extra profits from the colonies were an important element in the European case. Despotism finds fertile ground in Asia not only because of the backwardness of these peoples but also because of the imperialist, colonialist and selfish policies of the Western powers. And Russia, of course. The Russian "socialist," "anticolonialist" sun has been mortally wounded by the Yugoslav arrow and has begun to set on the bloody battlefields of Korea. Nobody expected honey from the imperialists. But after the bloody experience in Korea and the even bloodier Yugoslav experiences, the real nature of the USSR was revealed. Everybody wants to get along with this colossus and to benefit from its conflict with the U.S.A., but none believes it is the bearer of freedom. That faith still lives, but as something past, just as the October Revolution has passed. . . . If the Asian supporters of the Cominform—being so-called materialists and celebrating Lenin and October—do not understand that, Rada Khrishnon understands it, because he really is an idealist and pays real tribute to Lenin and October. Khrishnon's idealism stands for more lasting values: the freedom of science and culture, political democracy, anticolonialism and antimonopolism, and respect for human dignity. That is progress in comparison to feudal ideologies and colonialist practice. And what does Stalinist materialism stand for "in the name of" socialism and revolution?

Finally, how can Gandhi's unscientific ideas be so progressive? Doesn't that prove that ideas are only correct relatively? Doesn't that prove how the reality in ideas emerges in an unreal, distorted manner? And that the unreal form is the only real one, the way a given social reality expresses itself, and the only way to express it. Doesn't that show that things always turn out differently—better or worse, and in modern history usually worse—than what the courageous people were fighting for?

Nova Misao, No. 10, October 1953

IV
DOUBTS
AND SEARCHES

It seems essential to me that the *period of transition* from capitalism to social-ism not establish any *definitive* philosophy nor even less any *definitive* social system.

The "application of Marxism" to [. . .] reality leads to dogmatism. For since it is reality that is new and the theory that is old, the theory should be adjusted to the new reality, and not reality to the theory. The old theory can only be a starting point for both the new theory and the new practice.

The fundamental question for the transitional period is this: how to cross over from the class to the universal in both theory and practice. Every social theory claims to be fully universal, while at best each is a theory of only one class. Marxism admitted this openly, and therein lies its superiority over all other theories. Class Marxism claimed that it was possible to pass over from the class to the universal. But it has yet to develop the universal aspect it asserts is within itself, and, therefore, since they are also universal, logic (as the negation of philosophy), ethics and esthetics also remain undeveloped within it.

From the class to the universal—that is also the way for the withering away of the state and of the political movement in general.

An interesting psychological observation: whenever we Communists come upon hard times, we always recall some universal values, but as soon as we win—the class within us bursts out ever stronger. Why is this so?

Diary of Thoughts, 1953–1954 (unpublished)

7
The Vision Pales

In future parliaments, that which is new must have a powerful voice. [. . .] The new is already firmly established on the lower levels in the workers' councils and the people's committees and it was also beginning to appear at the top in the Parliament. [. . .]

Bureaucratism had almost displaced the principle of appointment on the basis of merit. [. . .] One of the urgent tasks of each deputy will be to struggle for legality and against abuses. Otherwise, the class of "patrons" will soon turn him into their own deputy and turn him against the people. It is the people who pay for all this fraud and favoritism. Most of all, it is the working class that pays. [. . .]

The issues are: the struggle against favoritism and privilege, against fraudulent and unwarranted assignments; the unmasking of abuses and arbitrariness, not only the minor cases, but the major ones which are rooted in the system itself; the maintenance of legality and the protection of the rights of individual citizens everywhere; and the establishment of political control over the bureaucracy. "Minor" issues they may be; but vital ones.

"Some Minor Electoral Issues,"
Borba, October 25, 1953

The Struggle for New Ideas

[Included in this section are edited versions of most of the articles that appeared in the party newspaper *Borba* between October 11, 1953 and January 7, 1954, articles that led to Djilas's expulsion from the party and the government. In them he asserts the need for a reorganization of the party and outlines the changes he believes necessary. The angry response of the party leadership compelled him to conclude that change in the party was impossible. The ruling elite was unwilling to relax its political monopoly. These articles fall into three groups: first were six articles, beginning with "New Contents," published between October 11 and November 22, 1953; next came five, beginning with "Without Conclusion," from November 29 through December 22, 1953. There had been some rumblings within the party in response to these articles, and Kardelj met with Djilas on December 22 to discuss toning down future writings. Djilas escalated the intraparty conflict with his next five articles, "Reply" (December 24), "Subjective Forces," "Objective Forces," "The Class Struggle," and "New Ideas." He received a second warning from Kardelj, Vulmanović, Dedijer, and Tito himself. This only spurred him to publish three more articles, before he was stopped: "Anatomy of a Moral" (January 1, 1954), "League or Party" (January 4, 1954), and "Revolution" (January 7, 1954).]

New Forms

Throughout all of history no great idea, no great movement, has ever succeeded unless it assumed specific, concrete forms and unless those forms corresponded to the real needs and the consciousness of the masses. [. . .] The question is, in what concrete, specific forms can socialism and democracy flourish and prevail? The answer to this question is more important, it appears, than the answer to the questions of what socialism and democracy are.

The problem is not which weapon to use, but how to use it. The weapons already exist: nationalized industry; workers' councils; organized power to defend the established order against illegal overthrow; a steadily increasing number of democratic social organizations; an international situation that, in spite of everything, is favorable; a certain level of culture and consciousness; and, most important, an improvement in the economy, which can no longer be called semicolonial. [. . .]

In our country, many forms are withering away voluntarily. The difficulty is that they have not been replaced by new methods and ideas but by old, prerevolutionary ones. This confuses many people. [. . .] But nothing ever dies or is ever born without a struggle. [. . .] As soon as the centralized control of the entire life of society—which was necessary during the war and immediately thereafter—disappeared, differences became inevitable. They are a result of the economic system. A free socialist economy calls for an appropriate form: socialist democracy. The economy can no longer be the domain of this or that institution, of this or that forum, or even of a political movement, which will decide how and where funds should be spent. That task belongs to representatives of those who created the funds. Discussion and controversy is inevitable. Conflicts arise concerning the rate of development, expenditures, methods of building things, etc. Such controversies arise in spite of agreement about the basic principles: defending our independence and strengthening the achievements of the revolution—socialist ownership, brotherhood and harmony. Different opinions are found at every juncture on almost all concrete problems. [. . .] But nothing new can arise without discussion, without listening to all sorts of opinions.

We must, therefore, learn to respect the opinions of others, even if they seem stupid and conservative (conservative from the point of view of socialism) to us. We must get used to the idea that our views will remain in the minority even when we are right and we must stop fearing that just because our views are in the minority, socialism and our revolutionary accomplishments will perish.

Irrespective of what anyone thinks—even what we ourselves think— socialism, the accomplishments of the revolution, the power of the working people, are today a reality.

Borba, November 1, 1953

The Importance of Form

[. . .] For a long time, Yugoslav Communists struggled through different and constantly changing forms to attain a new content: new property relations, new power relations, new ideological relations. For a long time they clung to the notion that content was primary and form secondary. [. . .]

Today, however, this attitude is no longer valid. Now, with the new socialist content already in existence, except in the villages, there is clearly no way to preserve it except by paying more attention to the disdained and neglected forms.

What are these forms? Above all they are laws, since laws largely regulate people's way of life. They are also moral and social norms, established habits in human relationships, ways of discussion, ways of reaching decisions. [. . .] Bringing form and content into harmony is a never-ending process because harmony is continually being destroyed. To bring them into harmony today means to nurture and develop democracy, a more permanent, far-reaching form of democracy; it means to nurture and develop natural, human relations among ordinary people. It means to enter into a new, socialist culture. [. . .] It means to enable discussion

and criticism to be carried out democratically, in a civilized way. [. . .]
It means to humanize the content of socialism and democracy because
this content is the only thing that is important to the common man. [. . .]

Borba, November 8, 1953

Without Conclusion

[. . .] One of the most serious "socialist" mistakes in our country
today is the demand that our present development be circumscribed by
precise conclusions and formulas. This demand is the remnant of that
tragic, dogmatic method that grew out of Stalin's brutal and antisocialist
despotism. Stalin was a master of expressing things in a formula, of
standardizing laws, human relations and human thought.

The nature of the material world—society and public opinion—cannot
be standardized. By the time a state of affairs can be expressed in a
formula and something conclusively proven about it, it has already
changed. Life has progressed, changed. Another, newer, formulation is
needed.

Description, analysis and explanation correspond to life, but expressing things in a formula does not. "Theory is gray. Only the tree of life is
eternally green." Perspective, flexibility, independent and individual
problem-solving are better suited to the nature of human thought than
some "definitive" and "irrevocable" formulation. Thought, too, is constantly changing, vividly and in the most varied ways.

Moreover, we have suffered from dogmas and "final" conclusions.
Once, in the remote past when we had to break the old capitalist ways of
thinking and to destroy the old capitalist world, these were necessary.
Only simple, invincible dogmas could concentrate all the revolutionary
energies on one single goal: the seizure of power.[1] That goal has now
been achieved. Today another life, normal and socialist, is developing.
Now it is necessary to build industry, to educate the peasants, and to
develop culture, democratic authority and social relations. How? Obviously life and all the various goals cannot be encompassed in a single
formula. Nor is it necessary. Today we are experiencing an evolutionary
social development and not a turning point when all forces must be
concentrated in one place, on the revolution, on the struggle for power.
In the revolutionary struggle dogma, although rigid, may have been
necessary because it grew out of a reality that was intolerant of "evasion"
and "analysis." Today, however, reality moves more slowly and normally.
New forces need help and old forces should be defeated.

1. As a matter of fact, though revolutions in themselves are the negation of everything
dogmatic and traditional, they cannot be brought about without the dogmatists,
without those who believe in ideals and ideas and stick to them until the end.

It seems more scientific and useful to socialism today to explain, to peel bourgeois and bureaucratic layers from the mind and ways of thinking, than to struggle for definitive dogmas.

I tried to explain this before, but it seems to me that I did not succeed. That is the reason for this and subsequent articles.

Borba, November 29, 1953

The General and the Particular

The problem is not whether "it is necessary" to differentiate between the particular and the general, that is, between individual and social interests. Proving that the particular is part of the general is even less meaningful. The world obviously consists of numerous diversities. Indeed, one need not be concerned here with eternal truths. It suffices to explain a thing particularly and specifically. The identification of subjective imperatives (ideas, concepts, morals, etc.) with social needs fulfills this requirement. In other words, subjective, personal and partisan should be identified with objective, social and legal requirements, thus making the subjective objective. In its simplest terms, the problem is whether the interests of any party or group of leaders are always identical with those of the people and of society. Under present conditions is there, or can there be, conflict between them?

During the revolution there was, on the whole, harmony between objective and subjective forces, between the general and the particular. Harmony was not the only characteristic of that period. The objective events were then so concentrated in the subjective (the organized, the conscious) forces that things were accomplished that objective forces alone could otherwise have achieved only in the course of decades.

As is typical of all revolutions, a section of these subjective forces got the impression not only that they were the representatives of the objective process, but also that they could replace it by their own actions. Today, they wish to play the same role as they did then. Then, the ideas, morals, feelings and even "petty" personal desires and "selfish" interests of these subjective forces were not basically opposed to the imperatives of the revolution. Not only did the flame of the revolution burn in them; they were the revolution. But that is not so today. No one party or group, not even a single class, can be the exclusive expression of the objective requirements of contemporary society. No one can claim the exclusive right "to administer" the development of the forces of production without simultaneously delaying the development of these forces and exploiting the most important factor in these forces—the people. This is so because, under present conditions, every reinforcement of the role of politics leads to delay and exploitation. What is required instead is a weakening of the monopoly of political parties over society, especially in our country under socialism.[1]

Pointing out the differences between actual conditions in the present and those that prevailed during the revolution is by no means to disdain the revolution or to sever connections between it and the present. Were it not for the revolution, our discussions would be held in prisons and would not be about new forms of socialism. The purpose of making this distinction between present and past conditions is the following. Since the forces of production have reached a higher stage of development, social relations today are not resolved by force of arms. Therefore the methods of struggle cannot remain the same. If people are unable to grasp this necessity for change, the result will be what it historically has always been: sooner or later, objective development achieves its own ends without regard for the fate of groups and movements and with even less regard for individuals. It achieves them in one of two ways: either it creates and organizes new forces, movements and men who rebel and destroy the old; or it removes the outmoded institutions and their living representatives by a long, slow, expensive and painful evolution through succeeding generations. And since the social conditions for the first process do not exist, the evolution of the second should be facilitated so that it is as smooth and painless as possible, so that institutions and political relations are more quickly harmonized with objective development and with the material and spiritual conditions of society. This is essential for socialism and for every little bit of real democracy. In short, it is necessary to adapt subjective (group, party, individual) ideas and interests to the progress of the forces of production. Furthermore, this must be done in such a way that the forces of production are less and less subordinated to subjective ideas and interests.

Every social order which made possible the development of the forces of production, that is, which enabled them to operate in the given conditions, was able to stabilize itself. This was true even under conditions of private ownership. It is only when private ownership becomes an obstacle to the relatively free development of the forces of production that it must be changed. An obstacle is nothing but a conflict between the subjective-particular and the objective-general forces of society.[2]

Such conflicts are inevitable in all societies. Our problem is not to

1. Things are now reversed. The change from the necessary monopoly of the party in wartime to the necessary abolition of this monopoly under socialism is the dialectic of reality. This approach is completely opposed to the usual, "normal," traditional petty-bourgeois or bureaucratic logic.
2. It goes without saying that subjective forces cannot be separated entirely from objective ones because they, too, are an objective factor of development, and without them there is neither society nor social progress.

avoid them, both because they will arise independently of our actions and because society could not progress without them. The point is how to "ameliorate" and to resolve them, in order to make possible the less hampered operation of objective socialist laws and the freer movement of society.

Present conditions are such that all groups, institutions, or individuals who identify their fate with that of socialism, who pretend that only their opinion is genuinely socialist theory and only what they do genuinely socialistic, must come into conflict with the real, objective, democratic, socialist process. There is no alternative but more democracy, freer discussion, freer elections to social, state and economic organs, stricter adherence to the law. It will then be possible democratically to repulse all those outmoded and reactionary forces which, because of their ideas or their temporary role, cling to the notion that they represent the whole of social reality, that they are the only "legal" representatives of society. And even if it is impossible to repulse those reactionary forces, they can be checked through the free struggle of ideas, they can be subjected to critical controls, so that the democratic process becomes possible.

Hairsplitting about harmonizing the particular and the general, the partisan and the social, the individual and the collective, is meaningless. Harmony does not and cannot exist. Moreover, it is unnecessary that it should, because it retards progress. As a matter of fact, to assure freedom for progress, no single subjective force must be permitted to hold down the other forces, and no single force permitted to monopolize social life. [. . .] It is not necessary to add that no single program, group, or trend is being considered here. Singling one out for criticism would only be another step backward toward a political monopoly of some kind, instead of a step forward to the creation of freedom from situation to situation, from question to question. This is true because the time for great theoretical and supertheoretical programs is over. We have had too much of them already. It is now necessary for the sake of democracy to take up concrete, ordinary, daily human work, to further and strengthen the progress of democratic forms.

Borba, December 20, 1953

Concretely

[. . .] In social conflicts, great and new ideas have been victorious only when supported by organized masses and when those masses, through parties and leaders, succeeded in discovering and realizing concrete forms of that struggle (uprisings, parliamentarianism, etc.). New ideas have always begun as the ideas of a minority. Although everyone thinks, people do not think collectively. The ideas of one or more individuals can, however, become collective ideas. No one can know in advance just which new idea will be progressive, which one will indicate that the future life of millions has begun, which one illuminates the first sprouts of new life. In our country, obviously it is not so necessary to organize the masses for the victory of a new idea as it is to create an atmosphere for free exchange of new ideas. Every social reaction has begun and ended its life with an ideological monopoly, by declaring its ideas as the only means of salvation. "Even the road to hell is paved with good intentions." The first duty of a socialist and every other real democrat is to make it possible for people to espouse their ideas without being persecuted. Only in this manner can new ideas, which up to that point were the property of individuals, of a minority, come to the surface.

The true Communist-democrat should never forget this. Least of all should it be forgotten in our country, where the entire system of ideas was so rapidly undermined that all new ideas initially seemed "stupid," "insane," and "illogical." The same is true of new forms. Didn't the idea of social revolution and the establishment of a regular army in an occupied country sound insane? And didn't the majority at first consider these forms and these ideas insane?

At this juncture, the most important thing is not new ideas, but freedom of ideas and the strengthening and development of new forms. Both must be supported. In practical terms, that means fighting for freedom of discussion everywhere, fighting for strengthening and developing certain democratic forms, like workers' councils, people's committees and voters' meetings; in brief, legality, continuing controversy, democracy.

It is well known that material and cultural backwardness are major obstacles to the development of democracy. This is apparent in the low social consciousness of individuals, groups, and even of whole strata (in our country this is called a low ideological and political level). But a rising standard does not automatically bring about a corresponding rise in democratic consciousness—witness Germany under Hitler, the Soviet Union under Stalin. How can such a rise be "accelerated"? Only by way of freedom.

Human thought itself should determine its own limits and correspondingly its real potentialities. Every limitation of thought, even in the name of the most beautiful ideals—and most frequently limitations are made in the name of ideals—only degrades the perpetrator. Giordano Bruno and the thousands like him were burned to save mankind from the hell of heresy. In the same way, in our own time, millions were burned in Hitler's camps to save the human race from the hell of Communism. Despised and demeaned, millions rotted in Siberia only because they did not believe in the validity of Stalinist doctrines. It is not ideas in themselves that are responsible. Not even fanatical belief in ideas is responsible. Ultimately, it is the reactionary fanatics who have a political monopoly and who produce this fanatical faith who are responsible.

No theory can protect us from despotism. The only protection from despotic dangers and tendencies is democratic forms and their permanent strengthening, as well as free thought and creative imagination. Specific practical action on specific questions can protect us wherever we are: in social organizations, settlements, committees, villages or enterprises. For that reason, such practice is necessary. It must, of course, be linked to modern socialist theory, and practice is essential for developing such theory.

And every real step toward democracy, every development of every kind of democratic form, means the progress of socialism and a further liberation of creative forces.

Borba, December 22, 1953

Reply

Recently, I have heard that this series of antibureaucratic articles has provoked widespread comment.

Comment falls into the following categories: (1) that I am a philosopher divorced from reality; (2) that I am writing for a foreign audience; (3) that I have begun to break away from dialectical and historical materialism, and from Marxism-Lenism; (4) that the forces of reaction have seized on my articles and used them against "our" people and "our" institutions.

My reply, or, if you prefer, my monologue:

Like most of the leadership, I, too, have been living in seclusion in my office and at home. It is not, therefore, surprising that I was one of the last to hear these comments and that I react to them "too sensitively." It is precisely this way of life and this kind of reaction that must be eliminated. It is unnatural in present conditions; it is inhuman; it is not even socialist. My purpose in writing these critical articles is to cause myself and others to emerge from the unreal, abstract world of the "elite" and the chosen and to enter as profoundly as possible into the real world of the simple working people and ordinary human relations. In short, the aim of these articles is to arouse socialist consciousness and to awake the conscience of ordinary people as well as that of the most progressive minds. In our circumstances and in present world conditions, these progressive minds can only be socialist, Communist, democratic. Such a new surge of conscience, in accord with new practice, is in reality an emergence from a crystallized form, from a closed circle (a party circle, if you like), into a "simple world" and a "simple life." And this is not a theoretical problem, but a problem of practical democracy. The problem is the greater unity of leadership with the masses, the merger of conscience and progress.

The reproach that I am an abstract philosopher is not only inaccurate but untrue. [. . .] If in the main I talk about abstract phenomena, it is intentional, because with readers who have been dogmatized—unfortunately they constitute the majority today—it is the best way to break down bureaucratic dogmatism, which is itself the ultimate in barren, primitive and malign abstraction. However, the admonition not to take me seriously only confirms that my criticism is not without foundation.

Those who say that all this has been written for foreign consumption only demonstrate that their consciences are not clear before their own people. They prove that their words and deeds are in conflict. This has always been, and remains, the symptom of decadence and social backwardness. Two moralities, two truths, do not exist in reality. Yet dualism does exist and it has camouflaged the lie with truth, hypocrisy with morality, bureaucratism with socialism.

I have no intention of defending myself against the charge that I have become a heretic of the dialectic, because the dialectic is the greatest heresy ever discovered and every real Communist should be delighted to serve it. Denial is the most creative force in history. [. . .]

I was aware that the forces of reaction would exploit my articles. But the real socialist forces could have exploited them too. It is not my fault that they have been used by the forces of reaction, but the fault of those who with their bureaucratic, illegal and arbitrary actions give the forces of reaction a halo of martyrdom. They offer the reactionaries the chance to show the masses the gap between words and deeds. [. . .] Focusing the argument on the fact that the forces of reaction have been exploiting my articles reveals only the Stalinist, bureaucratic character of that "criticism," though its wording may sound democratic, and reduces the validity of an argument to whether or not it is useful to the reactionaries. It is worth remembering that Stalin falsely accused the socialist opposition in the USSR, at first condemning it for helping the forces of reaction, subsequently for also acting subjectively, and finally for betraying socialism and the nation. He established the official "truth" and "unity": the worst dictatorship in history. True, he won temporarily, but in doing so he destroyed socialist social relations, although they were still only embryonic. And precisely because it is "socialist," our bureaucracy cannot avoid being a little Stalinist; to some extent, Yugoslav Stalinism. It therefore stinks of the same ideology and it proclaims the same "civilized" and "peace-loving" methods loudly and clearly These methods, however, are still not directed at those of us who are "on top," but at those who are "below."

Apparently there is no conflict about socialism-Communism as such, but about democracy and the method, form and tempo with which it should be realized. This is, in any event, the essence of the conflict. [. . .]

I do not think my articles are completely correct, and still less do I consider them original. I only wanted, and I still want, to stimulate thought on the questions which, for me, become increasingly burning questions. The root of these problems lies in the economy. Without a solution there, these problems cannot be solved. [. . .]

It doesn't matter whether the criticisms of my ideas are justified or not. They cannot silence the democratic struggle against bureaucratism, because it no longer depends on one theory or another, but on reality. This struggle is evident in every part of our society, and not only our society. We have been plunged into an era of struggle for democracy and we cannot escape from it, nor do we want to. The struggle may be hampered, held back, but never stopped. I am not writing in order to make a name for myself, or out of juvenile pigheadedness, and still less out of a desire to bask in democratic glory. I must write because, like many others, I am the "victim" of objective social processes that compel me to do so. And therein lies my source of passion and belief. Because of that, and precisely because I respect and want open, friendly socialist criticism of these ideas, I can have only contempt for any other kind of criticism.

Borba, December 24, 1953

Subjective Forces

Our socialist and revolutionary consciousness is often said to be on a high level, but this is true only to a limited extent. Our consciousness is really profound only when we speak of the basic achievements of the revolution and our present progress: nationalization, brotherhood and unity, and the defense of our independence. [. . .] However, as soon as new problems arise, we see individual consciousness searching for solutions. And what are these problems? Some of them we have already stressed (the contemporary class struggle, legality, new class structures, etc.), but there are many more (the role of authority, the role of political and social organizations, cultural freedom, real freedom of criticism, a real and not merely theoretical and verbal fight against bureaucratism, etc.). One does not see a zealous search for solutions to these problems;

but even if the answers are not yet available to the minds of many leaders and authorities, this does not mean that the problems do not exist, or that other people are not searching for and finding solutions to them. In our country everything is too circumscribed. We have too much pre- scribed truth, truth passed down from above.

The point is: since socialist reality exists and is developing, a new socialist consciousness must appear, independent of officials and forums and even against their will. Life does not wait to be approved. Today, conscious socialist forces exist alongside official Communist organizations, especially alongside and in opposition to many Communist bureaucrats and forums. The conscious, so-called subjective forces are not confined to Communists or politically aware workers alone (as they once used to be). These forces also include all who stand for an independent Yugoslavia, a democratic and socialist Yugoslavia, because only such a Yugoslavia can be independent, regardless of whether these forces' ideological and other conceptions coincide exactly with some so-called socialist dogmas ascribed to some bureaucrat, or even coincide with what is really socialist.

The dogmatic, bureaucratic theory that only Communists are the conscious forces of socialism ("a special type of man," according to Stalin) serves as an incentive to separate them from and place them above society as those predestined to lead others because they are the one group "aware of ultimate goals" and thoroughly trustworthy. This theory obscures the reality of the tendency toward building privileged positions in society, toward distributing jobs on the basis of political and "ideo- logical" conformity rather than by virtue of experience and capability. This theory and the associated practice can only drive a wedge between Communists and the masses and thus transform the former into the priests and policemen of socialism (as is the case in Soviet Russia). Such tendencies have always existed and still exist in our country.

Having once achieved a position from which they have centralized and regulated everything from ethics to stamp collecting, many Communists are unable to change their own opinions, much less their behavior, habits and manners now that the democratic wind has suddenly begun to blow. Democracy increasingly shows not only who the true enemy of socialism is, but also that the new enemy, bureaucratism, is more dangerous than the old one, capitalism. These conditions are quite different from what is written in good Stalinist textbooks and from what exists in the ossified brains of many bureaucratic heads. Democracy has revealed that the development of social consciousness is possible, first of all, through a real struggle against bureaucratism.

But precisely because of this, these bureaucrats cannot fight bureau- cratism. They were taught to fight the old capitalist class enemy, which, despite being bureaucrats, they were able to do. Yet, though the class enemy's role, power and importance have greatly diminished, bureaucrats still conduct a sterile search for them. When a few class enemies are eventually flushed, the bureaucrats bristle, which is not only nervous and naïve but also malicious (that's democracy!), and reveal their hidden desire to turn back the clock. They thus reveal their bureaucratism.

For the aforementioned reasons, the basic party organizations assigned to each street (and to some extent those in the various enterprises) have gone down a blind alley. From the top they are repeatedly told to be active, but they don't know what to do because there really isn't anything to be done by the old forms. The themes for so-called ideological and cultural work, which the committee offices invent, are dull and obsolete. [. . .] No activity takes place anyway. [. . .] The problem is very simple: the Communist organizations today no longer have that much authority, nor do they make all the decisions. The common people already live according to the new democratic forms. [. . .] In such circumstances, the basic organizations of the League of Yugoslav Communists and the Socialist Alliance do not have as much to do as before. In my opinion they should convene very rarely, when delegates are to be chosen or when a change of political line is involved. Yes, these are sinful thoughts! Who will look after the souls, the consciousness and the deeds of the people? Nonetheless, men have lived and elsewhere in the world continue to live without such meetings. They live the lives of normal people; they do not degenerate. They are even good and honest men, and even socialists.

I think that the conditions described above put the following question on the agenda: is it necessary to have a centralized political youth organization, such as we now have? And what about labor unions?

I believe that these conditions explain why professional party and youth leaders and other political workers are now superfluous and idle. They "direct" work, take care of "consciousness," and "inspire" activity. In their idleness, they invent and renew obsolete "revolutionary" bureaucratic forms. The conscious socialist forces (Communist-democrats and the people) can no longer tolerate these forms and those who impose them. Inevitably, the bureaucrats separate themselves from life irrespective of their virtues, and whether or not they are publicly criticized; and life is the better for it.

At one time men gave everything, even life itself, to become professional revolutionaries. They were then indispensable to social progress. Today, they are obstacles to it.

In spite of the best intentions, life has thrown all contemporary forms and ideas into a voracious mill which incessantly grinds them between its stones.

Borba, December 27, 1953

Objective Forces

Although strictly speaking one should not separate the objective from the subjective forces because social development affirms the unity of the two, such a simplification must be made if we are fully to understand reality. Roughly speaking, objective forces include all that which in a given situation cannot be changed by conscious and organized action but which in the final analysis determines the character of action itself (for example: the degree and rate of industrial development, the productivity of labor, the material wealth and the nature and degree of its utilization, the cultural level). But, looked at from the point of view of the internal development of a given country, all those external forces which that country cannot decisively influence, especially if it is a relatively small and underdeveloped country such as ours, are also objective forces.[1]

Thus, to determine the role of objective forces in internal development, it is not only reasonable but also unavoidable to take external forces into account. This is so because external forces have objective meaning for internal development, regardless of whether these external forces, considered by themselves, are objective or subjective. A thorough understanding of the objective forces based upon the changes taking place within them as well as upon the trends of their development is crucial for establishing a course of action at any given moment and for establishing human social action in general.[2]

During the last few years the objective forces in our country have altered significantly. They have changed to such an extent that their forms of operation, their organizational forms—that is, the subjective forces—lag significantly behind. In one way or another the two must be brought into harmony. Today the task of progressive social forces is clear: to bring the two into harmony with a minimum of disruption, that is, with as little discomfort as possible for society as a whole and with as much efficiency as possible for the further development of productive forces, that is, for the further development of socialism.

Let us look briefly at these changes.

Above all, our industrial strength has changed significantly, and with it the economic structure of the country. Our sacrifices, our efforts and

1. For example: we cannot significantly influence the internal development of Turkey and Greece, nor they ours. Nevertheless, we are inescapably compelled to a certain co-operation with them in external matters, despite differences and indeed disagreements about questions of social system.

2. I shall not discuss here why and under which conditions some people pay only scant attention to the role of objective forces, others assess its role more correctly, and still others almost fail to notice it. In each instance the role of objective forces cannot be ignored. How accurately these forces are assessed, their role and tendency discovered, in the final analysis determines the effectiveness and the nature of human action.

our *élan* were not in vain. Our country is, of course, still backward. Socialism is pushed back by the nonsocialist village, and the working class is largely semipeasant, young and inexperienced. But despite all that, the industrial revolution is taking place in our country and in a socialist form. And that cannot fail to have significant consequences, both economic and social, for thereby are established the preconditions for democracy, for a freer life of the cities and industrial settlements. The rule of bureaucratism over the economy, over culture and over political-social relations becomes more and more senseless and unnatural, both for the productive forces as a whole and for the producers.

At the same time, the external position of our country has changed significantly. We are no longer isolated from the rest of the world, neither economically nor politically. Ideological and political victory over the Cominform has been won. At the same time we preserved our independence vis-à-vis the West. As our independence became more firmly established, co-operation with the external world increased. Only an independent nation can realize genuine co-operation, equality and friendship. And we are such a country. Tito's heroic efforts and sacrifices were not in vain. Independence is the result of the economic, political and spiritual (ideological-cultural) transformation of the nation. Not only are we totally different from the old Yugoslavia but also from the new, postwar Yugoslavia. Immediately after the war we were fighting on all fronts a life-and-death struggle for independence and equality. We are still fighting, and we must continue to fight for a long time. But the important victories have already been won.

Due to that, a significant change has taken place in the consciousness of our citizens and our intelligentsia. Awareness of Yugoslavia as a country that can walk *its own path* grew stronger and stronger. Our peoples are no longer ashamed of their backwardness and poverty, because they know that it will pass. At the same time, selfless love for the common homeland has grown and we already feel a basic and previously unknown agreement about independence, equality and the dignity of the nation. Brotherhood and unity have already made decisive changes in the life of Yugoslavia.

Is that not a success? and a change?

As a result, the position and the role of the basic productive force—the working people—above all in industry (workers, the technical intelligentsia, and one part of the cultural workers), has changed significantly. It is becoming a new and independent force, a conscious factor further changing the society and economy of the country. Administrative force no longer need be the major factor of change. But administrative force had to be the factor of change until such time as the major productive force—the working people—became sufficiently strong in numbers and in consciousness. The working people themselves had to rely upon administrative force. Now they no longer have to use it in the same measure as before, and in some instances it is used very little.

Thus freedom that ignores the freedom of that basic productive force in its work, in making decisions, is not freedom. And thus any policy that does not start by liberating that objective, productive force, even gradually, can give birth only to a barren and often bureaucratic fruit. This is true even if the policy was adopted in the name of the highest ideals, with the most noble intent and through the most democratic political organizations. That is how freedom is transformed from an objective need of society and from the most important objective (that is, productive, human) force in society into something subjective and formalistic.

It might appear strange that just such new objective conditions—the strengthening of productive forces, the attainment of independence and brotherhood in the struggle to strengthen socialism—all contribute to the internal "disunity" of socialist forces, to the emergence of a struggle of ideas and to differences of opinion on certain internal questions. But only through "heterogeneity," only through the free expression of different socialist thoughts on different internal questions, can there be unity of socialist forces in conditions of expanding internal and external forces or in changed objective conditions. To look at socialist unity in any other way seems to be both outmoded and indefensible.

The genuine freedom of truly free socialist forces must become the major objective force of socialism and democracy.

Borba, December 29, 1953

The Class Struggle

The discovery of the class struggle inaugurated a new era in the social sciences. [. . .] The mystery that for some ten thousand years shrouded many events and personalities, and man and his fate, began to disappear. The way for Marx's discovery was paved not only by countless historians and philosophers, but also by revolutions and wars. [. . .]

Obviously, Marx did not invent the class struggle. He only found it an incontestable fact in past and present social reality, a law operating irrespective of organized human consciousness, opinion or expression.

The importance of every scientific discovery is that it permits the use of the so-called blind, elementary forces in everyday life.[1] The importance of the discovery of the class struggle is that it makes it easier to determine

1. After becoming acquainted with the laws of electricity, people built power stations and transmission lines, and new lights flared. However, people cannot invent or change natural laws. They cannot, therefore, reduce or increase electrical or any other kind of energy; they can only use these energies to the extent to which they extract them from nature.

who the opponents are. It does not, however, provide a universal key to every situation. Social reality is constantly changing, creating new conditions and enlisting new forces. Every new situation, therefore, involves a new struggle, the creation of new forms of the struggle, and the mobilization of new forces.

After Marx, all socialists and progressives, many of them even independently of him, came to the common conclusion that the history of modern society is fundamentally a struggle between labor and capital. Differences among socialists arose from their conflicting views on how the struggle could be carried on successfully. No one denies the existence of the class struggle and of class distinctions. Differences have arisen only about methods of eliminating them. As is usually the case, theory has proved no one right. Only practice can really do this. In Russia, as well as in Yugoslavia, practice has impugned all those theories that teach that this struggle in modern society can be resolved only by force and revolution. [. . .]

The class struggle did not end after the revolution either in Russia or in Yugoslavia, nor has it yet ended in the West, which has not had a revolution. The circumstances and shape of the struggle have changed and are continually changing; therefore, the theoretical aspects and political programs are also changing. [. . .]

What is the present nature of the class struggle in changed conditions? And, most important, how applicable is the theory and practice of intensification of the class struggle? The existence of the class struggle today does not in any event depend very much on the theory of class struggle, but, rather, on the existence or nonexistence of certain circumstances in reality. Yet the form and the success of the class struggle do depend on the theory. After all, the class structure of society has changed, but the theory remains more or less unchanged. The bourgeoisie is in every respect a vestige of a former class, and in the big cities, even the petty-bourgeoisie is gone.[2] Continuing the struggle against the bourgeois reactionaries exclusively on a theoretical basis and "line," and not on the basis of law, must now deviate into bureaucratism, into conflict with ordinary people because they hold differing opinions, or because of their frequently justified grumbling and objection to artificially imposed tasks. [. . .]

The duty of the state organs (primarily of the courts, the UDBA [political police] and the police) is not to intensify the class struggle, but, instead, to preserve and implement the law. In my opinion these organs must rid themselves of party interference, especially in those

2. They exist, and in great numbers insofar as thought is concerned, but they are not as numerous and important as a social stratum. They are almost all private merchants, private employees, or the like, or they are in the socialist network. The number of private artisans is small.

outlying districts where it is prevalent. Otherwise, even with the best intentions, they cannot avoid being undemocratic and unduly influenced by dogmatic ideological and political considerations as well as by local interests. They must become representatives of the state and of the law and thereby of the people, rather than representatives of the political interests and conceptions of one political organization or another. These are the inevitable results of the struggle for legality and democracy, and a step forward. If these officials continue to intensify the class struggle by disregarding the law, they must inevitably give special favors to those who share their opinions, and whom they consider sympathetic and "trustworthy." By using these same criteria, they must also inevitably judge the virtues of other citizens, and so divide them into lower, non-Communist and higher, Communist, classes. The class struggle is, in fact, intensified by such "theory" and practice. In so doing, they may appear to be distinguishing between socialism and capitalism, but actually they are working against the people.

In our country, only a democracy that continually makes progress can clarify class conflicts and diminish class differenecs.

Borba, December 31, 1953

New Ideas

Everything would be simple if new ideas in their nascent state were also the ideas of the majority. They are not, however, and never can be. In fact, if they were from the beginning the ideas of a majority, they would not be new ideas at all.

New ideas are always the ideas of a minority. [. . .] Every new idea, if it is really new, reflects some new reality, some change either in the material world or in scientific discovery or artistic creation. Restless, relentless reality constantly impinges on the human mind, which must react in order to explain, adapt and "lead" reality. Neither society nor the individual could survive if it stopped thinking, stopped seeking adjustment to reality, stopped explaining it and struggling within its confines. A human being lives only when he struggles (by working) and when he thinks (by explaining reality and adjusting to it). The less he is able to function in society and in reality, the closer he is to death as a social being, that is, as a human being. Roughly speaking, this is as true of classes and social strata as it is of individual ideological groups. They, too, come to life when they discover reality, but when they lose it, they die. [. . .]

Human beings can only live collectively, in society, yet as a society they are divided into opposing groups and classes, with divergent interests and ideas. However, they are not conscious of living collectively: they think as individuals, personally, though of course not "purely" individually, but as individual members of a society. They think as individuals who, roughly speaking, represent not only themselves but also a specific class, stratum of society, or interest. Whether the new ideas are political, scientific or artistic, they are formulated by individuals, or at best by groups, never in their own names, but in the name of some segment of society. A new idea manifests itself in the minds of human beings because social reality demands it; and whether the idea occurs to this individual or that one is a matter of chance.

However, all these simple, natural phenomena are complicated in society because new ideas represent new social forces, a rising social reality which tends to drive out the existing order in its attempts to secure for itself the "right to live." At first the old forces resist, always ideologically, protesting that the new forces' ideas are bad. They claim that the new forces are harmful, heretical, immoral and anarchic with respect to the existing society and to the established moral and other norms. [. . .]

This ideological struggle is an intellectual representation of a real struggle, which is not quite so apparent. The ideological struggle is, as a matter of fact, the struggle of various social forces projected upon human minds.

In such a relationship between old and new, the representatives of the old ideas and obsolete social relationships treat the new ideas and their representatives with "prejudice" and "without objectivity." This "lack of objectivity" and this "prejudice" are due not only to the fact that the old order represents conservative, "selfish" interests and inherited or usurped rights which have been turned into unjust privileges, but also due to the fact that the old ideas and concepts are unable to comprehend the new reality and the new movement. The new concepts and categories seem monstrous to them, immoral and unnatural, since they obviously differ so much from what is traditional. In reality, though, the old concepts have become unnatural, for their forms can no longer contain and accommodate the new reality and the new relationships.

No one can know in advance the extent to which an idea is new and progressive. Its worth can be proven only by experience. Such experience is possible only if the idea is disseminated, if people gather round it and fight in its name. That is why the old, resisting forces always try to have it "forbidden," as a means of preventing its dissemination. Conversely, new ideas and forces always seek free exchange of ideas, equality and freedom in the ideological struggle. Moreover, since the new ideas are more vital than the old, they can allow themselves the "luxury" of being more tolerant, more principled and more generous: they can avoid immoral methods. This is understandable because life and victory lie ahead of them.

Old ideas are still dominant among us, more prevalent than one would suppose. We have received a substantial part of our socialist ideas and theories not only in Leninist form but also in the Stalinist form of Leninism (for example, the theory of the party, and a great deal of the theory about the state, too). As long as our practice was predominantly bureaucratic, or tended to be bureaucratic, we were able to use these ideas. Although the revolution was not fundamentally "in accord" with these ideas, nor these ideas with it, later these ideas became more firmly rooted in bureaucratic reality. Our practice and the ideological struggle have broken Stalinist ideology as a whole but they have not destroyed it. It still lives in the minds of men, but not, of course, as Stalinism. Stalinism among us has become synonymous with Cominformism, that is, with betrayal of our country and of socialism. The Stalinist ideology lives on as "Marxism," "Leninism," etc.—the sum of inherited and formulated ideas and rules, with their corresponding organizational, political and other forms. It is not important whether or not these ideas have become obsolete; the crucial question is whether the practice for which they speak has become obsolete.

In our country only a free struggle of ideas can reveal—without a major social upheaval—which ideas and concepts are old and which new, but also, and more important, which are the valid forms of life. An ideological struggle is also necessary because one set of ideas always misrepresents the other. Our older ideas will always call the new ones "anarchist," "petty-bourgeois," and "Western," while the new ones will call the old "bureaucratic," "Stalinist," and "despotic." But the truth can be discovered only by experience, in struggle. The more this struggle is conducted on free and equal terms, the more one can talk about the real, if only newly born democratic relationships. Often the truth is somewhere in between. If a discussion has really been free and principled, the truth is not usually all on one side, at least not the whole truth.

Borba, January 1, 2, 3, 1954

The New Role of the League of Communists

Anatomy of a Moral

No one, least of all this young woman, could have guessed that life could suddenly become so bleak in the very midst of what seemed to the people to be so pure, so spiritual, so free of the petty, vulgar meanness and greed that naturally spring from privation and backwardness, and against which she had painfully fought all through her childhood and youth until those singing, shining summer days when she was married. But, to her, they were grim and distressing days.

She was a twenty-one-year-old opera singer and aware of her beauty, but that did not make her proud, not even in her own heart. She was conscious of her strong, slender body; she rejoiced in it as one rejoices in something one has but which does not really belong to one. She was without particular bents or passions. She was delighted in everything and sorrow was a stranger to her, at least until she met that profound and incurable sorrow which only disillusionment can bring.

Her only irresistible love was music. She devoted her entire being to it, not only in a special, intellectual way, but in the unusually passionate manner so characteristic of a musically educated person with an exceptionally fine ear. This insatiable passion burned in every nerve and fiber, and fired her imagination; it had sent her to conservatories for training and finally brought her to the stage. Because she came from a large and poor family, after her marriage she still retained a conspicuous and somewhat vulgar thriftiness, a spiritual naïveté, a directness and humility. Had her husband been less quick in reacting to everything, particularly where personal considerations were involved, she might have had no troubles and sorrows except those that life brings to everyone, even to the comfortable and the carefree. [. . .][1]

Her husband was a high official; he was handsome, virile, and strong. Above all, he was a famous wartime commander, which always appeals to women's vivid imaginations and evokes their envy: it makes them think of lost opportunities. [. . .] She anticipated, therefore, that the women with whom her husband had been intimate, as well as those who had failed to share his bachelor adventures but knew about them, would soon turn up with their petty intrigues, phone calls, anonymous letters and the like, problems that might frighten on old-fashioned woman, but that to her were simple. [. . .]

She was also cheered by the thought that if she entered this new, clean and spiritual milieu with her husband, as the wife of a high official

1. Matrimony has been and always will be, whatever the social order and its outward forms, one of the basic units and foundations of social life. It is one of the generally recognized achievements of civilized life, a value that belongs to no single class of society but is the result of a long, continuous process of humanization of social relations, an institution without which society would regress and turn savage. Hence, it has always been a generally accepted rule and duty to help young married couples establish as natural and warm relations between themselves as possible. It is an ancient custom, even among peoples of the most primitive cultures, for relatives, friends, acquaintances, or even casual guests, to show—by celebration, by giving gifts, by other kindnesses and courtesies—that they wish to help promote the best possible relations and understanding between the new partners, to help unite what at best is difficult to harmonize and not to make life more difficult for the new couple. This is especially true where bride and groom come from entirely different milieus, with conflicting social ideas and habits, and therefore react differently to the new situation.

among the wives of other high officials, all of whom seemed simple and unpretentious, these annoyances would soon become insignificant details, petty, loose-tongued maliciousness, and then, after a while, would stop altogether. [. . .]

And indeed that was the way it happened. The mean and malicious annoyances, the clandestine phone calls to her husband, the dirty stories told in sordid detail, the spiteful and bitter anonymous letters, became less and less frequent from day to day, from week to week. But, contrary to her expectations, her new milieu not only failed to show her affection, but also refused altogether to accept her. She faced a massive, icy and impenetrable wall which no one had warned her she would meet. [. . .]

Such was the mentality of this higher social circle. It grew, somewhat unawares, from a quite natural logic: namely, that favorable conditions should be afforded leaders so that they can work and live. This attitude, and the system it fostered, proliferated in all directions, from top to bottom, everywhere. Thus, people were classified into categories and strata, near-strata, kindred categories or professions, etc., each neatly placed in a secluded pigeonhole but bound together by a common solidarity that was not so much the product of ideological or moral unity as the product of the same way of life, of similar interests arising from the nature of the official authority they wielded and the manner in which they had acquired that authority.

On the lower, inferior social strata, life was franker, more brutal, savage and crude. A district secretary's new wife, for example, overnight becomes the first lady of the district irrespective of her intellectual and other adornments. She chooses her friends carefully and everyone regards it as a privilege to join her exalted set.

Friendships between husbands and between wives were made and unmade according to the political changes within the circle, and according to how one either climbed to higher positions or slipped to lower ones in the hierarchy. But in one respect every circle remained closed and impenetrable: in the common determination to keep out of the holy of holies any "unworthy" newcomer, or anyone not of the same, or close to the same, level of political importance. [. . .][2]

And so the young woman suddenly found herself—as a woman, wife, personality and actress—assailed from all sides and torn between her wishes and the impossibility of achieving them, between her dreams and the bitter realities of life. No wonder that slowly she was drawn by unsuspected, profound, and buried urges to return to the old Bohemian way of life, which, from time to time, might offer her joys and respite from her grief. With the invisible force of a gathering avalanche, life

2. In this case, however, they denied love and the right to love to anyone not a member of their own secluded circle, particularly where the love was of one of their caste for an outsider. Call it whatever you like, but not love.

itself was pushing her toward what one of the women in the exalted set had foretold: "Sooner or later, she will go down like the others. She belongs to that class." Nonetheless, the young woman kept struggling, resisting for her own sake, for the sake of her conscience and her love. But those people of the caste who boasted that they were apostles of the new had actually long ceased to be that and therefore, by their stupid, incomprehensible behavior, had clearly pushed the actress back into that world which she could not and would not give up, but which she had wanted to elevate and reform.

Therein lies the moral hypocrisy and inconsistency of this caste of people. On the one hand, they condemned and rejected her because, they said, she was an actress. On the other hand, they forced her to be one, and one of the lowest type, according to their own generally accepted standards. [. . .]

In the course of her painful life, pressed as she was on all sides and tormented by inner crises, she came to meet and to know other officially despised women. Some had been trampled down and forgotten, though they were first-class fighters—and what fighters!—in the war. Only now the brutal social reality burst open before her eyes in all its horrifying depth and scope. Only now could she see clearly that neither her profession nor her casual immoralities had provoked this stubborn opposition which knew neither bounds nor pity. No, the things they had said were shallow pretexts. The truth was—she could see it clearly now—that she was considered unworthy of that self-anointed circle, which craved pre-eminence and exclusivity. In that lay the spuriousness of their motives; in that lay the hypocrisy of their morals. Now she knew she could never be, and had no right to be, "one of us." And therein also lay the truth.

In the eyes of these people and in consonance with their secluded life, the "one of us" type soon became the only type that really counted. An old truth was once more confirmed. The more people dissociate themselves from the objective reality around them, from society and from life and its problems, the more their own small world begins to appear to them the only real world. Their own interests, concepts of life, moral codes, as they become increasingly abstract, are increasingly identified with the interests of society as a whole, with its absolute truths, its absolute moral codes. The old Aristotelian "eternal" truth which states that it is unnecessary to invent many moral laws, since they can be gleaned from the facts of life itself as we go along, put into formulas and fought for, has long since been forgotten in these secluded circles. They have also lost sight of another Aristotelian truth, that one of the foremost duties of politicians is to study the human soul first, particularly its ethics. [. . .]

Nova Misao, January 1, 1954

League or Party

This article is a little different: the discussions provoked by my article "Subjective Forces," because it was said that the article dealt too extensively with concrete and specific matters, prompted me to formulate my views on the problem in question in a more detailed and definite way. [. . .] I must emphasize, although it is clear from my articles, that no forum stands behind my opinions except me, personally. [. . .]

I consider the question of my proposals about changing the work within the League of Communists to be serious and as yet unresolved. My opinions seem to me to conform entirely to the Sixth Congress decisions and the statute approved by it, although some of my proposals may not conform to the letter of the statute. If the Sixth Congress decisions mean weakening the political-practical role of the League of Communists as a party and strengthening its ideological and educational role, as well as strengthening the political-practical function of the Socialist Alliance, then my opinions are identical with them. This cannot be said, however, for those practices that "strengthen" the League of Communists by imposing the form and content of ideological work, particularly ideological work that has no connection with either theory or reality. This is also true of interference by Communist organizations in all things, while all serious and systematic work of the Socialist Alliance is simultaneously neglected and treated as less valuable. [. . .]

The actual situation in the urban organizations is this: initiative in the new work methods increased among the membership after the Sixth Congress, but the committees have only slowly and "under pressure" accepted the new methods. [. . .] The actual work methods in the League of Communists (in the basic organizations and lower-echelon committees) have not developed, but remain basically the same as before the Sixth Congress: the apparatus plans and fixes everything in advance. The Communists separate themselves from the socialist mass of ordinary citizens; the organizations get involved in dogmatic, moralistic, useless and meaningless discussions, while life goes right on next to them.

Crisis in forms of work: [. . .] It is striking that the crisis in our methods of political work has emerged for the most part only in the most highly developed centers (the big cities) and in the most highly developed organizations.

For me, the crux of the entire problem lies precisely in that: the city is already quite socialist and democratic, and therefore does not permit obsolete methods because economic and political life has become freer. [. . .] New economic relations and increased urban democratic consciousness no longer tolerate old political methods and relations. [. . .] The increase of economic freedom conflicts with the old relations and ideas. Our entire inherited ideological and organizational system and apparatus (except the basic materialistic, Marxist, philosophical and sociological premises) are now called into question. The actual discrepancy between work methods and reality can and must be eliminated, but it is more profound than usual: a fundamental change is at stake. [. . .]

"Dissolution" of the League of Communists: Of all the ridiculous suggestions I have recently heard, this is one of the most absurd. [. . .] The question is not whether the Communist League should continue or not, but what its organization and work should be like. [. . .]

Facts and experience teach us: first, the League of Communists is no longer the old Communist party, not only because everything is no longer centralized in its hands and it no longer controls everyone and everything, but also because its membership is different, much broader in social origin and in the ideas inherited. Second, the burden of the battle against the Cominform was carried by the Communist old guard, ideologically and morally steeled and faithful to principles, and by the masses of the people. One part—and by no means a small part—of the party membership remained without initiative, in that it outwardly agreed to and slowly accepted as a matter of routine the new doctrines and the new criticisms of the Soviet Union and bureaucratism on the one hand, and, on the other, mired in its own Cominformist ideological conservatism, hindered the agreement concerning the supply of Western arms, a vital issue for our country. (Mention should also be made here of the fact that among the Cominformists arrested, there were no ordinary citizens, only party members and, though rarely, some so-called sympathizers.) Third, the Trieste crisis has demonstrated beyond our expectations the unity [of our people] in defense of our country. [. . .] Fourth, the last elections proved that the Socialist Alliance, with the Communists as its core (and not as a political faction), can successfully fight contemporary political battles. The elections have further shown that the classical, bourgeois urban forces of reaction have remained passive and impotent, while the subjectivism and arbitrariness of the political apparatus (particularly, I think, the party member section of the apparatus) have greatly asserted themselves. Fifth, and this is most important, socialist consciousness is no longer the exclusive domain of, nor represented solely by, Communists and their speeches and writings. It is held in common with the Communists by broad sections of society in different forms and intensity, beginning with the struggle for defense of the country, which the immense majority of citizens have in their consciousness, through the teachers who educate the children in it for this country, up to writers, painters, scientists and Marxist theoreticians. (Once, only we Communists were consciously for socialism.)

To be brief, one may say that before and during the war, the Yugoslav Communist party was the revolutionary party of the working class and of the revolutionary intellectuals. Because of the long duration of the war, and particularly the state of affairs afterward, the party increasingly took on "the garb of the peasant and clerk," so to speak, which correspondingly changed its internal life.

I do not mean to say by this that the League of Communists is "better" or "worse" than the Yugoslav Communist party, but only that they are no longer, and can no longer be, the same organization. Regardless of these things, one fact stands out indisputably: the Communist party, up to the time of its taking a clear-cut antibureaucratic position (which coincides approximately with its transformation into the League of Communists), was attractive to many people because it was the ruling party and, thus, membership in it, though it did not result in special privilege, was a certificate of trustworthiness and a recommendation with which one could more easily find a job. One could not say the same thing of the Communist party, either before or during the war. In those days, few people aspired to party membership. During the so-called bureaucratic era, however, membership increased overnight. [. . .] The old, prerevolutionary and revolutionary Yugoslav Communist party no longer exists in fact. What has survived is its positive revolutionary heritage and its old cadres, its Communists and the masses. No matter how great our nostalgia is for the old party, we must reckon with the facts, with people, and we must consider what we have to do in these changed circumstances, and how we are to do it.

The battle for democracy and against obsolete forms of society and outmoded methods of thought must be fought by the Communists, by those trained and experienced cadres who, through sleepless nights and efforts beyond human endurance (physical and mental collapse and even death), have shouldered the heaviest burdens during the reconstruction period. [. . .] Only such people, disinterested, imbued with the spirit of sacrifice, modest and discreet, as we knew them in the revolutionary days, are fit to carry on this battle. Only people who do not look on democracy and socialism through the prisms of their own personal interests, but, instead, see in the achievement of socialism the fulfillment of their own personal happiness, are capable of being and remaining driving forces in this process of our democratic transformation and re-education. [. . .] Without Communists there would be no Yugoslavia. This does not mean, however, that the Communists should continue to be organized and to work in the old pattern, for neither the old organizational forms nor the old methods were anything more to the Communists than means to achieve their final goals. [. . .]

New methods of work. Communists, real Communists, who are revolutionaries and democrats, will be more and more necessary in the future, but what I think are no longer necessary are some of the precisely circumscribed methods and functions, or the limitations of those methods and functions, inside and outside the League of Communists. The roots of the evil are in the present organizational structures, and in the style and methods of work. Old concepts and methods continue to be applied in new circumstances when the masses of Communists, and of the people, for that matter, can now influence decisions more directly.

That is why the present methods in the activities of the basic urban organizations are not only barren of results, but also have become a direct obstacle to more productive and creative activity among Communists themselves. [. . .] Present methods are a handicap to the Communists because these methods waste their precious time, kill their incentive to work, and are a source of confusion to their consciences. The final aim of a true Communist is not, and cannot be, some kind of abstract party as such, catering exclusively to Communists; it is, instead, elevating the people's socialist consciousness, educating the masses for democracy, and formulating concrete means of fighting for democracy, legality, the rights of citizens, etc. That is why I think Communists may now discuss current problems within the Socialist Alliance; that is, not first in the League of Communists, and only then, after they have been debated there, "passing them on."

It is not my purpose to propose work methods, but because we are dealing with that problem, let me have my say in that as well. The meetings of the basic organizations of the League of Communists are neither necessary nor useful if problems of daily political work are the only thing on the agenda. Unless there are some special problems (important political changes or political danger), these meetings should not take place. It is useful and necessary, however, for Communists to join the Socialist Alliance as ordinary members, and to work.

What remains of the basic organization of the League of Communists? The election of leaders and delegates, plus exceptional work, and something very important, more important than everything else: internal ideological work. This is the most sensitive point because people cannot tolerate it or be enthusiastic when they are ordered about and treated as immature human beings. Life can be organized only on the basis of personal desires and completely voluntary action. Such a life cannot be imposed on anyone. The only possible method is lecture and perhaps discussion, because it is voluntary and adjusted to the desires and the spiritual level of the audience. But it should not be restricted to Communists; it should be public and available to all who are interested. Lectures may vary, ranging from the most abstract theories and analyses of current political events to cultural, scientific and educational subjects. In that way we would break down the ideological differences between Communists and other citizens, granting no special privileges to either. And, most important, the personality of the Communist will be respected.

Thus, the League of Communists would change from the old party into a real and vital union of ideologically united men. Careerists and opportunists would lose their interest in party membership overnight. [. . .] Communists would be active everywhere they live and act as citizens. The number of Communists in various organizations would be small, but they and their ideas would be diffused throughout. No one would "control" their activities of "line," and no one would give them "directives." Moreover, on the basis of lectures and these discussions, they would take their stand on local issues, social life, and the unsolved problems of their own life and work.

The present League of Communists would "weaken," "wither away" as a classical party, and the conscientious role, comradeship and true discipline of pure Communists would be strengthened. The League of Communists would gradually take on the character of a strong, ideological, widely diffused nucleus, but would lose its party character. It would merge with the Socialist Alliance, and the Communists would merge with the ordinary citizenry. Why should that be bad for Communists and socialism? On the contrary, the Socialist Alliance would become a truly socialist factor and would not be a self-appointed elite of Communists. The role of personality would grow, on the basis of its quality and its function among the masses, and not only on the basis of its position in the party committee or administration. The direct political role of the masses would also grow, so that the people would decide most political problems by themselves and without imposed, patented and enforced leadership and formulas. Thus, the good, talented Communists would become ideological and political leaders, though not quickly or easily. Without either regular attendance at dull and meaningless meetings, or ideological indoctrination, it would become clearly known very quickly who was a *de facto* Communist, preferring the people, democracy and socialism to his own personal advantage. [. . .]

There are no working-class movements in the world today, except the Stalinist ones, which have the same working methods as our League of Communists. Nonetheless, there are non-Stalinist working-class movements which live and develop in spite of the fact that they have neither police, courts, nor press to support them. [. . .] Such working methods as compulsory education [. . .] [and] compulsory attendance at basic party organization meetings [. . .]—Stalinist party methods and organizational principles—ultimately became the forms of an authoritarian apparatus.

Although we can explain why these conditions still exist here, it is not clear why they should continue to do so.

The essence of the problem: Yugoslavia is the only country in the world with men and movements claiming to be Leninist. (The Stalinists and Trotskyists clearly are not Leninist.) We have no reason to be ashamed of that. On the contrary. But there is no reason for being that alone. [. . .]

We built our Leninist party, and later our state, with our own forces but under the influence of Lenin's ideas and Stalin's interpretation of Leninism. [. . .] If these theories and practices—with our own very important Yugoslav additions—were once appropriate to our reality, particularly at the time of our revolutionary struggle, they are no longer appropriate today. [. . .]

No one thinks of opposing the League of Communists. We only oppose the Stalinist remnants inside the League, or, to put it more accurately, Stalin's version of the Leninist party, because it retards progress, particularly democratic progress. [. . .] But the Leninist form of the party and the state has also become obsolete (the dictatorship based on the party), and must always and everywhere become obsolete as soon as revolutionary conditions no longer exist and democracy begins to live. [. . .]

Our progress can proceed in two directions—toward a centralist form of state and party which cannot be democratic today, or toward a renunciation of that form for a more democratic, free and decentralized form of political life and struggle. Freer and more flexible forms of political and ideological work are already appearing, if only as tendencies; we have less dogmatism and more democratic and humane relations among comrades and citizens of our country, so we can only delay the dilemma, but we cannot avoid it. [. . .]

Evolution and reform are creative and revolutionary; they are only possible in our country now, after the revolution, on the basis of the socialized ownership of industry and commerce, and in a time of developing democracy and strengthening independence.

Borba, January 4, 1954

Revolution

[This was Djilas's last article before his official dismissal from party and government posts.]

At the first reappearance of the old class, the vital forces of revolution are set in motion as if life and death were at stake. Yugoslav unity, social ownership, and independence have made the revolution a reality. The attack on the specter of the past is a surging of new life against something that no longer actively exists but is not yet totally dead.

The problem is no longer how to defend or explain the revolution, because it has already become an integral part of society; rather, it is how the revolution should be further developed without being perverted. [. . .]

As far as the violent struggle for power is concerned, the revolution ended long ago. What is actually taking place now is a revolution in social relations. Society could not continue to progress in the relations and forms that arose during the revolution. Two lines of development are now possible: transforming the revolutionary (therefore democratic) forms into bureaucratic ones, or transforming these same forms into truly democratic ones. Both are actually taking place. No single form changes easily and "neatly" into another, not even during longer periods of peaceful development. Inevitably ideological, political, organizational and other kinds of confusions arise. And so, today, bureaucratism sometimes disguises itself with revolutionary ardor and considers democracy as its successor. To some extent, bureaucracy is at least formally correct, because it insists on the forms of the revolution (concentration of all power in the hands of the party, and the absence of a written law). Democracy, however, is fundamentally the correct form because it considers the revolution the highest form of democracy in a class society, and therefore sees itself as the revolution's successor.

During the revolution, the party united in itself all democratic forces and aspirations. It did so and could do so because it was the representative of the will and action of the masses, the organized expression of that will and action. Accordingly, the party was the form of an objective process, a conscious, organized form—and a decisive one because of that organization and consciousness—for further progress. But if it was that then, and had to be so, this does not mean that the party automatically received a permanent option to remain in the same form, and so remain the expression of the will and action of the masses. Democracy in the revolution was expressed through the action of the masses, but also through its most conscious nucleus, the revolutionary cadres, and, first and foremost, the party was just that. It is not accidental that party forums and Communists were then not only the focus of the uprising, but also the source of justice, equality, altruism and humanity.[1]

Today, however, relations have changed substantially. This is no longer the same party that existed during the revolution, at least not for everybody nor in everything. The old revolutionary and democratic spirit is still strong and prevails in the leading cadres but it is not the only spirit. And this is also roughly true of the party's structure. Nor can the party play the same role in the same form as it did during the revolution; it is impossible under the present objective conditions. Its role must now be different and it must take on a different form. [. . .]

Continuing the revolution today means renouncing its obsolete forms for the sake of developing its democratic essence through new forms. As a matter of fact, today revolution is reform, peaceful progress, but progress.

---

1. And the majority of these are the old and real Communist democratic cadres still.

Progress is possible today only in democratic forms. Changes in reality and in methods mean that political and cultural progress, and progress of all other conceptual kinds, must take place, and has already, indeed, taken place. These changed conceptions will fundamentally influence, and already do influence, reality and social relations, and their progress. Precisely because of these changes, precisely because of the peaceful, reformist character of the actual progress of our revolution, all efforts to "raise" the League of Communists to the level of the prewar or wartime Communist party are impossible, not so much because it is impossible to raise hundreds of thousands to the level of tens of thousands, but because it is impossible to re-create those revolutionary conditions. If someone today really wants to separate himself from the past and from conservatism, he can do so only by fighting for new and concrete democratic forms. Today it is nonsense to struggle for power in a "revolutionary" form, not only because it is unrealistic, but also because it is counterrevolutionary. [. . .]

It would be much more useful to think about what can be done with the League of Communists as it is, and with the development of our certainly poor but real democratic forms, than to stagnate in old forms and to dream of things that used to be—even if those things were great, they cannot be re-created. Today's revolution is democratic practice, which demands a revolutionary vocation and spirit.

Nothing can diminish the importance of the revolution, nor can anything, up to now, be compared with it and its importance. The revolution's soul can be preserved, however, only in real freedom, because it was carried out by free men, for freedom, and in the name of freedom.

Borba, January 7, 1954

8
Tried
by the Party

[. . .] And just as victory by slander arouses the triumphant ardor of the victor, it leaves the slandered person in a hopeless position. He finds himself arguing pointlessly, trying to prove his point with primarily moral evidence—moral evidence that is monotonous and colorless, as all evidence is, and that becomes pale under the flood of slanders. [. . .] For slanders are infinite in number but there is only one truth. It is possible to slander indefinitely because one can always invent more lies, but the truth cannot be invented.

The "beauty" of slander lies in the imagination of the person who conceives it and in the obvious discomfort of the person defending himself. And its "advantage" lies in its unlimited possibilities. Slander progresses gradually, with calculation, and employs the vast power of tragedy. But the truth is sudden and involuntary, it is unpracticed and it is judged upon itself alone.

Slander comes forth in the name of the most beautiful ideals, with seeming passion and ardor, while in fact it is cold and deliberate. Truth is otherwise. The beauty and the advantage of slander lie in its forms and its possibilities. Truth is naked and powerless.

It will be said, Truth always wins in the end. Yes, but only in the end. . . .

Diary of Thoughts, 1953–1954 (unpublished)

[The material in this chapter contains excerpts from the trial of Djilas at the Third Plenum of the Central Committee of the League of Yugoslav Communists, held in January 1954. It includes excerpts from Tito's and Kardelj's attacks and Dedijer's loyal defense, as well as Djilas's three statements in the course of the trial. In these statements Djilas made one last attempt to reconcile the irreconcilable. This was perhaps the most humiliating moment of his life. Confused, exhausted, but still the disciplined, lifelong Communist, like many others before him, Djilas admitted

to ideological errors and promised, if only halfheartedly, to follow the
dictates of the party. But a few days later, when he regained control of
himself and reconsidered his position, he refused to apologize to the
party. This refusal made it impossible to heal the breach, and he was
then removed from all governmental and subsequently all party
positions.]

The Accusation

"Djilas Has Gone Too Far" (Tito)

The articles of Comrade Milovan Djilas were his own doing, were his
own ideas. It has been asked why we didn't do something about this
matter earlier. Since he was a member of the Executive Committee of the
Central Committee of the League of Communists of Yugoslavia, couldn't
we have resolved the problem with less commotion and less damage?

When the question is put this way, I must admit that to a certain
extent we are guilty. Comrade Djilas had written articles before and last
fall when he asked me, "Old Man, what do you think about what I'm
writing?" I replied, "You know that you say certain things I can't agree
with, but I don't think this is a reason for you not to write. On the
contrary. Mostly you have valuable things to say; keep on writing." I said
that because in his articles Djilas had presented matters about which we
had already written.

Only in December, when I read all his later articles, did I realize that
Djilas had gone too far. When I saw that Comrade Djilas directly
attacked the League of Communists (I will not mention other positions
he took which are invalid from a theoretical viewpoint—Comrade
Kardelj will speak about them later), I realized that he was proposing
the liquidation of the League of Communists and the abolition of discipline—proposals which could inflict enormous damage not only upon the
unity of our party but also upon the unity of the country. [. . .]

Comrade Djilas was aware of my opinion before he published his last
article in *Nova Misao*. He hurried to get it published. [. . .]

Are the articles in *Borba,* written at the rate of three articles per week,
some new original theory? Are these new ideas about our development,
new ideas about our reality? They are not, comrades! And when today
some of our comrades ask us, "Why did you attack him, why do you hold
a Special Plenum, when he only writes about things that you yourselves
have talked about?" I answer, "Correct. They contain some ideas and
formulations of my own, of Kardelj's, and also of some other comrades,

ideas and formulations which we have discussed publicly. I was the first one to talk about the withering away of the party and of the Socialist Alliance. But I did not say that this will take place within six months or a year or two, but that it is a long-range process." [. . .]

Why did Comrade Djilas part ways with the comrades with whom he had worked closely for seventeen years? Within our circle Comrade Djilas has always had an opportunity to say whatever he wanted—even more than he has written. We all knew him and discussed matters with him. We also joked, and a man can say many things when joking. But the questions raised in his articles were not discussed within our circle in the form in which they appeared in the press, nor did he consider it necessary even to mention them at meetings of the Executive Committee or of the Secretariat or to tell us what he was planning to write about. [. . .]

Up to now we have worked collectively and in the future we must do the same. Exchanges of opinion, heated discussions take place—and then what is deemed by the majority to be the most correct is accepted. That principle should continue to be followed within our circle. [. . .]

It is very curious—and revealing—that in his articles Comrade Djilas failed to mention the working class even once, as if it does not exist. [. . .]

If I see revisionism in Djilas's articles, it is not too hard to see why, comrades. [. . .] He is advocating democracy at any price, which is exactly the position of Bernstein, and of a whole set of revisionist circles in the West. Comrade Djilas does not see that. He fails to see that this is revisionism of the worst kind, reformist opportunism, and not the revolutionary dynamism that he tries to make it out to be. [. . .]

"Djilas's Theses—Shallow and Unscientific" (Kardelj)

Comrade Tito has already explained the position taken by the Executive Committee in regard to the articles of Comrade Djilas, that is, concerning their ideological and political character. The theoretical arguments in Djilas's articles are extraneous and unimportant. They are unimportant principally because Djilas starts with a political thesis and only later does he tack onto it hastily a schematic theoretical explanation—essentially superficial, unscientific and garbled—in order to make his theses appear more significant. Because they are unimportant, the Central Committee would not have interfered in the purely theoretical contemplations of Comrade Djilas unless his articles also had political significance.

However, since some are of the opinion that, although Comrade Djilas's theory is quite harmful in our concrete political situation because it is premature, it is nonetheless a "new" contribution to socialist theory, a "new" socialist idea, it is necessary to look at the theoretical side of these articles. It is clear that we have no time for a detailed analysis of these articles at this plenum. Therefore, on the basis of Djilas's articles, following the order in which he wrote them, I shall attempt to answer the following three questions:

1. Is the theory presented in the articles of Comrade Djilas really "new?"

2. Does his theory represent a contribution to socialist thought or does it drag socialist thought backward?

3. What is the significance of his theory in our situation, for our struggle for socialism and socialist democracy? [. . .]

I shall cite the content of one of my longer conversations with Comrade Djilas, that on December 22 of last year. A few days before that date I had mentioned to him my disagreement—as well as the disagreement of many other Communists—with the thesis set forth in his articles. On December 22 we met so that I could tell him the essence of my disagreement. In a friendly, comradely form, I presented my critical observations.

Comrade Djilas was very upset by my comments and, showing that he was hurt, he set forth the following theses:

1. that Comrade Tito defends bureaucratism and that sooner or later he will clash with him;

2. that Comrade Ranković and I are in agreement with him, Djilas, but that we are opportunists, and thus are evading a quarrel with Comrade Tito;

3. that within our movement—whether we like it or not—there exists some socialist "left";

4. that we must not exclude the possibility of developing two socialist parties simultaneously in our country.

Understandably those statements shocked me and I refuted all four of his theses. During our conversation—at least this is my impression— Comrade Djilas retracted all four theses, explaining that they were only ideas off the top of his head and that he himself knew that they were absurd. But I have no clear perception of how our conversation ended on the su ject of his articles in *Borba*. I did not mention Djilas's new theses to Comrade Tito. I believed they were just one of those foolish and fanciful journeys which were one of Djilas's familiar traits. I expected that in his future articles he would show more respect for the opinions of his comrades from the Central Committee. [. . .]

However, today, since Djilas's theory reached full expression through his articles, it is possible to say that the theses expressed during our conversation have a close connection with the theses in his articles. If there were not such a connection, I would not discuss them. And conversely: the theses that he presented in our conversation affirm what I just said—that Djilas's conception of democracy is not ours, it is not socialist but a mixture of anarchism and bourgeois-liberalistic forms. [. . .]

In opposition to the struggle for socialist democracy there exists still another process. Hiding behind the word democracy are petty bourgeois and anarchistic tendencies, all kinds of little socialist yearnings and various negative influences from abroad. Their goal is not democracy, although they hide behind its name. The pressure is very strong and it is no less dangerous for socialist democracy than are bureaucratic tendencies. Comrade Djilas, instead of opposing them, collapsed under their pressure. Here, in my opinion, is the source of the political conceptions of Comrade Djilas. [. . .]

Comrade Djilas reopens the dispute that Bernstein started fifty years ago and that was continued by many other writers and politicians, whether right social-democrats or left bourgeoisie. Bernstein formulated his conceptions in the well-known sentence: "What is commonly called the ultimate goal of socialism is nothing for me; the movement is everything." [. . .] From this position Bernstein concluded that the primary goal of the workers' movement is the struggle for democracy, the struggle to transform Germany into a democratic nation. [. . .] Although I am convinced that Comrade Djilas has never read Bernstein, did we not find the same ideas in the articles of Comrade Djilas?

MILOVAN DJILAS: I did not read Bernstein, but I agree with him that the goal is nothing and the movement everything.

EDVARD KARDELJ: Plekhanov, Rosa Luxemburg, Bebel, Parvus and other social democrats, even Kautsky attacked Bernstein (later Kautsky joined him). Lenin also stood against the revisionist thesis. As is known, Bernstein was expelled from the Social-Democratic party at the Hannover Congress in 1899 because of such views. I don't want to make some historical analogies. [. . .] But it is fair to compare several of Bernstein's sentences with those of Djilas, and to note the amazing similarity between the two. Djilas's theory is an old theory which has been restated in every conceivable manner in the last fifty years. [. . .]

If we want to draw any conclusion from all this, we shall have to state that the theory of Comrade Djilas not only failed to contribute to the development of scientific socialist thought, but that it represents a step backward, and that in its political essence it can only harm the ideological unity of the League of Communists in the struggle for socialism and socialist democracy.

What was the impact of Djilas's articles in our country? The impact did not derive from the theoretical content but from the general tendency toward uncontrollable anarchistic disorder. Such disorder is always acceptable to one stratum of people who want us to leap over the present phase—the effort to create the material conditions for socialism and socialist democracy—and to find ourselves overnight in the "land of plenty."

We have always had such tendencies. I must say that up to now we underestimated them and for this reason the present case has occurred. We must struggle against those tendencies by the further building of democratic organs of social self-management and other democratic forms and by the better work of the League of Communists and of the Socialist Alliance of Working People. *We must be aware that we have to battle on two fronts—against bureaucratic tendencies and against the tendencies of uncontrollable anarchistic forces.* Both can threaten the further development of socialism and socialist democracy. [. . .]

I do not believe that every Yugoslav citizen must be a Marxist or that every citizen must believe in the Marxist dialectic. But the League of Communists and its Central Committee definitely hold the Marxist position and consider Marxism to be a necessary scientific weapon of the working class and of socialism. Comrade Djilas can renounce the dialectic, but he has no right as a member of the Central Committee to force his opinions upon members of the League of Communists, and even less right to do so under the imprimatur of Marxism.

In "Reply" he writes:

> And precisely because it is "socialist," our bureaucracy cannot avoid being a little Stalinist, and to some extent, a Yugoslav Stalinism. It therefore stinks of the same ideology and it proclaims the same "civilized" and "peace-loving" methods loudly and clearly. These methods, however, are still not directed at those who are "on top" but at those who are "below."

The tone of his answer to his comrades is characteristic of Djilas's democratism. People who want to fight for democracy should first learn to speak democratically. This tone is typical of the language of the *pogrom* used against all who disagree. And the conclusion of Djilas's "Reply" expresses intolerance toward any other opinion and a shocking immodesty which has lost all sense of time and place. We read there,

> I am not writing in order to make a name for myself, nor out of juvenile pigheadedness, and still less out of a desire to bask in democratic glory. I must write because, like many others, I am the "victim" of objective social processes which compel me to do so. And therein lie my sources of passion and belief. Because of that, and precisely because I respect and want open, comradely socialist criticism of these ideas, I can have only contempt for any other kind of criticism.

This tone needs no comment. Comrade Djilas was unaccustomed to criticism. He was criticized for the first time—and from below. It is precisely

that which he could not stand. With his reply he wanted to cut off all
further criticism. And finally, doesn't the reaction itself show quite
clearly that Djilas's conception is not a contribution to our struggle for
socialist democracy but is instead a blow against it? I think that these
facts put into proper perspective Djilas's statements about freedom and
his so-called descending the "bureaucratic ladder" to be among the
people. They also show that the fear of some people that, after this
plenum, socialist democracy will not be able to develop is unfounded. On
the contrary, this plenum will put tendencies which are contrary to that
goal in their places and in that way will decisively contribute to our
further struggle for socialism and socialist democracy.

The Reply

"To Remain a Free Man and a Communist" (Djilas)

When I look over my past, I cannot say that I have been one of the
most disciplined Communists, but neither was I one who violated discipline or failed to carry out tasks entrusted to him. Discipline was for me a
conscious act and never conflicted with my feelings or wishes or with my
social action. I was the kind of Communist who conscientiously performs
his duty without thinking too much about discipline. I did not make any
"retreats" or act "hastily."

However, during the last several months I gradually began to be aware
of my ideological disagreement with the accepted theoretical views of our
movement on a series of fundamental questions. This is the real—and
basic—cause for my personal alienation from my closest comrades in the
Executive Committee of the Central Committee.

I reached these conclusions after long and deep reflection. I was aware
that my views have their weaknesses and for that very reason I presented
them as thoughts for discussion. Not even today do I maintain that all
those ideas were absolutely correct, although I believe that in the main
they are. It is probable that most of them, or at least a good portion of
them, should be changed or rephrased during the course of further discussion and the struggle of ideas.

Although in the top leadership there was no formal requirement to
present speeches and articles to be read by others, I did violate a long-
established rule, which amounts to a violation of discipline, although not
a formal one. [. . .] That violation is obvious because I was conscious
that certain of my views, especially on theoretical matters, differ from
those of other members of the leadership.

I thought, especially recently, that the differences among us could be eliminated during a discussion (better yet, a public discussion). I was convinced that as a movement and as a society we had already entered the phase where such discussions could be conducted without any danger for the unity of the movement—for unity is certain in all political, organizational and foreign-policy matters. I was not sure then, nor am I even now, that any of my political conclusions are either good or feasible. Insofar as I had time, I criticized all areas of our system, but I am not now nor will I be in the foreseeable future opposed to the system as a whole. [. . .]

During the entire period, including today, I have never been aware of any differences between myself and the leadership on questions of foreign policy or of the brotherhood and unity of our peoples. This is demonstrated by my recent election speeches.

However, looking over the past, especially in recent times, on philosophical and esthetic questions my views did differ in essence from the views of most of our theoretical workers. But I cannot understand nor can I accept the criticism that I abandoned materialism and dialectics (Marxism), or that I have become a skeptic or an agnostic. On the contrary, I believed that in our new progressive social and cultural development we try to expand upon and even to change significantly the previous ideological views, including those of Lenin. Marx's views were for me always and remain today the foundation of all my interpretations. [. . .]

My greatest mistake was failing to consult with my comrades. [. . .] Doubtless that was not only the proximate cause but also the essential cause of the present difficulties which could seriously harm the movement.

Stories are circulating that I am against Comrade Tito. I cannot accept that. Not one of my criticisms is directed against a particular person, and least of all against Comrade Tito. Comrade Tito was and, regardless of the present dispute, remains for me an incomparable figure in Yugoslav national and social development, the strongest and most active force for unity in our movement and in our country.

I shall always work with discipline to fulfill the decisions of the League of Communists and government organs just as I have in the past. Regardless of what I think, I am ready to renounce the publication of those of my positions that the leadership considers potentially politically damaging. You may think what you will about me or my work, but I cannot and could not imagine that socialism could be realized in our country outside the framework of the League of Communists, the Socialist Alliance and the governmental and economic organs.

I must say that my writing in "Anatomy of a Moral" in *Nova Misao* is too general and overdone—like all satirical pamphlet literature. Even more important, it deals with periods and with phenomena that are in many ways a matter of the past. Under certain circumstances that article could cause political harm. But I do not agree that my article is directed against any specific person or that it describes any concrete situation. Such a view of literature is naïve. If anyone feels insulted, I am ready to apologize in any manner that he wishes.

To me the unity of the movement is above all else, and I consider this to be the duty of every Communist and every citizen. In my opinion that unity does not contradict free thought but is realized with its aid.

Since my early youth I have always been a free man and a Communist and I hope to remain so till the end of my life. I cannot see that these two things contradict one another or that they could be separated from one another. And not only for me, but it seems to me that they are inseparable elements of the movement also: to say what one thinks and to do what is agreed or ordered. I shall do what is required without complaining and I shall speak without preconceived thoughts. I learned the one in the revolutionary movement and the other I was taught by a humanistic culture throughout my entire life.

I considered it my human and my political duty to send this statement first to Comrade Tito and to ask him his opinion. He has given his answer. Without asking his permission, I will read it:

> I think that you failed to understand the consequences of what you call "retreat" and "hastiness." I consider this basic to the entire affair, because just those consequences prove most clearly that such public discussions as you began in your articles are dangerous not only for the unity of the League of Communists but also for the development of socialism.

I will not try to interpret the words of Comrade Tito, because they are clearly stated. I pledge myself to carry them out in my political work. That is my statement. [. . .]

Now I should like to answer your statement very briefly, Comrade Tito.

I cannot accept some of the criticisms of my positions. I have stated that I did violate discipline. And it is correct that ninety per cent of those ideas, as Comrade Tito observes, are not mine but are taken from him or Kardelj or elsewhere.

It is clear that I cannot straighten out everything. I will dwell here only on the question of revisionism. In order to clarify some matters and to leave no doubt about what is involved here, I want to state some things clearly. I am a revisionist in relation to Leninism. I am of the opinion, and have no reason to hide it, that such an "ideology" no longer fits our country. Comrades, I am not a supporter of some bourgeois or Western social-democratic idea. I am not by my education or by my way of life, nor have I read about social democracy. If some of my ideas resemble those of some social democrats or those of Bernstein, which will be discussed later, that is not the result of copying those authors but the result of some objective conditions expressed in my mind, perhaps some possibly bourgeois tendency.

In order to understand each other clearly: I do not see any differences between myself and the leadership in regard to the policy, or the sharpness of that policy, of our party, our government and our economic organs toward the bourgeois elements in our country or in regard to the ideological struggle against those bourgeois elements. If our Central Committee or our Parliament [. . .] considers that our policy should be sharpened, and passes corresponding measures, I do not disagree. I never differed with our leadership on that question and have no differences even today.

Other differences are obvious and one should not hide them when they in fact exist. These differences concern the ideological questions about which we have already spoken.

I am convinced that many of my articles created a great stir within the League of Communists. I am not for liquidating the League. I am for organizational changes within the League of Communists. That is briefly what I wanted to say.

"The Party Needs His Strength and Talent" (Dedijer)

I have a feeling, comrades, that all of us will agree that we have never been through more difficult days in our lives than those today. [A VOICE: It depends. We had some pretty difficult days.] We found ourselves in a new situation. [. . .] I have become a persecuted animal. I was accused of being a traitor and also of disliking Comrade Tito. I felt this way until two days ago when Comrade Tito invited me to visit him. I found him also disturbed. Calmly, like a father, he let me tell him what was bothering me. [. . .]

Now, comrades, let me express my opinion concerning the articles of Comrade Djilas published in *Borba*.[. . .]

I thought it was good to have these articles published; the whole paper looked better with them, it had more substance. [. . .] I warned Djilas especially concerning the article "Is There a Goal?" mainly because it is very difficult to deal with such deep philosophical concepts in a newspaper article. Concerning his "Reply," I criticized his method. He was very upset by the comment of a comrade that he was trying to have Tito deposed. [. . .]

On December 25 I asked Kardelj . . . whether there was any fundamental disagreement between Djilas's articles and his own. He left me under the impression that there were no essential differences. [. . .] During these last few days, I have read all the articles written during the last two years by Comrades Tito, Kardelj and Djilas and I have concluded [. . .] that in essence there are no basic disagreements. [. . .] We elected Comrade Djilas as president of the Parliament on December 25. Up to that date he had already published 14 of his 18 or 19 articles. That means that he had already presented his thoughts. Yet with a unanimous vote we elected him president of the Parliament. [. . .]

I discussed the matter for an entire ten days with many comrades who are sitting among us, and the majority of them accepted more or less the articles of Comrade Djilas. Of course, the majority of comrades accepted those articles because they thought he was writing them in agreement with comrades from the Secretariat and that the Executive Committee stood behind him. But then the question arises, why do people accept articles without regard for their content, paying attention only to the authority behind them? Now we have a new situation. The Executive Committee examined the articles, reached its decision, and now these same people change their opinions. [. . .]

Finally, comrades, I am convinced that we must find a sensible solution. We have few people of Djilas's caliber. Such men are not born every day [laughter]. Yugoslavia and the party need his strength and his talent. If I am faced with a terrible choice, which finger of my hand I should cut off—Tito, Kardelj, Ranković or Djilas—which banner of the revolution I should pull out, I must answer: I cannot tear apart the body of my party. I would cut off my head to prevent my hand from doing it. We should rejoice that our revolution lives on, that it did not devour its children, that the children of this revolution are honest. [. . .]

"I Have Separated Myself from the Party" (Djilas)

I will dissociate myself from Dedijer's speech [. . .] because it is emotional. [. . .] I cannot hold it against you, comrades, if you consider that I have also separated myself sharply from the party. It is clear that I have dissociated myself from the party. I am aware of that today. But I did not do it because of any hostile intent, but for ideological reasons.

In that connection, Kardelj's speech is new both in tone and in the manner of exposition. We did not speak in this way [. . .] about Hebrang and Žujović. Regardless of how much I disagree with his opinion, Kardelj did discuss my theses. [. . . .] I accept ninety per cent of Kardelj's theses and can state that Kardelj criticized my work solidly. There are some points I cannot agree with, but I cannot categorically state that Kardelj might find something useful in some of my ideas. All in all, this is a struggle of opinions, and history teaches us that no one thesis is always right.

One area where Kardelj and Tito interpreted me wrongly is their contention that I neglect the role of the working class and that I fail to mention it. [. . .] In the trade-union periodical in 1951 or 1952 I stated that the working class is the major force in the building of socialism. [VOICES: That was earlier.] I stand by the same thesis today regardless of my unfinished articles. [. . .] Because whether I say socialism or socialist forces or the city, as you saw in my articles, that concept is for me almost identical with the working class. [. . .]

Some people speak about my skepticism and lack of faith. There is one thing that is absolutely true. [. . .] I do not really believe in the League as it is today. I do not want to say that all Communists are bureaucrats; but a large number in my opinion are not Communists. In my opinion peasant Communists are not Communists but are allies of Communists; peasant party members are our form of alliance with the village. Second, I think there is too much of the petty official element in the party in the city and that it plays too large a role within the party. I think that the role of the party apparatus is too vast to be democratized. [. . .] I think that things should be reorganized so that people at the lower level exercise initiative rather than receiving direct orders from committees. Thus, comrades, if our discussion were to lead to the reorganization of the League along these lines, all my differences with my comrades in the Executive Committee would vanish. [. . .]

Comrades, it has been stated that I sought to legalize factions. [. . .] That is not correct. [. . .] I did say that [. . .] neither socialism nor socialist theory makes the principle of one party an absolute. Kardelj said that this view was a retreat. [. . .]

When Comrade Kardelj says that I believe that the League of Communists is the chief obstacle to the development of democracy in our country, this is only partially correct; but I do maintain that the League of Communists, as it is today, is the chief obstacle to democratic socialist development in our country. [. . .]

Comrade Roćko told me that I have to repent. It is hard for me to understand this terminology in the League of Communists today. I have nothing to repent. If I made a mistake, I made a mistake and will be rewarded as I deserve. But I say openly what I think. To repent is a moral act appropriate to religion and not to our Communist organization.

"I Have Nothing More to Say" (Djilas)

Comrades, Communist self-criticism is very difficult. Mainly because there is a large complex of mistakes. [. . .] During these last two days in some way a devil broke in me. [. . .]

Today I am convinced that holding this Special Plenum was the best way to end the matter.

I have a strange feeling that this will be the most useful event for the Communist party of Yugoslavia since the Cominform conflict. [. . .] Last night [. . .] for the first time I slept normally. [. . .] From the criticism by Minić as well as Kardelj and Tito, I felt that the plenum is following an antibureaucratic course in struggling against my concepts. [. . .] I am in a situation here at the plenum where either I have definitely to part from Communist practice and Communist ideology and everything Communist or I have to try, at least as a private citizen, in some way to turn my face toward you, toward your work, toward Communists, toward the League, toward our entire politics. [. . .]

One of the comrades said that the article in *Nova Misao* is an integral part of the earlier articles, is even the conclusion. Quite correct. It is an integral part and carries things to the end, except for about ten more articles I intended to publish in *Borba*. That is the end and the entire whole. Comrades who say that is the case are correct.

After the Brioni Plenum I was not convinced that the plenum had chosen the correct path. I constantly had the feeling that the plenum was one-sided, that it neglected the struggle against bureaucratism. When I wrote my articles, I felt that someone should correct in some way the Brioni Plenum. [. . .]

Comrade Tito [. . .] said that there are men who are afraid of difficulties. I cannot accept this formulation as pertaining to me. [. . .] I was afraid of the victory of bureaucratism. I participated in the anti-Cominform campaign. Thereafter I started applying some of those criticisms to events in Yugoslavia. [. . .] In the Executive Committee I did not have any specific duty. Either I did not have one or I could not find out what it was or I preferred not to have one. This must have happened primarily because I always did intellectual work in the party. Those administrative-economic matters were hard for me to understand. But somehow I found myself in the situation that has already been discussed here.

MOŠA PIJADE: As far as I recall, you were in charge of social questions in the Executive Council.

DJILAS: That was done by Bobi. I traveled here and there. I had scarcely any contact with Bobi. I met him twice. But it does not matter. I had that job but I was attracted toward abstract intellectualism, and in the final analysis it doesn't make any difference. [. . .]

I only saw the external phenomena [. . .] but I did not see the entire process as a whole. [. . .] As I looked at those phenomena, I was afraid of bureaucratism . . . and I created an abstract theory which applied concretely means exactly what the comrades say it means: the mobilization of the petty bourgeoisie, of social democracy and the West, all of the things I really said. [. . .]

This plenum has convinced me that bureaucratism will not be victorious in Yugoslavia. My faith in the League of Communists is restored, the faith I openly denied yesterday. With this my faith in the Central Committee of the League of Communists and the Central Committee as the chief antibureaucratic force is restored. Obviously when confronted with these facts that I heard really do exist, my theory cannot operate in practice and nothing will remain of my theory. [. . .]

I have nothing more to say, comrades, unless someone else has something to ask me.

Komunist, No. 1–2, January–February, 1954

9
Reflections

No one is as stupid as a democrat turned imperialist or a revolutionary turned reactionary. When that happens the concepts get all mixed up. Just as it happens to each individual when his ideas come into conflict with the real trends of development, so also it happens to each movement. Desires, traditions and ideas either give in to developments or they are crushed by them.

For dogmatic—and not only dogmatic—reasons, we Communists proclaimed that the normal human concepts and ethical values are petty bourgeois. In this way we are creating two mutually irreconcilable worlds.

The more dogmatism—the less freedom.
The more talk about the ultimate ideal—the less freedom.
When reality is masked behind a revolutionary past and an ultimate goal, every policy that fails to take into account its weaknesses vis-à-vis the past and its illusions about the future must express itself as tyranny over society.

> Diary of Thoughts, 1953–1954 (unpublished)

Nordic Dream

[This piece is in many ways the most significant in this collection. A dramatic essay, it was written in the course of a single night, January 29, 1954. It is about the trip to the Scandinavian countries on which Djilas had been scheduled to depart at the time he fell from power. In the form of an imagined trip to the North, Djilas describes his feelings about the party purge, his loss of position, and his spiritual and physical anguish. Despite his realization that his actions could not be without consequences, he was unprepared for the totality of change. Thus this is an intimate memoir of the most traumatic moment of his life. In it, Djilas, one of the few men in power to have recorded his feelings at the time of

238

his downfall, reveals both his strengths and his weaknesses. (A second planned trip to Scandinavia was canceled when the Yugoslav government lifted Djilas's passport in the spring of 1970, a few days before his departure. A trip to the North thus remains an unrealized dream for Djilas.)]

It should have been called "Northern Sky," a sequel to "Eastern Sky,"[1] but it turned out to be only a dream. . . .

I was scheduled to travel to the Nordic countries,[2] but recent developments have made this impossible. And so, instead of the impressions and melodies of those unseen lands, I am forced to carry dreams about them within myself or within the grotesque reality that surrounds me.

But what is real? A world unseen or one visualized with such realness that it throbs in my blood, in my bones, in each thought, each desire, each dream?

Who knows . . .

That trip to the North was meant to be the reality. But now it is only a dream. . . .

Like all unrealized dreams, it is a little bit sad. But not something to feel sorry about any longer, despite—or even because of—this bitter and shattering reality which can once and only once be lived.

Although every reality, like every dream, can only be lived once, this reality is more intense than all others. At least for me. As least in the realness of the death I have lived through.

Dream and reality, colors and sounds, how it was all tangled up. How to unravel it? Or whether to unravel it? Maybe it is better to leave it snarled and tangled. Maybe that is the real life, the only genuine one. Is it possible to express that? How? Maybe, if one could use all means and all forms and still keep it all together. But that is impossible because of the limitations of a single person, of any single person.

Then at least a few lines. About reality and about the dream, "between reality and the dream."

I knew very little about those Nordic countries, Norway and Sweden, where I had been scheduled to arrive in just a few days. Mainly only the most general historical and statistical information, and even now that is fading away. All that remains are the strains of Grieg's melodies. We will not see those countries after all, all because of this unexpected uproar, this scene from an opera, which was anticipated, but not in the form it took. And this all occurred because of ideological disagreements expressed in a couple of newspaper articles and a few insignificant tentative proposals presented in them, and because of a trite and naïve portrait of

1. A description of my trip to Asia, published in *Nova Misao*, 1953.
2. The official visit to the socialist parties of Norway and Sweden was canceled after the Third Plenum, in January 1954.

our high society. In reactionary bourgeois times it would not even have been noticed, because it was superficial, innocuous and restrained, and really it is of no particular value, artistic or intellectual, except that it expresses a sense of what is fair and that the author had the courage to write it despite his premonition of the wrath that might descend on his head.

I could already see at the beginning of December (the realization struck me in the sleepless night of December 7–8, the night that, although things had been building up for months, was the most significant night of my life) that my views would not be accepted by even my closest comrades, at least not by all of them or even by the majority. But at the same time, being convinced of my ideas, I had an uncontrollable moral and psychological need to state them. Even if it meant that I would be thrown out, cursed and despised by the movement to which I had given my youth, my entire life, my every thought, my strength to the last drop, and by comrades with whom for seventeen years (and with some for even longer) —ah, what memories!—I had shared everything: bread and wine, the most intimate torments and joys, thoughts and dreams, tedious details and decisions of vast importance for the fate of the country.

There was a terrible spiritual and intellectual strain that had been building up unnoticed for months if not for years. Everything that up to that time had been my life and that made me what I am—the struggles, the understandings, the ideas, the creative urges, the loves and the hatreds, the blood spilled and the tears shed, youth and history, enthusiasms and dreams—all that pulled me in one direction, while dim forebodings, inklings of realization pulled me to the other side, toward the new and the unknown. Behind me everything was clear, appealing and beautiful; in front of me, everything was murky, clouded and uncertain. To remain with that which was or that which is, or to step forward into uncertainty? To break within myself my love for my comrades? To clash with the movement and its tradition, with a history that for me is so glorious and for which so much blood was shed, in which I, alongside the others, was someone and something, or? . . .

But I had to follow that other road, even if my steps were confused and indecisive. Otherwise I could not remain a man in my own eyes. For if I know something, even if only sensed in the darkness rather than known with certainty, if I discover something and I am convinced of its truth— how can I deny it, hide it from my closest friends, from the world and from myself? To think now about my career, my reputation or my family, about ostracism, about life or death, or even about ties to the past, would be as disgraceful as to be a thief or a traitor. In the final analysis one must subject himself to some internal "categorical imperative." Each person has his own "imperative," and so do I.

I knew in advance that the majority would be against me regardless of their personal convictions. I even told some of them that and wrote about it. I suspected that all of them might be against me. But still, it seemed better that way than to keep silent and to pretend. . . . There is some truth in the observation that nobody would have paid any attention to my "angry outbursts" had I not been in the position in which I was. But it is equally true that if I had not been in that position I would not have had the obligation to speak out. Had I in that position seen what I have seen and remained silent, I would have been sitting back enjoying life and lying. And whatever the consequences, that is impossible. . . . True, I had illusions both about people and about the forms of the confrontation. I envisioned two extreme possibilities: a general and academic discussion in the press, or a possibly brutal settling of accounts with me. But neither took place. Reality found itself in the middle and, as usual, it was "petty bourgeois," that is, common and average. But I didn't foresee all that. In the end it turned out worse than they promised me but better than I imagined.

I was not, nor did I desire to be, a "tactician." I could not believe that "our people" were so lacking in principles as to really oppose a discussion of principles, or that they could suddenly forget my own role in the movement or forget history generally, including the lessons from the history of the USSR and its settling of accounts with the socialist opposition (regardless of whether right or left, "correct" or "incorrect," but in no case bourgeois). But man and his character depend on the circumstances in which he lives and especially on his degree of social consciousness in a given situation. It is similar with the forms of struggle. . . . This society as a whole is obviously not yet ready for free discussion. Only those whose arguments are strong are ready for it, and these are very few and they are silent. Or perhaps these are just my "liberal illusions"? Whatever the answer, I was silenced as an agent of the domestic and foreign bourgeoisie and spit upon as a petty-bourgeois devil—after twenty-two years of membership in the party and over fifteen years within its highest leadership! And all without a real discussion about real problems. . . . This shocked me morally. Will this finally make me come to my senses?

Still, I am glad that it turned out this way. I have a certain peace of mind, if also a certain bitterness. Everything had to be and was, but could not be according to the "Stalinist ways." "These heights know no rules," as the saying goes.

I did not know before and I still don't know for sure how all this will be resolved. I don't know how all this will end for me personally—which is not important—or what will happen to the country. Nor how long all this will last. Probably for a long time. Years and years. Maybe for as long as I live. But it doesn't really matter! There is nothing wrong with being an ordinary person who loves his little pleasures and who lives from them. That is what life is all about. . . . Whatever the outcome, for me personally it is not very important because I did not have any "tactic," any "ulterior motives." Instead I threw myself into the storm, into the dense fog of uncertainty without heed for the consequences. More by intuition than by any conscious process I sensed that truth was on my side. And so I set out. . . .

I sensed that everything was coming to a halt and that it was my obligation to keep things moving or at least to clarify the standstill. It seems to me that the wheels of society turn only when lubricated with human blood and ceaseless, unimaginable suffering. This time I was the victim. I saw that I could not escape. Nor did I want to. Did I help the wheels move? Was I crushed in the process? I don't know. There was suffering, too much suffering. But in spite of everything one endures. . . .

And what history will have to say about it all, I don't know, nor can I even worry much about it. Probably everything will look less complex and we will all look more pathetic. But that is history's task, not mine. Perhaps it will condemn me as a madman and an intellectual adventurer, someone who strayed from the "correct road," "objectively selected" in unripe conditions and thus by his views served the forces of reaction. I don't really believe the latter, of course, because I start with an acute sense of consciousness. But whatever the case, history cannot dispute either the honorableness or the selflessness of my intentions in these political affairs which in themselves are usually dishonest and always selfish. No one can accuse me of being selfish and dishonest, because I saw clearly that despite the good wishes of my friends all this would accomplish nothing for me personally, not even when it appeared that it might accomplish something. Still, it was an unexpected blow, both for them and for me, and it turned them overnight into my enemies, who threw into the mire of oblivion the love, the ideals, the shared battles and misfortunes as if they had never existed. But there is no doubt that all that discussion, whose results were clear in advance, all that ridiculous campaign (against "anarchy" and "petty bourgeoisism," "the banner of domestic and foreign reaction," "the conceited intellectual," "the carrier of decadence," "the hope of the Tuzla Bishop," "the idol of drunkards," "Trotskyite droppings," "self-styled theoretician," "hanger-on of the revolution," "wrecker," "fractionizer," "Bevanite," "anarcho-democrat," "anti-Marxist," "McCarthyite," "antisocialist," "revisionist," "Bernsteinist," "Westernite," and "slanderer"), which spilled no blood and annihilated no physical being (and in this respect un-Stalinist), but only the social being (and in this respect Stalinist), all that setting of the stage to burn the heresy and the heretic but without the fire, showed that such "humane" and "democratic" behavior cannot serve the honor and glory of this country and its socialism.

I found myself the object of a planned and concerted attack, accused because my writings served the darkest reaction, especially foreign reaction, accused of trying to fragment or liquidate our socialist movement. Only the noble Dedijer, a man of principle and occasionally of too good a nature, surprised me with his courage and his clarity, which was in sharp contrast to the confused Mitra.* After ten sleepless nights, still tied by blood to those people and to that movement, confused, tired and obviously despondent, I finally stated that since they are not accepted by the authority that should accept them and that leads the country, many of my positions must be incorrect and dangerous. They asked me to do that for the sake of the unity of the movement. And truly, I didn't want anyone to follow me or to perish needlessly when nothing was planned and organized, nor could I accept such moral responsibility. I felt as if I were in some kind of religious ecstasy—I should sacrifice everything to avoid hurting the movement as a whole and to avoid harming those who agree with me but who are not organized. The ideas became unreal to me—even if correct for the distant future—precisely because existing practice and authority did not accept them.

And it grew to a crescendo, as each heavier stone was piled on my chest. But I did not renounce my fundamental (my philosophical) views. Or did I perhaps for a moment? But today no more! I cannot. They will accuse me, I know, of being insincere. But I can no longer accept the Stalinist code of sincerity, nor can I fall again into that rapture . . . they themselves have severed me so completely from themselves that I am without any illusions. Now I know many things that I didn't know before. I am still a member of the party but—as they themselves admitted—only because of foreign public opinion and only so that there wouldn't be a campaign claiming that we are just like the Russians.

Where are morality and principles here? They have written me off forever. Now it is only a question of finding the formal manner of doing so that is convenient for the state and for its elite. Naturally they could even grant me an "amnesty" if this suited them politically and if I "repented." Why not? It is fine to be generous if it doesn't cost you anything. Silenced and amnestied, I would not even be a blot on their consciences.

They are angry at themselves because they lost their tempers.

I too am writing off a few things, but by now without anger or bitterness.

Perhaps I should not have made my final statement. That will plague me for the rest of my life. At the very moment when I should have been great, I turned out to be small, and this precisely because for all of my life I belonged to something I believed was great, because I was part of a

* Mitra Mitrović, Djilas's first wife.

church—a member, and not just an ordinary one—and a believer in dogma.

It is disgraceful to renounce an idea, even its nonessential policy aspect! Of course! I am not seeking excuses. But I was not, nor do I want to be, the chief of any reactionary opposition, nor do I want to carry any banner but the socialist. I didn't know how to defend myself from those unexpected accusations. I only wanted to encourage domestic currents, not to change the system. Even though I was not satisfied with the existing government or system, I didn't want to change it, only to improve it. If that is possible . . . From a practical viewpoint, I almost got that far. In the realm of ideas taken generally, maybe even farther. I was trapped in that situation and surprised by attacks that were prepared in advance. And that is the essence of the matter. Everything else is just talk. . . .

And still, all this is progress, even if it tramples my political carcass and the consciences of many others. This could not have happened even in 1949, not to speak of 1946 or 1947. Regardless of how the dispute proceeds and what concrete forms it takes, it will be less "sharp" and more "civil"—regardless of how cruel—than if it had developed earlier or if it had developed in "the first country of socialism." . . .

Our country will not be bureaucratic and Stalinist even if it wants to and cannot even if it should be. Stalin was unique. His epoch is passing, and with it Stalinism. He rose to the top when the bureaucracy was rising. But today, the apex of bureaucratic Communism has already been attained and now the bureaucracy is in its decline. Its future may hold pain, tragedy and cruelty, but never again victory.

Our Yugoslav Stalinism, in part inherited but in greater measure developed on our own soil, can now only make retreats—longer or shorter, more or less painful. But Stalinism will not gain a foothold among the people and can never win them over again, if it ever had them at all. Stalinism in Yugoslavia is and will remain something alien, something imposed, which will never bring victory and glory to our country. It is not suited to us because we are already a part of democratic and humanistic Europe, part of democratic and humanistic mankind; or if we are not yet, we will be, we must be to live and to survive.

If there were as much wisdom in this country as there is power today, and did the thrust of the popular saying "Better a handful of power than a cartful of wisdom" not prevail, then, despite disagreements, matters would have been resolved in the following manner: I would have been "criticized" because I made some concrete proposals "on my own authority" and because of my position I created an organizational disturbance. For this breach of discipline I might have been removed from important positions (Secretariat, Executive Committee) . Philosophical and political discussions attacking me would have developed normally (even with the aid of the likes of Ziherl, who, if he thinks at all, thinks only those thoughts that come down from "above." [. . .] There would have been discussions. But they would still have allowed me to represent my country and to defend the country I love no less than anyone else, if not more. And more today than ever before . . .

But such a discussion is only a dream in this country as it presently exists. And maybe it is better that way because it will help me perceive the reality I am still not able to comprehend. . . .

But on with the dream. It is very beautiful and soothing and at the moment I have nothing else. It is cold outside. The frost heaves and contracts and hisses and cracks in thousands of corners. Nowhere is the wind stilled, nor is there shade or silence. . . .

Yes, a dream is a creature of the mind. . . .

I would like to travel north and defend my country and its socialist movement as it should be defended. Of course, at best this could offset the propaganda, frequently malicious but often quite accurate, against Yugoslavia and all that is new in it.

But we are where we are, in wild, primitive conditions where the dichotomy—either a faithful subject or an enemy of the state—is still routinely assumed. From whence there is no exit, nor can one appear. I must remain here. Without dreams. [. . .]

The most active and most ruthless were the newcomers and the hangers-on, the supporters of the "regime," hidden and overt Cominformists, "party members" who until 1945 were Četniks or Ustaši or who—not believing in our Partisan army—waited for the Red Army or the Western forces to liberate them from that terrible mess. Many of them are making their careers and are atoning for past sins. The omnipotence and the infallibility of the political apparatus had to begin again. Could anyone have foreseen such harmonious coming together? At the last moment I did, of course, and even worse. As for the others, I don't know. I shall bear the brunt. And the others? I don't know. I shall emerge from it stronger, more aware and without any illusions. This will happen to others too, but I don't know to which ones. New and younger forces will emerge. But where are they? I don't know, I don't know. But within myself I sense them somewhere, somewhere in the depths of this country and its difficult history.

Yes, there were difficult days. When they started to "unmask" me as a traitor and a Western agent, I decided quite stupidly that I must defend my honor and my dignity even to the death. And if things had not stopped at the halfway mark when they did, people might be talking over my corpse and they could easily say: This proves that we were dealing with a 100-per-cent petty bourgeois, a coward who could not hide his crimes and who had not the courage to appear before the party. [. . .]

I no longer know what is happening. The hypocritical and treacherous hunt continues. The train has already started and goes on and on. The engine has run over me and the train thunders on to the last car, to the grass-roots organization in some godforsaken village. [. . .]

Finally the train passes. But I don't believe that the railway dispatcher will appear with his cheerful lantern to say "all clear."

Of course, nothing is resolved except that I have been removed. Nor can it be resolved, because it does not involve me but the processes of socialism. I'm already removed from those events. Only the name remains, the idea, the live creature who bears them. Whether and how far this creature will be an obstacle? He might even disappear. He might even be forgotten, and probably will be. I don't know, I can't know, and don't really care. But social processes are complex. They are not just a question of the existence of a personality.

My conscience is as still as a closed book.

I wanted us to be a part of Europe, a part of democratic socialist Europe, not a part of the Balkans or of Russia. And we shall be Europe, even if I do not live to see it. . . .

Why does this preoccupy me so much? Even this was only a dream, a nightmare . . . reality was so terrible and inhumane. . . .

For a week I have been thinking in my cold villa on Dedinje, without hope for anything, even the security of a minimal existence. To be an ordinary loyal citizen of Yugoslavia—that's what I wanted, or at least that's what I told myself I wanted. Still, I am as calm and relaxed as if I had just finished some ordinary daily task.

All the members of this home are crowded into Mother's room. This is the only room that is heated. Once more Mother got the better of death, which almost held her in its embrace during those terrible days when she lay with fixed expression, all skin and bones, for days and nights without speaking, without breathing, without food or even water.[3]

Mother is better now and is waiting to move. We won't move immediately because "up above" it is considered "distasteful" to make someone vacate his villa the moment he ceases to be a minister. I shall wait a while for the sake of good taste.

It strikes me that this formality is important—such considerations did not exist earlier. But there is also something grotesque in it. Ministers—

3. During those days, and even earlier while everything was boiling inside of me and around me, I often regretted that she hadn't died earlier. But despite the gravity of her condition and the enormity of her suffering, I did not waver. (During the war she lost her husband and three children; now she was living to see the destruction and failure not only of her dream about freedom but also of her remaining children.) She had always said: Let anything else go, but for my sake save your honor. All else can be regained, but honor and honesty once lost cannot be restored. My "undeserved" troubles are heaviest of all for her.

or, in my case, the president of the Federal Assembly—are easily dismissed, even overnight, but so much attention is devoted to the formality of vacating the villa!

Together with the rest of us, Mother is "planning" the future, an uncertain life, an "ordinary" life. Complaining, I said that all this looks like a cross between the bankrupt aristocracy which tries to behave with "dignity" and "honor" and the petty bourgeoisie which worries only about what they will eat and where they will sleep!

Nothing is happening. Friends no longer come to visit. Not one, even for a casual call. No telephone calls. Those who dare don't want to; those who want to don't dare.

And that is the picture of society and the times. The sentence of one's own clan is the most terrible. It is total.

But still, all of one's life is not within the clan. Darkness does not yet prevail. At least not in our soul, not here at home. There is something infinitely resistant in human nature. Man is harder than rock.

No one came except relatives, and they seemed to be doing penance. The taste of power is so intoxicating that it is very difficult to forget.

Nor do we go anywhere, except to visit Dedijer, who lies in bed, half paralyzed by his old wound, which gets worse when he is overtired or psychologically tormented. Something terrible is happening to him! He is in such agony! Are they doing this to him?

Those evening walks to his house through the frozen streets, forcing our way through heavy frost and snow, are somehow pleasant for the two of us, for myself and Štefica.* These miserable icy days have brought us completely together although, at least momentarily, they seem to kill in us any desire or enthusiasm save for the new friendship blossoming before our very eyes.

Meetings with Dedijer, sick, tormented and lonely, are becoming more and more moving. He waits impatiently for us to come and already our visits have become a necessity of life. He gets worried when we do not come. I call him my Roxana, whom Cyrano visits every day at the same hour. But perhaps one day Cyrano will not come. . . .

It is cold. This cold ghastly January reminds me of other Januaries, icy but vague in my memory. It pulls me toward them, toward those long Januaries which are beautiful and warm in my memory. Which Januaries were those? Why can't I recall them and put the most important ones on paper?

No, I will not. But I must, I must! Why? Why?

Why this need to return to the past? Isn't that really just running away from reality? Or is it an instinctive defense of life? In front of me is a wall, thick, solid and insurmountable. There is no life there because it is

* Djilas's second wife.

impossible to either surmount the wall or break through it. But behind
me . . .

The human mind is designed well: it can forget as well as remember.
One can also live the past. By forgetting the present, the past becomes the
present, the living, the reality, despite the fact that it is already past.
How everything in it is beautiful, clean, radiant.

During those granite days and nights, motionless, frozen, accursed,
exhausted, everything runs together from different times and places,
everything mingles and glistens. [. . .]

Why this desire to stop, to return and to salvage past time? How fast
time passes, against all wishes and dreams, how unexpectedly! Has all my
life really passed by already?

What happened?

January 1929. I was in the town of Berane in my last year of high
school. I never dreamed that within my lifetime it would be called Ivangrad in honor of Ivan Milutinović, my friend and my comrade in politics
and in war. It was my fifth year there and already I knew its customs, its
smells, its colors, the distant mountain ranges and the gushing of the blue
Lim which constantly washed its shores.

That January twenty-five years ago the winter was also very severe,
more so than this one. As soon as I reached school the blood would rush
throbbing to my thawing nose. Our icy hands made the school benches
chilly. The little town seemed to bury itself underground and all life
took place round the stove and the fireplace. In the Mokva River the
bitter frost caught the wild geese and ducks unawares and formed crusts
of ice like shackles around their legs. The peasants would find them thus
imprisoned and slaughter them and sell them.

Politics did not interest me very much at the time. I was thrilled by
literature. Still, I was more interested in politics than my classmates and I
was perhaps the only one who read the newspaper *Politika*. Even then I
felt myself to be a Communist, partly due to eccentricity, but more as a
way of objecting to blatant injustice and cruelty. But it was the communism of Hugo and Tolstoy, and not the communism of Marx's political works.

Ever since the summer of 1928 I had been following the terrible
intrigues surrounding the murder of Radić, feeling intensely the injustice
and misfortune that had befallen both peasants and Croats. During the
winter term of 1929, on January 6, the Constitution was abolished and
King Alexander established a dictatorship. [. . .] During the following
week the entire atmosphere in the little town changed completely. It was
as if everything was dirty, poisoned, dangerous. People ceased to gather
together, or if they did they looked at each other despondently, with
shame, their eyes downcast. They dared not say what they wanted to say.
Their spirits were broken. They talked about daily household problems,

about their jobs and wages, but not about what was really bothering them, eating them up inside. [. . .]

But I did not think of the dictatorship as something terrible and tragic, even though I saw very clearly what was going on. This was not because I was eighteen and my painful boyish infatuations were transforming themselves into my first passionate love, which was taking root, becoming firm in my blood and my senses. My love for the fair, plump girl with large eyes, from a distance black but from close up like coffee, was unrealized and unrealizable. [. . .] She was my relative, a close one by our Orthodox Montenegrin standards, and because of that she could never be mine. I suspected that she liked me but I didn't really know. This bothered me constantly and I spent night after night thinking how to determine whether she thought of me only as a brother, or whether as something else. [. . .]

But those were not the reasons the dictatorship did not weigh heavily on my shoulders. [. . .] The dictatorship did not bother my conscience because I did not have to submit to it for the sake of a cause: my country, the state, the concept of unity, for those who had fallen in its name. It could not force such a dilemma upon me, a young man without the nationalistic illusions of the prewar generation. I hated it from the very beginning. With all its being it was alien to me, and my conscience was clear. But, terrible as it is to admit it, it didn't really weigh on my conscience very much. [. . .]

Less than a year after that first clear cruel day in January when those intoxicated words were uttered and caresses exchanged spontaneously, words and caresses that paralyzed and caused darkness to spread over everything, less than a year later we had started down our separate roads not knowing where they led, but always hoping for one thing and finding something else.

That love remained in my memory mostly as an unanticipated and unfulfilled sensual experience—a love started but never finished, for the two of us alone, broken off by our enslavement to social convention. I became a revolutionary and with that my love for her, my entire conscience, and all my behavior had gradually to change. And she had to do what all small-town girls from poor artisan families do—get married, no matter how, the sooner the better. This was as natural for her in the milieu in which we lived as it was for me, in my own environment, to be what I was. [. . .]

Now I am here in the small town with my relative; it is night. For a moment I got lost on Dedinje in someone's villa. For a moment I was traveling in the North, in the Nordic countries. . . .

There, people live simply and modestly, they have a quiet and warm family life, they love music and literature. And slowly, imperceptibly, they developed straightforward relations among people.

But it only looks that way to us who are accustomed to turmoil and plunder. Their dramas are different, more inside themselves, not taking place on fields trampled by conquerors; there are no mothers with crushed ribs; no children with their heads bashed in; there is less treason, less disgrace, less sacrifice, less struggle. But they also know both happiness and despair. [. . .]

For a hundred and fifty years there were no wars. (The expedition of Napoleon's general could hardly be considered a war.) When the reign of Karl XII ended, not only the glory but also the sufferings of war passed from these countries. Fortunately for them they found themselves on the periphery of historic battlefields, which in turn placed them in the center of human history, since human history includes, alongside of war, also peace, alongside of destruction, also the gradual development of social, family and personal life. Except for Hitler's adventure, there has been no serious fighting there for more than three hundred years. From generation to generation people inherited antique furniture, clocks. They modernize and add on to old houses with tall steep red-tiled roofs covered by green ivy and interrupted by slender chimneys.

This continuity of life through things, through small glass objects, jewels, through pleasantly furnished rooms and houses gives a special quality—calm, expressly humane and humanistic—to these people and these countries. To the foreigner it looks like a deep internal peace, even like a certain naïveté and slowness in reasoning. In reality this impression is very superficial, because, inside, their passions seeth and their uncurbed dreams and imagination are going wild all the more violently because the climate and social convention make their free expression more difficult. Life and man turn more deeply inward than in our country. Here's the difference: we are still struggling for a piece of bread to eat and a little bit of freedom, while they are immersed in the problems of the soul. They are moving faster, faster than one can observe. And social relations, at first glance imperceptibly and without any commotion, are moving continually forward according to some internal logic. Only the ceaseless duration of life "stands still," visible as nowhere else in the world. [. . .]

The Nordic peoples think of us as a warm, Southern country with green seas and blue skies, just like the travel brochures. Slim tanned girls with straw hats walk along our coasts, while inland, shepherds with turbans and embroidered vests tend sheep, play the flute or smoke pipes and—occasionally—fight. This is a sorrowful picture of our land and it is not our picture. For us they are quiet, frozen lifeless dwellers in a land of high living standards where there is perpetual harmony among classes and a trite petty-bourgeois contentment. Our picture of them is more deceiving than theirs of us. But in both cases the picture is inaccurate. Reality differs from the notions obtained from postcards and tourist ads, from the ideological schemes and from shallow Marxist-Leninst propaganda or from well-intentioned social democratic prejudices. [. . .]

Finally I am finding myself again. . . . Cast down all alone from the Balkan heights onto an iceberg, as smooth and hard and gray as metal. An iceberg, and I am an iceberg on an iceberg and inside of me there is an iceberg in this unreal transparent icy darkness of January; my strength is tied in a knot, my heart is only a flicker, my thoughts are full of ominous foreboding. . . . Here I am wandering along the coasts of those countries. I fly into their villages and cities, I squeeze down their chimneys past electric fireplaces, which dance with the reddish flames of centuries past as if they were burning large oaken logs, next to them sitting ancient grandmothers like etchings, listening till they fall asleep to the ancient endless embellishments and the countless Bach arias or else talking, murmuring and warm like the waters of spring, telling the ancient, beautiful, cruel Nordic legends. [. . .]

Sweden is mainly flat forest land. Its low shores, gray and hard, like tin, are flayed by brittle howling waves, slashed by the pale icy sea. . . . At night along the shore sprinkled with settlements, endless cheerful strings of light and endless hope and endless warm fires burn in the icy night for the hearts and minds crouching on the decks of ships in this infinity of metallic water that pours out of a million gorges and whips with a million steel lashes. [. . .]

A look at a workers' settlement, if one can call it that—it is so luxurious. And a bit monotonous because of the white of the houses against the parklike green of the spruces and pines. It shows how much these countries, being beyond wars and revolutionary tempests, were able to move not only ahead of us but also far ahead of the rest of Europe. People usually say that their lives lack dynamism. But I don't know what that means. Obviously they don't miss it. If dynamism means wars and mutual extermination in the name of progress, we could do without it too. If only we were able to . . . But if we cannot, if we must endure uprisings and wars, then let us not flinch before our destiny.

Here in Sweden the state stepped into the national economy both as regulator and as owner. The old relations will never be restored here. But the old relations don't scare anybody and no one can conjure up their specter to justify establishing their own scheme of things. [. . .] No thinking person, however, maintains that there are no conservative tendencies in Sweden or that there is no danger of bureaucracy and bureaucratism. Those tendencies are alive and make themselves felt in the demand for an increased role for the bureaucracy, especially the technical bureaucracy. Politically speaking the bureaucracy alternates between the two major parties, not knowing which will be the "ultimate" victor, for if it knew, it would attach itself to the winner. But this is not the real bureaucracy. It is dependent on the real one, on the political bureaucracy, which has power and privileges only because it belongs to a specific political organization and, so it believes, adheres to a specific ideology. But in the North the political bureaucracy is weak. . . .

One conclusion emerges: where the political institutions of democracy are not developed, control by elements of the political oligarchy—the political bureaucracy—will inevitably emerge and it will be stronger in proportion to the weakness of freedom. That is the rule in the contemporary world.

What they could not show us was workers' councils, our workers' self-management, which even here is of interest. But for that our country would not be particularly remarkable except for its heroic struggle for independence. True, our steps in this direction are small, but nonetheless qualitatively new. When we point out to our Nordic friends that this is the most likely road to the withering away of democracy itself, of parties and of the state, that it is the form of continuous liberation of human labor and thought, they do not deny the value of our experience for us, but . . . they do not think it is the only way or the ultimate solution. They do not point to any specific feature of their own as a contrast, but they obviously cannot be shaken in their belief in the permanent and irreplaceable value of spiritual freedom and political democracy.

Still, it is clear—how is it that no Yugoslav who visited Scandinavia ever noticed it before?—that the trade unions, especially in Norway, remain independent from the government and that in the nationalized enterprises they reach collective bargaining agreements with the state. The workers instinctively refused to let themselves be guided by "wise leadership," even by the leadership of their own socialist government, and they do not consider the state as their own but as a specific social instrument they can also make use of.

It seems to me that these questions are important for socialism everywhere. In the case of Nordic socialists, it is as if nothing is final, established once and for all, as if they have no ultimate goal, especially no goal to which existing reality would be subordinate. Not even our discovery of "new" roads to socialism is accepted as anything final. [. . .]

They do not denounce our revolution. I think they even secretly admire our heroism. Like all social democrats, they feel sick deep inside because they are not and cannot be revolutionaries. Their revolutionary origins have not completely vanished from their blood. But, they say, today conditions are different in their country, and we agree with them there. Not only does it not even enter their heads to make the revolution at home, but also they don't even think of making any revolutionary moves. Yet one cannot deny that they are correct.

Once there were revolutionary Communists, and there still are some. But the masses do not support them and there is not the faintest hope that they will ever get their support. Because of the specific circumstances here, where class relations unfold gradually and where the nation and society live and function alongside of old capitalist relations, to talk about revolution not only would be utopian and a forcing of "Russian" or Yugoslav models upon a different reality, but also would make the majority of ordinary people ask, "Why? For what fantastic religious purpose should there be all this poverty, devastation and bloodshed?"

How strange. What we Yugoslav Communists most fervently yearned for, what was our greatest glory, our magnificent accomplishment, here looks unreal, shallow, strange. Such is historical reality. It changes and meanders throughout the world. It does not like anything to be absolute, to be "the best," the "most beautiful." And frequently it gleefully cracks ideological models, transforming what were previously realities into utopias and what were until now the "creators of history" into historical ghosts. [. . .]

It is not an entirely good thing that we came here in the winter. There is something oppressive in this endless two-tone landscape—snow and evergreens—it is both vast and bizarre.

True, while traveling from the north of Sweden to its southern tip in a train that looks more like a sanatorium than a dirty threadbare train compartment, we were intoxicated and lulled by the endless undulating spaces dotted with groves and covered with boundless forests. We were cheered by the gentle hills adorned with evergreens and astounded by the stark contrast of the dark blue of the evergreen and the glistening white of the blinding bareness. We were continually surprised by the flat whiteness of the fields, the frozen lakes, the elegant hotels, sportsmen in gray sweaters with their colorful scarves flapping in the wind. [. . .]

In the summer the meadows are probably pale green, a soft watery green, with sheep white like field poppies and cows yellow, all as if they were painted with solid colors for greater visibility, for the simplicity and for the purity of the landscape itself, to differentiate everything in it— this is grass, this is stone, this is animal, this is a golden-haired freckled girl in a blue dress with white flowers. [. . .]

The squares are tidy and symmetrical. All that developed mostly in the last hundred years, although it is an accumulation of something older. People either go to church or not, but they are not bigots. The vast majority seem to be believers. In any event, it is obvious that religion is a private question, not a political one. We did not ask about it because it would be out of place—like asking an Englishman why he is a monarchist.

Their men are not like ours. They are strong, tall, well-proportioned. But they lack our vivacious expression and our contrast in coloring of eyes, hair and complexion. In general there aren't very many different types. The women, too, are well-proportioned, although large boned and perhaps too athletic and thus not feminine enough for our oriental erotic tastes.

Nordic life continually strives for bright colors because there are so many cruel days here—they don't have our warm sun and sky. Here in Sweden, where everything is white and frozen and where there are neither subtle shadings nor intense colors, the yellow and green door frames and the dark-red brick walls and tiled roofs do not look like pastry decorations, as they would in our country. Even the factories, most of them new and modern, are built in parks next to clear rivers and azure lakes. They are white, with various colors like some modern cathedrals, but they are low and harmonious from all aspects.

In the same way everything else turns toward the sun. One can see here that the sun is the source of life.

For traditional architecture the problem was to capture as much sun as possible while at the same time providing protection from the long harsh winters. Traditional Nordic architecture expresses that conflict. This is probably why the old buildings have so many narrow stylized apertures. Modern architecture lacks that conflict. Perhaps it is more harmonious, although one cannot say it is more beautiful. It turns itself effortlessly toward the sun. New buildings with their large windows expose themselves completely to the farthest corner to the sky and the air. The new architecture evolved slowly, and one can see how the new forms broke through step by step. In the same way democratic forms which imply a larger role for the common people in social affairs broke through old forms slowly.

Everything is visible here. There are no sudden breaks. History did not begin here with this or that generation. The continuity of history is undeniable here. And this is the value, the uniqueness and the beauty of the life of the Nordic peoples. . . .

Their standard of living is high, the highest per capita after the United States. But it is more equally, more equitably distributed than in the United States. Neither a high standard of living nor happiness for its own sake ever seemed to me to be goals in themselves. They are only means for people to develop more humane relationships, to enrich their lives with spiritual meaning and activity instead of being exclusively preoccupied with the inhumane but inevitable struggle for existence. Do people here strive for the same things? Do these people who live so well attain them? What is it like to attain them?

We have been here too short a time to answer with certainty. But are not those values found above all exactly in that steady if slow movement of society? In the absence of significant obstacles to that movement? Because from this stems respect for the human personality and its dignity, the assured right to make decisions freely without bothering others, to seek and to experience the infinite world and to express itself freely. [. . .]

Although the Nordic countries lack our enthusiasm, our drunken sincerity and our uncontrollable outbursts of friendship and love, they also lack our treacheries and our rapid changes in mood.

People say what they think, even if they don't say everything they think; but they will not say something they do not believe.

Relationships among people have long been nurtured and developed here. These relationships are both valued in themselves and are one of the major causes of the gradual nature of social change and of the relatively good relations between political parties. Their entire culture is the product of a long, uninterrupted spiritual development and material prosperity. In this environment the free-thinking Nordic peasant—unknown in the rest of Europe—transformed himself into an employee: of the bank, the factory, modern commerce. Perhaps the free Nordic peasant was only a more convenient vehicle than other peasants for eliminating barbaric relationships. But no matter how progressive he might have been he could not have eliminated those relationships by himself. It was the factory and the machine that forced people to humanize life and their mutual relations. Otherwise they would have destroyed themselves in the mutual struggle. [. . .]

Viewed from the outside, the cultural life—theater, literature, etc.—is not nearly as rich or as exciting as ours. There is less of it, and there are no instant successes, no great hubbub, no self-adulation. But they are incomparably more cultured and refined than we are. Refinement is part of the way of life. They never say of someone, "He is refined." Refinement does not happen, it cannot be produced, it does not stand out, as in our country, but it endures, it radiates in everything. And here is another difference: in our country everything is giddy and unexpected, and here everything is understood in itself, is evident.

Between trains travelers leave their suitcases in parks and railway stations. Where there are few thieves, it is very easy to catch them. This proves another point—where there is no extreme misery, neither is there much crime. Crime does not follow from human nature, or does so only exceptionally, but is the product of social conditions.

Many aspects of their social relations appear to us idyllic and a bit strange to our semioutlaw ways of thinking. We could even have visited the King. Here in Sweden and in the other Nordic countries this is not at all difficult or unusual; it is not even a very special privilege, although it is valued as a sign of attention and respect on both sides. The King's life and the court have no mystical splendor. They are symbols of state sovereignty, but it would be giving them too much authority to say that they are crowned presidents of republics.

Slowly some inborn need for simplicity and politeness captures us. . . .

But enough of this! I am bored by it! What did I accomplish by escaping into fantasy?

Am I escaping from one reality and idealizing another?

Yes, and no . . .

I am not seeking a reality more beautiful than ours, even though ours shreds my every nerve into a thousand pieces every second, even though it drives my thoughts into a dreamlike muddle. To remain here and to burn myself out in our reality and for our reality. Only he who wants to be free of his conscience can lose it, only someone for whom everything was over in 1945, finished with the revolution and his own personal destiny in it. . . .

And that wandering, that dream, that excursion is nothing more than a transposing of oneself and of this Yugoslav world into another world in order that this one become clearer and closer, more terrible in all of its murderous, unattainable grace and its hideousness.

I don't like you Nordic countries, with all your wealth, your social harmony, your distant black mountains and your white plains. I want my country!—its bitterness and its poisons, its joys and its splendors. I want to plunge into its dank, foul cellars and into its misery and dirt, its lies and betrayals, so that I may ascend into its sunny and drunken assault on the stars, on unattainable bliss. . . .

January again, the year was 1932.

The first demonstrations against the dictatorship—they were student demonstrations—had just ended. They were provoked by the elections of November 1931, in which there was only one electoral list, that of the Commandant of the King's Guard, Petar Živković. Just before one demonstration I was the speaker in the assembly hall of the Law Faculty. After we left the hall we went out onto the narrow Karadžić Street intending to march down Knez Mihailova Street in the center of town. But the police attacked us and broke up our march just as we reached our destination. The site of the demonstration was immediately transferred to the student dormitories, which became the real stronghold of the movement. It was the natural gathering place of students, and the police could have seized the dormitory only by using weapons, which the regime did not dare to do because of the strong tradition of university autonomy and because of public opinion. [. . .] After the demonstration the police searched for me, and as soon as I could get away, I disappeared for a month, going down to Kotor to stay with the Mitrović family. At the end of December, when everything had calmed down, I went to visit my family in Lješnica, near Bjelo Polje, for the month of January. [. . .]

In January 1934, two years later, I was already a political prisoner in the Sremska Mitrovica jail. Impatiently I counted the days of the three months of solitary confinement which was just coming to an end. I

listened with excitement each evening as I heard, each time as if for the
first time, the revolutionary songs of my fellow prisoners resounding from
the bowels of the neighboring buildings. And as always, before each new
experience, I could hardly wait to join them. But as always, before each
new experience, I was overwhelmed by anxiety: had I done everything I
should have? Hadn't I done something wrong and brought shame upon
myself? Was I worthy to pass through the gates to this new life?

Then came the years of illegal activity and jail which at first glance
may appear undistinguished and monotonous but in reality every moment of which was exciting.

Eight years later it was January 1942, and the Četnik and Italian
forces had attacked Nova Varoš. I had to retreat into the forests across the
Lim River. Day and night marches through blizzards and drifts with the
wounded and the refugees, the patient Serbian Partisans, the nostalgic
Sandžak Partisans. [. . .]

As I see it, we are fighting the war for freedom and for socialism; it is
our final debt to the USSR. Is this war the revolution we waited and
longed for, only in a different form? How long will it last? The Germans
will lose. We Communists must win. Only we are fighting as one should
fight. There will be many more marches and offensives, there will be
hunger, injuries and death; but after that—happiness and freedom, the
ultimate dreams of mankind, will be attained in our own country. . . .

January 1944. After a minor offensive, a nervous and tedious waste of
time, in Drvar, we are waiting for winter to pass and for the thaw so that
we can begin the last and most powerful campaign of the war.

And now . . .

What remains of the prewar and wartime dreams? Of the jails, the
bloodshed, the hunger? East Europe is covered with stakes and gallows.
Revolutionary consciences are ground down by the treads of Stalin's
tanks, either making peace with reality or willingly accepting sentence
for treason. There they do not just shoot people—that would be too easy.
First they rip out their souls, they destroy their awareness and their will,
they crush human feelings. There . . . And in the West there is fear and
hysteria and a spineless collapse before the prophets of doom who play on
the fears of war to attain mastery first of their own country and then . . .
Fear, religion and continual entertainment lull the people into acceptance. There . . .

In Yugoslavia both East and West are contained in a single cup into
which are crowded all the contradictions of the contemporary world. We
were . . . Focus . . . Splendor . . . Fire . . . And now, we are the cup
of all bitterness. . . . It seems to me we shall have to drink it, all of it,
drop by drop.

And now, I am in Norway. . . . In my dreams . . . Am I running
away from that bitter poison? There should be no running away. One

must drink all of it, not escape. But to dream is not to run away. The dream is life, the life that survives, the life that cannot be destroyed as long as one lives.

Why is everything in such sharp relief in dreams, sharper and more precise than in life? [. . .]

Norway is the country for me.

Norway, with its wild cliffs and its gentle fields and fjords carved into granite mountains, with contrasting lights, from nights as dark as tar to mornings glaring as if the sun shown down from the sky onto the metallic water and reflected directly onto us—this country is more for me and my moods. Lots of wilderness and unruliness, very little that is tame, but at the same time somehow gentle and complete. A country that is sudden and unpredictable in everything, at each step. I shall try to make Norway come alive in me,[4] with its abruptness and its contrasts, its beauty harder than granite that engraves itself into one's memory with the permanence of granite.

Here in Norway the land conquered the sea, and man conquers nature.

The icy ocean, the freezing weather and the storms gnaw at the granite and crumble it, streak it, extrude it, sharpen and pound it—now needles, now heavy black monstrous crags, now cliffs so smooth and polished, so shiny black that the eye does not halt in the thousand-meter sweep from sea to sky. Now ominous and dark, now pale and diabolic, but always hard, the water cuts to the very nerve, to the marrow of the mountains and crumbles the land into thousands of islands scattered along the shore like a routed army, stretches it into narrow, low peninsulas, cuts it into straight heavy slabs. . . .

But the land resists, as peoples and nations resist in their perpetual struggle with misfortune and foe, and when each wave breaks, new islands arise from the depths of the sea and warn the tireless razor-sharp waves which slice incessantly that they are there and that when they disappear there will be others to spend themselves, to be killed defending their body—the land and the shore.

Perhaps some mathematician could compute how many years or even days or hours the sea would need to erode, undermine and finally topple the Norwegian land mass. But to us, as far as the human mind can project, it is the land that has defeated the sea, defeated it once and for all, even if there is ever less of it. The land rose and rebelled against the

4. I am not the first Yugoslav to write about this country. More poetic pens and more observant eyes and greater knowledge than mine have been here. Forty years ago Isidora Sekulić was here and brought to us in Yugoslavia a picture of this country in her incomparable "Letters from Norway." [. . .] These Norwegian pages are as much hers as mine, with maybe the difference that she traveled here as a writer and I as a politician, she in a different and perhaps less confused time, and I now, and—most important—she in reality and I in a dream. . . .

sea, against its external might, and stands defiantly; it rends the sky and thrusts its extremities in all directions, striding fearlessly into the ice-cold steel water which has no bottom or limit. . . . And thus the land stands defiant as only human thought can be defiant, and will stand as long as there is man to admire it and to learn from its example.

The clash of the elements and the extreme contrasts in form, color and sound are the characteristics of Norway. The gloomy and ponderous Ibsen next to the contented and reflective Grieg; peaceful blue fjords in black clouded cliffs . . .

In this cruel climate, with this landscape torn by the rough sea and storms, there is little fog. This is not a land of fog but of natural furies and of something else—of a wild and angry sun which appears either briefly or which shines day and night, a frightening violet radiance that penetrates everywhere, into all corners, into the dreams of children and the secret thoughts of adults, from which none can escape because it attracts with its horror and its murderous beauty.

As the land wrested itself away from the sea, so did man withstand nature—the land, the sea, the vast pale sky, smooth and cold and motionless into which jets fly and lose themselves as gently as in a dream.

And nowhere more than here in the clash of the elements with human toil does man seem more a part of the cosmos or more one of the terrible, incomprehensible games of nature.

And nowhere does one feel more the force of man than here in this harsh inhospitable landscape. Nowhere are his efforts more visible, mainly because nature so resists. Perhaps nowhere as much as here should one pity, love and admire man. Here he has shown what he can do when he must and how his courage and his strength is spent without measure, without limit, without mercy. [. . .]

Norway is a living picture of this continual struggle. As a country of the most meager, the most inadequate natural possibilities, it is still a marvel even for the modern world and its technology.

It does not suffice, it seems to me, to explain its standard and the degree of its development only by its high level of technology, which made superprofits possible, or its temporary monopoly profits in the shipbuilding industry. The question is how did Norway manage to master such technology. And here the inherited social relations—nurtured and further developed by the struggle of the working class—played an unusually important role.

Freedom is the best builder—the most diligent, the most economical and the fastest. Norway is the living proof of that. Civil liberties and socalled bourgeois democracy existed here even before modern technical progress and obviously made the development of the latter easier.

We Yugoslavs must not lose sight of this, especially after our bitter Soviet experience.

Because just as the despotic forms of Eastern Europe and of the East in general were and are still in some places necessary for the nation to liberate itself from colonialism and technical backwardness, in the same manner democratic political forms were necessary for industrial growth and for the completion of the Industrial Revolution in Western Europe and in the West in general. There in the West that process was accompanied by bourgeois revolutions and by bourgeois democratic forms; here in the East, much later, it was accompanied by socialist revolutions and state capitalist bureaucratic forms. This division is crude and oversimplified but it is nonetheless valid. It pertains to the past. But the present has not yet abolished this division, although forms are converging and signs of each one are appearing in the other so that the differences are no longer as clear.

Norway added new content to old freedoms.

If in the past Lenin could say that Western democracy was merely formal, that it applied only to the bourgeoisie, the owning classes, today that is completely untrue. No one can seriously maintain that any longer. The working class pushed its way in, scraped out the old molds or pushed them aside with its crude creative strength and created new relations and transformed the old ones into instruments of its struggle. Change is certain within democracy itself, and democracy is no longer what it used to be.

Norway is not only a living example of a different—democratic—route to socialism, but also an affirmation that without ordinary simple freedom for ordinary people, there can be not only no socialism, but also no real progress of any kind.

Contemporary Norway understood the significance of science for modern industrial development. That knowledge does not come from the high technical level of the nation, from some intrinsic or inherited feeling for machines and innovation, but from painful and expensive historical experience. This nation, which conquered the sea in order to live on it and from it, almost lost the sea. The steam revolution took Norway by surprise; it destroyed overnight its shipping industry, based on the sail, and it impoverished the nation. Decades were necessary for Norway to recuperate before the face of the country shone again. Now Norway invests vast sums of money in the development of atomic energy and in modern science. [. . .] Investment in science is really investment in industry, in the standard of living, in better dwellings and in a bigger piece of bread. Each industry, no matter how modern, can fall behind overnight if it is not backed up by modern science. Norway, like England, understands that lesson, learned that lesson well.

And this lesson is more important for us than any ideological lesson. But we Communists think of ourselves as destined to teach others.

Instead of shamefully cursing intellectuals because of their "petty bourgeois" backgrounds and their "ideological backwardness," and instead of wasting funds on all kinds of nonsense, it would be better to concentrate on science and to leave men of science and learning in peace. In postwar Yugoslavia less was spent on real science and research than was spent for bureaucratic office posts, and for the latter there is, of course, no accounting. [. . .]

How do the Norwegian people live? How do they live socially?

The average man is only slightly engaged in politics between elections, mainly by following the press. He is not forced to participate in politics, nor is he condemned to be a silent observer of mysterious games in the party elite. Even the activity of the party is only felt minimally. Party feelings run high before elections but otherwise feelings are lethargic, made weak by the lack of interest of the average citizen. Social relations are stable, political forms established, and at election time the consciousness of the masses grows. But that does not mean that the people are disinterested in world events or that they are unaware of what is going on. But still they don't get very excited about politics. Somebody will win and somebody will lose at the elections, but life as a whole will not suddenly change with the results of the election, because things move slowly, they do not leap, they live continually and not by sudden revivals.

Family life here is relatively closed. There are outings every Sunday, active participation in the social organizations that the people themselves formed and that the chaos of life forced upon them. They read a lot, they have a small circle of close but lifetime friends, they struggle stubbornly for their standard of living and for each penny, they love music to the point of losing themselves in it but in it they come alive—very strange for Nordic people—in some inward, more reflective and perhaps even more emotional manner than we do.

Norwegians are on the whole religious, regardless of their political party, but this does not mean that they deny the achievements of science or the existence of the objective material world. Religion seems to be some kind of convention, some inherited obligation of society and life which existed before and from which man arose. Science and scientific discoveries are understood for themselves, and just as religion is a habit, it is assumed to be possible, it is assumed that there is some law above those we can discover. [. . .]

They don't have any fixed philosophy, not even socialist. It seems to me that empiricism is most suitable for people who wrestle with the catastrophes of nature but who at the same time secure fairly easily their basic existence.

That, it seems to me, is the greatest weakness of this nation and its leaders. But maybe it isn't. Perhaps it is a virtue.

We Yugoslav Communists think that we must have an ideology—a single ideology, one not only for us but for the entire nation, despite the fact that willy-nilly we transform our ideology into fanaticism. Norway can obviously exist without that, without monopolistic ideologies. Such ideologies would obviously be destructive and stifling there.

Really, for everyday life and for ordinary people empiricism is both convenient and attractive. That is the way they think and live. But despite all that, it seems to me that when great events are involved, historic dramas, nations rising from the dust into the sun—it is a philosophy of lethargy.

It seems to me that social progress would have been quicker and relations among people more humane if theories had been more realistic. But here they can obviously live without theory, perhaps because they are prosperous. Obviously they don't need any social philosophy above and beyond what corresponds to immediate reality and its problems. But we who are poor, we can only fall to lower levels without some ultimate philosophy, even if it is preposterous and unrealistic. . . .

Is it true that those developed nations are moving more slowly spiritually than they should be, based on their technical degree of development? Or does it just seem this way to me? Few stand taller than the average, but the average is quite high. Or is this the real, natural life of people and nations toward which one should aim? I was too long in a closed—Communist—world to be able to comprehend the world outside of it easily.

And we, we tear ourselves apart with convulsions to break away from the average, from technological backwardness.

But for what purpose all this confused "philosophical" torment? Perhaps I am searching for myself and my country in space, all alone? What is the purpose of ideology and philosophy if they cannot. . . .

But my country and my party no longer have an ideology, they have no principles. Naked power cannot be either an ideal or a goal. This must not happen. One must not let it. . . .

What is the purpose of all this?

In the end, for every society, what matters is freedom.

Only a free man—and freedom is relative, of course—could have wrested a living from this cruel environment and from man himself who was accustomed to dominate other men. [. . .]

But perhaps none of this is real. Perhaps it only seems more beautiful because of the contrasts, because of the confusions and suspicions that have taken hold of my country and of myself.

Let it be so. Let this be a dream about my country, even if not about what I would desire for it, what I would dream for it, but only about that which might have been. Let those cliffs that reach to the sky be the men of my country, those quiet vales the women and the girls!

Toil and struggle, no matter how—isn't that freedom? Isn't that for the free man?

Near the Lofoten Islands, among the richest fishing grounds in the world, we saw what the Norwegian wrests from nature without drama and without bragging and what patient and unostentatious acts of bravery he is capable of. [. . .] The Lofoten Islands are in the Gulf Stream, and although they are much farther north than the continent, in this cold and gray weather these mild islands cheered us the moment we sailed into their green waters. [. . .] At midnight, dressed in warm waterproof coats and boots, we sailed out on the first fishing boat. [. . .] Morning found us in waters so full of fish that the ships appeared to be sailing in a hearty fish soup. [. . .] Just when the tempo of work reached its highest pitch, still orderly and with no confusion, an old bearded fisherman, sweat dripping from his face, tugging slowly on a rope, with a pleasant smile on his broad firm lips that showed his large even teeth, asked us, "They say your fishermen are brave. Why don't they come to the northern seas?" . . .

Our fishermen will come because they are brave and proud. They will sail across all seas and cross all mountains and overcome unforeseen obstacles. They are moving slowly and uncertainly on their own soil with a strength they were not aware of and still aren't and with skills they barely know they have. It isn't so far from the South to the North in this world that day by day comes closer together and that merges despite contradictions, conflicts and insularity.

For nothing can destroy a world that exists because it is in motion and that is in motion because it exists; a world that does not exist but becomes, that exists by being. Equally indestructible is the thought radiated by society—each time anew through the individual—the essential, the most subtle, the most beautiful emanation, without which the world would not know of itself and without which man would not know of the world. . . . Thought can be neither destroyed nor cut down nor imprisoned, because it is matter and energy. Imperceptibly and untiringly it roots about and taps ceaselessly in minds whether asleep or awake; it moves hands to work and souls to rapture. Even now it burns low but is not extinguished in our people, in myself, in our fishermen who will yet come to the Northern seas, because they do not fear ice and desolation, nor do they fear loneliness and endless expanse.

The embers smolder on; thought dissolves walls, compresses distances. And I am here in this little room, all alone, by myself. And yet it is as if the entire human race were right here, with all its bitterness, and were about to burst into song—sometime, "for some distant generation"—with a joy and love that could not exist without the desolation and the bitterness.

It is night.
How much longer the darkness?
Ice and frost attack from all sides.
When will the thaw come? When will the dawn come?
Why do the stars fall
    in the sky and new ones fail to rise?

January 29, 1954 (unpublished)

10
Jail Diary

In the contemporary world—at least in the world in which I live—as a rule, ambition governs men.

I have never known a man who was totally free of ambition. That includes myself, although I controlled myself with skill and with determination.

The worst of all is that ambition—even the most innocent and most justified ambition—warps one's understanding of men and of relations among men.

Friendship is relative. In bureaucracy and in state capitalism, since all categories of conduct are overturned (that is, all categories of the normal, inherited morality of common man), friendship is meaningless. Moreover, a bureaucrat is even commended and thanked if he manages to rid himself with ease of a past friendship, naturally with the good excuse that it is all for the sake of the "revolution."

What the term Marxism means today has no more connection with the real Marx and his theory than does the contemporary church with the Bible. Even if "Marxism" is a logical extension of Marxian thought, it should be rejected as reactionary since by its ideological monopolism it stifles the freedom of the human spirit. In that "Marxism" there is nothing new, nor is it capable of creating anything new. It is nothing else but petty politics and politicking, which defends *naked power* and authoritarianism, covering itself clumsily with ideas and ideals, some of which could even be real.

Diary of Thoughts, 1953–1954 (unpublished)

Thoughts about Prison and the Outside World

January 21, 1958
Tonight snow fell, and from the light outside one could see on the wall shadows of snowflakes, like butterflies fluttering by. It is more pleasant

with the snow and the frost; the rain and fog lasted too long, and I didn't feel good. [. . .]

I observe here in solitary confinement, where a man focuses his thoughts upon himself, that I know several hours in advance, depending on my mood, what the weather will be. Even changes in the weather! This morning I am feeling chipper. [. . .]

January 30, 1958

The cold weather continues. Hoarfrost on the arbor vitae makes them even more beautiful. Not even the sun, which breaks through and clears up the fog during the day, succeeds in melting the snow on the paths and the hoarfrost. Every evening around six they turn on the heat for about fifteen minutes. Not much help in that, except one can go to bed a little more comfortably.

My day looks like this: 5:30—rising (in the summer, an hour later); 6:30—emptying the chamberpot; 10:30—walk (an hour and a half; up to now the walk has usually been at 8:30 and lasted only an hour); 1:30—dinner; 3:30—an hour's walk; 7:00—p.m.—supper; bedtime, by regulation, is at 9:00 (the bell rings 15 minutes before that). I now go to bed around suppertime because I am cold. I seldom take supper, and sometimes not even breakfast (chicory coffee). During the day, I lie dressed underneath three blankets and read with gloves on my hands. [. . .]

During the winter I give some crumbs to the sparrows. They have already gotten to know me and they are waiting. I want to help them during these cold, snowy days.

The weather remains cold.

I looked at the calendar and remembered that I have already been here a year.

Fog in the morning. But during the day, beautiful blue skies. [. . .]

January 31, 1958

Food:

Breakfast: always chicory coffee.

Dinner: Potatoes, beans, cabbage (in winter, sauerkraut, very good), rice. The food is thicker than a chowder. There is little fat or spices, but it is well cooked and clean.

Supper: like dinner. Sometimes, as at dinner, split peas or noodles.

Quantity: always a ladle of a half liter. Also, half a kilo of bread (very good wheat bread), except for those doing heavy work, who get 700 grams, and those who are on discipline (in solitary confinement), who get only 300 grams.

Meat: three times a week (Tuesday, Thursday, Sunday)—cooked in with the food, in very small pieces.

In comparison with the prewar food here in Sremska Mitrovica Prison the fare is no worse today. There is no less bread; it is even somewhat tastier. Without the addition of lard, sugar and vitamins, the food would be insufficient.

Packages: 10 kilograms a month. And the right to buy in the prison store food up to a value of 1,500 dinars (including 1.5 kilograms of lard and a maximum of 1.5 kilograms sugar. [. . .]

February 9, 1958

I have grown quite accustomed to life in a cell, and sometimes I even feel good. Is that the human power of adaptation? Or is it something changing in me? [. . .] Sometimes I feel freer than ever before in my life—my thought is free, my conscience at peace.

It is thawing fast. It's a nice day—scrubbing time! I have neglected my room during the winter. [. . .]

February 10, 1958

It was accidental that I began this diary. And now I like it: I note down trivia and minor thoughts—anything that comes to my mind. [. . .]

February 13, 1958

In everyday political reality humanism shows itself to be unrealistic and unreal. But it is a reality of the greatest spirits—an irresistible and unquenchable yearning of man for ever greater humaneness. Choosing between Erasmus and Luther, I would always choose Luther, but wish to be like Erasmus. Striving for the good in the battle against evil, man does not dare renounce evil methods. When among wolves, one must have sharper and stronger teeth. And evil is all that which is used by others to strengthen their might and mastery.

February 14, 1958

I add the following to the above: coercion and evil generally win over humanism and good, but the latter always regenerate themselves and are born anew. They are creators of the great and the beautiful, even when defeated. They change history. They are what is noble in man, trampled and tragic, but indestructible, pure, and brilliant.

February 17, 1958

One should always be opposed to any monolithic party ideology in socialist parties. Monolithic ideology brings with it centralism and the rule of one small group of doctrinaire men. Men should be united by realizable, accessible ideals, and not by some abstract formula of impossible ideals. [. . .]

Marriage is a very great sacrament and can represent for many people one of the greatest moral bonds and obligations. Even people who are not good can become so in marriage; marriage can be the strength that bends their characters toward the good. Because marriage is—regardless of its different forms through history—one of those enduring and eternal characteristics of human life. Therefore, one should honor it, and not interfere in it. This applies to both individuals and the state. The state should secure marriage as much as possible by noninterference. [. . .]

March 1, 1958

It is absolutely untrue that in jail, and especially in a cell, one's senses become sharper. It only seems so to a condemned man, and also to myself. There is so little to which one can react, so that when something is observed—something unusual, out of the ordinary—it stands out sharply and appears as if one's senses are especially acute. [. . .]

March 7, 1958

A note: although I am an atheist, I think that it is not so good to be without a church here. The majority of the prisoners are religious, and for them a church would be a great consolation. Anyway, by means of it, the principle of freedom of conscience would be realized. Surely, it might prove useful too for the re-education of some of the convicts. But I don't think that one should abolish the movie (now located in the prewar church building) in order to re-establish the church; the introduction of movies was a very sensible and useful decision. [. . .]

March 9, 1958

The regime over me is finally completely stabilized: I have two guards who follow me everywhere: on my walks, bathing, and when I go to the toilet or for water. They stand, sit, or walk in front of my door. [. . .] I scarcely meet anyone in the corridor except for the orderlies when I receive food.

A good mood is still upon me. I would even say that my internal peace is getting stronger and deeper. [. . .]

March 17, 1958

My son, Aleksa, Štefica told me, is always dreaming up ways to set me free. And in that connection he asked me yesterday, "Which is stronger, tanks or airplanes?" When I answered him, he said, "You know I have tanks, and I could liberate you." In imagination he has probably accomplished that already. In his wonderfully innocent world there is already a grain of evil—father is in jail—there are struggles to free him. [. . .]

March 23, 1958

As I think back—I have been cold all my life. In primary school I was poorly dressed. In high school, the same. And I lived far from the school.

At the University—not a single winter did I live in a room with heat (except for the last winter, when I slept on the cement floor in a steam-heated kitchen). In my first jail term, I was cold. When it was over, I was still cold. Then came the war; and again it was cold. During the winter after the war we did not heat our first villa. In the second villa (Ninčić), it was warm. But I spent the winters of '50 and '51 in the city and it was cold there again. When I returned to the villa, there was electric heat, but it was expensive. I didn't use it. Instead, we made a fire only in the bedroom. We were thrown out of the villa into the cold again—at Palmotićeva 8. The heat was not strong enough to allow one to sit for a long time, and we had a fire only in the afternoon. Often I stayed up working until two or three in the morning! And now, this place . . . I have grown accustomed to cold; it doesn't bother me any more. But I often think that if I save myself from jail and ever have some money, I will spend the rest of my life being warm. Because of that recurring wish, I make a note of this. [. . .]

March 24, 1958

While in jail before my second trial I finally turned against war. Not for humanitarian reasons, for I know that people will wage war as long as tyranny and evil and the conditions that create them exist. Whether they will ever vanish, no one knows for sure! In my decision to oppose war, two factors played the major role: first, the conscious knowledge that the social relations within Communism are capable of change—over a long period of time, of course—without war; and second, the spontaneous feeling that it would be best for my country to stay out of war, that is, to remain neutral. [. . .] Obviously, this does not mean that I think there will be no war. On the contrary, I believe that war is inevitable. But a true democrat or socialist must fight against it, though not in such a way as to give in to evil and hegemony. If in a future war anyone should be victorious—ultimately there would be a victor—then he would have so much power that it would mean the beginning of a new evil and a new war. For the same reasons, I am against atomic weapons except in self-defense. The killing of women is incompatible with democracy, with human decency and with chivalry. It is stupid to try to determine in conventional ways who is responsible for the Cold War. We are not speaking of the First World War or, even less, of the Second World War. Such an attempt leads to the dogmatism of just and unjust wars, and that is not applicable to the present conflict. [. . .]

[. . .] Each theory, each philosophy transforms itself into a myth the moment it ceases to be relatively true, that is, at the moment when it ceases to be the most believable and the most truthful theory. But there is no knowing when that will happen, when it will pass into myth; it is only when an opposing theory appears or when life itself makes the old theory superfluous. Among all the philosophies that have existed so far, Aristotle's is perhaps the closest to science, and despite that, it too became a myth—that is, it became accepted without questioning—at the very moment when science began to challenge it and new theories (Copernican and Galilean) began to oppose it. Marxian ideas were inspired by science and rested in part upon science. So did Lenin's ideas and those of others. Where today is the classless society or the withering away of the state that Marx imagined? It is a myth. A classless society is, perhaps, possible, but we have no empirical evidence for it. It is obvious, even in situations where events developed in close accord with Marx's theory, that society is not coming closer to, but is moving farther away from abolishing class differences. The Leninist party and its unity also became such a myth. Many things in it today are just the religious expressions and ecstasies of atheists, and yet it began as the negation of everything religious and mystical.

Such, it seems, is the fate of ideas.

And yet, people cannot exist without ideas. Moreover, ideas are one of the conditions of their life and movement, of their humanization. I underestimated myths earlier, maintaining that everything is "conditioned by matter" (of course it is, but not in such a mechanical way). At the Third Plenum in January 1954 when they toppled me, I felt quite strongly about the indestructibility of ideas, especially contemporary ideas, and, as I expressed them, correct ideas. I still firmly believe in them. Men cannot live without ideas, for ideas are the means of orientation in a given reality, that is, in the everyday life of man. Ideas can be destroyed only by time and by other ideas, providing, that is, they have absorbed and expressed the real course of events in the world around us. Moreover, other means used against ideas serve only to affirm them more and even strengthen them. We are talking here about "progressive" ideas—those that most accurately represent the given reality of hopes, wishes and efforts of specific men—whether nations, classes or strata. Great and beautiful in given conditions, they are small from the viewpoint of eternity. Yet people do not live in eternity; they live in time.

April 24, 1958

Contemporary men admire power. I do not know how much or in what way this admiration is expressed in the West, since I do not know the philosophies of those men, but I believe that it exists in some form there also. It exists within all men, or within almost all men, no matter how educated and intelligent they are.

I cannot explain this to myself. Such reasons as fear, material dependence, flattery and blind worship are insufficient. Of course, for those reasons power is admired by many persons. But is seems to me that there is a special and deeper reason: human communities cannot thrive without power; it is "inherent" that no human community can survive without power such as corresponds to the external or internal circumstances and to the nature of the community itself. Of course, a primitive tribe has no governmental power in the form of police or courts, but it has spiritual power administered by priests. The latter punish only those violations against blood relatives or against the tribe as a whole. The modern state is characterized by force, which is its typical and perhaps its basic characteristic. But it has another characteristic: the expression of the consensus of the community. These two elements—force and consensus (the latter as inevitable as life within the community) go hand in hand.

And the moment something is inevitable it receives a higher meaning in the eyes of men, especially if it is supported by power. The worship of power is only one expression, a distorted one at that, of the inevitability of power within human communities and human life.

And power—both its specific form and the institutions that exercise it—acquires even sooner the mythological form.

Finally let me end this discourse about myths. They contain within themselves at first something real and rational (as an attempt to explain something). Their roots are to be found in some need—material, social, or spiritual. But the moment they separate themselves from that need, the moment they perfect themselves as a form, the moment men forget their origins—the myths disappear. Man's life is full of myths and men are barely aware of them. The past lasts through myths, within them. Because the spiritual world still goes on. Because, because, because . . .

April 25, 1958

The reasons for the rude attacks on me at the Congress are becoming more obvious. The major reasons were to stifle any rational discussion of my views within the party and to react to the complaints from without, that is from the East, about the party's "lack of determination" toward me. In any case we live at a time and within a country where everything is visible and where everyone wants to find the truth. This is not the Stalin-Trotsky era, when ideological disagreements could be resolved within the closed circle by simply accusing opponents of being responsible for all the evil in this and in the future world. As far as I am concerned, I do not see any concrete consequences from those "new" accusations, and I remain steadfast in my positions, as I have thus far.

But this train of thought interrupted the earlier one, which is the continuation of my notes from yesterday.

I never wanted to be in power, nor did I seek power, either subconsciously or otherwise. I paid little attention to titles, decorations and the like. I was interested in bringing down the old system and old ideas. Even when I was in power I was full of anxiety, for I realized that one thing was not good, that another should be changed, that still another progressed too slowly, or that something over there was outdated. I could not even comprehend why power is so dear to men. I did not comprehend that power, along with property, is the major material motivater of human struggles, desires and passions. Those two are the major levers of social struggles. However, I was not even very interested in material goods. And everything that was made for me and given to me—villas, automobiles and the like—was done mainly against my wishes. My resistance to things is seen even by the fact that when I was thrown out of my villa on Dedinje, my furniture was so poor by petty-bourgeois standards that I barely had anything to sell except for some personal possessions— hunting rifles, books. And how did all that look in other, comparable homes? I do not regret this. On the contrary, I just present it as a personal fact.

When I fell from power, however, not only did I feel all the significance of the fall, but I also realized that power is the most terrible human passion—even within me, despite the fact that I was indifferent toward it while in power. That does not mean that I craved power or crave it now, since I was mostly interested in ideas. Yet each struggle contains within itself a struggle for power and influence. Alas, there are no pure ideas—perhaps not even in arts and science. Yes, power and property. [. . .]

April 29, 1958

Yesterday they gave me my new prison number: 1732. Up to now I have been number 6880. I bought scallions and radishes. I took much pleasure in the green leaves of the young scallions. They reminded me of my birthplace. There in Podbišće scallions grew in the summer. I was sent to cut their leaves. Many handfuls were put on the table and we all grabbed at them.

This anger and excitement because of insults against me [at the party Congress] diminished yesterday. I felt quite pleasant, despite the cold and rainy weather. Yes, changes in the weather affect one's disposition— any steady weather pattern maintains also my steady disposition, as a rule. But one's good mood often is the result of reasons other than weather.

I see, after all, that isolation has already made me painfully sensitive. How far will this sensitiveness go? What kind of person will I be after three, or five, or seven years?

I observed one characteristic within myself which has developed spontaneously: I am careful not to step on any insect or worm I find along my path. In my room I gather them onto a piece of tin and empty them into the wastebasket. Only the spider is permitted to roam at will. But outside I do not step upon anything, except unintentionally. That is not because of any philosophy. I just feel respect toward life, toward every living thing, as if each form were one of the stages culminating in human life and from which the latter has sprung up. It sometimes seems to me that the differences between myself and the benevolent ladybug whom I meet along the path are really minimal. Even the ladybug in its own way "thinks" and struggles in the world and lasts as long as it is allowed to. Life is neither beautiful nor ugly, neither happy nor sad. [. . .]

May 22, 1958

I was told that all foreign books are forbidden to me. They kept the review of *Land Without Justice* from the New York *Times*. I wrote immediately in angry protest. Obviously some pettiness—a "tightening" up. For what purpose? Still, this made me a little angry—and throws me off in my spiritual life and my work.

I lost all interest in ants, bees and bugs. And maybe I did not. During my walks, I stroll a little and then lie down to sun myself if there is sun, and then I think about what I am writing. That is so precious to me that nothing else enters my mind.

I planted an apricot, and it has sprouted. It progresses poorly. If someone does not pull it out, I hope to nurse it and make it grow. The arbor vitae and the pepper are not sprouting. [. . .]

June 4, 1958

They confiscated the letter from Milka [his sister]. Disgusting. I can bear more pain than they can impose on me. A little war of nerves. I am writing a protest—like Yugoslavia protesting to the USSR. [. . .]

June 15, 1958

In order to prevent me from sunning myself, they changed my walk back to 7:30 in the morning instead of 9:30. Must not react!

Yesterday *Politika* announced the shooting of Imre Nagy and other comrades. I am very sorry for him. I often thought that a similar fate awaited me. I always felt that he and I were alike in many respects. Except that I wrote. Perhaps he would have done the same, had he had the chance, although he was not a writer. I had just finished *The New Class* when the Hungarian Revolution took place. Nagy died an honest death. And that means a lot. Even more than if he had remained alive. I believe that he will remain a great man in the history of Hungary, although he was not able to accomplish much of anything. He proved that in Communism there are democratic and socialist men, although they are mostly utopians, who end up like us. His views remained unknown, but his practice did not, and it guided him. It would have been better if some things had been clearer to him. Perhaps he would not have been caught. His cause, however, did not suffer from his death. His cause does not exist, because it was not formulated. But he does, and he chose Hungary at the decisive moment. His cause: Hungary and freedom.

From here, upon hearing the news of his death, I pay him my respects, which any honest man owes to martyrs.

His death is also the symptom of the resistance to change in the East. And a symptom of the international sharpening of tensions. [. . .]

June 20, 1958

They restored my walk again to 9:30. Do not react. Since last night I have again been seriously considering a hunger strike.

The only real and justified ideal in politics is freedom.

Politics which in practice (and thereby also in theory) loses its ideal, that is, its ideas, sooner or later must come to a dead end. The same applies to politics which loses its morality, that is, politics which chooses not to select among the means, which in the final analysis is equivalent to subordinating the end to the means, or, as it is better known: the end justifies the means.

Although ideas do not mean much in politics—nothing is possible without them. Although the only realizable goals are immediate and direct, without goals one can do even less. The ideas, the goals, determine the direction of movement. They also enable a particular politics to be moral, even if it resorts to cruel means. It needs only to fall into justifying the means by the end.

Man cannot live without ideals, and yet they are unreal. Man lives in reality, and only in it, but he always strives for something more beautiful than that reality, for something ideal. It is exactly the same in politics. The moment that ideal disappears—politics finds itself in a dead end. [. . .]

June 24, 1958

A little plant sprouted in the can where I planted seed from the arbor vitae. I hope it is arbor vitae, although it does not look like it. First, two little leaves came out, and then two on the opposite side, and now two new ones have sprouted again. I woke up last night and thought that the rain would break its weak stem. It was raining all night. The violet in the other can is thriving. The cans are in the yard, and the gardeners know that they are mine and don't bother them. I water them often. To the guards I must appear to be a slightly crazy man in isolation who has lots of time. But what else am I anyway? [. . .]

June 26, 1958

In jail some elements of one's internal life must sort themselves out. Not in the case of all people, but in the case of political prisoners. Doubts, difficulties and crises do not seize political prisoners equally, nor do they equally affect them intellectually, morally and psychologically. In my case there was never an intellectual or moral crisis, not even difficulties, but psychological difficulties cannot be avoided, even when one is not in jail, but especially when one is. [. . .]

July 5, 1958

It is clear to me now why I am overburdened with reminiscences. This is not solely due to jail and solitary confinement. I was really already isolated from the conflict in 1954. The thing is that up to 1954 I had a very intensive life, and from then on I did not have it—I lived alone with only my immediate family. My intellectual life was alive, but there was no other life. Thus a void was created, a chasm. And because man must live—if he wants to live normally—an intellectual and a practical, day-to-day life, in the absence of the latter I inevitably turned to reminiscences. From time to time to those things I do not want to remember. Jail, solitary confinement, encourage all that. [. . .]

July 10, 1958

The weather is changing from clear to cloudy. But I am noticing that the atmospheric conditions less and less influence my attitudes. Almost no influence on my attitude. That is true only recently. All in all I keep my good mood.

Yesterday a small sparrow flew in from somewhere—it can barely fly. I wanted to save it and put it on the arbor vitae. It fell again; it is hopping around, and many older sparrows are surrounding it. And there is a spotted cat. The little sparrow hid. The cat did not come out. We are all happy—I, the guard, and the little sparrow. Only the cat is unhappy, but not everyone can be happy. As among people. [. . .]

July 13, 1958

Yesterday I saw a Chinese film about a boy who helped the Partisans against the Japanese. Not only was it worse than our worst film, but it was even worse than one the Bosnian Četniks might make about our Partisans. During the performance a prison official asked me what I thought about the film. I answered him that if Chinese development continues along this path for a hundred years—which I don't think it will—they will succeed in uniting the entire white race against themselves, regardless of ideological system. [. . .]

July 15, 1958

I have been thinking about the role of the West in the Middle East. I know very little about the situation. But I hope the West will not intervene, because those people have the right to free themselves from foreign vassalage. That the Middle Eastern countries are changing to military dictatorships is in part the responsibility of the West. I don't view this through Western glasses or through Eastern glasses, or as the weakening or strengthening of democracy. But I see the entrance of these peoples into the world arena serving to unite the world further and to enrich it with new beauties and values.

The Russians are certainly waiting for some turmoil in the Middle East in order to jump in as defenders of the rights of suppressed peoples. The intervention of the West in the Middle East would give the Russians the opportunity to enter as defenders of the freedom that the Middle East lost long ago. The peoples of the Middle East want neither West nor East but only their own path, which they have just begun to tread. [. . .]

July 19, 1958

I don't believe much that war will break out now, but I don't exclude that possibility. In any event the USSR will immediately descend upon Yugoslavia and the Adriatic Sea. Nobody knows with what means and with what speed. I suppose that the Yugoslav government will leave me here so that the Russians will catch me and finish me off as they did Nagy. With that my road would end. And that wouldn't be so bad. I would choose to be one of the martyrs, I think, if it came to that. Besides, if there is some commotion, perhaps our authorities could place me somewhere else.

Because of that fear, I have ripped the diary in two, between the 21st and 22nd of July, in order to put it behind the radiator, in the hope that someone will find it. I am sorry to destroy it. I will do the same if I succeed in the rewriting of *Montenegro*. That is, I will also hide it there. It isn't any great hiding place, but better something than nothing, for the moment. [. . .]

July 28, 1958

Around 3 P.M. three prisoners came to my room. [. . .] I was allowed to go with them for the afternoon walk, which for our room takes place behind the building on the abandoned volleyball court. There was commotion during the making of beds, getting to know each other and just chatting.

Solitary confinement is now over. It will be much more pleasant. [. . .]

August 2, 1958

One of the convicts approaches me and tells me that 24 prisoners were called in by the secret police and asked to spy on me. [. . .]

All in all, I still think that such a regime is better than total solitary confinement. Better for my nerves. [. . .]

August 3, 1958

Much activity. Whitewashing, scrubbing, new straw for the mattresses. Convicts approach me and tell me who the informer is. [. . .]

August 21, 1958

The beauty of life is in its variety, that is, in continual happening. Because of that, jails are boring to people—prison takes away that concreteness, that experience of change. Man without happening is crippled; without any changes, he is dead. Because of that suspension of events, isolation did not seem so long to me. It was a gradual and mild dying. And now it is the same, but in less measure, for I am not alone. I can't say what is better, because isolation, in some ways, has advantages. More precisely, one should ask which condition is worse. [. . .]

Without exception criminals endure jail with difficulty. Much worse than the Communists before the war. [. . .] But we Communists hid and learned better to suffer. Apparently, conscience is the chief reason why some bear up with greater difficulty than others. Not only conscience, but also belief in some ideal not exclusively one's own. That is conscience, and yet it is not—if by conscience one means to understand the sum of knowledge or the totality of particular national formulations, of human, class, and individual roles. It is more correct to speak of faith. Faith makes up for the lack of change, that is, for the absence of possibilities for concrete living.

August 22, 1958

Man is a dual creature although not completely and totally separated into two spheres. He is self-oriented and, on the other hand, sociable. When he asserts himself, he seeks to bend society to his will; and when he acts socially, he personally surrenders himself to society. This is true of all people in different measure. The two spheres are concentric. A dictator will evolve the social from the personal; he will assert that his private goals are public goods.

And these criminals are social beings too. But the personal element is most accentuated in them. They, of course, do not equate their position with the needs of society—and in that they differ from the dictator. Instead, they maintain that they have no obligations toward society— that they can take from others, revenge themselves, and in that manner satisfy their passions. They are very self-centered people—intensely so. Their passions are stronger than those of the average man. [. . .] I hold that violation of society is inevitable for some people; it seems innate, just as the desires for power, riches, glory, or—what is most fortunate— conscientious work belong to some men by nature. There is an unwritten, spontaneous "division of labor" without which people could not exist. Crime is inevitable among people. It springs out of their nature and out of the nature of each society. But the struggle against it is also inevitable and natural.

Re-education of convicts is a utopian ideal. What the state should do is to increase the opportunities for prisoners to better themselves. Each must be given the chance. [. . .]

August 30, 1958

All in all, imprisonment is now easier, as far as conditions are concerned, in comparison with old Yugoslavia—less harshness and many more conveniences: tobacco, newspapers, radio, movies. [. . .]

September 14, 1958

It is interesting how in the case of these convicts—thieves, informers and murderers—there exists a very developed sense of betrayal. They themselves betray one another, but if someone betrays them—they get very angry. [. . .]

As far as I'm concerned, although I think that nothing should be reported to the prison authorities and that all informers are most repulsive, I do hold that betrayal, in fact, can function like any other ethical norm. To attack something dishonest is not betrayal. But to report one's friends of yesterday is of course immoral, even in the opinion of amoral people. [. . .]

September 16, 1958

Convicts mostly dream about how to outwit the authorities, that is, how to live as easily as possible and to escape punishment. [. . .]

Besides, Building No. 2 is the worst because all the prisoners here are repeaters. We who live on the ground floor are considered to be better— we are isolated from them in our walks. [. . .]

It is interesting that convicts most readily throw the blame on social conditions to excuse their crimes—it was the same before the war. All thieves do that. The same with cheats. [. . .] Each looks better to himself than in fact he is. Each seeks consolation in his conscience.

And that is one of the characteristics of human beings. [. . .]

November 23, 1958

I did not expect a visit today. [. . .] Štefica was by herself; she wanted once to visit me alone and to talk with me. She told me immediately that Jenny wrote me—Jenny Lee [Bevan]—and sent me greetings. The agent intervened maliciously: "Who is that Jenny?" I answered: "A friend from London." He cut short the visit, and ordered me to go to another room. [. . .] I did not raise any fuss. [. . .] Poor Štefica— denied the visit, she went into the wintry night.

I was very sorry for Štefica; I woke up several times during the night thinking about her. [. . .]

Obviously a tightening of control over me. Why? All this is senseless. [. . .]

December 3, 1958

Although it cannot be considered a thankful task, whenever I talk with some of the convicts I try to persuade them not to steal or kill in the future. [. . .] Among most of them, resolution to avoid crime increases with the fear of punishment, that is, with disgust at prison life, which is void of any pleasures and family responsibilities. I should remark that in each of them there is some resistance, something that prevents them from seeing their crimes and violations as their own humiliation. Most believe—and for them it is a very important belief—that their sentences are too stiff. That is the form their social resistance takes. [. . .]

From this I draw two conclusions: the entire system of re-education (not necessarily measured by political results) that tries to make convicts over into "socialist citizens" is wrong, because it does not lead toward real understanding of mistakes, but toward giving up under pressure. It leads only to shallow and uncertain results. Religions go deeper into these questions, and one should draw some lessons from religions. I myself do not know what should be done, but it is clear to me that one cannot become a good person until he tames something within himself—and is it even possible?—to tame the evil part of one's own being? In any case, the present system is not good.

It seems to me that one should create better conditions for improvement, hold ethical lectures and similar activities; leave everything else to itself. [. . .]

December 4, 1958

Last night I dreamed about Mother, as if she were on her deathbed—I took her pulse and barely felt it, as if at a great distance. I was trembling all over.

It seems to me that yesterday, while talking about the problem of acknowledging crime, I put my finger on the essential point—that the perpetrator recognizes and admits his crime with the greatest difficulty. Now I wish to add that any system of imprisonment that does not lead toward that recognition misses its goal. But any system that *forces* the wrongdoer to acknowledge his wrong completely, that is, to bear full responsibility as the initiator of crime, is a terrible form of oppression of the convict's personality. Forcing a convict into such recognition (though the intention is to correct him) at the same time destroys him as an individual, even if he is an evil person. I believe that the only human approach is to create conditions that do not make it difficult for the convict to improve himself, that is, the least senseless, arbitrary, and primitive conditions. Of course, there must be very strict measures taken against violators of that order. In addition, good books and movies, ethical, informative lectures—nothing more. My thought boils down to this: convicts are more or less human, like everybody else, except that their passions are stronger. No measures concerning them are justified except those that protect society and the prisoners themselves, especially the men who want to serve their sentences peacefully and to improve themselves. Present measures that work for re-education often end in mere verbiage or in deceptive behavior by the prisoners. It is especially bad when a prisoner who behaves no better than others convicted of the same or less offensive crimes is released on condition, or he gets a pardon, before others in his group. This creates an impression of total lawlessness, and, obviously, it happens because of "good connections" and outside intervention. In matters of pardon and release, only the prison administrators and the court should officiate, not politicians. The latter must concern themselves with law and penal policy, but not with individuals. [. . .]

December 29, 1958

Rade told me two months ago about the Belgrade policemen who (during the war) turned criminals, instead of rich and prominent people, over to the Germans to be shot in reprisals. He says that he almost perished that way, and he was very happy when they transported him to work in Germany. I noted this theme as an interesting one. [. . .] Really there is some depth in that idea, not only a curiosity. This is the basic problem: Have people the right to kill other people—those worst in society—in order to save those who are better or, at least, more useful to the specific society? [. . .]

December 30, 1958

The end of the old year is nearing. [. . .]

December 31, 1958

For the last two New Years I remained silent until midnight and thought about my family. [. . .]

This year I will do the same, although I am not alone: at midnight I will think about my family—about Štefica, about Aleksa, about Mother, Milka, and all the others. But since I will not be able to go to sleep immediately, I will think about them for some time, until my thoughts trail off and I sink into sleep. [. . .]

So ends this diary for 1958.

A piece of life, a human life, my life. I thought for a long time to end this year's diary with those words. And I have now written them here.

Let it be: a piece of life. [. . .]

January 21, 1959

What is crime? To this question, as to any other social and human problem, there is no final answer. I don't pretend that I have the solution to such a problem. But there are several observations one can make.

Crime is undoubtedly also a passion—a thirst for achievement, making up for some insufficiency, or inferiority. The most frequent reasoning is: "If he can, why can't I?" This is also the motivation for political crimes, with the additional idea, of course, that in order to survive, we must do such and such—that is, we must commit the crime.

I am convinced that crime is part of the nature of man, and that in one measure or another it is true of every man. But in some a tendency toward a specific kind of crime prevails—pickpockets scorn murder, and murderers scorn picking pockets.

All criminals are of a passionate, exalted nature.

Social reasons for crimes are, of course, essential, and perhaps the most important reasons for crimes, but not exclusive.

And criminals—even the greatest ones—are men like everyone else, with all human faults and good points, but many are without any moral criterion. [. . .]

From the viewpoint that criminals are as human as anyone else, only they cannot stop committing crimes—and are therefore abnormal—the death penalty is unjustified; instead, such men should have the most humane treatment in jails that would not deprive them of anything except the possibility for them to carry on with their crimes. They would be isolated from the conditions that tempt them to commit a crime. I am convinced that the present type of punishment, that is, imprisonment, is senseless and based on revenge, even if it has the most humane form.

I don't believe much in re-education, especially in political re-education. But its opportunity must not be excluded, especially in the direction of making people unlearn crimes and see the essence of their own crime. Spiritual cure seems to be the most important. [. . .]

I want to say that even criminals are still people. They too have a country, and suffer and love and hope and sacrifice. [. . .]

February 4, 1959

It is cold but I am working normally in the morning—happy to see that I have ideas to write about, particularly in this place, in fact, quite a few ideas. [. . .]

February 5, 1959

Since they are locating old people and sick people on the ground floor, this morning they moved out my cellmates. They departed as if we didn't know each other—such are the forced jail acquaintanceships. Taki even kissed me good-bye. I went to Supervisor Petrović to see who is going to be with me. He told me that I can choose for myself from among the old people. This is unsatisfactory to me. [. . .] I absolutely cannot bear to be with old people or people who spend all day in the cell—it would be better to have anything else. [. . .]

We agreed that in my room will be the fellow who works in the canteen selling things, and the librarian. It was a matter of indifference to me as long as I don't have old people and sick people. And the authorities did not want me to remain in an isolation ward: it might have been interpreted as a sign of bad treatment. I don't like isolation either, but I would rather have that than be with the sick and the old. [. . .] Thus there are three of us—there is now no bed above me, and this is more convenient. They are out all day on their jobs, so that even in that way I am going to be spared. I am already more comfortable and I breathe with greater ease. It is strange how the room is completely comfortable with three people while with four it was very crowded. [. . .]

February 28, 1959

The thought I mentioned earlier is now more clearly formulated.

Besides all its evils, the Cold War has also many good points. Above all, like all modern wars, it has speeded up technical development, primarily in military technology but also in other technology, since the former is not isolated from the rest. Its second, even more important, good point is that it puts to the test all social systems, forcing them to compete and to change. Inherited ideas and forms of power that show themselves to be weak are inevitably torn down, and must be torn down, even without a real war. The rapid disintegration of colonialism—that part which survived World War II—could not have been imagined without the Cold War. That process is continuing. Not even a crisis in Communism would have emerged so soon without the Cold War. Nor would the so-called crisis of private enterprise in many areas of the USA and in other capitalist countries have emerged without it. Such as it is, the Cold War still brings about the unification of the world. This might seem absurd: by tearing the world apart you unite it. But it is true that the world is split even without the Cold War; the Cold War just made this split visible; so that the crisis is reached, and thereby is opened the process of unification. Besides, in politics, very little good has ever been accomplished without much evil, without force and injustice. The same is true of the Cold War. [. . .]

March 3, 1959 (in the afternoon)

This morning while looking at the draft of "The Legend of Tsar Dukljan" and reading *Ann Vickers* by Sinclair Lewis, I formed an opinion of how one should set up jails. [. . .]

Jails should be totally abolished, that is, such as they are at present, since criminals are people spiritually disturbed in a specific manner.

Criminals [. . .] are people who are ethically sick. I cannot see why we don't recognize that they are sick people, just like other kinds of patients. Not a single convict whom I have come into contact with gave me the impression that I was talking to an abnormal, disturbed person, but only to a man who was in some way unwilling to give up some sin. In fact, there come terrible moments of intoxication with some kinds of crime. The effect is similar to that of narcotics, but deeper, because it embraces the entire person and makes the criminal submit to it.

If this proposition is correct—and it is—then jails that do not rehabilitate anybody are an absurdity, as irrational as beatings during interrogations. They are today, in essence, revengeful, and even those who would want to be the least cruel are bad.

In some manner society must protect itself from criminals. That means that people susceptible to crime must be separated—but in such a way as not to be denied a single human right. They should come under the care of psychologists and psychiatrists, and not under the care of jailers and political supervisors.

This would, of course, cause a change in the judiciary and in the judges, since, during the trial and the interrogation, psychologists would participate. The accused would be classified according to the required type of treatment, and the essential task would be not to determine how long they must spend in isolation (not our present form of isolation), but to ask when they are going to be cured.

In order to begin the introduction of such a system it is not necessary to change the entire society. Such a total change is impossible. The essential thing is to understand properly the problem of offenders and their crimes, and to introduce a greater degree of democracy than exists in any country, especially in relation to political offenders, who are, in fact, not offenders but opponents of the ruling ideas and system. It is essential to understand that no single idea in a system is absolutely good and should have absolute sway. Therefore, those in power cannot treat their opponents as absolutely evil. [. . .]

All these and similar reasonings led me only more fully to become conscious of how deep an injustice was done to me when I was thrown into jail simply because I could not prevent myself from stating my views. Those who did this to me probably believed that they were humane—they made some fine distinction between execution and a sentence of nine years in jail, not to mention their humiliating me and slandering me in the dirtiest way without any chance for me to defend myself. [. . .]

But let's drop this musing about myself.

The sun will shine further, and, as always, time will put everything in perspective. When we are no longer among the living, it will be all the same how we lived, but—a lesson for the living. [. . .]

March 7, 1959

As the concept of time has changed here for me, so too has the concept of space. Already grown accustomed to this confined space in a room 6 by

12 feet, and in a yard 600 by 600 feet, I have forgotten, no, I have lost, my sense of space. For the same reason, perhaps, prisoners in literature and in life always crave the sky and are overjoyed by it because sky, with its clouds and stars, returns to them the lost sense of spaciousness. [. . .]

When the regime of total isolation was forced upon me, I had to learn to live in total silence, which in practice meant not asking questions of my guards. I achieved this immediately even though in the beginning I had to practice self-control. Probably I would not have succeeded in that so fast had I not had a strong feeling of pride. [. . .]

March 11, 1959

I have been thinking about De Gaulle for several days. He has not yet given all of himself. Anyway, he is an interesting and, basically, a conservative personality. But he is conservative in such a way that he must introduce something new, that is, the most French France, which will be an Americanized France. He is introducing into France the modern industrial way of life. If his *détente* with Germany is not a temporal one, it may be the promise of something new in Europe, and in any case will help in the creation of Western Europe as a separate force. Great Britain will have to bend and join, or be lost in her splendid isolation. The USA cannot oppose such a development for now, since it is anti-Soviet. But when USA-USSR contradictions are resolved in one or another way, a united Europe could stand up to the American giant, unless Fortune helps mankind to unite through some kind of world parliament which would respect national identity. Today all peoples have so much in common that one such parliament does not seem so unreal. In his hope to raise France, De Gaulle is a pioneer of something that will come independently of and contrary to his will. And so are many others. [. . .]

March 14, 1959

Today is Aleksa's birthday. My son. For several days I have been preparing to devote this day in my thoughts to him. I have already been thoughtful in my preparation. Today—Štefica and he—will mention my name, today, in the afternoon around five o'clock when he blows out his candles. It is a cold and rainy day, but I feel very pleasant. Is it because of thoughts about Aleksa and my gentle and deep love for him, for them?

When I decided to embark on the road that I am following, I thought about Aleksa quite a lot and asked myself the following: Do I have, as a father, the right to sacrifice him too and expose him to unforseeable difficulties? Today I ask myself, if he lives through all these difficulties, will he understand that I had to do as I did and that it did not mean I loved him any less? On the contrary, exposing him to uncertainties, I loved him even more. It is so even now. [. . .]

Happy Birthday, my son.

Wishing for your well-being is the only thing I can do for you. Even if I cannot provide what you really need, my wishes are for me some kind of consolation that enable me to feel at a distance a happiness because they express my enormous and unfulfilled love for you.

March 14, 1959 (in the afternoon)

In connection with my thinking about evil—a topic that I also want to write about—I feel that evil is, of course, inescapable and is an exclusively human category. In a certain way it is even a good thing. And what is the origin of evil? It is inevitable that forms and techniques change; and any lag behind this process or outdated form appears to be evil in comparison with technical progress and new forms. This is true of social evil. As for personal evil, no absolute border exists, because what is involved are the inevitable, specific violations of the rules of human behavior, with some kind of abnormality in each case. But there are also "positive" abnormalities, such as those shared between geniuses and madmen, between wise men and criminals, and the distance between the two is not so great.

My theory about good and evil is that they are only a special case of the general relation between such opposites as freedom and oppression, progress and reaction, etc. I use those terms as the most popular and as the most convenient to bring out the relation to ancient thoughts and teachings and also to our traditional thought and problems.

But nothing is more wrong, and more dangerous, than belief in some kind of progress in human nature, that is, in its ability to change. Such a belief leads to oppression, to the attempt at perfecting that nature according to one's own view of progress. "New man" would be pure utopian nonsense if it did not also mean oppression and deceit. In technology there is progress, and, along with it, changes in the forms of social and private life. I am sorry that I put down those little dark thoughts on Aleksa's birthday, which, at the same time, is the date of Marx's death. But perhaps my thoughts about the uncertain future of the boy also led me to it. [. . .]

March 24, 1959

Last night I dreamed a sentence word by word: "Evil is when someone is the chief cook in his country but is not also the chief taster of what he cooks." [. . .]

I must say that I do not believe in classless society, even though capitalism has heard the last bell toll for itself. Each future society will be a class one. Marx's mistake was that he equated the collapse of capitalism with the collapse of classes. That was a small mistake in comparison with impressive visions and wise proofs predicting the collapse of capitalism and the bourgeoisie. In order to destroy one world, Marx had for sure to promise an ideal, utopian vision, otherwise, he would not believe himself, and, even less, would others believe him. A product of his time, a great scientist, he was also a great utopian. To establish the goal of a classless society was to make a logical mistake: to take for a hypothesis something that should be proven only by experience (*partitio principii*). The goal of socialism—of course, a democratic one—can be only a society of mixed economy (governmental, co-operative and private), of nonviolent struggle between free classes, if we are already talking in "class" language. In short, an unperfect or, better yet, a normal society.

One must not nurture illusions about the things people fight over, since ideas are mostly banners, around which rally interests and drives; they remain almost invisible to those who struggle for their fulfillment. And the chief theme of that struggle centers on *the way of life* already existing, or, for others, on that which should be achieved and which seems possible. Of course, so society is completely harmonious, since each specific way of life represents and is guided by some class, authority, or group of classes. The way of life is not only material, but also spiritual, psychological, etc.—in short, life in all its complex puzzlement. Men therefore fight not only for material interests—money or position—but for other things that make the essence of their life. [. . .]

April 9, 1959

Between the lie and the truth, regardless of how absurd it may sound, there is something in common. From the moment man begins (for one reason or another) to defend a lie, he grows increasingly passionate in his defense, and understandably so, because the lie is one of the numerous forms of his existence, as are truth and honesty to the person who chooses them. And as the latter person, who is dedicated to justice and truth, can burn out all his passions in the bosom of his conscience and find peace in himself, so can the one who is a supporter of the lie become intoxicated with the lie to the point of insensibility. Especially miserable is the position of one who, discerning the truth, must speak a lie; his wishes are put down, and the lie is taken as reality—such a man has no internal peace. On the other hand, the passionate supporter of the lie often believes that he represents truth and justice. When one deals with politics, reliable measurements for truth do not exist except for the one that is taking place, that is, human practice. Then, too—at least it seems to me—conscience and morality are the least frequent and the most reliable criteria of truth in politics and, generally, in human relations. The burden of conscience was, not without reason, felt by such a criminal as Hitler, or else he would not have called it a prejudice and told his generals that he freed them from it. Since he was passionately more devoted to the lie, he totally repressed conscience and honesty. But despite that artificial similarity, there remains forever the Aristotelian difference between the lie and the truth: the truth is singular, while the lie can be varied infinitely, and those who lie, in one or another way, do so in each new situation in a new manner. There is no end to their lie until someone gets wise to it and stops them from lying. [. . .]

April 16, 1959

Milka is right: if I did not write about my imprisonment, it would be senseless. Therefore, write, write, write. [. . .]

Prison isn't so difficult, really, for a person of spirit. Even if one did not have the minimum conditions of work, and I do have them. The problem of prison for politicians is really the problem of morality and conviction. [. . .] Last night I talked with Petrović about God and the immortality of the soul—he believes in both. I told him, finally, there is no God. But man has in himself many godlike things, much that is good, that is, characteristics that he ascribes to a god—the power to shape matter, to create spiritual goods, and to protect the conditions of one's own life. He agreed, but this power is given to man by God, says he, and does not derive from man's own evolution. Soon we fell asleep. I slept sweetly without his god, and he slept sweetly with him. [. . .] This morning something came to my mind: What is there is not good and evil, but only forms of human existence that one group of people understands as good and others as evil! [. . .]

Look at that man who slaughtered the Hungarians* who told me that even now his conscience doesn't bother him, although he remembers and is quite depressed when he is alone. [. . .]

I started to write with cheerful thoughts, but now that I begin to think everything turns dark. [. . .]

The loudspeaker bothers me—it is located right in front of the window. I must again learn how not to hear what I don't want to hear, as I did last year and the year before that. Here history repeats itself, only it is not real history. [. . .]

May 5, 1959

It is now 4 P.M., and I hear the sparrows chirping. Until I came here I didn't even think that they could sing nicely—those wise, angry, somewhat gentle, and freest of birds who fear everybody but who are acclimated to the least favorable conditions. Isn't that too a kind of freedom? [. . .]

July 27, 1959

Interesting talk between Khrushchev and Nixon at the [Moscow] fair. The former is attractively offensive; the latter cunningly seems per-

* See the story "An Eye for an Eye" in *The Stone and the Violets.*

plexed. Another great literary theme. If I were only free and could go
somewhere, I would write about it more. [. . .]

August 2, 1959

The real reason for this note is Nixon's visit to the USSR and its effect.
That man really presented himself as the good representative of his
country: dignified and stern, peaceful but firm. He is not a simple man.
He must have generated admiration among his countrymen. In any case,
the Russians could draw a lesson: the USA is not afraid of their growing
strength. Such a conclusion could be fateful for the peace of the world, if
the Russians reached it. But one must also fear that the Russians will see
in Nixon's behavior only a propaganda stunt. [. . .]

August 9, 1959

It seems to me that I was right in my interpretation of the meeting
between Eisenhower and Khrushchev, namely when I did not consider it
to be "crucial and historical." Of course, the meeting should be viewed
positively, despite the fact that Khrushchev wants to increase his personal
standing and attempts to divide a West that is united only in its resistance to the USSR. The USA wants to penetrate the USSR and gain
time. It is ridiculous to imagine that the publication of speeches of Soviet
leaders can have the same impact in the USA as publication of American
speeches in the USSR. Despite all that, there will be some good for both
sides. But there is no room for great expectations yet. [. . .]

August 30, 1959

I am really happy with today's visit. And Aleksa observed: "It would
be better, Father, if you had been in jail when I was born, so that I
would not remember you. There would be now fewer years of waiting
until you came out." [. . .]

September 18, 1959

I'm still in a good mood, and more peaceful, as I remove myself further
and further from direct reality, and my imprisonment becomes longer. If
some excitement comes, it is of short duration. I also have medicines
against it—writing, work, reflection, thinking, and, especially, examination of my conscience. [. . .]

September 21, 1959

Khrushchev's visit to the United States interests me very much. I won't
comment in detail, but that man seems to feel some uncertainty. I don't
want to say that he also has a feeling of inferiority. How else can one
explain his great effort to convince American capitalists that he is a
Communist when they are even more sure of it than he is himself? Other-

wise some of the demonstrations against him seemed to me not only stupid but also ugly, since politeness toward guests is a moral obligation. [. . .]

October 1, 1959 (in the afternoon)
The newcomers show no interest in me. Last year I was an attraction. Time erases everything. [. . .] Yet I do not feel any more unhappy, and even less isolated. Hermits must have felt similarly. Of course, they had faith. I have it also—in human thought and in the inevitability of good! History is not created only by the victors, but also by the vanquished visionaries. Although I am not a creator of history, I am one of the visionaries—one of the smallest and least significant ones. It is not nice to think about oneself. But people live with that also when they have nothing else to do. [. . .]

November 4, 1959
The line from Hamlet is really beautiful: "This above all, to thine own self be true." [. . .] Behave according to your conscience. That at the same time means to be on the conscience of others. It is rainy and dark, but I know that the sun is born anew every day. [. . .]

December 28, 1959
I am conscious that in a specific way I am re-enacting from the beginning the same drama that was experienced by all Communist heretics, especially under Stalin. It seems to me that those who decide about my fate are not conscious of that, and in order to "work me over" and "break me down" they in fact go from mistake to mistake. [. . .] They kept me in solitary confinement for 20 months. [. . .] I must admit now that spying and provocation by the convicts has ceased. In the final analysis, those above me could only take revenge, while I will emerge from this experience strengthened and purer than I was. I will suffer: that is correct. But I will not go crazy or kill myself, or die. It seems to me that it was part of my fate to suffer—in order to affirm myself. [. . .]

January 12, 1960 (morning)
Although I said yesterday that the West is retreating, I stand by my observations dating from the time of Khrushchev's visit to the USA: All this is temporary and on unstable foundations. Moreover, I am convinced that a new worsening of international relations will occur within a year or two. Like that of any young nation, Russian appetite can only grow as it tastes success, while the Western countries will become bitter defending their existing positions. But this is only the psychological side; the conflicts are basically not psychological, but material or systemic. Differing systems have always coexisted, but today mankind cannot live peacefully

if those systems are as closed and exclusive as they now are: the situation is worsening and threatens everything because of opposing trends. [. . .]

January 15, 1960 (in the morning)
Last night was very cold, perhaps 5° below zero. We closed our window. The cold weather caught me unaware while I was writing, and my right hand, especially around the joints, is so chapped that it is bleeding. Now there is steam in the morning and in the evening. Until yesterday it wasn't so cold. This weather is not so unpleasant for me, because in the cold weather one thinks clearly and precisely. [. . .]

January 21, 1960 (in the morning)
Since yesterday one thought runs through my mind: he who ceases to fear death fears nothing.

Raoul Roa, the Cuban foreign minister who is now visiting Yugoslavia, talks about the similarity of the Cuban and the Yugoslav revolutions. He is both right and wrong. The two revolutions are different in all respects, but all contemporary revolutions, and even more so all contemporary dictatorships, have something in common: industrialization through governmental force. And the origin is the same: the struggle against backwardness and technical undevelopment. The Cuban revolution is no different. I am sympathetic to the Cuban revolution not because of its leaders or ideas, and not because of the forms into which it is transforming itself, since it is obviously becoming the personal dictatorship of Fidel Castro, but because the Cuban people want to and must live in modern conditions and because the American companies and the domestic landowners were unwilling to begin any real technical progress or to give an ounce of freedom and a crumb of bread to the common man. There is no other way except through revolution and dictatorship.

As far as the people's democracies are concerned, there were no people's democracies and probably there can't be any. Democracy always involves the ruling classes or a ruling class. The people, even if they are united and concrete, can never—except for brief revolutionary moments, that is, in the periods of struggle for bare existence—exercise power, and the moment the people exercise power through elected or imposed representatives, that power is no longer exclusively the people's authority. In fact, a pure people's authority does not exist. But that does not mean that it does not matter to the people whether there is more or less democracy or in what manner its representatives are selected. Because if those who rule or wish to rule fight among themselves with democratic—that is, equal and lawful—means the people themselves—the common man—gain something from the struggle. In fact, I wanted to say that the moment a regime begins to call itself "popular," in modern times this is the surest sign that it is turning into a dictatorship (all dictatorships, especially those today, are personal dictatorships) . The same fate awaits Cuba as awaited Egypt. But this is better, at least in the beginning, than Batista and Farouk, until they become new Batistas and new Farouks. But therein is the sense of the people's struggle and the fate of man—the task of Sisyphus, eternal struggle for the new and the unattainable. As for parliamentary democracy, it is the product of free trade and developed capitalist countries; of course, it is good for them and for the thin layer of intellectuals who want to express their thoughts. This is the basis for my sympathies, although with some reservations. But the peoples of backward countries are not willing to adopt that form even if it looks ideal, because it does not offer them the possibility of life but transforms them into the instruments and objects of wealthy nations. Each person lives with that form with which he can and must live, and not with forms from the minds of philosophers or strangers. [. . .]

February 14, 1960

The Russians are absolutely wrong about Germany (and Berlin) when they justify hanging on to East Germany because of German revanchism and the danger of German imperialism. No matter how real the danger is, the Russians still attempt to justify hegemony and imperialism of a new kind. [. . .] The German question cannot be resolved by force or by pressure—since both lead to an arms race and to cold war. But its resolution cannot be postponed forever. It is impossible to keep the Germans forever divided, even if that were the way to resolve German revanchism. Let us hope that they will not be the only ones to remain dependent after all the colonies have gained independence! The Russians have the right to guarantees against another German attack. They have also secured the right by their military power. But if they continue to secure all other things by force, they must recognize that it will cause a reaction of force on the opposite side. Such is the state of affairs today. [. . .]

There are so many socialisms in the world today and they are of so many varieties that an entire institute would get lost trying to unravel them. Even the Russians realize this and derive conclusions that will give greater flexibility to their foreign policy. [. . .] These new processes are becoming understood even in the West, at least the fact that peoples can live without their (Western) parliamentary systems and democracies and that even without them it is possible to move forward. Freedom is not limited to and expressed through only one form, but in the short run, alas, even sometimes through despotism. [. . .]

April 20, 1960

. . . I only note here my thoughts and wishes at the moment—whether they are correct or incorrect doesn't matter. Again and again I come to the conclusion that despite its economic and political successes and despite its growing strength, Communism, both ours and that in the USSR, cannot escape internal processes which weaken its foundations despite all efforts to protect itself. [. . .] And as it seems clear to me that Communism is not moving toward capitalism, so it is also certain that capitalism is not moving toward the Communist form of socialism. But despite the fact that these systems move in different directions, their internal and external necessities force them toward unification of the world, that is, unification of the world through contradictions and variations of their extreme forms. [. . .] The dissolution of the colonial system weakens classical captalism, but it also has an impact from within upon Communism, since the latter must fight for its existence also outside its territory and must present itself as being more beautiful than it is. Words in politics signify nothing except when they are needed to beautify reality. But little by little words also oblige. [. . .]

I was and I will remain a malcontent within Communism. Perhaps that circle has no exit. But I do not wish to exit from it, since outside of it I would be nothing, just as I would be nothing if I renounced my nonconformism. This is not a question of will or spite, although there is some of that in it too, but of the essence and the survival of one's individuality. (One's essence is destroyed in one or another manner, but in greatest measure from within; it never changes of its own will, since that will is only an expression of the essence—of the individual's forms and ways of existence. [. . .])

April 28, 1960

It really seems that in East-West relations very little has changed. [. . .] It seems to me that the problem of disarmament, although everybody calls it "the most important problem of our times" will hardly escape a blind alley without the resolution of political problems, which, unfortunately, are barely touched upon. [. . .]

May 19, 1960 (afternoon)

I read Khrushchev's statements at the press conference in Paris. They above all are very primitive—and that wouldn't be so disastrous if they were not so uncultivated—which is very tragic for the leader of such a nation. I think that Russia has ripened for a smarter head than his. Now many who had illusions about Khrushchev will have the opportunity to see the truth for themselves. He is, of course, a vital man with a flexible mind, but very unstable and ruthless. There won't be any immediate larger crises in international relations, but they are around the corner. Berlin will certainly be the culmination. [. . .]

June 16, 1960 (8 P.M.)

De Gaulle's invitation to the Algerian government really opens new vistas. . . . If De Gaulle succeeds—that would be his most beautiful and most significant act as a statesman and, finally, the end of Western colonialism. [. . .]

July 29, 1960 (morning)

The world has changed while I have been under house arrest and in jail. Many things have happened, some contrary to my expectations and some as I expected, and many things remained unchanged. But all in all, the world has changed in a direction for the better, and in the present world, despite the existence of the atomic apocalypse—which, just like the Biblical apocalypse, did not occur—it is not so bad. The most important changes are that many new nations in Asia and Africa until recently oppressed and unknown, have entered upon the international scene and have become the subject of human history. Another, no less important change, is that within those new nations one sees the beginning of new forms of relations and property which resemble socialism but are not the same as those of the Russian type and—even more important—are not dependent upon the Russian model. The changes are the least within the USSR and the USA. But those countries are extremes—they do not change generally but destroy one another. The role of the USSR grew enormously in many ways and even beyond its real capabilities, and the role of the USA, wherever it was the keeper of the old order, declined and suffered failures. But it was shown that the world moves on despite the USSR and the USA and that their mutual quarrel will make it easier for other nations (China, India) to gain a more prominent place and, in the future, to replace them.

Western European socialists finally confined their role to Western Europe. The Algerian and Latin-American socialists pursue their own paths. If Communism continues to make gains outside the East bloc, not, of course, in its classical variety, one may expect that it will not be a carbon copy of the USSR but that it will retain certain forms of independence. In any case, it is obvious that socialism does not cover the same territory the USSR controls and that socialism can exist even if the Soviet state tomorrow were to cease to exist. India, Yugoslavia, Egypt and Cuba are good examples. It follows that the USSR and the USA must recognize this fact, even though they do not like those countries for quite different reasons. It is confirmed that both states can live with different systems and with independent countries. [. . .]

The world is more and more united through independent nations and conflicts. [. . .]

And finally, we are very far away from the realization of the classless society, and I would say that it was a dream—perhaps one of the most beautiful dreams ever—and one of great significance for the cause of social struggles and changes, but only a dream, as were Christianity and Buddhism, which, despite being dreams, nonetheless changed the world.

Upon the ruins of old worlds rise new ones, and new classes will replace the old ones. That is so, and such is the fate of mankind. The moment communism accepts this fact, and that will happen, in time, real and essential changes will begin within it. But it does not seem that we are close to that day, since communism as a system, despite all its internal and external contradictions, is still progressing with great strides. One cannot say the same for capitalism, although there is significant progress there too. Capitalism as a whole is a system in decline, and although I do not believe that the USA will change into a socialist state of the soviet type, I doubt that its social system will survive another century.

No one knows what things will happen or how, but we do know that only such a form of society, property and power will prevail as will permit the people's further existence. Civilizations replace one another not by one growing out of another but by one destroying and pushing aside the other, turning it into archeological data. [. . .]

August 13, 1960
Yesterday two dangerous burglars attempted to escape as usual in a very clever manner: they jumped into the truck and drove through the gate, which was open because it was being painted. The guards went after them, also in trucks—as in America. But the escapees had the misfortune to drive into a hole—they didn't know their way, or they were afraid to drive through the guards' buildings. They jumped out of the truck and began to run across the field. The shooting began, and yelling, and we heard it. They caught them—no one was wounded; they only beat them up, as it must be when there is a settling of accounts between those who represent order and those who represent disorder, especially when the latter are irritating the former. Although I am not on the side of the criminals, I always like it when they think of something clever. This is only a proof of how much senseless energy is buried there and how the human spirit works tirelessly, despite all limitations. As always, escapes are simple. One should have a special sense to uncover the possibilities that exist in this respect, as in anything else. [. . .]

November 1, 1960
I got up a little tired and more puzzled than depressed. But, as usual, with a slight pressure in the back of my neck and around the left ear. I decided not to report to the doctor unless the same thing occurs again.

11:30 A.M. Sušak called Dr. Kalibarda this morning. After taking my blood pressure, listening to my heart, and examining my reflexes, Kalibarda concluded that my last night's fainting is nothing serious and that it was due to the suddenness of my getting up. I share his view. During the visit I told Sušak (in front of Kalibarda) that I will not seek outside doctors but will go through normal procedures, that is, through the prison doctors, in the treatment of my nerves, which really bother me. [. . .] And as for my nerves, nothing more was done, and the reason for this is the prison conditions, more than anyone's evil intent—and more was done for me in that respect than for any other prisoner. [. . .]

November 7, 1960

The American elections are tomorrow. Although I would like to see Kennedy win and although all predictions published in our press give him the advantage, it does not seem impossible for Nixon to win. The amazing thing is the absence of any essential differences, but Nixon's personality did not charm me, while Kennedy possessed a fresher, livelier and more flexible spirit. . . .

November 10, 1960 (in the morning)

Kennedy won. That is good, and in any case better because the USSR will only in him find the real opponent—more rational than the passionate man Nixon would be. As time goes by, changes might be even greater, especially if Kennedy, as he promises, increases economic growth in the USA. This would have enormous consequence in all aspects of American life and throughout the world. . . .

With Khrushchev began the new era of Soviet politics—the struggle of the USSR to achieve world domination.

It does not seem impossible to me that with Kennedy begins a new era for the USA—which is hard to describe in advance. Possibly, the essential characteristic for that era will be an attempt to maintain world leadership and to wrest it away from the USSR. Kennedy represents and points very clearly to a new America—which I do not know well enough, though I discern some things about it: Kennedy is young, wise, handsome and rational. Both Eisenhower and Nixon represented the conservative, self-satisfied part of the USA. Nixon had possibilities to retain support but not to gain new support. Besides, the Democrats are more known throughout the world than the Republicans due to Roosevelt and the Second World War. Kennedy will offer new encouragements and ideas in the struggle against the USSR. These are my expectations, and even they are something to a man who has nothing and from whom everything has been taken away. Of course, in this situation it is of no use to me who rules America, Kennedy or Nixon, but it is not so to the world or even for the future of my country, whose fortunes are inseparable from the fate of the world as a whole. [. . .]

December 17, 1960 (morning)

When I went to bed last night I was seized by terrible nerve attacks. I don't think the pain was more intense than in the attacks I had in November of last year. Everything was throbbing—chest, head, stomach,

and with such a force that it seemed to me that the back part of my skull
would explode. But the psychic fears were not so great—perhaps because
of my recognition from experience that this condition will pass. After
long agonizing and pondering, I finally took some meprobamate and
gradually calmed down. This morning I got up drowsy, but also quite
calm—it is always so after a dream. [. . .]

January 9, 1961

My nerves have been dangerously tense this morning, especially those
hot flashes in the brain, of several minutes' duration at a time, which
spread from the skull into the brain itself. But that pain (in the brain) is
no more painful or more unbearable than the one felt in my skull; and
neither is the fear any greater when it spreads to my brain, despite the
fact that the pain attacks the organ I try to take the best care of and
cherish the most.

Tomorrow is the end of the week—the period within which I asked the
jail warden to notify me of the reason that I am not yet freed from jail.

January 19, 1961

On Thursday at 1 P.M. they took me again to Penezić, who was sitting
in the room of the superintendent of the jail. I had no particular idea—I
proposed only as a possibility to write to Tito after my release and to give
him my word, and Penezić proposed the following text:

> To The Federal Executive Council of the Federal Parliament of
> Yugoslavia.
>
> Convinced of your positive decision, I am honored to present
> the following statement:
>
> Bearing in mind that events and our entire postwar develop-
> ment in internal and foreign policy has reversed all that by which
> I caused an opening of criminal proceedings and passing of
> sentence upon me, I anticipate that the Federal Executive Council
> will review my case and decide to permit me to be released from
> jail. It seems to me that the basis for my release from jail would be
> my will and firm determination to steer clear of any activity like
> those which have led to the present relations between myself and
> the political and governmental organs.
>
> I am determined to preserve my integrity and to adhere to any
> solution you propose which is acceptable according to my moral
> principles: thus, my intentions are sincere and well-intentioned.
> Therefore, after release from jail I will not undertake any political
> activity contrary to the laws of the Federal Peoples Republic of
> Yugoslavia, which would put me in a position of criminal respon-

sibility, nor will I seek to do my country any damage, and in the future I will permit no one to print anew the book *The New Class.*

I would like to emphasize that this statement is sent in the belief that the decision to release me from jail would, at the same time, abolish the lesser punishments—such as the taking away of my decorations, my pension, and other items.

In conclusion, I would like to assure the Federal Executive Council that I will remain true to my statement, expecting that among leading comrades I will find good will and understanding.

signed: January 14, 1961   Sremska Mitrovica   Milovan Djilas

Everything was written word by word, and much of the text was composed of quotations from my letters to Kardelj, Ranković, and the members of the Central Committee (during the last four months). To sign such a text, which is something in the nature of a petition, although penitence is circumvented, I was led by the desire to meet them partway, because their wish was obvious—to change my conditions from the present ones. Besides, one cannot exclude the possibility of future new contracts between me and them. I never renounced socialism, or left Communism, even though I criticized it and think that it should be criticized further. Besides, I pointed out to Penezić that I do not renounce *The New Class*, and that I have no regrets about my past—a fact that can be seen from the entire correspondence—and so, relations in that respect remain as they were, of course, with obvious mutual concessions. Of equality, one cannot even speak. They represent the state and the power. About my renunciations and humiliations, however, there was not and could not be any talk (although one paragraph smells of it, it is not formulated in an obsequious-penitent form). Everything therefore belongs to the future.

At the last meeting with Penezić, which lasted about an hour and a half, I discussed all other questions. He told me that I will be freed under conditions—he did not hide that this is necessary for the first time as a pressure and a safeguard for my behavior. [. . .] In view of our future cooperation, I expressed a readiness to talk, but also skepticism that we can come to any agreement, because the fundamental differences of principle between us are great. Also, as he pointed out, I am very obstinate.

The solution cannot make me very happy. But [. . .] everything belongs to the future and depends on the development of circumstances, which I believe will not go against me. But even if they were to go against me, it is unimportant because I have my ideas and my literary creativity. [. . .]

The Second Imprisonment

[Djilas was released from prison on January 20, 1961, and rearrested on April 7, 1962 for publication of *Conversations with Stalin,* which was alleged to have violated the conditions of his release and to have revealed state secrets.]

July 4, 1962 [transcribed from toilet paper]
Man is like a fortress—people and nature created him and no matter how many times people put him down, something of himself remains to show what kind of person he was. [. . .]

July 8, 1962
Man is the link between the eternal and the momentary—a moment of eternity. Man was and will be a fighter, according to the immutable laws of his existence. And although it is an illusion that it is possible to abolish despotism and establish freedom in the world—they need each other—the struggle itself is not illusory. The results of each struggle, even the great ones, are temporary and inadequate to achieve the ideal. But the struggle alone in itself is great and creative. The struggle transforms itself into a myth, and people live by myths. [. . .]

July 16, 1962
In the press they talk frequently of the lower instincts developed by viewing criminal movies. I don't know which are the low or which are the high instincts. Low is only that which is damaging to someone else; but that is not an instinct—it is a conscious act. [. . .]

July 10, 1963
Sentenced by themselves, in a world unto itself, people are forced to build bridges between each other, in order to endure and to persevere, to survive and to preserve their essential human characteristics. This is tragic and majestic human fate—separation and linking. Man is also *a person,* and thus a world in itself; but he is also the collective human being—he must link himself with other people and with the world around him.

I am tearing up each draft of *Worlds and Bridges* the moment I finish the next—in the same manner I did with the text of *Lost Battles (Under the Colors).* I say: I will make it easier for the authorities to get to my manuscripts, that is, they will have an easier time getting them if I ever leave jail. [. . .]

August 30, 1963
One thought: dogmatists are the greatest tragedy of humanity, but unfortunately they most frequently move humanity also. [. . .]

December 2, 1963

A thought: each theory that tends toward absolute inevitably acquires the form of religion. Truth about human destiny can only be complex like that destiny itself. (It is beginning to get cold—another winter in an unheated cell.) [. . .]

August 8, 1964

Today half of my sentence (six and a half years) has been completed. A bittersweet day. I didn't have anything to celebrate it with save that I divided a piece of chocolate with my cellmate. But this is not important. [. . .]

November 23, 1966

Two days ago I sent to the authorities a petition to give me some way of heating my cell. Today the Assistant Superintendent called me to his office and gave his permission to install an electric heater. Good. At least this winter I will not have trouble about it—after so many years. [. . .]

March 14, 1967

Aleksa's birthday—at last I am celebrating it at my home. [. . .]

"Jail Diary" (unpublished)

V

REALITY
AND
IMPERFECTION

The question is whether the democratic and socialist movement will follow the road of the hegemony of one socialist state and one movement over the others, or follow the road of equal relations among them. [. . .]

The present experience of Yugoslavia shows that a socialist country can be thwarted and threatened in its development by another socialist state that attempts to establish its hegemony and mastery over other socialist countries. That means that the problem of peace, the problem of the free development of individual countries, is not so much one of the different social structures of states as one of the containment of hegemonic tendencies regardless of social structure.

"On the Occasion of the Election of Yugoslavia to the Security Council," *Borba,*
September 24, 1949

11
Lenin and Stalin

The personal role of an individual in history is not only relatively minor but also fleeting. It generally comes to an end when one's life ends (with the exception of philosophers). The individual nonetheless performs a small task and is a necessary link of history, for the chain of history cannot exist without individuals, since history is the story of men.

Diary of Thoughts, 1953–1954 (unpublished)

Appraisals of Stalin

Stalin

When the humming of Hitler's planes woke everyone up early one clear spring morning in Belgrade, when bombs started slashing the beautiful and innocent body of the city, with their gray smoke spreading death among the parks, streets, buildings and tree-lined avenues, the vision that came before the eyes of the shocked populace was that of Stalin—fatherly, concerned, and smiling. When columns of tanks trampled through peaceful, innocent villages and when German boots echoed on the cobblestone streets of our cities, our people sensed that there is one leader in the world, teacher and father of mankind, who thinks of us and will never forget us. And when around the bends of the roads the first shots were fired by those who seek revenge and when in Hitler's headquarters the first bombs exploded, Stalin became our closest and dearest comrade. He commiserates with the suffering of our people, he rejoices over the successes of our fighters for freedom, he sits with us as we wait in ambush, he soothes our wounds, he gives courage to our people not to lose faith, he commends us for our bravery and our noble deeds.

Can there be any greater honor and happiness than to feel that one's closest and most beloved friend is Stalin? Can there be any greater happiness and honor for peoples and for fighters than to be commended in the most fateful hour of humanity by Stalin, the builder of a better future for mankind? [. . .]

Our peoples began to sing a simple but emotional song of battle, a song about the great Stalin, a song about our Russian brothers who must save the Slavs from extermination and save all of humanity from relapse into barbarity. Stalin became the most beloved face in our villages and our cities. Didn't you see his name embroidered with coarse wool thread, written on the wall with charcoal, carved into the bark of the tree with the shepherd's knife? Our heroes are dying before fascist firing squads with his name on their lips.

Stalin courageously led the great and mighty land of socialism along the road of happiness and prosperity. He developed the teachings of Marx, Engels and Lenin and made them the daily life of millions. He plotted the passage of the first worker-peasant ship of state, a ship capable of resisting any storm. The ship of the Great October, which Lenin led bravely into new seas, toward bright new shores, is tempered by Stalin with socialist construction into the hardest steel ever known and is powered with a new kind of energy—the spirit of Soviet Man. [. . .] What would the world be today without the Soviet Union? The darkness of fascist barbarity! Without Stalin the sun would shine with sorrow. [. . .]

Stalin is the bitterest enemy of all that is inhumane, he is deeply concerned, he is the wisest person, he nurtures human kindness. Man is the greatest treasure! At a time when the rest of the world struggled in misery and shrank under the oppression of reaction and when imperialist cabinets knitted nets to strangle European nations, Stalin created that magnificent poem of freedom and brotherhood among men and peoples —the Stalin Constitution—and with an open heart he showed peoples the road they should follow, the road they would follow one day. The Soviet Union is the only country without hidden motives. It will not enslave peoples but will give aid to enslaved peoples in their war of liberation against Hitler's tyranny. Stalin is the only statesman with a pure conscience and an unselfish heart. He is so because he is the pupil and the collaborator of the great Lenin, because he is the best son of the working class and the glorious Bolshevik party, because the Great October spirit lives in him, because in him breathes everything that today is great, noble and freedom-loving in mankind.

Stalin is Marxism-Leninism revitalized and enriched. He is a man who never wavers, a man before whose eyes are unraveled future events, entire centuries. Should someone be waiting for the Red Army to weaken, he will live to see Hitler defeated and the Red Army strengthened. Stalin is the most complete man. Yesterday he was concerned about the quality of wheat, kindergartens, workers' dwellings, heavy industry, world politics and dialectics. He knows all and sees everything; nothing human is alien to him. Today he worries about the children of fighters, feeding the people, scientific discoveries for war technology, vitamins, and warm gloves for the army. He leads the Red Army, he plots its moves and prepares its victories. There are no riddles in the world that Stalin cannot solve; thus his hand leads only to victories. He can see the weak side of the enemy and the enemy cannot hide from him in any darkness, and thus the Red Army will be victorious. Destroy the life force and the technique of the enemy! Master to perfection the military skills, enter into the soul of the weapon and become its master! Stalin is the greatest strategic genius of all time, the builder of peaceful, happy working life.

Stalin—he is an epoch, the most crucial epoch in the history of mankind.

Stalin—he is the Lenin of our times.

History knows no greater love than that of Stalin for Lenin. And no one deserved Lenin's love as does Stalin. Lenin will live as long as there is world and life. Stalin made his accomplishment eternal and indestructible. Stalin is Lenin living among us. Lenin is alive and will never die. It is a great honor to live in the era of Stalin, to fight under Stalin's leadership, which means to be a part of something that will live forever. Stalin is the thought, the spirit and the emotion of millions of ordinary people who are fighting for a better life. Through loving him the small become great, eternal, they become part of the eternal Stalin, the Lenin of our day. [. . .]

When the din of war quiets down and peoples sail into the port of peace, into the happy life that knows neither slave nor master, wherever man looks he will in all things see Lenin and Stalin. They made it possible for man to rejoice that he is alive, to be with other men, to work. They gave joy and radiance to the spring, scent to the flowers, song to the birds, and soul to mankind. They made it possible for the sun to shine over mankind brilliantly and joyously.

Humanity's sufferings and temptations are greater today than ever, but we shall overcome them. The sufferings and temptations of our peoples are painful and vast. But they arouse in us all that is great and warm, even though it be covered with the ashes thrown at us by the enemies of our people.

They forbade us to love the Soviet Union. We are proving today, with weapons in our hands, that we always loved it. [. . .] Our love toward the Soviet Union is undying because it became our life through flood and fire, our soul, our future, our survival, our daily bread! That love is eternal because it is ennobled by the spirit of the great Stalin, it was magnified by the Great Fatherland War of the socialist country to save humanity from the darkest power in history—German fascism.

Our cause is just. Victory will be ours.

Borba, November 7, 1942

Meeting with Stalin

We entered the Kremlin at dusk. The day had quieted down and the night had not yet begun—everything was covered by violet shadows. The Kremlin looks beautiful from the outside, with its high, long walls, its mighty towers and turrets, and gently curved palace roofs. However, inside everything is quite different. It is like a university or a museum. Outside, one can see centuries of the history of Russia; inside, one walks through it, passing by the mouths of old cannon, beside the bell of the tsar and the cannon of the tsar, beside the proud, well-ordered and victorious church of Ivan the Great.

The yards are almost empty. Here and there one can see a soldier walking along the clean-swept alleys, and in arbors there are the thin trunks of leafless, gloomy trees.

In the Kremlin, where Soviet leaders work, there is no luxury. Everything is simple, unusually clean and orderly, in gray and brown colors that attract no attention. And yet, in that architecture of centuries some harmony awakens in one, some gentle, common, bright and simple peace.

We entered a large, simple building, took the elevator up one floor and started down a long corridor. The officer who acted as guide showed us into a waiting room where we left our coats and caps and from there into a smaller office. The clerk, who sat behind a desk below a life-sized picture of Stalin, stood up, offered us seats and left to announce us. He returned soon, showed us a door that led from his office and told us to proceed.

We thought that we would pass through several more rooms and have a chance to compose ourselves for the meeting with Stalin, but before us opened a sizable room. To the left of the door was a long table with oak chairs. It was covered with a brown tablecloth, and at its farther end stood the solid figure of V. M. Molotov. On the right side in the corner of the room was a large working desk, and above it Lenin's picture. From this area one could see through an open door another, smaller room, which held an enormous globe. From the room, partially obscuring the globe, emerged J. V. Stalin.

He walked with a long stride, his head a little inclined, his arms falling at his sides. He wore the everyday marshal's uniform and high soft boots.

He did not resemble the pictures of him. His mustache and especially his hair were everywhere equally grayish white, and his face was white. Rosier cheeks, and rough. He was of lower medium stature; he had nice, small hands with quite long fingers, long legs, narrow shoulders and a large head. Stalin's face is not only pleasant because of its strange, gentle hardness, because of the Nordic expressiveness, because of the thoughtful, lively, smiling, stern but caring dark-yellow eyes, but it is also beautiful in its harmony, its simplicity and its ever-lively calmness and expressiveness.

All this is missing in the photographs. Neither do they express the motions of Stalin's body, his head and his hands, which are never still but are never sudden or abrupt, his index finger rising from time to time to emphasize a point.

When we introduced ourselves to him, he shook hands with us simply and replied casually, "Stalin." And, after shaking hands with Molotov, we were asked by him to sit down.

One could not say that we were not excited and even confused.

But this lasted only a few moments. I don't know exactly how long, perhaps just a few seconds, and our confusion disappeared. The conversation began with Molotov's inquiry about our impressions of the Soviet Union. We answered that we were thrilled, and Stalin, smoking his pipe, interrupted: "We are not thrilled. We are doing everything possible to make things better in Russia."

Stalin then started the conversation.

He conducted it in a special manner. He posed questions to us, to Molotov, to himself, and, in general, to all. He himself spoke, and listened to others, all the time doodling on the paper in front of him figures of different forms, some random, some geometric, which during the conversation he crossed with horizontal and slanting lines, both straight and wavy. He never gave a straightforward, clear answer or conclusion. Rather, from Stalin's comment or proverb, from his exclamation or joke, a conclusion emerged in the course of the discussion, and he did not finish his doodles until each question was exhausted. With the emergence of a new question there emerged a new figure on the paper, not separated from, but a continuation of, the previous ones.

We were immediately aware of Molotov's participation in the conversation and of the relation between the two of them. They talked to one another intimately, Stalin always asking Molotov about something, and Molotov adding something more to Stalin's comments. For a moment one got the impression that one person was talking to himself. It was as if a younger comrade, or, more precisely, a younger brother, were helping his older brother, both coming from the same home, from one father and mother. That atmosphere prevailed for the entire hour's conversation. And Molotov's broad, fair Russian face smiled heartily at Stalin's jokes, which, it seems, were always new and fresh for him. Never did I see between two persons a relationship that was so obviously cordial and, at the same time, so intimate, so serious and understandable. What had happened to make our initial confusion disappear so suddenly?

The behavior of Stalin, his entire personality, is so unaffected that it rapidly plunges a listener into the real, human world, into relations that are neither too intimate nor too cold, but simply human. Stalin's movements are simple, ordinary. He leans with his body and his head toward the speaker in order to hear him better or so that the speaker can hear him. With the pencil he uses to doodle, he also packs a pipe that is always in motion, and then he wipes the pencil on the tablecloth. His marshal's uniform does not fit him like a uniform, but like a suit. [. . .]

Stalin is unusually modest, something that has already been written about many times. [. . .] He is, simply stated, a man, and that is more a man than most. From movements, humor and appearance to his brilliant theoretical and philosophical works, there is nothing discordant in him to upset the whole man.

There are no small or unimportant things about which Stalin is unwilling to talk. He asked about procurements for our army and about our international position, but he also inquired about the sufficiency of our small shops for repairing machine guns and about the food that our army eats. He resolved the greatest problems simply, as if he were dealing with trifles, and he doggedly called our attention to matters that seemed trifling to us until they finally became clear and precise. Only when one talks to Stalin does one realize, after some of his comments and short explanations, how something that appears so trivial is, in reality, of great significance. A question that was discussed with Stalin turned, in time, into a new question. Nothing was left unclear. A precise and clear position prevailed that forced one to find its fulfillment.

What one reads about Stalin in books proved true after the first moments of genuine talk with him; and it becomes immediately clear why Stalin is so beloved in the U.S.S.R. He is a man who does not need to seek the way to understand men, or the working class in general, or to seek the historical road they should follow to happiness. He himself is the embodiment of those masses in one man, of their wishes, their hopes and thoughts. His life is the history of the contemporary epoch, and as his index finger directs individuals, so his thoughts direct all honest workingmen. [. . .]

Looking at Stalin, one can see that he is aging. He is gray and wrinkled. But his age is not felt during his conversation. Stalin will not age because his thought is eternal, always new, completely mature, and thoroughly formed. There is nothing that one can add to it. He is completely saturated by thought, and there is not a single atom in his body that would not live or breathe that thought. [. . .]

Leaving Stalin in the bright spring evening, we did not even realize that the conversation had lasted an hour and a half. It seemed to us that all that had lasted only a moment. [. . .] It seemed to us that we were not walking through specific streets, through Red Square, but instead that we were bathing in the sun at unattainable heights, which are not for dreaming and daydreaming, but hard, granite peaks without abysses or valleys. It seemed that we were moving through history, in its essence and its direction. We moved and lived by Stalin's words, by his thoughts. And then I suddenly realized why, upon seeing Lenin, a simple worker exclaimed: "He is a simple man!" Stalin is a man simpler than anyone alive in the world today, and thus—an unsurpassable, magnificent genius of our time.

Borba, December 21, 1944

Conversations with Stalin

Immediately upon my return to Yugoslavia, I had written an article about my "Meeting With Stalin" which pleased him greatly. A Soviet representative had called my attention to the fact that in subsequent editions I ought to throw out the observation that Stalin's feet were too big and that I should stress more the intimacy between Stalin and Molotov. [. . .] The affair with *Novoe Vremia* led to more serious trouble. [. . .] They diluted or ejected practically everything that had to do with affirming the originality and extraordinary significance of Tito's personality. [. . .] It was only at the second conference—when it became clear to me that in the USSR no one can be magnified except Stalin and when the editor openly admitted this in these words: "It is awkward because of Comrade Stalin: that's the way it is here"—that I agreed to the other changes; all the more so since the article had preserved its color and essence.

For me and for other Yugoslav Communists Stalin's leadership was indisputable. Yet I was nonetheless puzzled why other Communist leaders—in this case, Tito—could not be praised if they deserved it from the Communist point of view. [. . .]

Everything occurred with surprising speed. [. . .] I thought that I would pass through two or three offices before reaching Stalin, but as soon as I opened the door and stepped across the threshold, I saw him coming out of a small adjoining room through whose open doors an enormous globe was visible. Molotov was also here. Stocky and pale and in perfect dark blue European suit, he stood behind a long conference table. [. . .]

But the host was the plainest of all. Stalin was in a marshal's uniform and soft boots, without any medals except a golden star—the Order of Hero of the Soviet Union, on the left side of his breast. In his stance there was nothing artificial or posturing. This was not that majestic Stalin of the photographs or the newsreels—with the stiff, deliberate gait and posture. [. . .] He toyed with his pipe [. . .] or drew circles with a blue pencil around words indicating the main subjects for discussion, which he then crossed out with slanting lines as each part of the discussion was nearing an end. [. . .]

I was also surprised at something else: he was of very small stature and ungainly build. His torso was short and narrow, while his legs and arms were too long. His left arm and shoulder seemed rather stiff. He had a quite large paunch, and his hair was sparse, though his scalp was not completely bald. His face was white with ruddy cheeks. Later I learned that his coloration, so characteristic of those who sit long in offices, was known as the "Kremlin complexion" in high Soviet circles. His teeth were black and irregular, turned inward. Not even his mustache was thick or firm. Still, the head was not a bad one; it had something of the folk, the peasantry, the paterfamilias about it—with those yellow eyes and a mixture of sternness and roguishness.

I was also surprised at his accent. One could tell that he was not a Russian. Nevertheless his Russian vocabulary was rich, and his manner of expression very vivid and plastic, and replete with Russian proverbs and sayings. [. . .]

One thing did not surprise me: Stalin had a sense of humor—a rough humor, self-assured, but not entirely without finesse and depth. His reactions were quick and acute—and conclusive, which did not mean that he did not hear the speaker out, but it was evident that he was no friend of long explanations. Also remarkable was his relation to Molotov. He obviously regarded the latter as a very close associate, as I later confirmed. Molotov was the only member of the Politburo whom Stalin addressed with the familiar pronoun *ty*. [. . .]

But I was to have still another, even more significant and interesting, encounter with Stalin. [. . .]

For Stalin, too, everything was transitory. But that was his philosophical view. Behind that impermanence and within it, certain great and final ideals lay hidden—his ideals, which he could approach by manipulating or kneading the reality and the living men who comprised it.

In retrospect it seems to me that these two, Molotov, with his relativism, with his knack for detailed daily routine, and Stalin, with his fanatical dogmatism and, at the same time broader horizons, his driving quest for further, future possibilities, these two ideally complemented one another. Molotov, though impotent without Stalin's leadership, was indispensable to Stalin in many ways. Though both were unscrupulous in their methods, it seems to me that Stalin selected these methods carefully and fitted them to the circumstances, while Molotov regarded them in advance as being incidental and unimportant. I maintain that he not only incited Stalin into doing many things, but that he also sustained him and dispelled his doubts. And though, in view of his greater versatility and penetration, Stalin claims the principal role in transforming a backward Russia into a modern industrial power, it would be wrong to underestimate Molotov's role, especially as the practical executive. [. . .]

An uninstructed visitor might hardly have detected any difference between Stalin and the rest. Yet it existed. His opinion was carefully noted. No one opposed him very hard. It all rather resembled a patriarchal family with a crotchety head whose foibles always caused the home folks to be apprehensive.

Stalin took quantities of food that would have been enormous even for a much larger man. He usually picked meat, which reflected his mountaineer origins. He also liked all kinds of specialities. [. . .] He drank moderately, most frequently mixing red wine and vodka in little glasses. I never noticed any signs of drunkenness in him. [. . .] As all to a man overate at these dinners, the Soviet leaders ate very little and irregularly during the day. [. . .] It was at these dinners that the destiny of the vast Russian land, of the newly acquired territories, and, to a considerable degree, of the human race was decided. And even if the dinners failed to inspire those spiritual creators—the "engineers of the human spirit"—to great deeds, many such deeds were probably buried there forever. [. . .]

Every crime was possible to Stalin, for there was not one he had not committed. Whatever standards we use to take his measure, in any event—let us hope for all time to come—to him will fall the glory of being the greatest criminal in history. For in him was joined the criminal senselessness of Caligula with the refinement of a Borgia and the brutality of a Tsar Ivan the Terrible.

I was more interested, and am more interested, in how such a dark, cunning, and cruel individual could ever have led one of the greatest and most powerful states, not for just a day or a year, but for thirty years! Until precisely this is explained by Stalin's present critics—I mean his successors—they will only confirm that in good part they are only continuing his work and that they contain in their own make-up those same elements—the same ideas, patterns, and methods that propelled him. [. . .] The ruling Party followed him doggedly and obediently—and he truly led it from victory to victory, until, carried away by power, he began to sin against it as well. Today this is all it reproaches him for, passing in silence over his many greater and certainly no less brutal crimes against the "class enemy"—the peasantry and the intelligentsia, and also the left and right wings within the Party and outside of it. And as long as that Party fails to break, both in its theory and especially in its practice, with everything that comprised the very originality and essence of Stalin and of Stalinism, namely, with the ideological unitarianism and so-called monolithic structure of the Party, it will be a bad but reliable sign that it has not emerged from under Stalin's shadow. [. . .]

If we assume the viewpoint of humanity and freedom, history does not know a despot as brutal and as cynical as Stalin was. He was methodical, all-embracing, and total as a criminal. He was one of those rare terrible dogmatists capable of destroying nine tenths of the human race to "make happy" the one tenth.

However, if we wish to determine what Stalin really meant in the history of communism, then he must for the present be regarded as being, next to Lenin, the most magnificent figure. He did not substantially develop the ideas of Communism, but he championed them and brought them to realization in a society and a state. He did not construct an ideal society—something of the sort is not even possible in the very nature of humans and human society, but he transformed backward Russia into an industrial power and an empire that is ever more resolutely and implacably aspiring to world mastery.

Viewed from the standpoint of success and political adroitness, Stalin is hardly surpassed by any statesman of his time. [. . .]

However, let us not be unjust toward Stalin! [. . .] Unsurpassed in violence and crime, Stalin was no less the leader and organizer of a certain social system. Today he rates very low, pilloried for his "errors," through which the leaders of that same system intend to redeem both the system and themselves.

And yet, despite the fact that it was carried out in an inappropriate operetta style, Stalin's dethronement proves that the truth will out even if only after those who fought for it have perished. The human conscience is implacable and indestructible.

Conversations with Stalin, 1962
(Trans. Michael B. Petrovich)

About Stalin, Probably for the Last Time

I thought that my "conversations with Stalin" were finished. But I was mistaken in this, as I was in many other things, such as in my recent hopes that after *The Unperfect Society* I would not have to deal with "ideological questions."

But the ghost of Stalin will circle the earth for a long time to come.

Almost everyone renounced his legacy, but many still draw their strength from him. Most of them even unintentionally take their example from Stalin. Khrushchev disavowed him but admired him. The present Soviet leaders do not admire him but they bask in his glory. Even in the case of Tito—fifteen years after the split with him—respect for his statesmanship revived. And I even have to ask myself: Isn't thinking about Stalin in itself a sign that he has left his mark on me?

What is Stalin: a great statesman, a "diabolic genius," a victim of dogma, or a maniac and a criminal who seized power? What did Marxist ideology mean to him and for what purpose did he use its ideas? What did he think about his own achievements, what about himself and about his place in history?

These are only some of the questions that the figure of Stalin raises. I emphasize them because as great as is their effect on the fate of the contemporary world, especially the Communist world, equally great is their—I would say—broader significance beyond time and place.

1.

From my meetings with Stalin, two of his positions now stand out to me as especially important. The first, if I remember well, was stated in 1945 and the second, I am quite sure, in the beginning of 1948.

The first position runs something like this: if our ideas are correct, then everything else must follow of itself. The second position is related to Marx and Engels. In conversation, someone—I think it was I—emphasized the continuing validity of Marx's and Engels's view of the world, at which point Stalin remarked, as though he had thought about the matter for a long time and had arrived, perhaps reluctantly, at an irrefutable conclusion, "Yes, without doubt they are the founders. But they also have their shortcomings. One must not forget that Marx and Engels were too much influenced by German classical philosophy, especially Kant and Hegel. Lenin, however, was free of such influences."

At first glance these positions do not appear particularly original. The Communist classification of views and approaches into correct and incorrect depending upon their conformity to dogmatic orthodoxy is generally familiar; and no less familiar is the myth of Lenin as the sole defender and continuer of Marx's teachings. But in Stalin's positions there are some aspects that make them not only personally his, but also particularly significant for our discussion.

What does Stalin mean when he says that ideas are the foundation and the condition for victory? Isn't this position contradictory to the basic tenet of Marxism according to which "the economic structure of society"[1]

1. Karl Marx, Foreword, "Introduction to the Critique of Political Economy," in Karl Marx and F. Engels, *Izabrana dela* (Beograd: Kultura, 1949), Vol. 1, p. 338.

creates the foundation of all ideas? Doesn't such a view come close, even subconsciously, to philosophical idealism, where the mind and ideas are primary and decisive? It is obvious that Stalin was not talking about Marx's notion that "theory becomes a material force the moment it catches hold of the masses,"[2] but, instead, about theories, about ideas before they "catch hold of the masses." How does all this fit in with Bukharin's observation about Stalin, in his conversation with Kamenev in July of 1928, that "at any given moment he will change his theories merely to get rid of someone."[3] And finally, what accounts for Stalin's late and unexpected criticism of Marx and Engels?

But despite this flood of questions, one finds very little in the cited statements of Stalin that is contradictory. Moreover, it doesn't seem to me that Bukharin's judgment about Stalin's lack of principles, even if we ignore the fact that it was made during a period of fractional fanaticism, is inconsistent with Stalin's attributing decisive importance to ideas.

If not the most important, then at least one of the most important reasons why Stalin's enemies within the party—Trotsky, Bukharin, Zinoviev and others—lost the battle lies in the fact that he was a more original, a more creative, Marxist than any of them. Of course, his style lacks Trotsky's pyrotechnics and his analysis lacks the scholastic acumen of Bukharin. But for that very reason, Stalin's expositions are a rational view of social reality, signposts and inspirations to new victorious forces. Taken out of context, out of the specific conditions and atmosphere, his ideas really appear dull, biased and invalid. But this is only the appearance.

The essence of Marx's teaching is that theory and practice are inseparable. "Philosophers explained the world in many ways; the problem is to change it."[4] Communism and Communists could not be resisted wherever and whenever that unity of their theory and their practice could exist. And his stubbornness and skill in linking Marxist-Leninist theory with power, with the force of the state, gave Stalin an incomprehensible, diabolic strength. Stalin is not a political theoretician in the normal sense: he writes and speaks only when the political struggle, whether within the party or within society, but most frequently in both at the same time, forces him to. That tie between reality and thought, that unimaginative, unmeditated pragmatism, in fact is the source of the strength and originality of Stalin's views. . . . One might add that failure to perceive that property of his views, that is, treating his writings formally, makes it difficult today not only for dogmatists in the East but also for conscien-

2. Karl Marx and F. Engels, *Rani radovi* (Zagreb: Naprijed, 1967), p. 98.
3. Cited from Robert Conquest, *The Great Terror* (New York: Macmillan, 1968), p. 81.
4. K. Marx and F. Engels, *Rani radovi*, p. 339.

tious students of Stalin in the West to understand his personality and to comprehend the conditions of his rise. . . .

One should emphasize again that Stalin's Marxism, Stalin's views, almost as if they didn't exist, never appeared outside the needs of post-revolutionary Soviet society and the Soviet state. This is the Marxism of the party which of necessity transforms itself into power, into the "leading," ruling power. Trotsky called Stalin "the most prominent mediocrity in our Party,"[5] and Bukharin ridiculed his hopeless desire to become a noted theoretician.[6] But those are incomplete, fractional judgments, lacking in reality. Stalin's thinking, it is true, is not theoretical in the ordinary sense of the word, that is, it is neither scholarly nor analytical. But as the linking of ideology and the needs of the party, that is, of the party bureaucracy as the new elite, it is theoretical in far greater measure than was true of all his opponents. It is not just a coincidence that the party bureaucracy lined up behind Stalin, just as it is not a coincidence that Hitler's tirades, which sound incredible today, enthralled millions of "rational" Germans and sent them off on suicidal assaults. Stalin was not victorious because he "corrupted" Marxism, but precisely because he made it a reality. . . . Trotsky continuously strewed around himself the paradoxes and constructions of the world revolution, Bukharin immersed himself in dogmatic details and in the probable bourgeoisifying of the colonies, while Stalin in his reports on "future tasks" equated the existence and the privileges of the transformed and newly emerging party bureaucracy with industrialization and the strengthening of Russia.

In so doing, Stalin, like any genuine politician and capable administrator, appropriated the ideas of others and dressed them in more realistic garb. Stalin's most famous undertaking, "the building of socialism in one country" (the USSR), was originated and developed as a theory by Bukharin in the struggle against Trotsky. This might be considered literary theft or a lack of originality, but in politics it is called taking advantage of opportunities.

No one ever questioned whether Stalin was a Marxist. No serious person even today does so. Differences of opinion exist only in evaluating his qualities as a theoretician and his legitimacy as Lenin's heir.

2.

A few moments ago I stated what appeared to me to be Stalin's most significant qualities.

Any attempt to determine who is someone's heir seems to me superfluous and irrelevant. Only those who are not gifted with vision and who have no creative capabilities can be consistent and true heirs. Here we

5. Cited from Robert Conquest, *The Great Terror*, p. 71.
6. *Ibid.*

are talking about politics, where myths are inevitable everyday occurrences; but in the concrete case, we are talking about refuting the dogmatic and demagogical treatment of Lenin's legacy by "citation." By citation one can prove that each of the possible heirs was faithful to Lenin, or equally well that no one was faithful to him. Only comparing Lenin's intentions with what Stalin accomplished and also with what his opponents proposed can bring us closer to the truth.

Still, we cannot altogether avoid analysis of Lenin's so-called "Testament." [. . .] Although it deserves separate and more detailed attention, we can safely conclude that Lenin did not transfer authority to anyone and that in Stalin he found no *political* deficiencies but only personal shortcomings. And this corresponds to the historical facts: Stalin was always a Bolshevik, a Leninist. Stalin had good reason to boast at the plenum of the Central Committee of October 23, 1927, "Characteristically, there is not a single word, not a single hint in the 'Testament' about Stalin's errors. There are only comments about Stalin's crudeness. But crudeness is not and cannot be a deficiency of Stalin's *political* line or position."[7]

But what is the truth regarding Lenin's heir? Who really continued his work? [. . .] Different interpretations are inevitable, of course, because the Stalinist past of the Soviet Union and of the Communist movement are still today in many ways a living reality, and different ideas and different forces are still fighting over them. But if one rejects the deterministic view according to which such a backward Russia and such a total ideology could only be put into motion by total administrative despotism, then it seems to me that Stalin is the most logical, the most natural heir of Lenin. Such a conclusion is not even inconsistent with the hypothesis that Stalin would have liquidated even Lenin himself. The substance of Lenin's theories leads to this conclusion: in contrast to those—including also Marx—who preached the ideal society, Lenin fought for and obtained the *total power* necessary to build such a society. Like Marx, he calls this power the *dictatorship of the proletariat.* But while Marx envisions that power as the control and the pressure of the working masses, in the case of Lenin that power becomes a reality through "the avant garde of the proletariat," that is, through the party. To the hypothetical ideal society corresponds the nonhypothetical ideal power, that is, total power.

One may accuse Stalin of many things, but not of betraying the power that Lenin constructed. Khrushchev did not understand that—he could not and dared not understand that. He proclaimed Stalin's power a "mistake," a retreat from Lenin and Leninism. In so doing, he failed to root himself in the intelligentsia and in the people, but he did under-

7. J. V. Stalin, *Ob Opozitsii* (Moscow: Gosizdat, 1928) , p. 723.

mine himself within the party bureaucracy, whose own history, like that of any community, is an integral part of its existence. George F. Kennan observed that in Germany after 1945, the authorities did not have to renounce the Nazi crimes (although the measures taken against the Nazis are inadequate), for there the continuity of authority was interrupted, while in the Soviet Union no leader disavowed his continuity with the party and with its history. Although some of the methods changed, Lenin's power continued in Stalin. And not only his power. But it was power that was essential. That power—somewhat altered—continues today.

3.

All of Stalin's opponents within the party, some more so and some less so, moved in an unreal world. Trotsky was obsessed with revolution, nothing less than world revolution, Bukharin with the economy as the basis for anything and everything. They lamented bygone "camaraderie" and projected an "ideal" future. Stalin, however, following in the tracks of Lenin, gradually perceived that the new order could not survive without changing the position and the role of the party. In the revolution, in the union of power with party, the balance had been on the side of the party. The change consisted in shifting the balance to the side of power, which is in exact accord with Lenin's leading the state in the direction of coercion, organs of oppression, the secret police and its troops. Of course, all of this developed gradually, under the guise of preserving "the leading role of the party," that is, prejudices about ideology and form. If one at the same time bears in mind that power as such brings privileges and "a place in history," it will be clear why from the very first day in power the party developed a desire to stay in power. Stalin did not invent the totalitarian party bureaucracy; it found in him its leader.

Exactly because he understood the emerging and potential reality, Stalin was able to surprise and outplay his opponents. Their ties to the party ultimately became their weakness and also Stalin's chief method: total "unarming oneself before the party" had to be confirmed by confession of the most heinous crimes—treason, sabotage, murder. Today it is known that Soviet instructors brought that "ideological" experience to their younger East European brothers in the postwar trials of Slansky in Czechoslovakia and Rajk in Hungary and perhaps others. Of course, just as in the case of medieval heretics and witches, all that could not have been accomplished without torture and without executioners; it was only the motives and the instruments that were new.

Stalin did not destroy the party, but transformed it, "purified it," and made it the weapon of the powerful. Like the Grand Inquisitor of *The Brothers Karamazov,* he understood that it is necessary to kill God (party camaraderie and the society of equality) to save the institution (the Soviet order and Communist organizations). Not only did the political bureaucracy follow him obediently but so did the majority of Communists throughout the world, forced by circumstances to link—even to identify—their survival with that of the Soviet state. . . . How else can one account for the fact that such fine minds as Togliatti's or such heroic personalities as Dimitrov "failed to comprehend" Stalin's blatant lies and even acquiesced before his monstrous terror?

With his "victories" not only did Stalin's prestige grow, but also he became intoxicated with them. Power and idea became identified with him and he with them. . . . It is as if Hegel's Absolute Spirit, in reckless identification with the world, finally found two forms of itself: the mystical materialist in Stalin, the intuitive mystic in Hitler.

4.

Stalin first presented the entire theory of "Leninism" three months after Lenin's death (in his lectures "On the Questions of Leninism," April, 1924). It was an impoverishment but also an institutionalization of dogma, just as Engels' *Anti-Dühring* was a dogmatic systematization of Marx's writings. Stalin, of course, did not do it by chance or hastily; he had already grasped the essence of "Leninism" and made it his own symbol. His views and endeavors triumphed in the Soviet Union and within Communist movements. Successes and victories—the politician's reality—gave him ample "confirmation" of the decisive importance of "our" ideas, that is, his own ideas.

I believe that for these same reasons Marx's theory diminished in importance in Stalin's eyes, although he remained faithful to its essence —to materialism as the basis of the "scientific" view of the world and as the basis for the construction of the ideal, Communist society. [. . .] Of course Stalin never publicly reappraised Marx and Engels. To do so would have jeopardized the faith of believers and thereby his own power and his deeds. He was aware that he won primarily because he most consistently developed those forms that linked theory and practice, conscience and reality. It was incidental and unimportant to Stalin whether or not he altered this or that principle of Marxism. Had not all great Marxists, and most assuredly Lenin, emphasized that Marxism is a "guide to action" and not a collection of dogmas, and that practice is the only judge of what is correct? But the problem is broader and more complex. All systems, but especially despotic systems, tend toward stability. Marx's theory, by nature dogmatic, had to solidify into dogma the moment it became the official state and social ideology, because the state and the ruling stratum within it would fall apart if its members had to change their uniforms every day, not to mention their ideals. And they have to live so as to adjust, through struggle and work, to changing reality both external and internal. Leaders are forced to "retreat" from ideals, but in a manner that preserves and, if possible, even increases their brilliance in the eyes of their followers and the people. The determinism or "scientificness" of Marxism, the hermetism of society and the totality of power, led Stalin unwaveringly, with the most cruel methods, to weed out ideological offenders, while at the same time life was forcing him to betray and to alter the "most sacred" principles of ideology. Stalin carefully preserved ideology, but as an instrument of power to strengthen Russia, to strengthen his own prestige. It is thus clear why bureaucrats who identify the Russian people and Russia with themselves even today believe that Stalin, despite his "mistakes," accomplished much for Russia. It is also clear why, under Stalin, lies and coercion had to be raised to the level of highest principles. . . . Who knows, perhaps Stalin in his piercing and merciless mind thought that lies and coercion are that dialectical negation through which Russia and mankind will finally arrive at absolute truth and absolute happiness. . . .

Stalin brought the idea of Communism to maximum life and to dogmatic extremes, from which point that idea and "its" society began to decline. The moment he destroyed his internal enemies and announced that a socialist society had been constructed in the Soviet Union, as soon as the war was over, a new motion began in Soviet society and in Communist movements. . . . In any event, when Stalin emphasized the decisive importance of "ideas," he was merely saying, in the only language of his reality, the language of his ideology and his movement, what other political leaders say: "If our ideas reveal the directions of society and if our ideas inspire people so that they organize themselves for the task, then we are on the right path and we shall be victorious. . . ."

5.

[. . .] By purges and by his obstinacy, Stalin destroyed even his own family. At the end only fear and desolation surrounded him. Before his death he pasted photographs of children from an illustrated magazine on the walls of his room, but he refused to see his own grandchildren. . . . This could be an important lesson, especially for dogmatic "one-dimensional" minds who place "historical necessity" ahead of human life and human endeavors. For although Stalin belongs among the greatest victors known to history, in fact he is one of the most defeated personalities. After him there remains not a single lasting, unrenounced value. Victory transformed itself into defeat—of the person and the idea.

What, then, is Stalin? Why is it that way?

In Stalin one can find all the characteristics of past tyrants from Nero and Caligula to Ivan the Terrible, Robespierre and Hitler. But regardless of how much he resembles them, he is a new, original phenomenon. He is the most complete and the most successful. . . . And although his oppression is the most perfidious and the most total, it seems to me that it would be not only oversimplified but also incorrect to view Stalin as a sadist or a criminal. In Stalin's biography, Trotsky states that Stalin enjoyed watching animals being slaughtered, and Khrushchev in one place confirmed that during his "last years" Stalin suffered from paranoia. I do not know any facts that would either confirm or disprove their observations. Judging by everything, though, Stalin delighted in the execution of his opponents. Etched in my memory forever is the expression that appeared on Stalin's face for a moment during a conference of the Yugoslav and Bulgarian delegations with Stalin and his colleagues on February 10, 1948, in the Kremlin. There was a cold and somber delight over the victim whose fate had already been sealed. I had seen such an expression in other politicians in moments when they "broke their canes" over "errant" compatriots and followers. But all that—even if true—is not sufficient to explain the phenomenon of Stalin. [. . .] The phenomenon of Stalin is very complex and not only affects the Communist movement and what were then the internal and external possibilities of the Soviet Union, but also impinges on the relations between ideas and men, between leaders and movements, on the role of oppression in society, on the role of myths in human activity, and on the conditions for peoples and nations to come closer together. Stalin belongs to the past, and discussion about such questions had barely begun. . . .

Yet I shall add that Stalin was—as far as I could tell—a lively, passionate and abrupt person, but also a highly organized and self-controlled one. Otherwise how could he rule such an enormous modern state and conduct such a horrible and complicated war?

Thus it seems to me that such concepts as criminal and maniac are unreal and miss the point when one is talking about a political personage. Here we must guard against confusion: in reality there does not exist, nor can there exist, pure politics free of base passions and motives. If only because it is the sum of human tendencies, politics cannot be purified of either the criminal or the maniac elements. It is difficult if not impossible to draw a generally applicable line between crime and political oppression. With the appearance of each new despot, philosophers are forced to search for new analyses and new generalizations.

But if we still believe that a border exists between the rational and the emotional, between the necessary and the subjective, then Stalin, even if we could not find criminal or maniac elements in him, nonetheless belongs among the most monstrous oppressors in history. For if one maintains, for example, that collectivization was rational and necessary in the given conditions, it is still obvious that it could have been done without exterminating millions of "kulaks." But even today one can find dogmatic objections to such statements: Stalin was caught up with building the socialist society, the Trotskyite criticism of opportunism pressed him, fascist attacks threatened the nation and could have found support in the "class enemy." But what, then, can be said for the contrived accusations and bloody purges of the "opposition" within the party who not only did not threaten the order and the ideology, but also, precisely through their dogmatic ties to it, revealed their weakness and their loss of direction.

Stalin's terror is not limited to the purges, but they are its most specific form. All the party opposition was more or less in agreement with the repression of the "kulaks" and other "class enemies." All of them voluntarily placed their necks in the noose of ideology—in the ideal goals that were the same as those of Stalin. Complaining that Stalin wasn't doing anything specific, Bukharin affirmed his own illusions that he was dealing with science—economy and philosophy. Not a one of them had any essentially new visions or alternative ideals. There was not a single one of them who was not also shaken by Stalin's purges. By means of the purges, Stalin separated himself from them and became what he is and established the foundation for his actions.

With ruthless uncurbed purges in the thirties Stalin made identical the idea and personal power, made identical the state and his own person. Could it have been different—in a world of absolute truths, with faith in the classless, perfect society? The end became the means. Stalin's deeds renounced all moral foundations and by the same token renounced all claims to live long in the lives of men. Herein lies the riddle of his person and herein lies the real measure of his accomplishment.

July 1969 (unpublished)

Reflections on Lenin

Lenin

Even during his lifetime Lenin's historic achievements were being attributed, in the writings of Soviet historians, to predetermined events in his personal world—an approach which, with the passage of time, has transformed him into an infallible sage and saint. The truth, however, speaks otherwise: it was Lenin's undiluted and realistic revolutionary nature that moulded him into a fervent and implacable dogmatist. In a different society and a different age he would have made a fine advocate, or an excellent professor of sociology, or a mediocre preacher. But history, or rather the need of the Russian people for a new social system, the need of the international revolutionary movement for new ideas, found in Lenin an incomparable architect.

Lenin, the party pseudonym of Vladimir Ilyich Ulyanov, was born on April 22, 1870, in Simbirsk (now Ulyanovsk), the third child in Ilya and Maria Ulyanov's family of six. There was nothing remarkable about any of his forebears, except their mixed blood, a subject upon which Soviet historians have been devoutly and conspicuously silent: his paternal grandmother was a Kalmuck, his maternal grandmother a German.

Lenin, an intelligent and mettlesome youth, with red hair and mongoloid features, spent the first 18 years of his life in a dull Russian province, untroubled by any major emotional upheavals. Then, inescapably invading the recesses of his unshaped personality, the shadow of the gallows passed over him. In 1887 his elder brother, Alexander, "Sasha," the favourite, was hanged for his part in a plot to assassinate Tsar Alexander III.

Lenin was to follow in his elder brother's footsteps although his creed and his weapons were different. Neither among his papers nor in his published work, however, is a single word to be found about Sasha's tragic fate, although there is ample evidence that it shook him to the very roots of his being.

Lenin's personality seems to have had no subsistent being apart from the theory and practice of revolutionary Marxism. His relationship with Nadezhda Krupskaya, with whom he became intimately associated in 1894 and who remained completely devoted to him until his death, and indeed later, was as much as political, even a party, relationship as one of sentiment.

Moreover, even his infatuation for Inessa Armand, whom he met in Paris in 1910 and with whom he remained in close touch until her death in 1920, did not, it would appear, step beyond the bounds of party comradeship, nor did it leave any visible signs upon his personality. No human being ever succeeded in capturing his affection, nor on the other hand did anyone ever become the object of his personal hatred.

And in every other respect Lenin's character showed the same pattern. In the 50 volumes of his writings there is not a single word that is not functional: a clarification of revolutionary theory, or a counsel for revolutionary practice. Although he possessed a good working knowledge of German, English and French, his interests never strayed outside political and social confines. His spirit was indomitable, but it moved tediously in its single groove. His energy was inexhaustible, his intelligence sharp and penetrating, his conviction unshakable—at all times exclusively in the service of the revolution.

Only a personality of this mould, a personified idea, could have engineered the Russian revolution and carried it to completion.

After graduating in law, Lenin went to Petrograd in 1893, and in Marxist circles there he became involved in propaganda and organization activities. He was arrested in 1895 and banished to Siberia for three years.

In 1900 he emigrated, and apart from brief visits to Russia between 1905 and 1907 he remained abroad until April 16, 1917, when he returned home via the battle camp of Germany. Less than eight months later, on November 7, 1917, he presided over the demolition of Kerensky's liberal, so-called provisional government, and the establishment of a Soviet Government. On August 30, 1918, he received two bullet wounds from a revolver in the hand of a non-Marxist revolutionary, Dora Kaplan; but he recovered without any major complications.

This was the precise moment when the Russian state's measureless multinational expanses came into the grip of a harsh and devastating war that was to last for three years, a war in which the mind of Lenin was to show a versatility and power never before seen in a revolutionary leader. But the critical problems of the new social order marked the beginning of the end for Lenin, although his genius did burst into flame again just before the end of the Civil War. He was suffering from cerebral arterio-sclerosis; and on January 21, 1924, after two years of torment, he died in the village of Gorky, near Moscow.

It would be hard to find in history any figure who from the very outset was so firm in his faith as Lenin and who at the same time contrived the instruments for making a reality of that faith. Lenin, in spite of unimagi-nable obstacles, kept his feet on the same path—the path of revolution.

In the days of his exile in Siberia he had written a revolutionary critique of Russian society in *The Development of Capitalism in Russia*, and by the time of his departure abroad he was elaborating his doctrine of the revolutionary party of a new type for the periodical *Iskra* (The Spark).

The actual establishment of such a party was achieved after long fac-tional struggles; but its beginnings are to be found at the second congress of Russian Social Democrats in London. Here Lenin won a majority of votes (the Russian word is *bolshinstvo*—hence the name of the Bolshevik Party), while the minority vote (*menshinstvo*—hence the Menshevik Party) fell to Martov, hitherto his friend. The main dispute arose out of a qualification formula for party membership. Lenin demanded "per-sonal participation in one of the party organizations", while Martov was satisfied with "regular personal assistance under the aegis of one of its (i.e., the party's) organizations."

This, ostensibly minor, difference contained within itself the fate of Russia, indeed, to a large extent, the fate of the whole world. Lenin insisted on personal devotion to the party, i.e., subservience to its forums and its ideology. He realized that the goal, in this case revolution, was illusory, even worthless, unless the means for achieving it were first secured—and this meant an ideological, militarily disciplined party.

Even in those early days European socialists were not favourably dis-posed towards Lenin, and later they were to accuse him of having a party split in every pocket of his clothing. Nevertheless, the Bolshevik Party i.e., the Russian Communist Party—and following its example, the other communist parties, were born of this second congress dispute. Therein lay the embryos of the professional revolutionaries; and these, in their turn, developed after the revolution into the professional party bureaucracy. Here, too, were planted the seeds of the dissensions in the world as we know it today.

In the 1905 revolution Lenin and the Bolshevik Party played an active but secondary role. But from this revolution Lenin drew fateful conclusions about the transmutation of a democratic revolution into a proletarian revolution. Previously, socialist thinking had been unanimous in taking the view that the overthrow of the Tsarist autocracy must necessarily be followed by a longer or shorter period of economic and democratic transformation during which Russia would become ripe for socialism, ready for the socialist revolution. Lenin, on the other hand, regarded both revolutions as two phases of one and the same process.

From the doctrinaire point of view it is a moot point whether the October Revolution was in fact a proletarian revolution, and whether the social order after the October Revolution was socialist; but it is incontestable that Lenin alone recognized the social currents and potentialities at the disposal of his idea.

At the very beginning of the First World War, Lenin, as opposed to the majority of social-democratic parties, favoured the defeat of his own country's government and the conversion of the "imperialist" war into a civil war. He, at that time an isolated émigré, was thus the initiator of the split in the world social-democratic movement, a split which he made complete after the victory of the revolution by founding the Communist International (Comintern).

The revolution of February, 1917, came as a complete surprise to Lenin in his Swiss retreat. But he realized at once that it was the beginning of the revolutionary process which he had predicted in his political writings and for which he had been preparing the Bolshevik Party.

The Bolshevik Party leadership, with Stalin among its numbers, had meantime organized itself into a legal opposition against the provisional Government. As soon as Lenin arrived on the scene, he switched this policy: in his celebrated *April Theses* he insisted that the immediate task was to carry on the revolution and convert the bourgeois democracy into a "dictatorship of the proletariat". The war and its reverses had put an end to the already crumbling structure of autocracy; and Lenin, as opposed to the bourgeois parties and the Social Democrats, insisted on the urgent need to make peace. In this, Lenin was joined by Trotsky, who until that moment had been outside the Bolshevik Party and in disagreement with Lenin on a number of issues.

With uncanny infallibility, Lenin chose November 7 as the date for the revolutionary coup (October 25 according to the Orthodox calendar; hence the name—October Revolution) ; and here Trotsky, as president of the revolutionary Soviet of Petrograd, was to play an all-important role in carrying it through.

Obsessed by dogma and revolution, Lenin was incapable of understanding the criticism of Rosa Luxemburg, the German communist. Without personal freedom, she declared, no kind of democratic society, and hence no socialist society, was possible. But after victory in the Civil War he began to plumb the depths of Russia's inveterate oriental despotism and the all-pervading backwardness of the peoples of the Russian empire. With unsparing and painstaking energy he bent himself to the task of restoring the economy.

But his successors did not maintain progress along this path. The party bureaucracy, which had begun to wax monstrous in the revolution and the period of terror, became, even in Lenin's lifetime, a force above society.

Even Lenin was powerless to escape the chains of his own visions and to stride ahead of his own time. He failed to understand that the party bureaucracy was a new social phenomenon, a new parasitical stratum. His criticisms of the bureaucracy were confined to demands for a better party spirit and more efficient administration.

After Lenin, Russia shed her backwardness and became a first-class world power. But in respect of freedom the changes were actually retrogressive: Tsarist autocracy was replaced by the totalitarianism of the party oligarchy. Even today Soviet society, rent with unresolved contradictions, languishes under injustices.

Even more sorry in its aspects today is the plight of the body of dogma built up by Lenin's successors and classified under the name "Leninism" for political reasons, more often than not with underlying authoritarian and great-state motivations.

It was not Lenin who introduced Marxism into Russia—that had been done by Plekhanov. Neither did Lenin found the Marxist (Social-Democratic) Party in Russia. But with his unhesitating grasp of the revolutionary side of Marx's teachings, he was the first to give meaning to the party and to build up a cadre capable of carrying through a revolution.

This is not to deny Lenin's importance as a Marxist theoretician and original political writer. On the contrary, it is no exaggeration to say that he evolved the revolutionary side of Marxism, particularly in matters concerning the party, power, and revolutionary strategy and tactics.

But nothing could be farther from the truth than the claim that Lenin was the founder of Leninism, or indeed that any system of ideas for which this would be a suitable nomenclature actually exists.

Lenin regarded himself as Marx's disciple. And indeed he was. He could even be regarded as the most steadfast and profound protagonist ever to wear Marx's revolutionary mantle. During Lenin's lifetime the word Leninism was not used. The myth of Leninism as the new, higher stage of Marxism, "the Marxism of the age of imperialism", rose after Lenin's death out of the struggle for the succession between Stalin, Trotsky, Bukharin, and other contenders, and from the need of international communism for a standardized, definitive dogma.

It was no accident that the first and most important codifier of Leninism was Stalin. Three months after Lenin's death, at the beginning of April, 1924, he delivered a series of lectures on "The Fundamentals of Leninism". Further, Stalin included many of his later articles and speeches in his book *Leninism*, grouping them under the general title *The Problems of Leninism*. Nevertheless, it is misleading to argue that all this represented a falsification of Lenin's ideas: in the same way that Lenin's revolutionary dictatorship was carried on under Stalin's personal and oligarchal despotism, so his ideas could only become comprehensible and acceptable to revolutionary movements outside Russia, and mandatory in Russia itself, if they were presented as dogma, as Leninism.

The theoreticians of Leninism are in disagreement in determining the essence of Lenin's views. This is due very largely to their diverse opinions about the actual state of affairs in the post-Lenin era and about communist tactics. But the most deep-rooted of these disagreements have their origins in Lenin himself. He was not concerned with founding a new doctrine; nor was he capable of doing so.

His mode of thought was not a philosophical one; nor were his methods scientific. Facts, particularly statistical data, which he amassed with zeal, were exploited by him, not as tools for uncovering the hidden truth but in order to prove, or "to put into practice", Marxian principles which he had already accepted as being "scientific". For scientific work, or for philosophical thinking, this sort of method has fundamental flaws. But for the revolutionary it offers unique advantages.

Lenin's Marxism differs from Marx's own only in so far as its theoretical postulates are an integral part of its practical application. The scientific, theoretical approach has hardly any place in Lenin's thinking unless action is involved. Since Marx's theories were the only scientific ones for Lenin, and since the party was the sole instrument of their implementation, Leninism is theory for the sake of party activity, and from Leninism to the Stalinist abolition of all forms of thinking there runs an unbroken, if devious, path.

The deficiencies and wishful thinking in Lenin's views are most glaring in just the areas where they are usually considered, and with justification, to be basic and most original: viz., in the doctrine of the dictatorship of the proletariat and the theory of imperialism as the highest stage of capitalism.

The doctrine of the dictatorship of the proletariat was made to follow, to a large extent, the lines of the experiences of the Paris Commune, the revolt of the proletariat and army after the defeat of France by Prussia in 1871; but it was taken over by Lenin from Marx. Marx had conceived of the dictatorship of the proletariat as the direct rule of the masses, while the Paris Commune was a multi-party state. Lenin's idea of the dictatorship of the proletariat was the rule of workers and poor peasants under the leadership of an "avant garde" proletariat, i.e., Lenin's party, "conscious" of the "ultimate" aims and centrally organized.

In the event, that is to say in the October Revolution, the dictatorship of the proletariat was exercised by the Soviets—or councils—of workers, soldiers, and peasants under the leadership of the party. According to both Marx and Lenin the state was supposed to begin withering away, overnight as it were, after its inception. But things turned out very differently from these theories. With the consolidation of the party monopoly of power, the unreal and unrealizable dictatorship of the proletariat gradually degenerated into a dictatorship of the party bureaucracy.

Nor was Lenin's theory of capitalist imperialism an original one. This was first developed by a British reformer, J. A. Hobson; but from it Lenin drew his own conclusions—schematic, revolutionary conclusions. He evolved the theory that societies in developed countries (capitalism) were coming under the domination of an ever-decreasing number of capitalist monopolies, the trusts; and these were sharing out the undeveloped world among themselves. This was the process by which the societies were entering into their highest, i.e., final, stage; and after this, as a result of the combination of rebellions in the colonies and proletarian revolutions in the metropolises, the dictatorship of the proletariat and the socialization of production were inevitable.

Lenin's analysis was constricted and schematic. The societies in developed countries today are obviously in a state of change—but it is not the change that Lenin envisaged. The colonies, for their part, have achieved independence, but they did so very largely in agreement with the metropolises, and nowhere has there been a revolutionary combination of colonial peoples and proletariat.

The metropolises have not fallen as a result; on the contrary, they have prospered. As a matter of fact, colonial conquest is not the highest stage of capitalism; it is the lowest, the initial stage. Monopolistic tendencies have not vanished; but a monopoly over the government and economy exists today only in Lenin's own country and in countries dependent upon it.

In short, imperialism can be seen to be not an absolute property of a specific social order but, as it has always been, one of the aspects of the essential nature of great powers.

Lenin's ideas have been devoured by time and the betrayal of his successors—Stalin, Khrushchev and Brezhnev. In fighting for their own survival, and that of the party bureaucracy, they even managed to convert Lenin's mausoleum into a shrine of power and authority, and his body into the relics of a Russian Orthodox saint. Lenin's International was disbanded and communist solidarity transformed into the hegemony of the mighty over the weak, with all the unprincipled embranglement entailed.

Today, after the unprecedented enormity of the sufferings and sacrifices of the Soviet peoples, and after last year's occupation of Czechoslovakia, there is a tragic topicality in words written by Lenin in 1895 at the outset of his visionary design and his struggle to achieve it.

Only if Russia is free and under no necessity to subjugate the Poles, the Finns, the Germans, the Armenians, and other small nations, or constantly to incite France against Germany, will she allow contemporary Europe to breathe in freedom, relieved of the burdens of war, with all the reactionary elements in Europe crippled and the power of the European working class enhanced.

Few men bear comparison with Lenin in respect of the suffering and solitude of his dying. But it is not this that makes him a tragic figure. He was one of those rare historical figures who lived to see the triumph of his ideas. His tragedy lies in history—in the transformation of his life-work into its inverse, of his creed into duplicity and wishful thinking.

The Times Saturday Review, December 6, 1969
© Times Newspapers Ltd., 1969 (Trans. Anon.)

12
The New Class

Contemporary Communism is that type of totalitarianism which consists of three basic factors for controlling the people. The first is power; the second, ownership; the third, ideology. They are monopolized by the one and only political party, or—according to my previous explanation and terminology—by a new class; and, at present, by the oligarchy of that party or of that class. No totalitarian system in history, not even a contemporary one—with the exception of Communism—has succeeded in incorporating simultaneously all these factors for controlling the people to this degree. [. . .]

I believe that power will remain the basic characteristic of Communism.

Communism first originated as an ideology, which contained in its seed Communism's totalitarian and monopolistic nature. It can certainly be said that ideas no longer play the main, predominant role in Communism's control of people. Communism as an ideology has mainly run its course. [. . .] This could not be said for the other two factors, power and ownership. [. . .]

To date, Soviet Communism, the type which has existed the longest and which is the most developed, has passed through three phases. [. . .]: revolutionary, dogmatic, and non-dogmatic Communism. Roughly speaking, the principal catchwords, aims, and personalities corresponding to these various phases are: Revolution, or the usurpation of power—Lenin. *"Socialism,"* or the building of the system—Stalin. *"Legality,"* or stabilization of the system—"collective leadership."

The New Class, 1957
(Trans. Anon.)

Ideas on the New Class

[The first hint of Djilas's concern with the failure of the Communist bureaucracy to implement democracy occurred in 1946 when he noted certain failures and shortcomings on the part of the people's committees

("Perversion of the People's Power"). His doubts about the bureaucratic aspects were temporarily displaced, first by the fervor with which he set out to construct socialism, and then by the threat posed by the Cominform Resolution of 1948. But by 1950, especially in his "Speech to the Students and Professors of Belgrade University," he returned to the theme, by that time seeing the bureaucracy as responsible for the behavior of the Soviet Union toward Yugoslavia. This theme was reiterated in 1951 in "The Brutality of the Bureaucracy."

His article "Class or Caste?" in 1952 marked an important step. It was his first attempt to analyze seriously—although still within the Marxist framework—the nature of the bureaucracy. In it he applied Marxist analysis to determine whether the Soviet bureaucracy was a class, in which case to oppose its development was futile, or a caste, in which case it could and should be resisted. The article appeared in *Svedočanstva* in February 1952, and an abbreviated version was published in *Borba* on April 6, 1952. *Komunist* published a "Discussion of 'Class or Caste?' by Stanovnik, Kristl and Djilas" in its March–April 1952 issue. Djilas's position was that, although the Soviet party bureaucracy enjoyed some of the property rights characteristic of a class (the rights to use, enjoy, and dispose of property), due to the collective nature of those rights, it lacked other rights (transferability and hereditability of property), and that therefore it was not properly a class, but, rather, a caste. As a caste, it could effectively be opposed. This conclusion was compatible with his own view of Yugoslavia at the time—namely, that the victory of the bureaucracy was not inevitable, but should be prevented by a thorough-going reform of the party before it was too late.

Between 1952 and 1956, when he concluded that the Soviet party bureaucracy constituted a historically new class, Djilas in fact had tried to reform the party in his own country. Indeed, Tito had even encouraged him to become involved in party reform. When Djilas encountered opposition from the party to his proposals, he became more convinced that he had to develop his ideas on party reform to the fullest possible extent. Although initially he believed that reform was possible, he later came to recognize that the overriding principle governing the new class was the maintenance of its own monopoly of power, and that therefore, while protest or dissent might be morally necessary for the individual, its chances of changing the course of history were slim.

By his own account, during the first three months following his party trial in January 1954 he was disoriented, isolated, and depressed, but after a few months he started writing about the party again. In March of 1955, a little more than a year after the whole affair had started (and a few months after his state trial in January 1955), his ideas were beginning to gel. He wrote the first draft of what was to become *The New Class*. During the summer of 1955 he made extensive revisions in "The

Omniscience of Folly," a lengthy essay started in 1954 examining the competence and personal interests of the party's inner circle and the rationale employed to justify their retaining a monopoly on political power.

In January 1956 Djilas completed three articles about the USSR and world Communism (prompted, he says, by the evident failure in the West to understand the changes taking place). Many of the ideas in these articles found their way into *The New Class*. In "The Essence of the Soviet System," (the companion piece to "The Soviet Union Today" and "Contemporary Revolutions"), Djilas presents his analysis of the political bureaucracy. He argues that the ruling class of the political bureaucracy manages property, distributes the proceeds, and establishes the evaluative criteria; that these rights over property are absolute because of the administrative monopoly of the political bureaucracy; that these absolute rights constitute, or are equivalent to, ownership; and that therefore the political bureaucracy is a class. (Though in 1952 he declined to identify the party bureaucracy as a class precisely because of the absence of transferability and hereditability of property rights, in 1956 his conclusion was different because he has altered his definition of class.) He further notes that these property rights are necessary to preserve the status of the political bureaucracy as a ruling class, and that this particular class has a previously unknown degree of monopoly of power, ideology, and ownership rights which it uses to protect those property rights. He also observes that because the individual has no rights except as a member of the group, each member is fundamentally insecure as an individual and is thus fanatically dedicated to the survival and prosperity of the group.

On May 1, 1956, he completed an article he titled "The New Class." He soon realized that the "new class" was the concept he had been looking for, and he set to work revising the old manuscript. Indeed, he found that his ideas had changed so much that he could scarcely use any of his old material. He completely revised his manuscript, which he finished shortly before he was sent to jail on November 19, 1956.]

May 1, 1958

Without any relation to today's holiday, May the First, I want to write down some details about *The New Class*. For a long time I have been planning to.

Had I not personally lived through what I did, I could not have written it. It was clear to me at once, the moment the conflict arose and sentence was passed on me at the Third Plenum, that the controversy was not about socialism but about the fact that presentation of ideas outside the established framework threatens the existing power. After the first trial (January 1955) I went for walks in February and March in the park on Topčider. It was there that the idea was first born that my thoughts might be of international significance.

During the summer of 1954 I had written three articles, "The Way Out of a Circle," for the *Daily Herald* of London, because the Labourite Davis, with whom I had a meeting, had said he would ask me for something like it. But he never wrote, and so nothing came of it. In March of 1955 I started the first draft and finished it within the month. It lay around until the summer of 1956. Then, in May, I think, I sent out *Land Without Justice*, which I was forbidden to do. American publishers showed an interest. I had the intention to revise the draft and had already started. The offers mentioned spurred me to speed up the matter. When I looked at the draft, however, I saw that I would barely be able to use any of it, so much had my thinking developed in those two and a half months. It was with great difficulty that I freed myself from the existing outline—divisions into chapters, etc. I should add that earlier in the winter (January 1956) I wrote three articles for *Life* which contained the basic ideas of that book. I felt compelled to write those articles because of the failure, throughout the world, to understand the essence of the changes in the Soviet Union. Those articles were not published. In the spring of 1956, for my own satisfaction I wrote an article called "The New Class." Thus I was moving gradually, and when I undertook to revise the book, the article "The New Class" was simply included with minor revisions.

Thus the book developed gradually. During this entire process my personal knowledge and my experiences played a great role. Here is one detail: At the Third Plenum and also afterward, I felt as if I had been through a Stalinist trial. I had the feeling for months that I was the only one who had experienced something like that. The subsequent measures against me, although I never wavered on questions of socialism, forced me to seek an explanation for these events. And if one bears in mind that I began those questionings and criticisms while I was still in power, then it is clear how I went in my thoughts and how I had to go.

If they had treated me differently, things would not be different, but perhaps they would have developed more slowly and had a milder and more humane form—without arrests, without damnation in the press, etc.

For a long time I could not find a title for the book. The draft from 1955 carried the title "Freedom and Property." In the spring of 1953, sitting in the car in front of the present Secretariat for Foreign Affairs, the thought struck me that capitalism had not resolved the problem of property and that socialism had not resolved the problem of freedom. For months I lived under the obsession of those two ideas: it seemed to me that the contemporary world is troubled by those two unresolved questions. That obsession entered the first draft. When I had rewritten the book in the summer of 1956, I saw that it must have a new title. For a long time I could not find it, and I kept trying the titles "Face of a World" and "Likeness of a World." Finally I found the most natural solution: I took the title of one chapter—"The New Class"—as the title of the book. It also provides the basic framework of the book.

One might think that the basic idea—the new class—is not original. But it is. Two Yugoslavs—Kristl and Mandić—took the position earlier than I did that the Soviet bureaucracy is a class; in 1952 Kristl polemicized about it to me. But their arguments were completely different and dealt only with Soviet bureaucracy. And in no way at all did they influence me. Of course, they would have gone further with their views (or someone else would have) had not the discussion about those questions died out in our country, especially after my dismissal and the unfortunate Third Plenum (January 1954). Kristl made an entire study of it, which I have not read, and Veljko Vlahović, as a member of the editorial board of *Nova Misao* or *Komunist*—I forget which—rejected it. And I see now, from one passing sentence, that also Bertrand Russell, in his *History of Western Philosophy*, takes the position that it is a class. I was not familiar with that view. If I had been, I would have cited it.

This much I can say: I arrived at my views independently. And I repeat: Unless I had traveled the road I did, I could not have arrived at those conclusions by pure reasoning.

The first draft ("Freedom and Property") took the position of "improving," so to speak, the ideal Communist society, although my criticisms of dogmatism and monopolism went quite far. I did not feel any passion while I wrote it. But while I was thinking about the composition of *The New Class* and writing certain parts, I felt the same excitement that one feels when writing poetry. I felt that the entire world was opening before me, that with my thought I was modeling its material, uncovering its secrets.

I knew that the book would be a success. But I did not expect so much uproar about it. While I was writing it, I supposed that I could be tried and sentenced, but not so severely. It was the same when I decided to publish it. It seemed to me that it was a matter of vital concern to me and that I owed it to my conscience to say what I had to say.

I do not regret anything. On the contrary. Something may not be the truth but if one feels that it is the truth and is convinced that it is, then one should treat it as one treats truth, that is, one should make all else subordinate to it. I am convinced that this document will live longer than I, even when it loses currentness. While writing it, I had a vision of how thousands of people throughout the world, inspired by it, were fighting. The vision was concrete, sensory, in which there were crowds, in columns, with steel helmets and banners. I am talking about a vision, and not about a real belief that it will happen. For I knew even then that people fight for concrete interests and under concrete slogans, but my work could only help in some intellectual way, especially socialists, who, I had discovered earlier, without any reason have a guilty conscience because they are not such good socialists and revolutionaries as the Communists. But I also knew that explanations, if they are correct, can give direction to thought, to different thoughts and theories, and through them influence the orientation of the masses. Probably that was behind all these visions. Was it conceit? No. I say that this is correct and that it must bo so. It had to be so. The words written here are only a document and not an excuse or an attempt to prove anything. [. . .]

Jail Diary (unpublished)

An Early Version of *The New Class*

The Soviet Union Today

Soviet Communism, like all other Communisms, passed during its development through two phases. The first was the revolutionary phase, the so-called Lenin period. The second was the dogmatic phase, the so-called Stalin period. Now it has moved unobserved into a third, unnamed phase. This phase, in my view, could best be called "nondogmatic Communism."

The first phase was characterized by the fight for power, the demolishment of the old society and the abolishment of property relations. The second phase was characterized by industrialization or, to put it better, by strengthening the new forms of property and by establishing in all fields of social life the totalitarian power of the political apparatus—the party and the secret police. These two phases were distinct from each other psychologically and intellectually. The first was one of impetus, faith and ideological uplift. It was brutal in its relations to its enemies, but had a certain ideological tolerance, at least within party ranks. The second was realistic and severe. The General Secretary, Stalin, and his Politburo were the only ones who could define and develop dogma as political power. A secondary element of that phase was the intermittent nationwide purge and annihilation of even the best-intentioned ideological adversaries.

The third phase began only with the death of Stalin, although its first symptoms could have been observed even during his lifetime.

Today the changes in the Soviet Union have already gone so far that one can not only recognize their existence but can also define many of their essential characteristics. In that way we can at least understand the direction and methods of present-day Soviet policy with respect to internal and foreign policy. The Soviet Union plays the leading role in the development of world Communism. Whatever happens in the Soviet Union may be applied to all other Communist movements and is, in principle, the measure of them. That is why I speak here only about changes in the Soviet Union.

Before going further, the following points should be mentioned. When I say there are three phases, I do not imply that aspects of the first two may not be found in the third. By making this distinction I only want to point out that each phase of Communism has its own characteristics in addition to aspects of the other phases. Each new phase is indeed the child of the preceding one. Communism changes and develops only as necessary to conserve its essence and its principal characteristics.

By overlooking this fact, even if the fact of the change has been correctly noted, many an observer of contemporary Soviet events has reached the wrong conclusions. Some observers saw changes so profound relative to former phases of Communism that they were able to believe that the Soviet system itself was changing. Other observers went to the opposite extreme, likewise wrong, concluding that because the system remained essentially the same, the changes were unimportant.

The truth however is that the changes are deeper and more far-reaching than is commonly supposed. But they take place with the aim of giving ever greater support to the base of the system, not to alter it. The results confirm this.

Today the Soviet system has such an appearance that at first glance Stalin might be alarmed at what happened to his work. But the teacher and master of today's Soviet leaders may rest in peace. In fact, what he might be astonished at is the strengthening, in a new manner, of the same system which he took over from Lenin. Actually, he would not be surprised. He would know that these are only new ways of strengthening the same old system.

The more recent changes were prepared by developments in the earlier phase, which, as is known, lasted for a quarter of a century.

The industrial development begun by Stalin has gone so far that the organizational control that made it work has now become worn out. In connection with this, relations between the social forces have also altered. The party bureaucracy and the technical intelligentsia have become the new, more important social forces. Governing only by secret police and party secretaries has become a hindrance. Organizational and other changes as well as a more tolerant atmosphere can no longer be avoided. The most outstanding and most important characteristic of today's situation is that we no longer have individuals (personalities) like Stalin who represent in their person all the ideological, political and other aspects of Communism. There is not even any chance that a new

Communist personality will come forth in Russia even if one of the present Communist leaders took the reins completely in his own hands. The era of the cult of a leader and personal dictatorship has come to an end. It would be an impediment to the established complex activity of contemporary Communist society as well as to the new, more sophisticated scientific production. Therefore governing by party-political oligarchy or so-called collective leadership instead of personal dictatorship has become not only possible but also unavoidable. This is the essence of the evolution of Communism from Stalin to Khrushchev.

For the Soviet system internally this means much more than it may seem to those living abroad. It brings with it a diminished role for the political police. The police had "out of a good servant" become "a bad master" even for the party oligarchy itself. By gaining more legality and security for themselves, the party oligarchy for a short time, at least, had to offer a little of the same to the masses. Social unrest was thereby avoided. However, it also meant that different tendencies of the political bureaucracy had a chance to come to the fore. By ending the power of a personality one ends also the ideological monopoly of that personality. This in itself meant a great deal to a nation living under dogmatic compulsion.

Superficially, everything is changing in Soviet Russia. But the one thing that does not change is the essence of the Soviet system, that is, party monopoly of power (which for a long time was actually transformed into the power monopoly of a very small circle of party and political functionaries). One can even say that there is no chance at all that this party monopoly will be threatened by future changes. We can be sure that the leaders on whom this depends do not have the will to change it. The totalitarian power of a political apparatus over society changes in form but remains unchanged in essence. From a preponderantly administrative dictatorship it now becomes a preponderantly political control. The latter may be milder but it is no less solidly entrenched.

The essence of the change is that instead of administrative centralism in the hands of party functionaries and secret police, which expressed itself by a complicated and ineffective administration, now party centralism within the leadership prevails. Therefore a certain administrative decentralization in economic and other fields cannot be avoided. This goes along with a strengthened role of the party in control and also in administration.

All these changes have already had and will have consequences for Communism in other countries, especially in the satellite nations, depending on what the international situation will permit. Contact and coordination of the work of foreign Communists and satellite nations is now done more through political and party activity than by direct administrative commands. This is important for Communist countries and parties—if not for the outside world—because it gives them greater freedom of action. However, unity on general aims remains essential and is even strengthened.

Another important fact is that the changes in this third phase of Communism are not followed by serious dogmatic fights or by the development of important new theoretical ideas. This is quite understandable. The present Soviet leaders are not constructing a new system, such as Lenin and Stalin did, but are giving the final polish to an existing system. Although dogma in no way loses its importance, it is in fact being transformed slowly from an orientation and an inspiration into a direct means of governing. The leaders will pressure the people to adhere to dogmatic orders only if it is a practical necessity. Thus ideological prosecution becomes milder. [. . .]

In any event, these changes can lead to a lessening of Communist fanaticism. [. . .] The present changes in Russian Communism will introduce into the Communist movement a more flexible, more adroit and more realistic attitude. These changes have not only eliminated the possibilities of severe social clashes internally but also facilitated and speeded up a new economic expansion of the country. Externally, these changes will give the Soviet leaders the means for a more varied penetration into the non-Communist world. That penetration is made not only through the activity of Communist parties but directly by economic and political actions by the Soviet government.

Some observers are confused by changes in Soviet foreign policy. It is not in the interest of the Soviet government and the Communist leaders to be as exclusive, brutal and dogmatic in foreign policy as they were in Stalin's time. I remember times when Vishinsky, speaking about the Arab world, said that "all this feudal capitalistic mash is not worth one Soviet division." Such an attitude belongs to the past, not only because the Arab world convinced the Soviet leaders of its importance but also because these leaders understood that it was necessary for them to change their attitude toward the non-Soviet world if they wanted to avoid isolation. Also, the Soviet Union is not now compelled to be such a carefully closed country as in the earlier phases of Communism.

It is therefore important to bear in mind that the possibilities for Soviet economic penetration of the non-Communist world are far greater than one might imagine. The Communist economy is always at the service of the political needs of the Soviet government. For Communists, direct profit and efficiency are secondary to basic political aims. Furthermore, today's Soviet economy also has a direct interest in emerging from its self-contained Stalinist isolation. By this act it would strengthen its essential meaning. It must safeguard its monopolies of managing and distributing material goods for the party bureaucracy.

Of course, these changes do not happen by themselves alone, but are also the result of the reaction of the Communist world to the technological revolution abroad. The leaders of world Communism have realized that their system, which is momentarily technically inferior, can be more easily moved forward if they abandon their Stalinist isolationism. The device to end this isolationism is the theory of so-called coexistence between different systems, which has become acceptable to them (for the time being) despite the fact that the Soviet internal system excludes not only every other system but also every other way of thought.

One cannot deny the attractiveness of tendencies surrounded by an aura of Gandhi's humanism to the protagonists of peaceful coexistence, especially its attractiveness in Southeast Asia. But the problem of peace today is not whether different systems can exist together (they always have) but the impossibility of developing modern technology within the degeneration of a politically closed system. Stable peace in the world is possible only through the gradual coming together of mankind, which in practical terms means through the active interaction of different systems. There are two prerequisites for peace: freedom and national sovereignty. Whatever the desires of its leaders, the closed Soviet system by its nature excludes such a mixture of different ideological systems. I had occasion to hear Stalin say, in 1945, that modern war differs from past wars by the fact that today's victor brings with him and imposes his own sociopolitical system. He already knew that his closed totalitarian system could maintain itself more successfully if it were more widespread. His aim was deepening of differences, not easing or overcoming discrepancies of various social systems.

Behind concrete crucial questions—Germany, Korea, Eastern Europe, Indochina, disarmament, the Middle East—lies something far more important. Of course the solution of those questions would point toward a solution of the fundamental problem, and therefore every step in that direction is useful. But in regard to that basic point, let us look at the Geneva foreign ministers' meeting. It was by no means accidental that the fourth point on the agenda—the exchange of ideas—met with the greatest possible objection from the Soviet leaders. Superficially it was not important, but when examined carefully, in fact, it was the main problem: the gradual removal of the impediments that above all Soviet isolationism had erected between nations—in other words, the elimination of ideological, political and other monopolies of one group over the nations that constitute the Communist world of today. [. . .]

One can conclude that the so-called stalemate (balance of power) was acceptable to Soviet leaders for a short time. It was however only a momentary condition. They have now convinced themselves that they can perfect their totalitarian system more easily if they shift this balance of power in their favor. Incidentally, Russia did not accept this momentary stalemate only because of the hydrogen bomb. It was also accepted because the Soviet leaders wanted it, because they detected in their own system new and as yet unexploited possibilities for internal and external expansion. The truth is that a nondogmatic attitude and a flexible approach have already helped them to upset the balance of power. But because they did not have to do it with weapons, as Stalin did in Korea, or with threats, as he did in Yugoslavia, they were able to present themselves as fighters for peace and to continue with their propaganda.

I had the opportunity to make the acquaintance of many Soviet leaders, among them Bulganin and Khrushchev. Their behavior and their way of speaking have changed and become more simple and direct. However, Bulganin, methodical and self-controlled, has not changed at heart. Neither has Khrushchev—that robust man cast in a single mold. Coming out of Stalin's shadow, in a simple but also more flexible and winning way, they strengthen (at home and abroad) the system to which they belong. And the essence of that system is and remains the total ownership of men's bodies and souls.

To sum it up: all these changes do not weaken, but, rather, strengthen the Soviet Union and Communism throughout the world. Communism today has become more dangerous, not only in its traditional threats to life and property, but also, and more important, in threats to the basic human freedoms without which we cannot have a righteous social system, progress in the world, or the unity of peoples.

Leaders and peoples who fail to understand this will be compelled to pay the high price of bitter experience for the lesson. In politics, all else can be excused or compensated for, except what is lost because of one's illusions.

Winter 1956 (unpublished)

Contemporary Revolutions

By "contemporary revolution" I mean revolution of the Bolshevik type, which has given completely new political, social and spiritual aspects to our age. There are other revolutions, of course, national and political revolutions, but they did not produce anything absolutely new, even though they may have had some characteristics in common with Communist revolutions.

When we speak about revolutions of the past—so-called democratic or bourgeois revolutions—we usually refer to the French Revolution. Democratic and bourgeois revolutions, especially the latter, had some important characteristics in common. They were all carried out after the new economic and social systems had already infiltrated and so shaken the old ones that only the old political system remained. The social and economic situations were ripe for change and only the political system hindered their full development. These revolutions did not create a new society but only removed the obstacles that stood in the way of an already acceptable new society. As soon as they had overturned the old political system, the revolutionary methods and organs became in their turn a hindrance to the development of the new society. Therefore they had to be dissolved quickly. The role of the revolutionary forces also ended with the revolution itself.

As a rule, bourgeois revolutions took place in the most developed countries—Holland, England, France and even the United States. They broke out because feudal and similar relations prevented modern social and economic forces from developing more fully. In all these revolutions, the judiciary played a special and important role. The chief revolutionary aim was the establishment of a legal system under which all men were treated equally. This is because these revolutions tended to go no further than the development of a new political system. One prerequisite was the establishment of a legal system giving equal rights to all and replacing feudal rights and aristocratic privileges of the old system. Although facilitated by favorable surroundings, these revolutions did not need an outside factor to bring them about. Conditions were already ripe and favorable in the life and conscience of entire nations. For those nations, it was not necessary to have a special event such as war or foreign occupation to break down the old state and social system.

In all those revolutions foreign elements played a minor role. The revolutions were first of all national revolutions. In earlier times there was no world market to link nations economically. Although these revolutions had a great influence on other countries, they were almost exclusively revolutions taking place within a single nation. Even the French Revolution, although it shook feudal Europe and spiritually affected the entire world, remained within its national frame.

Because of this, all these revolutions, even when they ended with the despotism of those who carried them out, led in the final analysis to political freedom. The Jacobins, the Napoleon and the Cromwell dictatorships were bound to collapse once they had accomplished what was necessary for the establishment of the new order.

Contemporary revolutions are a completely different story. Their most outstanding feature is that they occur in countries that have never had, or have had only to a limited extent, bourgeois revolutions and that therefore have never had a free political life. The only exception to this is Czechoslovakia, and possibly Hungary. But the new system in both of these countries is not the product of internal revolutionary process, but of occupation by the Soviet army. For the East European countries, except Czechoslovakia, it is also characteristic that their Communist movements were weak. Even in Czechoslovakia the prewar Communist movement was much more parliamentary than revolutionary in character.

All these revolutions occurred under the special conditions of a war that to a great extent had already demolished social relations and the state apparatus and that at the same time had compromised the ruling classes and their parties. This was true even of the Chinese Revolution. While it is true that the Chinese Revolution started with a series of local uprisings and then went over to a period of twelve years of guerrilla warfare in the remainder of the country, it ultimately won out in conditions that had been created during the Japanese occupation and the Second World War.

Contemporary revolutions are like national revolutions in that they are also national revolutions, but they are national in a different way and form. Contemporary revolutionists feel, ideologically at least, a part of the entire Communist movement and that their activity is related to that of the leading Communist state, the Soviet Union. Thus, outside influences play a greater role in Communist revolutions than they did in earlier revolutions. Also these Communist upheavals took place at a time when the world was linked not only by a world market but by the export of capital and the world system of production. Thus these revolutions are national only in that they are the national expression of the clash and struggle that is taking place throughout the entire world.

As I have stressed, contemporary revolutions take place in underdeveloped countries and in those countries that have not evolved through political freedom to free social and economic development. The countries having revolutions of the Soviet type, due to special circumstances, lagged in their development, and when they wanted to move toward freedom and industrialization they could not do so. By the time they were ready to move out of feudalism and anxious to have industrialization and parliamentary rule, technology elsewhere had developed so far and had become so expensive that they, the backward countries, could not hope to meet the competition of developed nations. Foreign capital, which had taken excessive profits from these underdeveloped countries, now showed its "selfishness" and refused to give them aid, and the poor nations lacked the financial means to help themselves. These nations had either to collapse or to make up their minds to use extreme measures, which meant to accomplish by political means what they could not do by economic means. They used political pressure to extract the necessary funds from the masses. They attempted to carry out their industrial revolution by political means alone.

Unlike bourgeois revolutions, however, in modern Soviet-style revolutions the use of force does not end with the victory of the revolution. Instead, force develops a verve and refinement that it never possessed in earlier revolutions. Instead of being the midwife of the new society, force becomes the creator.

The dictatorship resulting from a Soviet-style revolution had to change itself in the process of changing society in order to industrialize. Lacking sufficient capital and in constant conflict with the outside world which resented the loss of semicolonial territory, the dictatorship had not only to mobilize all of its human and material resources but also to extinguish all opposition. Under these circumstances, it was necessary to control all spiritual and even personal life. Dictatorship became totalitarianism. The evolution of Russia from the Communism of Lenin to the Communism of Stalin parallels the development of the raw revolutionary dictatorship into totalitarianism and parallels the transformation of Russia from an agricultural into an industrial nation.

While the development of every revolution leads toward a dictatorship, even if only for a short period, modern Soviet-style revolutions must inevitably develop into totalitarianism.

One might expect—and there have been such illusions even among the Communist opposition in the Soviet Union—that with the attainment of industrialization, the dictatorship would cancel itself out. But it has happened the other way around—dictatorships have become stronger and stronger in Soviet-style revolutions, altering only their outer forms.

It is thought that the reason for this is the reluctance of those who have seized power to give it up. That is partly right. Few can resist the temptation to rule over others, even where such rule brings no material gain. The Bolsheviks are no exception.

But, in addition, the Bolsheviks were not really disinterested in material gain. In order to bring about industrialization, it was necessary to have a group personally interested in achieving industrialization. Thus was created a class of privileged administrators and managers. That class became even larger than society's needs required. Thus was created a class that was better paid than all the others. This class also ensures the stability and survival of the Communist system by ensuring the contributions of the masses. The moment such a class is created, it develops its own way of life and transforms itself into a privileged group possessing special power within the given social order. Without this privileged and in fact parasitic class it is impossible to make the system either operate or continue in existence.

But there is an even deeper reason for the continuation of the dictatorship. The leaders of Communist revolutions cannot bring about industrialization as they had planned, or even as the West did in the past. They are forced to separate themselves from the outside world in order to perpetuate themselves and to industrialize. Materially and spiritually the Communist country must be closed to the outside world. However, despite the prophecies of Communist theoreticians, the dictatorship finds itself in a perpetual race with the Western world because the West is constantly advancing industrially. The dictatorship must compete so that it will not end up at the same comparative level of industrialization, vis-à-vis the outside world, as when it started.

It seems that dictatorships go around in circles. Wishing to raise their standards of living by industrialization, they at the same time have to keep them low in order to invest. Shut off from the outside world, in a constant bitter struggle both at home and abroad, dictatorships became suspicious of everything and likewise everyone becomes suspicious of them. Therefore heavy and war-related industries become the main tasks of their economic development. [. . .] In order to hold their position in competition with technically more developed enemies, they have to fight, to enlarge their territories and to exploit foreign territories. The alternative, to link their production and their exchange of goods and to bring them into line with those of other countries, is not acceptable to Communists because it would mean that they would gradually have to give up their closed system. [. . .]

In this way a contemporary revolution that begins with the nation's need to develop and also to rid itself of a nondemocratic regime transforms itself into a totalitarian and aggressive state. The expansion of revolutionary ideas evolves itself into the aggressive politics of the state.

At the same time that the contemporary revolution developed into the struggle with foreign capitalism and underdeveloped local capitalism, the working class and the socialist movement developed. Democratic revolutions, struggling against those medieval prejudices that tried to preserve feudalism, fought in the name of freedom and free thought. In the same way, in our time, the fight is carried out in the name of socialism and of a future Communist society conceived in the most idealistic manner.

It is not our task here to measure to what degree those revolutions have been really socialist. However, we must again stress that today's revolutions in underdeveloped countries carry out with force applied by the state those tasks that in the past in developed countries were carried out by private capitalism, with its economic elements. We may therefore conclude that modern revolutions wear an ideal socialist and democratic garb but in reality are supporters and proponents of state power. The judicial aspect of these revolutions is merely formal and propagandistic. The real goal is power and spiritual monopoly.

Dictatorships of the Soviet type and all other modern dictatorships possess similar characteristics: the establishment of a closed economic and political system, nationalization for political but not necessarily economic reasons, social demagogy, etc. The Nasser military dictatorship talks about Arab socialism in a way similar to the way the semifascist Perón dictatorship spoke in the name of the working class. In other words, every contemporary dictatorship, no matter from what ideological and social factor its leader is derived, tends toward totalitarianism. This is a mark of the epoch.

For people from the non-Communist world it is hard to understand how masses of humans can endure such long-lasting deprivation and such a strange and oppressive form of terror. But this is explained to a certain extent by what we have already said. They had no choice except that which the dictatorship brought them.

Dictatorship brought terror and deprivation, but it also brought with it the only industrialization these peoples had known and without which the nation would disintegrate. The masses were deeply discontented, but a serious and organized resistance could not arise because no other solution to the historical dilemma into which they had fallen—industrialization or ruin—had any chance of being realized. The only alternative offered to the masses was a return to the old way of life. However, they knew from experience that they could not and would not want to live in the old way, which was in some respects even more unfavorable than those conditions that now exist. In fact, there have been no serious suggestions from within or without for an alternative to despotism and totalitarianism. Any such suggestion must start from the recognition of the country's need to industrialize and to transform itself from its semi-colonial status.

History confirms that the masses will endure any system as long as there is no real possibility of a change for the better. People must be able to see the possibilities in advance and must believe that those possibilities will guarantee not only a change for them but also a better life for those who will come after them. Only then will the masses desire change and desire freedom. Until then, freedom, in this or that form that is dear to so many peoples, remains something nice but abstract and unreal, and life would have to get a great deal worse before they would be willing to die for it. [. . .]

Winter 1956 (unpublished)

Later Ideas

The New Class

In reality, the Communists were unable to act differently from any ruling class that preceded them. Believing that they were building a new and ideal society, they built it for themselves in the only way they could. Their revolution and their society do not appear either accidental or unnatural, but appear as a matter of course for a particular country and for prescribed periods of its development. Because of this, no matter how extensive and inhuman Communist tyranny has been, society, in the course of a certain period—as long as industrialization lasts—has to and is able to endure this tyranny. Furthermore, this tyranny no longer appears as something inevitable, but exclusively as an assurance of the depredations and privileges of a new class.

In contrast to earlier revolutions, the Communist revolution, conducted in the name of doing away with classes, has resulted in the most complete authority of any single new class. Everything else is sham and an illusion. [. . .]

As in other owning classes, the proof that it is a special class lies in its ownership and its special relations to other classes In the same way, the class to which a member belongs is indicated by the material and other privileges which ownership brings to him.

As defined by Roman law, property constitutes the use, enjoyment, and disposition of material goods. The Communist political bureaucracy uses, enjoys, and disposes of nationalized property.

If we assume that membership in this bureaucracy or new owning class is predicated on the use of privileges inherent in ownership—in this instance nationalized material goods—then membership in the new party class, or political bureaucracy, is reflected in a larger income in material goods and privileges than society should normally grant for such functions. In practice, the ownership privilege of the new class manifests itself as an exclusive right, as a party monopoly, for the political bureaucracy to distribute the national income, to set wages, direct economic development, and dispose of nationalized and other property. [. . .]

To divest Communists of their ownership rights would be to abolish them as a class. To compel them to relinquish their other social powers, so that workers may participate in sharing the profits of their work—which capitalists have had to permit as a result of strikes and parliamentary action—would mean that Communists were being deprived of their monopoly over property, ideology, and government. This would be the beginning of democracy and freedom in Communism, the end of Communist monopolism and totalitarianism. [. . .]

Although he did not realize it, Lenin started the organization of the new class. He established the party along Bolshevik lines and developed the theories of its unique and leading role in the building of a new society. This is but one aspect of his many-sided and gigantic work; it is the aspect of his work which came about from his actions rather than his wishes. It is also the aspect which led the new class to revere him.

The real and direct originator of the new class, however, was Stalin. He was a man of quick reflexes and a tendency to coarse humor, not very educated nor a good speaker. But he was a relentless dogmatician and a great administrator, a Georgian who knew better than anyone else whither the new powers of Greater Russia were taking her. He created the new class by the use of the most barbaric means, not even sparing the class itself. It was inevitable that the new class which placed him at the top would later submit to his unbridled and brutal nature. He was the true leader of that class as long as the class was building itself up, and attaining power.

The new class was born in the revolutionary struggle in the Communist Party, but was developed in the industrial revolution. Without the revolution, without industry, the class's position would not have been secure and its power would have been limited.

While the country was being industrialized, Stalin began to introduce considerable variations in wages, at the same time allowing the development toward various privileges to proceed. He thought that industrialization would come to nothing if the new class were not made materially interested in the process, by acquisition of some property for itself. Without industrialization the new class would find it difficult to hold its position, for it would have neither historical justification nor the material resources for its continued existence.

The increase in the membership of the party, or of the bureaucracy, was closely connected with this. In 1927, on the eve of industrialization, the Soviet Communist Party had 887,233 members. In 1934, at the end of the First Five-Year Plan, the membership had increased to 1,874,488. This was a phenomenon obviously connected with industrialization: the prospects for the new class and privileges for its members were improving. What is more, the privileges and the class were expanding more rapidly than industrialization itself. It is difficult to cite any statistics on this point, but the conclusion is self-evident for anyone who bears in mind that the standard of living has not kept pace with industrial production, while the new class actually seized the lion's share of the economic and other progress earned by the sacrifices and efforts of the masses. [. . .]

It would not be important to establish the fact that in contemporary Communism a new owning and exploiting class is involved and not merely a temporary dictatorship and an arbitrary bureaucracy, if some anti-Stalinist Communists, including Trotsky as well as some Social Democrats had not depicted the ruling stratum as a passing bureaucratic phenomenon because of which this new ideal, classless society, still in its swaddling clothes, must suffer, just as bourgeois society had had to suffer under Cromwell's and Napoleon's despotism.

But the new class is really a new class, with a special composition and special power. By any scientific definition of a class, even the Marxist definition by which some classes are lower than others according to their specific position in production, we conclude that, in the U.S.S.R. and other Communist countries, a new class of owners and exploiters is in existence. [. . .]

The ownership of the new class, as well as its character, was formed over a period of time and was subjected to constant change during the process. At first, only a small part of the nation felt the need for all economic powers to be placed in the hands of a political party for the purpose of aiding the industrial transformation. The party, acting as the *avant garde* of the proletariat and as the "most enlightened power of socialism," pressed for this centralization which could be attained only by a change in ownership. The change was made in fact and in form through nationalization first of large enterprises and then of smaller ones. The abolition of private ownership was a prerequisite for industrialization, and for the beginning of the new class. However, without their special role as administrators over society and as distributors of property, the Communists could not transform themselves into a new class, nor could a new class be formed and permanently established. Gradually material goods were nationalized, but in fact, through its right to use, enjoy, and distribute these goods, they became the property of a discernible stratum of the party and the bureaucracy gathered around it. [. . .]

Collectivization was a frightful and devastating war which resembled an insane undertaking—except for the fact that it was profitable for the new class by assuring its authority.

By various methods, such as nationalization, compulsory cooperation, high taxes, and price inequalities, private ownership was destroyed and transformed into collective ownership. The establishment of the ownership of the new class was evidenced in the changes in the psychology, the way of life, and the material position of its members, depending on the position they held on the hierarchical ladder. Country homes, the best housing, furniture, and similar things were acquired; special quarters and exclusive rest homes were established for the highest bureaucracy, for the elite of the new class. The party secretary and the chief of the secret police in some places not only became the highest authorities but obtained the best housing, automobiles, and similar evidence of privilege. Those beneath them were eligible for comparable privileges, depending upon their position in the hierarchy. The state budgets, "gifts," and the construction and reconstruction executed for the needs of the state and its representatives became the everlasting and inexhaustible sources of benefits to the political bureaucracy. [. . .]

The new ownership is not the same as the political government, but is created and aided by that government. The use, enjoyment, and distribution of property is the privilege of the party and the party's top men.

Party members feel that authority, that control over property, brings with it the privileges of this world. Consequently, unscrupulous ambition, duplicity, toadyism, and jealousy inevitably must increase. Careerism and an ever-expanding bureaucracy are the incurable diseases of Communism. Because the Communists have transformed themselves into owners, and because the road to power and to material privileges is open only through "devotion" to the party—to the class, to "socialism"—unscrupulous ambition must become one of the main ways of life and one of the main methods for the development of Communism.

In non-Communist systems, the phenomena of careerism and unscrupulous ambition are a sign that it is profitable to be a bureaucrat, or that owners have become parasites, so that the administration of property is left in the hands of employees. In Communism, careerism and unscrupulous ambition testify to the fact that there is an irresistible drive toward ownership and the privileges that accompany the administration of material goods and men.

Membership in other ownership classes is not identical with the ownership of particular property. This is still less the case in the Communist system inasmuch as ownership is collective. To be an owner or a joint owner in the Communist system means that one enters the ranks of the ruling political bureaucracy and nothing else.

In the new class, just as in other classes, some individuals constantly fall by the wayside while others go up the ladder. In private-ownership classes an individual left his property to his descendants. In the new class no one inherits anything except the aspiration to raise himself to a higher rung of the ladder. The new class is actually being created from the lowest and broadest strata of the people, and is in constant motion. Although it is sociologically possible to prescribe who belongs to the new class, it is difficult to do so; for the new class melts into and spills over into the people, into other lower classes, and is constantly changing.

The road to the top is theoretically open to all, just as every one of Napoleon's soldiers carried a marshal's baton in his knapsack. The only thing that is required to get on the road is sincere and complete loyalty to the party or to the new class. Open at the bottom, the new class becomes increasingly and relentlessly narrower at the top. Not only is the desire necessary for the climb; also necessary is the ability to understand and develop doctrines, firmness in struggles against antagonists, exceptional dexterity and cleverness in intra-party struggles, and talent in strengthening the class. Many present themselves, but few are chosen. Although more open in some respects than other classes, the new class is also more exclusive than other classes. Since one of the new class's most important features is monopoly of authority, this exclusiveness is strengthened by bureaucratic hierarchical prejudices.

Nowhere, at any time, has the road been as wide open to the devoted and the loyal as it is in the Communist system. But the ascent to the heights has never at any time been so difficult or required so much sacrifice and so many victims. On the one hand, Communism is open and kind to all; on the other hand, it is exclusive and intolerant even of its own adherents. [. . .]

The new class is most sensitive to demands on the part of the people for a special kind of freedom, not for freedom in general or political freedom. It is especially sensitive to demands for freedom of thought and criticism, within the limits of present conditions and within the limits of "socialism"; not for demands for a return to previous social and ownership relations. This sensitivity originates from the class's special position.

The new class instinctively feels that national goods are, in fact, its property, and that even the terms "socialist," "social," and "state" property denote a general legal function. The new class also thinks that any breach of its totalitarian authority might imperil its ownership. Consequently, the new class opposes *any* type of freedom, ostensibly for the purpose of preserving "socialist" ownership. Criticism of the new class's monopolistic administration of property generates the fear of a possible loss of power. The new class is sensitive to these criticisms and demands depending on the extent to which they expose the manner in which it rules and holds power.

This is an important contradiction. Property is legally considered social and national property. But, in actuality, a single group manages it in its own interest. The discrepancy between legal and actual conditions continuously results in obscure and abnormal social and economic relationships. It also means that the words of the leading group do not correspond to its actions; and that all actions result in strengthening its property holdings and its political position.

This contradiction cannot be resolved without jeopardizing the class's position. Other ruling, property-owning classes could not resolve this contradiction either, unless forcefully deprived of monopoly of power and ownership. Wherever there has been a higher degree of freedom for society as a whole, the ruling classes have been forced, in one way or another, to renounce monopoly of ownership. The reverse is true also: wherever monopoly of ownership has been impossible, freedom, to some degree, has become inevitable. [. . .]

The new class cannot avoid falling continuously into profound internal contradictions; for in spite of its historical origin it is not able to make its ownership lawful, and it cannot renounce ownership without undermining itself. Consequently, it is forced to try to justify its increasing authority, invoking abstract and unreal purposes.

This is a class whose power over men is most complete known to history. For this reason it is a class with very limited views, views which are false and unsafe. Closely ingrown, and in complete authority, the new class must unrealistically evaluate its own role and that of the people around it.

Having achieved industrialization, the new class can now do nothing more than strengthen its brute force and pillage the people. It ceases to create. Its spiritual heritage is overtaken by darkness.

While the new class accomplished one of its greatest successes in the revolution, its method of control is one of the most shameful pages in human history. Men will marvel at the grandiose ventures it accomplished, and will be ashamed of the means it used to accomplish them.

When the new class leaves the historical scene—and this must happen—there will be less sorrow over its passing than there was for any other class before it. Smothering everything except what suited its ego, it has condemned itself to failure and shameful ruin.

The New Class, 1957
(Trans. Anon.)

The Faceless New Class

With the overthrow of Khrushchev in 1964, the Soviet party bureaucracy finally freed itself from the nightmare of a purge—in this case an "anti-Stalinist" purge—that could have resulted in an unenviable and hazardous loss of the bureaucracy's preponderance over the remaining forces of power, especially over the governmental and the economic apparatus. In this way the party bureaucracy attained peace and security, but at the same time it lost the creativity and vision which from the revolution onward had comprehended and been accompanied by purges in the ruling ranks and the weeding out of social forces "condemned by history." It sounds horrifying and absurd, and it is: in a totalitarian system, such as the Soviet system is today in the main, new forms of social existence are unrealizable and inconceivable without a cleansing within the ruling stratum and without mass repressions.

The fall of Khrushchev, however, did not mean the suppression of some group opposed to the party bureaucracy or separated from it. In fact, the governmental and economic apparatuses, mainly because they are led by and composed of party people, are parts of the same political-party organism, and accordingly each of them has a separate structure, caste characteristics and narrower interests. But in spite of the uniformness of the three basic apparatuses of power—the party, the governmental and the economic—differences and friction between them are of enormous significance for Soviet society and indirectly, since what is involved is a world power, for the whole world. Roughly speaking, all changes within the Soviet system have been the product of shifting relations between these three apparatuses of power. Under Lenin, there was the ideological leadership of the party along with relative equality and established boundaries between the party, governmental and economic organs. Under Stalin, initially we had subordination of all other organs to the party apparatus; later, the party was brought under personal control or control by the secret police as the selected governmental organ. Under Khrushchev, an attempt was made to establish equality of the apparatuses. "Collective leadership" reflects the formal supremacy of the party apparatus.

Obviously, the Soviet Union did not lose in Khrushchev a genius who could lead it from despotic shackles and schemes into free, democratic currents. The structure of Russia is still today such that reforms are realized by the personal power of the despot-reformer. And even in Khrushchev's case reformism was inseparable from personal power, that is, from his own "cult of personality." A dynamic pragmatist, but still the child of party bureaucratism, Khrushchev behaved as if it were possible to change the established system and the experienced ruling stratum by means of the surrogates of ideas without the movement of new social forces. To the party bureaucracy even that was too much: Khrushchev became inconvenient, even dangerous, the moment his "anti-Stalinist" campaigns threatened the party bureaucracy's monopoly of power and of mind.

All Soviet leaderships up to now have presented themselves as "collective." The present leadership differs from previous ones only in that there are no outstanding personalities within it. This is—or so it appears to be—the ideal condition for the party bureaucracy: members of the forum are equal, if in nothing else, at least in evading any radical, personal initiatives.

At present, conservatism is the most visible, chief characteristic of the Soviet "new class." That "class" is capable of maintaining itself, but it is not capable of creating. Satisfied with its own social position, it trembles in the face of change. The Soviet oligarchy has frozen its own dogma out of fear that any debate, any rethinking of its dogma, could break out into an epidemic and lead to the disintegration of both the ideology and the "new class." But the party apparatus seized that collective bliss through concessions to the other organs of power, in the first instance to the governmental, or, more precisely, to the corps of higher officers. The strengthening of the role of the army began with Stalin's death. Beria and Molotov were brought down by the army's active support. That strengthening continues under the current "collective leadership." Stalin has been rehabilitated, principally as the wartime commander-in-chief; heavy industry and armaments, and especially the naval fleet, have priority. The military chiefs are more prominent and incomparably more able than the party *apparatchiks*. This strengthening is also related to modern military technology, the only field in which the Soviet Union keeps pace with the West. It is especially significant that all foreign policy successes—the occupation of Czechoslovakia and the untangling of it, the curbing of China, penetration into the Mediterranean and the Middle East—are primarily the work of the army. But the army lacks the sanctity and the unifying role of the party apparatus. The present situation within the ruling stratum of the Soviet Union in reality is characterized by the specific balance between the party apparatus and the military apparatus.

But like all balances in society, this one cannot be of long duration. A shift of the scales in favor of the party apparatus seems the least likely; the ideology and creativity of the party are in decay, on an irreversible decline, not only within the USSR but throughout Communism. And besides, Soviet society no longer develops in isolation from world relationships and events. Whether the balance of power will be disturbed in favor of the army, military production and a global strategy, or in favor of the economy, international understanding and rising standards of living, will depend heavily on external developments.

A shift in the scales in favor of the economy is the most complex, although it would be the most useful to the Russian peoples and would be gladly welcomed in the world. But regardless of relations among the ruling groups, the heresies of freedom are spreading; in the Soviet Union disagreements and political groups are sprouting and political trials are multiplying. These forces, however, do not have any visible chances of success in the near future. But today it is essential that they exist, that they can no longer be uprooted, and that those who rule today or who will be rulers in the future will not be able, due to their existence, to rule with complete peace of mind.

Uncut version of "The 'New Class'—Faceless, Fearless,"
The New York Times, January 7, 1971

VI

UTOPIA AND BUREAUCRACY

Whereas the "classless society" in Stalin's time was a society of shattered classes, today the classless society is one of classes lacking cohesion, legitimacy or institutions. [. . .]

But with the disintegration of ideology, that is, with the crisis of totalitarianism and of the "new class" of the party bureaucracy—which is taking place exactly in our time—the working class in "socialist" countries will gradually appropriate its class and social roles. [. . .] Each "thaw," each move toward freedom sets in motion the working class and pushes it forward. That was turbulently visible in Hungary in 1956, in Czechoslovakia in 1968 and in Poland in 1970. [. . .]

The party bureaucracy is not a stable, monolithic stratum. In assuming all functions of society, the party involuntarily becomes susceptible to the changes and trends in society. Society becomes stratified with technical progress and the accumulation of wealth. A "socialist" "middle class" also emerges, composed of managers, the free professions and technical experts. A part of the party bureaucracy belongs to that middle class. New ideas appear—ideas about more efficient production, about more democratic and more socialist management. That is the climate and those are the perspectives that make it possible for the working class to accept society as its own, for only in that way, in such a society, will the working class have its own class rights. But "socialism" is just at the beginning of that process: the basic form of the workers' struggle is still passive resistance and occasional outbursts.

The results often mock the makers. Thus one must conclude with sorrow that the workers in "socialism" have yet to obtain what their brothers in "capitalism" have long had as inalienable rights—the right to strike, the right to professional organization, and the right to their own beliefs, free from any ideology.

"The Worker and Bureaucratic Society,"
February 1, 1973

13
Soviet Hegemony and Imperialism

All the demons that Communism believed it had banished from the forthcoming as well as the real world have crept into the soul of Communism and become part of its being. [. . .] Communism [. . .] has become transformed into national political bureaucracies and states squabbling among themselves for prestige and influence, for the sources of wealth and for markets. [. . .] The communists were compelled [. . .] first to wrest power—that delight above all delights—from their opponents, and then scrabble for it among themselves. This has been the fate of all revolutionary movements in history. [. . .]

Communism has not only failed to become a religion, a "scientific" one, in fact, but it also disintegrated as a world ideology. [. . .]

In reality, Communism no longer exists. Only national Communisms exist, each different in doctrine and in their policies practiced and in the actual state of affairs they have created. What binds the Communists together today in international relations, or makes them want to be bound together, is fear of perils at home and abroad, or is the result of pressures from one of the Communist superpowers. [. . .] Soviet Communism has become the mainstay of conservative forces at home and abroad, while Yugoslav Communism is a model of the weakness and disintegration of Communism, both in theory and practice, and at the same time is a model for national Communism and a hope for a democratic transformation. [. . .]

The crisis of Communism is not brought about by economic, so-called objective factors, but almost exclusively by human, so-called subjective factors. [. . .] They are individual acts, a human defiance of coercion, whether that coercion takes the form of brute force or of spiritual domination or, as is most frequently the case, of a mixture of the two. [. . .]

Communism, like every other revolutionary despotism, has failed to bring itself into harmony, let alone identify itself, with unidealized, natural desires, and with the ordinary life of the people.

The Unperfect Society, 1969
(Trans. Dorian Cooke)

Socialist Colonies

Press Conference

Question: What position does Yugoslavia take toward the international Communist movement? Does Yugoslavia favor a new Communist International?

Answer: Yugoslavia is steadfastly against the creation of a new Communist or similar international. That position follows from our general stand concerning the workers and democratic movement. The workers and democratic movement should develop independently on the basis of the conditions and position of their country.

Q: Does Yugoslavia think that the Communist parties of different countries must have mutual ties?

A: The workers and democratic movement should and must co-operate mutually on the principle of equality. The creation of any centralized leadership in which any individual country or movement would play a leading role would only complicate real co-operation because contemporary development moves toward greater equality and independence and at the same time toward greater economic and other interdependence.

Q: How do you assess the strength of the anti-Comintern forces in East Europe, including the U.S.S.R.? Do you think that other countries might join Yugoslavia in its position against domination by the U.S.S.R.?

A: The anti-Cominform forces of East Europe should be divided into two types: one is the forces of bourgeois opposition and the other is those forces that seek equal relations with the U.S.S.R. The first cannot gain serious support among the people because the people do not want to return to the past. The second cannot be destroyed because they resist en masse and because they are the progressive forces. I have insufficient information to predict the concrete roads along which socialism will develop in general, and especially in Eastern Europe. [. . .]

Q: Can Communist Yugoslavia and capitalist United States of America co-operate over a longer period of time in the political and economic sphere?

A: Yugoslavia believes that it is possible to have peaceful co-operation among all countries, and therefore between socialist Yugoslavia and capitalist United States of America, with one proviso: that such co-operation is based on respect, on mutual independence. [. . .]

Q: Could you tell us something more about reports that Dimitrov supported Marshal Tito?

A: Dimitrov personally told me, in his private railroad car near Belgrade at the end of April, 1948, when the Bulgarian delegation was on its way to Prague, that we should stand our ground. He spoke in connection with a letter of the Central Committee of the CPSU (b) which had just arrived a few days before and which signified the beginning of Soviet pressure against our country. I replied that the Yugoslavs have plenty of firmness and asked him what the Bulgarians would do. He replied that the most important thing is for us to stand fast, and the rest will come by itself. During that short conversation there was another Bulgarian present, whose name for understandable reasons I cannot disclose. That meeting with Dimitrov was very cordial, but his tone changed noticeably when Chervenkov and others entered his car.

In the subsequent campaign against Yugoslavia, all the Bulgarian leaders came out against Yugoslavia. But Dimitrov kept silent. He attacked Yugoslavia at the Congress of the Bulgarian Communist Party with only one weak and unconvincing part of his general report. During his illness and after his death, the Bulgarian leaders sharpened their anti-Yugoslav position.

From previous relations with Dimitrov we knew that he was an honest supporter of co-operation with Yugoslavia and that he was close to our beliefs. He believed that Bulgaria should develop independently but in co-operation with Yugoslavia.

We did not announce this, in order to avoid making trouble for his supporters in Bulgaria. But now the situation is changed, and the Bulgarian people should know what we thought.

Q: What measures will the Cominform countries take against Yugoslavia?

A: One should expect further diplomatic and political pressure and provocations against Yugoslavia by the Eastern European countries, but this too will end in failure, as all past measures did.

Q: What is the strength, if any, of the pro-Cominform position within Yugoslavia?

A: The strength of the Cominform inside Yugoslavia is almost non-existent. This is the weakest opposition to the new Yugoslavia in its course toward progress. The expression "opposition" is not accurate, since Cominform activity in Yugoslavia does not go beyond simple espionage and diversion.

Q: Do you think that the United States will attach political conditions to the economic aid to Yugoslavia?

A: The present development of relations between Yugoslavia and the United States does not provide a basis for any conclusion that the government of the United States will make aid contingent upon Yugoslavia's yielding politically. The Yugoslav government will not under any circumstances give in to any country that threatens its independence in domestic or foreign policy. The Yugoslav government will attempt to develop co-operation on the basis of mutual respect with all countries.

Q: Do you think that the Chinese Communists will develop in their own specific way or will they be tied to the Soviet Union?

A: I think that the Chinese People's Democracy will develop in its own specific manner, regardless of what relations they have with the Soviet Union.

Borba, November 5, 1949

Anti-Semitism

The bloody prologue in Prague ended so that the bloody drama could begin. The legal miscarriage of justice, as usual, is only a preface to the mass campaign that will be carried on outside the law and the courts. The legal masquerade only serves to justify and to set the stage for what is to follow.

This time it is not just a gory play with a monstrous plot and scenes and characters designed to shock and paralyze the spirit of the Czechs and the Slovaks.

This time it is something else, something quite new.

It seems to me that this was not sufficiently recognized, even in our own country.

The bourgeoisie gladly warms its hands around Stalin's pyres. Its press presents those fires as a quarrel within the Communist family, as a revolution devouring its own children, and as an aspect of Soviet foreign policy (in this case, its utilization of the Arab-Jewish conflict). Although there is some truth here, there is very little, for all this is superficial. Bourgeois public opinion condemns itself to blindness on just that question where it thinks itself freest. The struggle against Communism, against socialism as an ideal, makes it impossible for it to perceive the anti-Communist, anti-socialist reality of its Soviet adversary.

The problems are very simple.

In January of 1948 I was dining with Stalin. Other Soviet leaders were present. The atmosphere was unlike any before; there was reserve on both sides, many thoughts remained unuttered, and we had a few flare-ups. Stalin asked me: "With the exception of Pijade, why don't you have more Jews in your Central Committee?" I explained to him how our movement had developed. He started to laugh heartily and sarcastically. With sympathy he called me and the other Yugoslav Communists anti-

Semites. I heard a lot, talked a lot about this anti-Semitic theme in the USSR. One man from the apparatus of the Central Committee of the Soviet party bragged how Zhdanov had weeded out all the Jews from the apparatus of the Central Committee. The deputy of the Chief of Staff of the Soviet Army, Antonov, had by chance been discovered to be a Jew. This had ended his brilliant career.

The struggle against "cosmopolitans" in the USSR is really a covert struggle against Jewish intellectuals in the USSR. During the war anti-Semitism was more or less openly expressed in the army. In Moscow in 1948 there was a lot of discussion about the Hungarian Central Committee, which, as is well known, is made up mostly of Jews. And in the Moscow trials Jews always played a major role. There are no longer any Jews in the public life of the USSR. They are citizens of the lowest rank of public life in the USSR. The same thing is now taking place in Eastern Europe. And all that over a handful of people—sufferers who survived the fascist extermination. And all this happens, and continues to happen, regardless of whether some of the Jews are bourgeois or socialist.

The Prague trial revealed the conscious, organized anti-Semitic line without any doubt. It showed, as is common in the case of Stalin, that reality is often disguised. Anti-Semitism is hiding behind the struggle against Zionism and Americanism and even behind the struggle against anti-Semitism—which is quite in the style of Stalinist absurdities. [. . .]

Anti-Semitism has already become the rule in Eastern Europe. It attains monstrous forms, which would be grotesque if they were not so bloody. The Hungarian leadership is the most anti-Semitic in its propaganda just because it is made up primarily of Jews. They want to prove that way that they have freed themselves from the "Jewish cosmopolitan mentality" and that they are totally faithful to Stalin and his "Great Russian" imperialism. They are not only crawling, but they are also attempting to guess the hidden secret wishes of the master. This is not strange. The Hungarian leadership finds itself doubly despised by the Hungarian people: because it is the servant of Moscow and, traditionally, because it is Jewish. The past bane of capitalism, which was presented to the Hungarian peasants and craftsmen in the image of the Jew-miser, today becomes the "socialist" bane, again in the image of the Jew, but this time a bureaucrat. This is convenient for all kinds of combinations of the Soviet government. Stalin only smiles like a devil while Rakosi and Gero and others of the Jewish bunch, with their anti-Semitic propaganda, braid the rope that will hang around their necks. Ilya Ehrenburg can sing paeans to Great Russian imperialism at peace congresses. But in the Kremlin they know what they need to know about him. During the war I heard Stalin describe him as sly and cunning, at the very time when Ehrenburg was at the height of his anti-German glory. His spirit is too cosmopolitan to be claimed by them. He is still necessary because of

French and other cosmopolitan intellectuals. But those are some of his last songs, and in reality are the hoarse barks of an old dog who begs a last bite from his master.

From history we know that each order became reactionary the moment it began to turn anti-Semitic; the pogroms against the Jews were the surest sign of the blackest social reaction. History does not repeat itself, but it is very seldom wrong. Great Russian bureaucratic state capitalism had to become not only nationalistic but also racist. This is inevitable, for how else can one justify the struggle for world hegemony and the oppression of other peoples except through one's own "special" merits? Thus it must inevitably become, indeed, it already is, anti-Semitic. Because of their history, Jews became the carriers of trade and of the city way of life, creating channels through which flowed the separate regions into the first common life. Some of them some of the time tried to be feudal lords and good Christians, but they didn't succeed. Their usury and trade, regardless of how callous and inhumane, undermined feudal relationships and spread ties among regions and peoples. They were the yeast of the new civilization. Those who condemn them are thus undermining their own world. But it has been a long time since the Jews were such an "evil" yeast. They are not the only channels or the only merchants. Christian usurers and merchants are greater "Jews" than the Jews themselves. The cosmopolitan spirit remained and still remains, but only there where they are scattered. It is also mainly because they are scattered that they are persecuted. In Palestine they are as nationalistic and as socialistic as the people in any other state.

The Prague trial is really in the first instance a part of the struggle against Palestine and, through being coquettish with the Arabs, for the Middle East. In essence it is anti-Semitic. It is a struggle against the "last" remnants of the spirit that binds East European peoples with the rest of the world, the socialist or "cosmopolitan-Jewish" spirit. The moment any order becomes exclusive, closed within itself and sufficient unto itself—and thus becomes also reactionary—such an order must also become anti-Semitic because of the spirit that lives within Jews. This spirit cannot be dangerous to progress and socialism, despite the fact that it is a remnant of the past, mainly because it is a remnant of the past. To liquidate the socialist spirit completely can be most conveniently accomplished in the East through an anti-Semitic form. And thereby one liquidates the Jews also as carriers of something international, even if this is not socialism. And therein lies the essence of the matter. But also in this: by forcing Gottwald and others to spill the blood of their own friends, to commit treason and perjury, they appear completely servile in the eyes of their people and they remain the formless agents of Moscow. All the rest is merely historical decoration or arrangements for the practical requirements of the moment.

It is not easy to understand how during the last war the Jews, helplessly, stupefied, paralyzed, waited without struggle patiently for Hitler's slaughterhouses and "obediently" walked into them. But is it not also true that other reactionary regimes excluded them from the life of the nation. Had not the USSR already begun to exclude them from its life? Did anyone in the world really protect them? Isn't it true that everything was done to exclude them, to cast them out of the history of each people and out of history in general? What can such a neglected people do? This was a people without a stable class, without a territory, without stable fighting organizations, a people saturated with the traditional spirit of adaptability and obedience. Yes, that resignation in the face of extermination was "unexplainable," especially in our country where revolutionary struggles were going on all around us. This is exactly the most tragic historical event of this quiet and meek people—which through prior development was so handicapped that it could not struggle to save itself even there where the struggle could have been successful. They died peacefully or ran aimlessly. Imbued with a spirit of the past, as in the past, as in the Middle Ages, they gave themselves up to a fate they could not explain and thus could not resist.

At the execution ground many Jews tried without success to convince the Nazi's that they were anti-Bolsheviks. Today in vain they are doing the same thing—trying to convince Stalin that they are not against the USSR, that they are for socialism. They are supposed to stop being that which they are—a people of specific characteristics formed through historical development, a people imbued with an international spirit (regardless of which one, because it is not the same for all Jews). And they are imbued with that spirit mainly because they are a people scattered throughout the world. The spirit is strongest there where they are persecuted. They cannot kill the spirit within themselves, and thus they have to be persecuted wherever there is a regime enclosed within its own fortresses.

But because of that, the fully human and humanistic duty today is not only to uncover anti-Semitism as the basic element in Stalin's bloody game, but also to struggle for the defense of this small, unfortunate but beautiful people, to whom all despots in history have denied the right to breathe the air and to enjoy the sun and of whom one can say that, although persecuted, resettled and scattered, burned, tortured and exterminated through thousands of years, of whom one can say—if such comparisons were not senseless—that it gave to humanity nothing less than any other "chosen" people, and further they did not give its part, part of the progressive, democratic forces, in isolation, but always within the framework of, and together with, the people with whom it lived. It is not a question of defending capitalism or socialism, or, least of all, Palestine, which is a state the same as any other, with its own way of life and its ties and which will defend itself as best it can. It is a question of defending a people who are still subject to the most terrible and longest-enduring crimes known to history. And not in medieval times or even in Hitler's times, but in "socialist," "revolutionary" countries. Precisely socialism and democracy must come to their defense if they do not wish to undermine themselves, to lull the democratic and peace-loving consciousnesses and the revolutionary spirit of their own people into some kind of Stalinist socialism. For Stalinism is nothing but common imperialism, chauvinism and racism, new only in that it emerges in a state-capitalist form, decorated with "socialist" feathers and hostile to private capital, but in reality it is even more deeply hostile to real socialism and real democracy. That struggle must be carried on for the sake of that small and unfortunate people and also because of the spirit for which that people is persecuted. And also for the sake of socialism, which preaches the idea of the brotherhood and equality of all peoples.

Anti-Semitism soils and extinguishes everything human and democratic in man. The imprint of its shame cannot be erased from history. The intensity of anti-Semitism is the measure of how much a reactionary order has succeeded in enslaving its own people. History also proves that those who use it, even if their power is still growing, are at the beginning of their own end.

Borba, December 14, 1952

The Storm in Eastern Europe

With the victory of national Communism in Poland, a new chapter began in the history of Communism and of the subjugated countries of Eastern Europe. With the Hungarian people's revolution, a new chapter began in the history of humanity.

These two events, each in its own way, sharply express the internal condition of the East European countries. If the events in Poland encouraged the aspirations of Communist parties—particularly those of Eastern Europe—for equality with Moscow, the Hungarian Revolution made a gigantic leap and placed on the agenda the problem of freedom in Communism, that is to say, the replacement of the Communist system itself by a new social system. If the former event had encouraged both the people and certain Communist circles, the latter encouraged the popular masses and democratic tendencies.

Between the two events, although they happened almost simultaneously, there lies a whole epoch. The changes in Poland mean the triumph of national Communism, which in a different form we have already seen in Yugoslavia. The Hungarian uprising is something more, a new phenomenon, perhaps no less meaningful than the French or Russian Revolution.

In short, these events have brought to the fore the following new questions: (1) the further possibilities of national Communism; (2) the replacement of Communism by a new system, and, along with this, the right of a people heretofore under Communist rule to choose its own—non-Communist—path of development; (3) the problem of the future foreign (and, in my opinion, internal) policy of the Soviet regime.

The experience of Yugoslavia appears to testify that national Communism is incapable of transcending the boundaries of Communism as such, that is, to institute the kind of reforms that would gradually transform and lead Communism to freedom. That experience seems to indicate that national Communism can merely break from Moscow and, in its own national tempo and way, construct essentially the identical Communist system. Nothing would be more erroneous, however, than to consider these experiences of Yugoslavia applicable to all the countries of Eastern Europe.

Yugoslavia's resistance to Moscow in 1948 was possible, first of all, because the revolution took place in the course of the struggle against foreign occupation; in this revolution, an independent Communist country was formed, and with it a new class, the Communist bureaucracy. Not one of the Eastern European countries had this kind of a class, because their Communists received power from the hands of the Soviet regime. For this reason, a united, autonomous Communist bureaucracy could not have been formed. Therefore, there were and still are essential differences between Yugoslav national Communism and that of the Eastern European countries, even though their common keynote is equality with Moscow.

Yugoslav national Communism was, above all, the resistance to Moscow of the Communist party, that is, of its leaders. Not that the people opposed this resistance, not that they did not support it and benefit from it—quite the contrary. But the interests and initiative of the leaders played a crucial and leading role. The resistance of the leaders encouraged and stimulated the resistance of the masses. In Yugoslavia, therefore, the entire process was led and carefully controlled from above, and tendencies to go further—to democracy—were relatively weak. If its revolutionary past was an asset to Yugoslavia while she was fighting for independence from Moscow, it became an obstacle as soon as it became necessary to move forward—to political freedom.

In the countries of Eastern Europe, the reverse is true. There, Communist resistance to Moscow resulted from the discontent of the popular masses. There, from the very start, unbridled tendencies were expressed to transcend the bounds of national Communism itself. The leaders cannot everywhere control and subjugate the popular masses; therefore in some cases they try to halt any further estrangement from Moscow. That is the case, for example, in Czechoslovakia and Rumania. In Bulgaria and especially in Albania, further de-Stalinization and the strengthening of national Communism have been halted—only partially because of fear of Yugoslav domination, although that plays some role. Other motives were decisive: The victory of national Communism in these countries would probably have meant the beginning of the end of the existing system.

Yugoslavia, both as an example and through the initiative of its leaders, played an indispensable and important part at the beginning of the transition of Eastern European countries to national Communism— but only at the start. As the price of reconciliation with Belgrade, Moscow was induced to recognize verbally the equality of Yugoslavia and its "independent path" to "socialism." In that way, the deep disaffection of the Eastern European nations received legal possibilities for expression. Limited but sanctioned protests against inequality with Moscow began to turn—and in Hungary did turn—into protest against the system itself.

Yugoslavia supported this discontent as long as it was conducted by the Communist leaders, but turned against it—as in Hungary—as soon as it went further. Therefore, Yugoslavia abstained in the United Nations Security Council on the question of Soviet intervention in Hungary. This revealed that Yugoslav national Communism was unable in its foreign policy to depart from its narrow ideological and bureaucratic class interests, and that, furthermore, it was ready to yield even those principles of equality and non-interference in internal affairs on which all its successes in the struggle with Moscow had been based.

The Yugoslav experience has thus determined the tendency of the national Communists in both their internal and external policies—that is, it has determined the limits to which they are willing to go. But wishes are one thing and possibilities another.

In all this, Moscow, with its imperialist appetite, is not a passive observer but an active participant. In order to avoid an uprising in Poland and to gain time, it yielded to national Communism there. Gomulka's accession to power was not only the result of the efforts of the Polish Communists; to a larger extent, it represented a compromise between Moscow and the turbulent masses of the Polish people. Given independence from Moscow, Gomulka took a historic step forward. But with half-hearted reforms he will soon reach a dilemma—which Moscow had foreseen. He will have to choose between internal democracy, which has become inseparable from complete independence from Moscow, and the ties with Moscow required to maintain the Communists' monopoly of power. The events in Hungary have only accelerated this dilemma, which Gomulka will not be able to avoid. The victory of national Communism in Poland is not the end, but rather the beginning of further disagreements and conflicts inside the country and with Moscow.

It is difficult to say whether national Communism in Poland will choose freedom and independence rather than totalitarian rule and dependence on Moscow. But without a doubt many Communists in Poland will not hesitate to choose their own country and freedom. Knowing Gomulka, a man who is unusually honest, brave and modest, I am convinced that he himself will not long hesitate if he is confronted with such a choice.

In Hungary, however, such internal conflicts are over: Not only did the so-called Stalinist set vanish, but the Communist system as such was repudiated. Moscow at first tried to cover its intervention by bringing national Communism to power through Imre Nagy. But Nagy could only install national Communism with the assistance of Soviet bayonets, and this threatened the very end of Communism. Having finally arrived at the choice between Soviet occupation and independence, Nagy courageously decided to sacrifice the party and Communist power—which had already been crushed—for the sake of his country and freedom. Sensing Moscow's equivocal game, he asked for the withdrawal of Soviet troops, declared Hungary's neutrality, and appealed for the protection of the United Nations. His government, up to that point insignificant, became overnight the symbol of national resistance.

Moscow could no longer preserve Hungarian Communism; it now faced the choice of either leaving Hungary or occupying it. Thus, its imperialism dropped its last "socialist" mask.

Had the Hungarian Revolution not only brought political democracy but also preserved social control of heavy industry and banking, it would have exercised enormous influence on all Communist countries, including the USSR. It would have demonstrated not only that totalitarianism is unnecessary as a means of protecting the workers from exploitation (*i.e.*, in the "building of socialism"), but also that this is a mere excuse for the exploitation of the workers by bureaucracy and a new ruling class.

Moscow fought the Hungarian Revolution not only for external but also for internal reasons. Just as the Yugoslav revolt revealed Moscow's imperialism with regard to Communist countries, so the Hungarian Revolution threatened to reveal the Soviet internal system as the totalitarian domination of a new exploiting class—the party bureaucracy.

Had the Hungarian Revolution been saved from Soviet intervention, it would have been difficult indeed for Moscow to obscure its internal conflicts by means of foreign conquests and the "world mission." The Soviet system would soon have been confined to its own national boundaries, and there, too, the citizens would be forced to reflect on their position and their destiny. And not only the citizens, but also the leaders. They would have to break up into different groups which could no longer carry out mutual purges within their own closed circle, but would be forced to bid for popular support. Thus, new processes would begin in the Soviet Union, too.

The attack of Israel, Britain and France on Egypt cannot permanently divert attention from the events in Eastern Europe, although it certainly encouraged the most reactionary and aggressive elements in the USSR to settle accounts with the Hungarian people. Human history is changing in Eastern Europe, and that is its center today. The outmoded colonial war in the Middle East will have to be stopped.

Moscow and all the other Communist regimes, each in its own way, now face a dilemma which they never faced before. The Communist regimes of the East European countries must either begin to break away from Moscow, or else they will become even more dependent. None of these countries—not even Yugoslavia—will be able to avert this choice. In no case can the mass movement be halted, whether it follows the Yugoslav-Polish pattern, that of Hungary, or some new pattern which combines the two.

The view that the movement in Bulgaria and Rumania must be slow because of their undeveloped working classes seems dubious to me. In these countries, the peasantry is deeply nationalistic and, once the process starts, may well play a more important role than it did in Hungary. In Czechoslovakia, despite an advanced working class, no significant movement has yet emerged. But if it does, it is likely to go much farther than that of Hungary.

Nobody can predict precisely what Moscow's ultimate course will be. At the moment, it is playing a dual role: recognizing national Communism verbally, simultaneously undermining it by not renouncing its hegemony and imperialism. Of course, the USSR falsely depicts its intervention and pressure as "aid" to and "security" for Communism as such in the subjugated countries. But that plays only a minor role in its actions. Moscow's policy toward Communist countries clearly reflects a will to resist the breakup of the empire, to preserve the leading role of Soviet Communism—a will demonstrated in its efforts to use national Communism as a means and a mask for its imperialist, expansionist policies.

At the same time, however, all these actions involve Moscow not only in external strife, but also in internal conflicts. One can declare with certainty that there is a split within the Soviet leadership, and that even the most reactionary and imperialist (the so-called Stalinist) group is hesitant in its actions. The influence of this group prevails today, especially in regard to the Eastern European countries. But that does not mean that the other group is for the independence of these countries. The difference between them lies in their methods: whether to stick to the old army and police methods (Stalinist imperialist methods), or apply new ones in which economic and political elements would be dominant. Attempts at introducing the new methods led to the Polish case, the return to the old ones led to Hungary. Both methods proved ineffective. From this spring the splits and conflicts in the USSR.

Hesitation, duplicity, ideological and political controversies, inconsistency in the use of methods, reversals of attitude, and a consistent and feverish insistence on keeping their own positions—all of these things reveal cleavages and contests among the leading group of the Soviet Union. Further changes in this group seem most plausible, and they will be of great importance both for the USSR and for the rest of the world.

There can be no doubt that the rest of the world—perhaps for the first time since the Bolsheviks took power—can directly and positively influence the direction of these changes. Despite the Soviet repression in Hungary, Moscow can only slow down the processes of change; it cannot stop them in the long run. The crisis is not only between the USSR and its neighbors, but within the Communist system as such. National Communism is itself a product of the crisis, but it is only a phase in the evolution and withering away of contemporary Communism.

It is no longer possible to stop the struggle of the people of Eastern Europe for independence, and only with great effort their struggle for freedom. These two struggles are gradually becoming one. If Moscow's imperialism suffers defeat and is prevented from war adventures, the USSR, too, will have to undergo considerable internal changes. For, just as it is compelled to be national in its forms, in essence Communism is one and the same, with the same historical origins and the same destiny. The events in one Communist country necessarily affect all other Communist countries, as in one and the same living organism. And just as Yugoslav Communism, separating itself from Moscow, initiated the crisis of Soviet imperialism, that is, the inevitable birth of national Communism, in the same way the revolution in Hungary means the beginning of the end of Communism generally.

As in all other great and decisive historic events, the Hungarian fighters for freedom, struggling for their existence and country, may not have foreseen what an epochal deed they had initiated. The world has rarely witnessed such unprecedented unity of the popular masses and such heroism. The unity of the popular masses was so strong that it appeared as though there had been no civil strife, as though a ruling class had not been wiped out overnight as if it never existed. And the heroic intoxication was so high that bare-handed boys and girls were stopping the tanks of the interventionists who, like the Cossacks of Nicholas I in 1848, tried to suppress their liberty and enslave their country.

This event will probably not be repeated. But the Hungarian Revolution blazed a path which sooner or later other Communist countries must follow. The wound which the Hungarian Revolution inflicted on Communism can never be completely healed. All its evils and weaknesses, both as Soviet imperialism and as a definite system of suppression, had collected on the body of Hungary, and there, like festering sores, were cut out by the hands of the Hungarian people.

I do not think that the fate of the Hungarian Revolution is at all decisive for the fate of Communism and the world. World Communism now faces stormy days and insurmountable difficulties, and the peoples of Eastern Europe face heroic new struggles for freedom and independence.

The New Leader, November 19, 1956
(Trans. Anon.)

The Unquenchable Fires of Czechoslovakia

The tragedy of the Czechoslovak leaders—Dubček, Svoboda, Smrkovsky and Cernik—is not that they had illusions, but, rather, that they were lacking in them. It is precisely here that their sacrifice lies. Deprived of illusions, and to ease the tragedy of their peoples, they agreed to the dictates of the Kremlin and thereby risked bringing upon themselves the permanent shame of unvaliant betrayal. Such could have been done only by men who cared more for their peoples than for their own places in history, by men who discovered truths and ideas capable of cleansing and vindicating all temporal weaknesses and inconsistencies. What they consented to while Soviet prisoners pains them and will pain them for a long time. But their consciences should be clear: the freedom they proclaimed and the tragedy that befell their country are already an integral part of the experience and consciousness of mankind and cannot be extinguished or forgotten.

What really happened in Czechoslovakia? What is the meaning and significance of the changes brought about and proclaimed there?

Even before the Czechoslovak events it was apparent that Communism as an ideology and as a world movement had fallen into conflicts and crises from which there was no escape. First it was the leaders of the Yugoslav revolution who in 1948 defended their national independence and their revolutionary morality against Soviet hegemony and Stalin's methods; in 1961 the leaders of the Albanian revolution similarly defied Khrushchev; in 1963 the leaders of the Chinese revolution contested Moscow's monopoly over Communist movements and Communist doctrine; finally all parties now rise against any kind of a center, and all sorts of heresies and sects burst into flames and spread throughout the world. A special significance is reserved for the tragic national and democratic uprising of the Hungarians in 1956, which revealed the irreconcilable conflict between the existence of central European peoples and the Russo-Soviet state and its societal forms.

It was only after the overthrow of the Novotny regime in January of this year that the democratic Communists and the people of Czechoslovakia made the first conscious, real steps in the direction of transforming the Communist party into a nonideological, democratic party and transforming the Communist authority into an elected authority dependent on the free will of citizens. Freedom of the press had already been realized and a guarantee of the rights of the party minority had been drafted. For the first time the policy of a Communist party in power became public and subject to criticism, and the ideas of its top leaders ceased to be directives for the entire society. The visions of reformists of Communism about the union of collective property with personal freedom became a reality, and Czechoslovakia, in mediating between East and West and in bringing them together, found her true being and realized her mission.

All these changes, doubtless, are organically linked to the history, culture and character of the Czechs and Slovaks and likewise were imposed by economic sluggishness and by the aspirations of the spirit. At the same time they took place in a unique world ideology (Communist), which is already torn apart and disunified and in a unique system (Communist), which, although diverse and divided, pretends to be a model for all nations and all societies. And since today almost half of mankind lives under Communism and since Communism in one form or another is present in all quarters and in all ideas of today's world, the Czechs and Slovaks and their leaders, in their reforms, built a construct of worldwide significance. It exposed new horizons and gave new hopes to all those who strive for the convergence of peoples and for a freer human condition. For a single moment, Czechoslovakia glistened with the hopes of the entire world.

But the Czechs and the Slovaks and their leaders knew, unlike the Hungarians and their leaders in the 1956 uprising, that they could not escape from the commonwealth of states and from the social and ideological foundations in which their construct had taken root, even though from the very beginning these foundations had been hostile. The Czechs and Slovaks endlessly apologized, even though they knew it was not possible to seek pardon from Gomulkas, dulled by outmoded "proletarian" and party dogmas, and even less from the faceless Russian *apparatchiks* fearing for their class and imperial interests. True, the international positions and situations of the other great powers were such that Czechoslovakia had no one to whom to turn, or from whom to seek aid. Aware of the foreign situation and convinced of the justness and inevitability of their cause, the Czechs and Slovaks and their leaders did not even attempt such an appeal. Their equanimity and strength lie in the fact that they remained faithful to their construct and stood their ground until the foreign power crushed them.

Obviously the occupation surprised even them, as it did all honest men, although they must have considered the possibility. But they perceived, they understood, that even an occupation could not destroy what had started under them. And even though the Czech leaders often had doubts and from time to time were fainthearted, they firmly and resolutely clung to the idea of human freedom and national sovereignty which life itself forced upon them with all the irresistibility and infallibility that only life can have.

They called those events, justifiably, a renaissance, and in reality it was one of those rare moments when new ideas unite with the existence, with the essence of a nation. These ideas inevitably arise from the vital needs of nations and societies under Communism. Party oligarchs and bureaucrats can stifle them but they cannot uproot them. These ideas are no longer heresies and revisionisms and abstract theories but social realities and national requirements and potentialities. That is why the Czechoslovak leaders could sign their names to the papers brazenly dictated to them like slaves in Moscow and still retain the trust of their people.

Czechoslovakia is occupied but not defeated. Soviet intelligence agents knew everything—by all accounts even the most secret deliberations of the Czechoslovak leaders. But they could not aid their masters in evaluating the determination and the will of the Czechs and Slovaks. The armies of occupation were met with neither flowers nor guns, but with the moral resistance of the whole nation, which astonished the world and restored its faith in the unquenchable thirst for truth and the indestructibility of freedom. The ideological, moral and political defeat of the Soviet Union is unprecedented and almost incomprehensible. The first country of socialism, the erstwhile center of world Communism, the liberator of Czechoslovakia from Hitler's occupation, the Soviet Union failed in a Communist country to find a single stooge capable of forming a government and was instead compelled to negotiate with its arrested leaders and to restore to them again their former perquisites.

As might have been expected, the occupation stifled free democratic currents and deepened the conflicts among the Czechoslovak leaders and the dilemmas within themselves and within the peoples of the Czech and Slovak nations. Viewed differently, these are conflicts and dilemmas between consciousness and action, between ideas and possibilities. These conflicts and dilemmas devastate all fighters and all nations, even the fighters in the USSR and the Russian nation under Communism. Today it is possible to outlast these conflicts and dilemmas and to develop peaceful forms of struggle, but no escape from them will exist in Eastern Europe until the replacement of the hegemonistic and monopolistic rule of the party oligarchy and bureaucracy in Russia itself and until relations between the atomic superpowers and between them and China are changed. . . . Communism is torn apart and disintegrated, but its existence and its fate are inextricably linked with the rest of the world. The dilemmas and conflicts involved are nothing but specific forms of the same conflicts and dilemmas that beset contemporary mankind and the world as a whole. In a torn and divided world, it seems that only dogmatists and despots can remain intact. . . .

The occupation of Czechoslovakia is not an occupation in the classic sense. By means of invasion, Soviet leaders obtained superiority of power and now attempt through the hands of the leaders of the Czechoslovak renaissance to extinguish the freedom and independence, to destroy the conscience and to poison the spirit of the Czechs and Slovaks. In this process they are very careful not to disrupt Czechoslovak industry, which is indispensible to them. They are even more cautious in their treatment of their "class brothers"—the Czechoslovak party bureaucracy—because only in the bureaucracy can they find support, and also because they do not wish to alarm or embitter people of the corresponding strata and currents in Yugoslavia and Rumania.

Under conditions of the occupation it is possible that some Czechoslovak leaders will lose their equilibrium and plunge headlong down irreversible dogmatic and subservient roads. But personal destinies are of no consequence. What is important is what is happening and what is going to happen: Czechoslovakia will smolder with freedom and will gather the forces of retaliation and—as once before, after occupation by Hitler in 1938—it will warn the world by its tragic fate.

On Czechoslovak soil was lost a great world battle. But there is no reason for despair. Not a single hope, not a single truth has been extinguished. All that is needed is more suffering, clearer visions, a more resolute struggle.

Czechoslovakia has become the conscience of the entire world.

The Central European Federalist (New York) , December 1968

The Conflict of Empires

The USSR and China: A Fundamental Contradiction

The fears of the anti-Communists (and the hopes of the Communists) that the victory of the Chinese revolution would not only eliminate traditional differences between the Chinese and Russian empires but also open the way for the world victory of Communism proved unfounded.

Indeed, the very opposite happened. Nothing in Communist reality follows the rules or the predictions of its dogma.

The present conflict between China and the USSR originated with the Chinese revolution. Every revolution, and certainly one occurring in a country as vast and significant as China, sets in motion forces and relations that differ not only vis-à-vis the old order, but also vis-à-vis the rest of the world. There is nothing more fatal for a revolution than imitation. Mao Tse-tung's dispute with Moscow and the emissaries of the Comintern, dating back to the very start of the revolution (1927), is well known. And as early as 1940 he insisted that the goal of the revolution was the "collective dictatorship of several revolutionary classes" and an order that differed from both the "soviet" and the "bourgeois."

But it was only with the consolidation of the revolutionary authority in China that differences with the USSR began to express themselves in the form of opposing visions and interests, especially in ideology and in interstate relations. . . . World Communism was thus irrevocably split. No one is now able to say which Communism is "right": each cell of Communism is beginning to rot away. The sacrifice of millions of lives, whether in revolutionary battles or by execution, accomplished nothing except that one-third of humanity now have the "new class"—the party bureaucracy—for their masters, and two new, closed great powers have made themselves secure. . . .

It is already obvious to any thinking person that the complicated disputations of Communists about "Marxism-Leninism" camouflages a struggle for power and hegemony. But ideological disputes are not only masks and motivations. Just like faith to the Scholastics of the Middle Ages, ideology to Communists is a higher reality: they live in that imaginary reality and are willing to die for it until the real world offers them security and comfort. In the USSR the ruling party has attained that condition and its ideology has been reduced to a weapon of expansion and power. The Chinese party bureaucracy still longs for the benefits of its own degeneration. In China, the revolution was carried out by the peasantry, not the proletariat, and the main role in it was played by the party in the army, and not by the party itself. As a consequence of the semicolonial position, the revolution was supported by a significant stratum of the intelligentsia as well as by the national bourgeoisie. China was more backward than tsarist Russia; the transformation of the party into a "new class" in China could only have taken place by depending on the Soviet party bureaucracy. Mao Tse-tung perceived that that would mean the limitation of the significance of the Chinese experience and the squashing of the independence of China. The Chinese leadership split, but Mao Tse-tung remained on top and openly resisted Khrushchev in 1963. With this, the Chinese revolution finally found itself on its own path. Soon afterward, Mao Tse-tung, drawing support from the army or, more precisely, from the military elements of the party, set the masses moving in the so-called Cultural Revolution, directed primarily against the party bureaucracy. By that he did not annihilate the "ideologically alien" strata, but he did extend the construction of the "classless society" over two centuries. China is a revolutionary autocracy, but it is not and probably will never be a totalitarian despotism.

Thus, two Communist centers have been established—a bureaucratic-conservative center in Moscow and a dogmatic-revolutionary center in China. Ideological "purity" is obviously on the side of the Chinese, and they will not easily yield that advantage. China is still so poor that ideology remains the major weapon of her internal cohesion and her penetration of the world. It is therefore irrelevant that the Chinese form of Communism (even if the "New Left" understood it correctly) has no prospects of establishing itself in the less-developed countries, let alone in developed countries. The important thing is that China for some time will continue to believe in the viability of her revolutionary myths and with them will undermine the influence of the USSR. Even if the gradual differentiation of still-kindred systems was not occurring, the common heart—ideology—is split. The struggle of Peking and Moscow for the souls of Communists throughout the world will not cease until they themselves lose their souls.

The USSR still holds substantial territories that the Russian tsars seized from China. Outer Mongolia, ethnically inseparable from China, is subordinate to the USSR. Thus state, national and even racial antagonisms feed the ideological dispute with unlimited irrationality. And, conversely, the Chinese ideological "logic" becomes a rational way of resisting "Russian revisionism" as the last white masters.

In this conflict, time definitely works in China's favor. Once China catches up with the USSR in "atomic kill," she will be in an incomparably better position. All the more so because China is socially and nationally more compact than the USSR, burdened by tsarist conquests in the East and by Stalinist hegemony over the developed nations of Eastern Europe. The Soviet Empire is not the British Empire, for the Kremlin is not Westminster. Hopes that the USSR would democratize itself, open up toward the West, or resolve the conflict with China proved premature and barren. The Russian people, as so many times in the past, may yet have to pay for the shortsightedness and recalcitrance of their leaders.

In brief, the differences between China and the USSR are more bitter and more explosive than the differences between either of these two and the United States.

But it would be senseless and useless for any government (I am thinking primarily of the United States) to build its policy on exacerbating the conflict between the USSR and China or on the subordination of either of them. That conflict above all stems from the structures, relations and interests of the USSR and China. As time moves on, the real interests and real possibilities will, as always, play a more decisive role than ideology in this conflict.

Not one of the three great powers—the United States, the Soviet Union or China—will renounce its own special role in the world. That disturbs and divides peoples and nations. But not one of these great powers is able to defeat both opponents, or even just one, without provoking the other power against itself. This ensures diversity and movement and a balance, of a kind, in the world.

New and complete version of "Moscow vs. Peking,"
The New York Times, April 1, 1971

14
Communism: National and International

The differences which exist between Communist states—differences that Stalin attempted futilely to remove by force—are the result, above all, of diverse historical backgrounds. [. . .]

International Communism, which was at one time the task of revolutionaries, eventually transformed itself, as did everything else in Communism, and became the common ground of Communist bureaucracies, fighting one another on nationalistic considerations. Of the former international proletariat, only words and empty dogmas remained. Behind them stood the naked national and international interests, aspirations, and plans of the various Communist oligarchies, comfortably entrenched. [. . .]

No single form of Communism, no matter how similar it is to other forms, exists in any way other than as a national Communism. In order to maintain itself, it must become national. [. . .]

Stalinism was a mixture of a personal Communist dictatorship and militaristic imperialism.

These forms of imperialism developed: joint stock companies, absorption of the exports of the East European countries by means of political pressure at prices below the world market, artificial formation of a "socialist world market," control of every political act of subordinate parties and states, transformation of the traditional love of Communists toward the "socialist fatherland" into deification of the Soviet state, Stalin, and Soviet practices.

But what happened? [. . .]

The Soviet leaders had to concede, after long vacillation and indecisive argumentation, that the Yugoslav leaders were falsely indicted as Hitlerite and American spies just because they defended the right to consolidate and build a Communist system in their own way. Tito became the most significant personality in contemporary Communism. The principle of national Communism was formally acknowledged. [. . .]

Today national Communism is a general phenomenon in Communism. [. . .]

Recognition of national forms of Communism, which the Soviet government did with clenched teeth, has immense significance and conceals within itself very considerable dangers for Soviet imperialism.

It involves freedom of discussion to a certain extent; this means ideological independence too. Now the fate of certain heresies in Communism will depend not only on the tolerance of Moscow, but on their national potentialities. Deviation from Moscow that strives to maintain its influence in the Communist world on a "voluntary" and "ideologic" basis cannot possibly be checked. [. . .]

The world center of Communist ideology no longer exists; it is in the process of complete disintegration. The unity of the world Communist movement is incurably injured. There are no visible possibilities whatsoever that it can be restored. [. . .]

National Communism per se is contradictory. Its nature is the same as that of Soviet Communism, but it aspires to detach itself into something of its own, national. In reality, national Communism is Communism in decline.

The New Class, 1957
(Trans. Anon.)

National Communism

The War in Vietnam: Misconceptions and Old Structures

The human mind is inclined to accept any situation that seems to it to be inevitable. Thus the present division of the German and Korean nations into separate states and opposing social orders seems to be "natural," although it was not foreseen by anyone except, perhaps, Stalin and Churchill. The victorious armies took possession of their zones of occupation and subsequently, with the flaring up of the Cold War between the two different systems, two different orders were established in these zones.

The division of Vietnam, however, occurred later, through the Geneva Accords of 1954. It is necessary to recall that even though the United States was not a signatory of those agreements, Secretary of State John Foster Dulles made it clear that if the division were not accepted, American troops would replace the defeated French army.

The Cold War had—mainly due to the death of Stalin—just passed its climax. All changes were subject at that time to the ideological schemes and the interests of the two antagonistic centers, Moscow and Washington. Experience from the divisions of Germany and Korea confirmed to the great powers that it was possible to divide nations into different social orders. But Germany and Korea were occupied territories where authority and order had to be established, while in Vietnam the territorial partition "divided" a specific social process—a Communist anticolonial revolution—which already had an army, had established its authority over significant territories, and had penetrated into all pores of the nation.

Although no one was enthusiastic about it, the division of Vietnam was at least temporarily acceptable to everyone. France finally comprehended the situation. The United States could hope—despite the fact that the strategic position it acquired in the south of Asia was heavily burdened with colonial mortgages—that with time it could encourage reforms that would secure stabilization. The USSR welcomed the chance, by representing Vietnam's Communists, to defend its own interests in Southeast Asia. China was then in the shadow of the USSR, that is, linked to it in "fraternal friendship." The armistice in Korea had been signed a year earlier, in 1953, and China consented to a similar solution in Vietnam all the more readily because she had borne the major burden of the fighting with the United States and the "consequences" of Soviet "internationalist solidarity." Albeit unwillingly, the Vietnamese Communists accepted the partition because they were still not ready to grapple with an opponent they sensed to be incomparably stronger and more determined than France. The unity and success of the movement over the entire national territory of Vietnam convinced them of the unnaturalness of the division but at the same time convinced them to accept the settlement temporarily in order to secure their gains and to prepare for further activity. The Vietnamese Communists thus interpreted the Geneva Accords as a lull in the revolution.

The Communist national revolution in Vietnam is not a novel occurrence. The Yugoslav uprising against the Nazi-Fascist occupation showed the Communist ideology could merge with national resistance. Such a revolution is unshakable in its confidence and inexhaustible in its perseverance. But perhaps the consequences of such a revolution—which had reached fullest expression in Yugoslavia—are even more important. Because Yugoslavia had passed through such a revolution, it was able in 1948 to reject subjugation to the Soviet government and to separate itself and become an independent Communist state. That was the beginning of national divisions and ferment in Communism. Later, for different reasons, other countries where the revolution had been victorious—Albania, China and Cuba—also separated from Moscow, while gradually the East European countries, although the Communists came into power there with the aid of the Soviet government, are also becoming independent.

The United States and the Soviet Union underestimated and perhaps even overlooked the significance of the Vietnamese revolution. Both superpowers were satisfied because they had established on that territory a border between systems that was acceptable to their own respective interests. But this settlement ignored the landlord. The revolution was growing stronger, making Hanoi more daring and independent and making Saigon more confused and dependent. Hanoi's maneuvering between Peking and Moscow shows that the Vietnamese revolution did not lose its independence—had it not been independent, it could not have survived. Saigon, on the other hand, was incapable of establishing any government, let alone a democratic government. . . . It is an old truth that the wisdom and determination of revolutionaries are worth nothing if the ruling circles are not mired in corruption and despair. Because revolutions are the choice of necessity, and not of freedom or slavery. . . .

The termites of the revolution nibbled away and within ten years they had undermined the crumbling structure of the Saigon regime to such an extent that they were unable to stop. Their job was made easier by the change in relations between the great powers: the Sino-Soviet split offered Hanoi greater possibilities for maneuvering, and with the slackening of the Cold War the conflict between "Eastern" and "Western" ideologies and systems was reduced to the conflict between "socialist" and "capitalist" great powers. This offered the revolution a new opportunity to affirm its national form and its social essence.

And it was also incontestable that the Vietnamese Communists, carried away by revolutionary enthusiasm, readily accepted the appraisal of the United States as a "paper tiger," a story which Peking was blowing around in its competition with Moscow for hegemony over the revolutionary movement. They did not understand that the United States is a new, technological-financial great power and not an old, colonial one. In determining the policy of such a great power, the character of a regime in a country is not always the decisive factor, but, rather, whether the regime is open and whether it means an expansion of the influence of one of the closed rival great powers—the USSR or China. The proof of this is to be found in independent Communist Yugoslavia, with whom the United States maintains normal relations, and even more drastically in Cuba, which the United States tolerates in its vicinity, blocking it as a revolutionary center of Latin America but threatening it with intervention only when the USSR attempted to transform it into its own atomic base. Conversely, the United States has very poor relations with Egypt, although its system is not Communist, mainly because Egypt, through its nationalism supported by the USSR, threatens United States interests in the Middle East.

The other side of this Vietnamese error of judgment was their naïve belief in the unconditional and unlimited solidarity of Communist states, despite the fact that "sacrosanct national selfishness," especially on the part of the USSR, had prevailed among those states for a long time. And once more "ideological goals" were sacrificed to national goals, to the interests of the state: for more than four years the "socialist" states supported their "sister" state, which was being thrashed by the largest "capitalist" power, only through arms and noisy resolutions. This fact had to make the Vietnamese revolution more dependent on the tactics and positions of the great powers, especially of the Communist ones.

Therefore, not only the intervention of the United States and the contest between the USSR and China over Vietnam, but also the Vietnamese revolution in part itself, in its new "anti-American" phase, are all expressions of inherited, still prevailing structures. The Vietnamese revolution was—let us hope that it is no longer to such an extent—overburdened with desiccated Marxist-Leninist theories. What supports it and is the wellspring of its strength are not dogmatic schemes but nationalism and the corruption of the Saigon system. Revolution is a social knot which must be untied in one way or another. That does not mean, however, that the revolutionaries have a monopoly on revolution and even less that they are infallible. The Vietnamese people must pay not only for the intervention of foreign powers but also for the errors of the leaders of the revolution. . . . The Vietnamese revolution gives one cause to contemplate the archaism of Communist revolutions. And not only because such revolutions are today impossible without the interference of the three great powers, the United States, the Soviet Union and China, but also because of the incapability of their totalitarian ideology to adjust to knowledge about society, and man, and modern technology. . . .

The catching fire and spreading of the revolution in the southern part of Vietnam has shaken the countries of Southeast Asia still overburdened with feudal and colonial relations. Laos is already destroyed by revolution and the same was about to occur in Indonesia on the eve of Sukarno's attempted Communist *coup d'état* supported by China. The structure and commitments of the earlier Cold War period, still in existence and still functioning, came into operation. South Vietnam was of crucial significance for American concepts and interests, still alive and unaltered since the time of the Geneva Accords, that is, since the time when the Communist world was still homogeneous, as yet unaffected by the "Yugoslav heresy." To China the Vietnamese revolution was welcome "proof" of its dogmas. It was also welcome to the Soviet Union because, involving the United States, its European and world rival, in unforeseeable difficulties, it opened to the USSR new possibilities in other areas, especially in Europe and the Middle East.

Politics does not exist without force; but force cannot replace creativity in politics. The Johnson administration reacted cautiously but routinely, as if this were a repetition of the 1950 invasion of South Korea. However, Communism was already fragmented into national movements, the struggle for which is not limited to the "socialist" great powers of China and the USSR. This is shown by the fact that American intervention in Vietnam was no longer to defend the "free world" from Communism, but primarily to maintain its strategic position in South Asia and vis-à-vis China.

But national Communisms are not now, nor is it certain that they will ever be, national to such an extent as to renounce the support of Moscow or Peking. It is especially dubious that China or the USSR could view the fate of Communist regimes and Communist movements the same way it looks at non-Communist regimes and movements. This all the more so because they are forced to make up for their technological and economic inferiority by their "ideological" influence. Although ideology is indispensable for China, the Soviet Union has not renounced it either. Even if they were not at odds with one another, neither China nor the USSR is willing to enter a war because of Vietnam. But at the same time neither China nor the USSR will renounce support of Hanoi. Because of that, a policy of "utilizing the Sino-Soviet conflict" has no possibility of yielding any significant results.

Especially barren were the hopes that Moscow, even if it wanted to, could significantly influence the policy of Hanoi. All the more so because Hanoi is nearer to Peking than Moscow in geographic position and in animosity toward "white colonials" as well as in doctrine. The keys for peace are to be found first of all in Hanoi and Washington, then in the relations between China and the United States, and only after that in Moscow.

Through the support of Moscow and Peking, the Vietnamese revolution secures for itself a continuous and invulnerable rear. The United States, however, is forced to a "war of limited objectives," that is, to the prevention of "infiltration" from the north and the preservation of the Saigon regime. Naturally, Johnson's "escalation" encouraged the Indonesian officers in their revolt against Sukarno and the Communists, but it could not bring victory to the United States. It is unlikely that that objective will be accomplished in the foreseeable future by "Vietnamization" of the war, although through it, alongside inflexible views one hopes also for more realistic views. Insofar as the war is prolonged, it makes a unilateral withdrawal on the part of the United States more difficult and less likely. In the existing situation such a withdrawal would mean yielding to China and the USSR, with unpredictable consequences for the United States in Asia and elsewhere. There is no hope that the American nation as a whole would support such a decision at present. The United States cannot win the war without risking either senseless conflict of much larger proportions or long and fruitless bloodshed. Obviously this is not a war in the normal sense of the word, but a national and social ferment which foreign interventions can suppress but not halt. For Hanoi and for the Vietcong, what is important is not winning or losing a battle, but maintaining the guerrillas and heating up the revolution. And for that they have very substantial material, moral, time and spatial possibilities.

A "war of limited objectives" is in fact a war without ideals. The war in Korea was different and the differences it provoked in the United States and elsewhere were only about the conduct and the scale of the war. At that time only the Communists were on the side of North Korea. The present differences about Vietnam penetrate into the war itself, that is, whether the war is necessary or superfluous, whether it is vital for American interests, or whether it is merely the product of inherited structures. Criticism of American intervention is carried on not only by leftist dogmatists but also by such persons as Walter Lippmann and Senator J. W. Fulbright, who are among the creators of a free-thinking America and who are attempting to bridge the gaps between nations that ideologies, oppression, wealth and history have created.

The slaughter of the civilian population in Vietnam, even isolated incidents, casts a dark shadow over the objectives of the supporters of intervention. Irrationality emerges wherever reason and law retreat. For that reason, men unburdened by ideological and nationalist prejudices are obliged to supervise the warriors, regardless of which side they are on. The so-called Russell Trial, however, failed because it was so pretentious and sectarian. And had the American press and television yielded to their nationalist myths, the world would have been made poorer by an overwhelming realization and enriched by horrible doubts about the conscience and the intentions of the most powerful nation of our time.

The war in Vietnam shook many beliefs and unsettled many relationships. Viewed from here, it is presented as an event of almost the same importance for the United States as the great crisis of 1929 or the Second World War. The war in Vietnam does not, of course, spare Communism either: it sharpens the quarrels between China and the USSR and undermines the myth of Communist solidarity. But at the same time it was very useful to the party bureaucracy within Communism, enabling it to present itself as the guardian of the nation and to revitalize its stale anti-imperialist and anticapitalist phraseology. It caused far-reaching moral and spiritual polarization without shaking social structures. There is no one who is not paying the price of the Vietnam war: outmoded structures, because it undermines them; nascent structures, because it stifles them. It confirms the Western lack of ideals, and also the absurdity of the Communist ideal. But out of horror and despair are born hope and progress. The Vietnam war is the nightmare of the past, but also the predecessor of more open systems and nonabsolute truths.

Time in this war is not on anyone's side. For that reason its duration depends no less on the comprehension of those who lead it, that is, on Washington and Hanoi, than on the strengths of the forces involved. And because this war is vital for world relations and for movements not only within "capitalism" but also within "socialism," it is perhaps more significant *what* peace will be established than *when*. A peace based on the power of the United States cannot long endure in Vietnam, just as contemporary consciousness is not ready to make peace with ideological slaughterhouses and "revolutionary" hegemonies.

Five years of war is too much to be able to comprehend the relationships and the possibilities, though only we who are outside of this war can think this way. The existing situation, however, does not offer any possibility for a rapid conclusion of the war. But mainly because peace could mean the beginning of a new epoch, it is the duty of all persons of good will to think about it and to work for it even if only those who set in motion the real war and who make decisions about it can find that peace. It seems to me that a decisive step along that hard road would be recognition of the Vietnam revolution on the basis of its being conducted within national borders and on the basis of guaranteeing the human rights of the citizens of South Vietnam. Exactly because they are so mighty and so rich, the United States can only gain by adjusting to the nationalisms of small and underdeveloped nations, just as the Vietnamese patriots and revolutionaries have no better way to affirm their patriotism and to gain undivided sympathy than by tolerance toward their brothers of different views and by comprehending the interests of their own people.

January 1970 (unpublished)

Bureaucratic Nationalism

Today the distinctive characteristic of Communist parties, even of those not in power, is bureaucratic nationalism. (Of course, it assumes different, national variations.) Despite that fact, bureaucratic nationalism has not yet been analyzed, and even the term is not yet established in use. This is understandable, for it is only now, when it has become a way of reacting and even a way of life, that bureaucratic nationalism has finally assumed a definite form and come to be used at all in the language.

Bureaucratic nationalism is immanent in Communism and has its own hidden and undisclosed evolution. Its previous stage was called "national Communism." That term came into use during the conflict of Yugoslavia with the USSR in 1948. The term "national Communism" itself expressed the contradictions and absurdities of Communism at the time: the movement to which internationalism was an inspiration and a sacred commandment was falling apart into national units which were beginning to conduct themselves in the light of their own interests and possibilities.

Furthermore, even then the term "national Communism" (like most "political" language) oversimplified and distorted a complex, still-developing reality. And, what is worst, with the use of that term was lost from view the truth that Communism, upon coming into power, transforms itself into a "new class" which cannot justify and maintain its mastery except by becoming identified with the "sacred national egoism." Because Communism is, above all else, power; and power can neither materialize nor survive except in specific national conditions. While struggling for power, Communism is internationalist, but after the seizure of power it is so only as much as it has to be.

At the time the term "national Communism" originated, insofar as there was awareness of these things, the facts did not yet fully confirm the transformation of classless illusions into class structures or the existence of conflicts among Communist states. But today the term "nationalism of the party bureaucracy" or, shortened, "bureaucratic nationalism," describes more adequately than "national Communism" the contemporary Communist movements and the relations among them.

East Europe is ruled today by bureaucratic nationalisms (of course, differing from country to country and unequally dependent on the Soviet center). This statement does not fully apply to China, Albania, Cuba and Vietnam, because those countries are still in revolutionary totalitarianism or in bureaucratic totalitarianism, which are the preliminary phases of bureaucratic nationalism.

Along with other firsts, the Soviet party was first also to transform itself into a monopolistic and nationalist bureaucracy. That process, complex and bloody, was finally completed under Stalin. But whereas the social privilege of the party bureaucracy in the USSR is obvious, its nationalistic character is obscured and is different from that in other East European countries. Stalin favored the nationalism of the Russian bureaucracy. Under Khrushchev, "balance" was restored, in that the role of the non-Russian bureaucracies (primarily the Ukrainian bureaucracy) was strengthened in the top party organs. The Ukrainian role did not diminish under Brezhnev. But that does not mean that one or another national bureaucracy in the USSR has a dominant role. In the same way that Stalin's Great Russianism utilized the darkest impulses of the

Russian nation to strengthen the mastery and imperial expansion of the "new class" as a whole, so also—at least theoretically—it would be possible to have cleavages and conflicts in the Soviet bureaucracy along national lines.

The Yugoslav party started the splitting of the world Communist movement into national parts. But Communism is an ideology, that is, a complete, closed doctrine. It is impossible to remove one pillar without shaking the other pillars and the entire structure. The abandonment of internationalism, necessitated by the hegemony of Moscow, strengthened the Yugoslav state but it also weakened the party ideology. Two other great crises followed in the Yugoslav party: the bureaucratic reaction after Stalin's death and at the time of "fraternal friendship" with Khrushchev; and—after the fall of Khrushchev and the failure of the ideological, bureaucratic economy—the collapse of the secret police as the guardian of ideology and monolithicness. New democratic dreams were suppressed, but at the price of spiritual disillusionment and disintegration into national bureaucracies. True, the national bureaucracies are no longer Marxist, not even declaratively. But not a single one of them is democratic; more precisely, they are only less nondemocratic than their predecessors. Insufficiently strong one against the other, and also within their own nation, not only do they make behind-the-scene alliances among themselves, but also they open the doors to anti-Communist, nondemocratic nationalisms. It can even lead to a merging of bureaucratic nationalism with chauvinism. We are witnessing the birth of a very specific kind of pluralism: the pluralism of nontolerant, nondemocratic nationalisms. The party bureaucracy does not develop, but, instead, disintegrates and transforms itself into new, for the most part authoritarian, structures. Of course, democratic currents also appear. All that creates a chaotic but freer atmosphere, but one without democratic institutions. Yugoslavia is freer but also less stable than ever before: now it is threatened by the still-unforgotten passions and tragedies of the Nazi invasion and the civil war.

But the changes in Yugoslavia do not have to develop in the same manner as those in other East European countries, let alone in the USSR. In Czechoslovakia there was a prospect of a democratic transformation, while in Rumania, despite its relative independence, there is none. Its "revolutionary" traditions, coupled with the possibility of maintaining its isolation and its imperial interests, make the Soviet bureaucracy more stable, despite its miscarried ideology and the cracks in its monolithicness.

The disintegration of the party monopoly frees people and nations from the drabness and the horror of ideological and political totalitarianism. But that disintegration does not automatically bring the freedoms that nations and peoples crave. It is necessary only to tap the irrational impulses and mythic heritage to escape into chauvinism and

into nationalistic ideology; to that extent to find ways out of bureaucratic nationalism requires harder and more conscientious effort. The
world faces a new situation which offers new possibilities, but also new
dangers.

October 6, 1971 (unpublished)

Ideology as a Means

Every theory tends toward absolutism, for thought would lose its way
amidst chaotic, complex reality and be ineffectual if it did not generalize
from that reality. In that sense every doctrine that seeks to be realized in
society is ideological. But only with the Industrial Revolution did ideology become established both as a word and as a phenomenon. At that
time was first revealed the possibility that decent living conditions could
be established for all people. Then first appeared the possibility of
merging the "scientific" theory of society with the movement "predestined" to bring about the ultimate transition from "the kingdom of
necessity into the kingdom of freedom." And ideology is precisely the
link between the "all-encompassing" "scientific" theory and the revolutionary movement. Obviously I am talking about "scientific socialism,"
since, despite Marx's good intentions, it was the first to evolve into a
complete ideology. Later, other ideologies emerged and in time that term
was expanded to include any complete political doctrine.

Total and final, ideology "replaces" religion (pseudoreligion). But no
religion was ever as exclusive or as total in its outlook, its means, or its
application as is ideology. Ideology tends toward totalitarianism and
once enthroned it becomes the very spirit of totalitarianism. Thus ideology transforms itself from idealized politics into the ideal means of
tyranny and oppression. And thereby begins the decay of ideology. And
the contemporary world, which is becoming united through diversity and
where each day science and art reveal anew the indefinable complexity of
nature, society and man, will complete the decomposition of ideology, at
least as we know it. This is the dramatic fate that awaits Communism,
which was once the most scientific ideology, the ideal ideology, the sole
world ideology.

But Marxist theory (that is, revolutionary Communist theory) even
from the start was never a science or even close to it. Its visions were
solidly supported by facts analyzed by the scientific method, and for that
reason the theory inspired and persuaded with the force of a new,
rational faith. At the time, it seemed that the movement and its militants
were the means of the ideology, and not the ideology their means.

But countries that had already had an industrial revolution—mainly in the West—proved themselves suited only for reforms. There, ideology began to branch off from the movement and, thereby, to dilute itself. In the East, above all in Russia, developments were just the opposite. There industrialization was just about to take place and—because of Russia's backwardness and subservience to Western financial centers—ideological, revolutionary movements were able to bring it about. There ideology and the movement merged together. That was the time of Lenin and the revolution: ideology nourished itself and even developed through polemics, especially in those aspects important for the revolution and for the new power (theories about the party and the "dictatorship of the proletariat").

But the revolution ignited by World War I and the postwar chaos quieted down. The Russian state had to survive in the existing surroundings and it could survive only as a Soviet state. Ideology and movement became subservient to the Soviet state as the "leading force" and the "center of revolution." Ideology was preserved by reducing it to formulas and phrases. Stalin did that; he became the sole ruler and supreme deity. At last, everything could be "explained"—and ideology needs only to be supervised. For only an unchanging, formularized ideology was suited for the party bureaucracy which establishes its total mastery and attempts to perpetuate that mastery as a means of deception and expansion.

For that very reason Khrushchev's "de-Stalinization" was least effective and least logical in the sphere of ideology. But Khrushchev was not capable of anything else, nor did the conditions exist for anything except the rejection of "Stalinistic" absurdities (for examples, "theories" about the intensification of the class struggle in socialism, the "necessity" of Communist revolutions in developed countries), and this only served to strengthen his opponents in the party bureaucracy. Ideology continues to be a means of power and expansion, but now more flexibly applied and no longer invigorated by bloody purges and rooting out of "alien" groups.

But even that modest "reforming" of ideology provoked significant developments: the new "ideological" superpower, China, affirms itself by dissociating itself from the "revisionistic" USSR, while the Soviet party bureaucracy in such "reforming" anticipates the undermining of its own monopoly.

Still, the toppling of Khrushchev did not return the USSR to the nightmare of Stalinism, but "only" stopped the budding and the changes. The party bureaucracy learned that ideology is already unchangeable, that is, that it is dead, but that it is all the more necessary as a means. Declarative statements for Marxism-Leninism are sufficient when it is not a question of "revisionism," whenever one deals with a spiritual vacuum. In such circumstances loyalty and conformism suffice, instead of the previously necessary faith (under Lenin) and awe (under Stalin).

But while domestically, through prohibitions and regulations, the reduction of ideology to a naked means can be concealed, in Soviet relations with Communist parties and "socialist" countries it has already assumed grotesque forms. In good old Stalinist times the mention of Marxism-Leninism was avoided in interstate declarations. Here, too, Khrushchev introduced an innovation, probably to muffle the "Stalinists" and his own conscience. Today ideological consensus is preserved primarily through diplomatic maneuvers and other pressures. Because ideology, even if it is no longer a spiritual bond, certainly remains an obligation for the weak, while for the strong it is the legitimization of control and intervention. "Ideological unity" is today the mythomaniac substitute for limited sovereignty. . . . Thus Belgrade *Politika* observed, "For the representative of Soviet students [. . .] all arguments which do not recognize the intervention [in Czechoslovakia] as legal [. . .] are taking a bourgeois approach to the question of the sovereignty of ideologies."[1] Thus, in the Yugoslav-Soviet statement made during Brezhnev's visit to Belgrade at the end of September, 1971, the ideological tie was strongly emphasized, despite the fact that both domestically and in foreign affairs Yugoslavia follows its own path and despite the fact that anti-ideological forces are dominant in Yugoslavia while in the Soviet Union, at least on the surface, ideological forces prevail. Moreover, in the declarations of the Soviet government and the governments of Arab countries was also underlined the identicalness of their socialist ideals, despite the fact that Communists are severely persecuted in those countries.

Ideology reduced itself to a currency for settling accounts, to a ritual form, to vassalage and blackmail. Ideologues can wail: "Ideology must be revived." But for that to happen there must be a different world, and there must be born another genius on the order of Marx or even Lenin. And the romantics who accepted ideology as their faith can cry: "Nothing is possible without some kind of faith." Of course; nothing is possible. But faith and ideals need not be, and cannot be, ideology.

November 1971 (unpublished)

Communist Contradictions

Chinese "Puzzles"

It is a peculiarity of Communist movements that the better they get on and the more successful they are, the more they become utopian, that is, the more they become convinced of their ultimate objectives. This seems

1. January 9, 1969.

absurd. However, politics is not logic but existence. A dogmatic conception of the world is realistic for peoples, classes or nations reduced to the bare struggle for survival. Even great religions—and Communism is a "scientific" substitute for religion—spread more irresistibly the more their supporters were convinced of the inevitability of the "heavenly kingdom." The most thorough transformations (and we live in an epoch of transformations of all forms and especially of those forms within which the underdeveloped countries eked out an existence) are not accomplished by pragmatists but by visionaries who found a path through the absurd, unbearable reality.

Communism is Communism only if it is realized; that is, if it struggles for power—its real and realizable goal. And power can be conquered and maintained only on real, national grounds. Exactly because of that, and not because of "revisionism" or "nationalism," despite the common internationalist teachings, Communism must split apart and come into conflict on national grounds.

Thus under certain conditions Chinese dogmatism and utopianism can achieve at least as much realism, if not even more, than can the idealess Soviet bureaucrats or the pragmatic American government. The Chinese enthusiasm for talking about "internationalism" and "world revolution" is the result of its national conditions and of its striving for a global role.

This corresponds to the domestic structure and the international position of China.

China is today the only country that still believes in a utopia of the perfect, classless society. Therefore, if by Communist one understands total subservience to the "scientific" ideology and practice of Communist movements, China is the only Communist country. In China ideology is placed ahead of production, and even class membership is determined by ideological orientation. North Vietnam is even more strongly infatuated with the Communist faith, but it is still struggling for survival in a hostile world, and for independence within the Communist world. The countries of East Europe in many respects can no longer be considered Communist. In each one of them—in a particular way and in different measure—society is stratifying itself and teachings are being reviewed and becoming ossified. Cuba and Albania are special cases, for there the withering away of ideals is obscured by total personal dictatorship.

Even were it not in a revolutionary rapture, China in its poverty and isolation had nothing else left except to feed on faith and to strengthen its position through the export of ideas. The religious aspect of Communism is the manner and condition of existence in contemporary China. Something similar happened in Russia in the era of Lenin and in the first years of Stalin's reign. Since that time Russia changed significantly internally, and its capabilities also grew. Today, in its emergence on a global scale, ideology is secondary to military power and even to economic power.

In politics, everyone interprets reality according to his visions and possibilities. The same is true of the leaders of China. Victory in the war and in the revolution and their increasing role and prestige convinced them of the correctness of their ideology, despite the fact that for the rest of the world, and especially for the developed world, China is extremely schematic and unreal, and even naïve. Naturally, there are among the leaders those who perceive the deficiencies of Chinese Marxism-Leninism for the rest of the world. Probably even Mao is aware of them. But such an ideology is essential today for the survival of the ruling forces in China and for their resistance to the external, hostile world. Unrealistic for others, that ideology is realistic for the Chinese Communists: it is the faith through which they and the Chinese masses survive and march forward.

It would be naïve to expect in the near future even a slight weakening or transformation of the Chinese religious fervor. For this to take place fundamental, painful and permanent changes are necessary, above all developing the capacity to ensure at least a minimal existence, and forming a productive, well-off elite. At the same time, Communist China cannot understand that the world is not receptive to its revolutionary, dogmatic schemes as long as that world is hostile to China itself.

For these reasons, the announced trip of President Nixon to China and the admission of China into the United Nations will be of direct but incalculable significance in transforming the "Chinese" world faith into a collection of outdated Chinese prescriptions. The oppressive and somber division of the world into ideologies will disappear. The twilight of ideologies has begun to fall, and now the uniting of the more life-bearing currents of humanity can begin.

The inclusion of China into the world community and the recognition of its rights are a formality and a process of bargaining. China was ready for this step a long time ago, but American pragmatism was more dogmatic and less flexible than Chinese dogmatism.

Chinese revolutionary utopianism is merely the other side of the pragmatic, realistic politics of the Chinese state. In practice the Chinese leadership will more and more retreat from proclamations and ideological schemes. Its ideological "sins" are already too numerous: support of West Pakistan against the democratic and national rebellion of East Pakistan—because of China's rivalry with Indian reactionaries; normalization of relations with the Yugoslav initiators of revisionism—in order to weaken the position of the Soviet Union. . . . In fact, the transgression, that is, the adjustment to reality, begins with the Communists' struggle for power. Thus Lenin, immediately upon seizing power, began to negotiate with the Kaiser's generals in Brest-Litovsk, although both up to that time and afterward he continued to cheer on the world revolution and the solidarity of the international proletariat. The opportunities for such retreats on the world scene will present themselves to China. Conditions are being created for the Chinese ideological faith to acquire a more measured, more realistic role—in order that it become an instrument of state policy.

No dogma or ideal can prevent the Chinese leadership from strengthening national and state interests. But such a leadership would be without a "guiding principle," and each renunciation would senselessly undermine its own power. . . . Communism cannot leave behind the framework of power. But for that very reason Communism, to an excessive degree and in an excessively elastic manner, must "explain" and "justify" everything that is in the interest of its power.

In this respect Chinese Communism does not differ from its "revisionistic" predecessors and rivals. Only the means and motivations are different, since it is a different epoch, and a different nation, with its own specific conditions.

The Chinese are the largest nation on earth. In addition, China is the only nation that has been in continual existence since the beginning of human history. And although its four-thousand-year-long history and Confucian teachings affirm the alternation of order and disorder (*ho-p'ing* and *luan*), China evolved almost entirely within the same social system. For that reason Mao Tse-tung was able to say that China is an unwritten page. Because of philosophical and social immobility, China was forced to import ideas. Chinese Communism is less autochthonous than Russian Communism, and perhaps because of that, Communism means a more fundamental and a more significant transformation for China than it meant for Russia. It shook China's millennia-long existence and for the first time really united it and brought it onto the world stage. Such a history and such a transformation could only be favorable to the conviction of the Chinese leaders that the "center of world revolution" had passed from Russia into their own country. And that conviction of the Chinese leaders could not exist without their perceiving China as a global power.

I believe that the Chinese leaders are correct when they view their country as a world power, but that they are suffering from a dogmatic illusion with respect to China's potential as a "center of world revolution." If one considers the economic power and technical level of China, then it could not be considered a world power or superpower. Moreover, neither its area nor its population in themselves can ensure it a global role; its revolutionary attitude and its atomic weapons are not sufficient for that. And yet it was a global power, and has been indisputably and consciously so since the breach with the USSR and the escape from its shadow. That split is probably the most significant event since the end of World War II. It irrevocably split Communism as a unified ideology, as a world movement, and as a commonwealth of states. With that, the Cold War became absurd. The might and domination of Western powers (including also the USSR) in Asia have been undermined and are now unsustainable. The USSR and the USA cannot by bypassing China resolve mutual conflicts, and even less can they dominate the world. Thus, for example, the agreement on nonproliferation of nuclear weapons, whose signing was directly connected with the revelation of the Sino-Soviet dispute, is worthless and meaningless because of the Chinese nonparticipation and the French withdrawal. . . . China is a super-power primarily because of its role in world processes and world relations, and only secondarily in its potential, uncontainable possibilities.

However, China's influence as a world revolutionary force has no great prospects; it cannot even approximate the influence of the USSR either after the October Revolution or during and immediately after World War II.

China spreads Communist teachings at a time of the spiritual decline of Communism. Chinese propaganda is unoriginal, a schematic imitation of the Marxist-Leninist theories which *in the past* excited revolutionaries and destroyed specific realities. The *Quotations from Chairman Mao Tse-tung* is obviously distinguished by an exceptional belief in the "universal truths" of Marxism. But it is original only in its analysis of the conditions and tactics of the Chinese revolution. . . . Today both the essential content and the possibilities of Communism are known. Communist parties are no longer classified according to their degree of orthodoxy but according to their national and even momentary interests and positions vis-à-vis Moscow and Peking. The division into "pro-Russian" and "pro-Chinese" parties coincides almost exactly with the range of influence of the two centers—Moscow in Europe, Peking in Asia. There exist, of course, also some "disputed" areas in Latin America and Africa, and also the semi-independent and independent parties. Roughly speaking, the parties tied to Moscow are no longer revolutionary parties. But even the parties oriented toward Peking are not as totally lacking in independence as were the Communist parties that were oriented toward Moscow in the era of Stalin. Communism has split into two global forces, with a tendency toward becoming independent of both of the national parties and the Communist states. Experiences with Moscow are too bitter to be unquestioningly repeated with Peking. Moscow fed and encouraged Communist movements, but not only did it never carry out any revolution, but also it came into conflict with all revolutions. Peking will not have any better luck. There have to be revolutions, but not on the Chinese model, not in slavelike dependence on Peking.

The existing situation in Communism itself offers no prospects for any kind of unity, and least of all for the establishment of a world revolutionary center. The contemporary world is not well adapted either for any kind of centers or for a unified ideology. Technology, the needs of nations, and human knowledge all force social systems—even conflicting ones—to mix and intertwine.

Maoist groups are today most active in the developed countries of the West. But this is primarily a case of a misunderstanding; anarchist currents in the West take Mao as the symbol of total negation, and Peking seizes upon them as the beginnings of a "Marxist-Leninist" party. Only in China are the Red Books of Mao's quotations substitutes for prayer books. In the West, at best they are symbols of defiance or are the requisites of the revolutionary mythology. Because the "Western" way of thinking, even when it is Communist, is incomparably more complex and flexible. Time and circumstances will have their effect even here. In the West the revolutionary imitators will become disappointed and will disperse, and Peking will narrow its world revolutionary mission to the framework of its state interests.

The Soviet Union especially has no reason to fear Chinese revolutionary zeal. Not only do the people know that song very well there, but they also know the long-lasting—alas, in many respects still going on—totalitarian oppression. And in addition to this, the "first country of socialism" is protected even more powerfully than by these horrible experiences from the Chinese orthodoxy by the state rivalries and by the long Russian memory of a century of enslavement under the Mongols. Slight dogmatic differences between the USSR and China conceal ancient, but still very much alive, national, state and even racial contradictions.

The Soviet "Stalinist" past hovers like a nightmare over China. In its party "monolithicness," its ideological monopolism, the "dictatorship of the proletariat," "internationalism," and the "cult of personality," China resembles the Stalinist Soviet Union. Moreover, like the USSR under Stalin, China is also building the "classless society."

But that does not mean that China is passing through the bloody darkness of "Stalinist" totalitarianism. There are significant differences between contemporary China and the USSR under Stalin.

The roots of these differences are to be found in the nature of the respective revolutions and in the levels of development and the specific characteristics of Russia and China. Russia was European in its progressive and democratic tendencies, and when it carried out its revolution it was incomparably more developed than was China. Inspired and led by Marxist intellectuals, the Russian peasants in uniforms and the Russian workers rose to arms against the rotted state and against the bourgeois defenders of the senseless and devastating war. At the head of the Chinese revolution were also Marxist intellectuals. But that revolution was primarily a long guerrilla war by the peasants, first against the landed gentry and the war lords, and then against the Japanese colonialists. The long duration of the fighting and the leading role in such a war of Communists in uniforms made the military part of the party the leading force of the new power. The Chinese revolution from the beginning separated itself from Moscow and the Comintern. Already by 1940 Mao Tse-tung had set as his goal the "joint dictatorship of several revolutionary classes" and not only the "dictatorship of the proletariat," while in 1945 he emphasized the peasantry as the mainstay of the revolution and the new power.

Its specific development, its history and its state could only encourage the Chinese leadership toward differentiation from the USSR. The cult of Mao is similar to the cult of Stalin, but without as much oppression. Because the prestige of Chairman Mao is more similar to that of Lenin than to that of Stalin, he was not forced to legitimate his power and his visions by slaughters of "revisionist" currents and by the extermination of "socially undesirable" groups. Open repressions in China have traditionally been considered a sign of weakness. The "re-education" of the intellectuals and functionaries through physical labor in villages is senseless, wasteful oppression, but it cannot be compared with the horror and arbitrariness of Stalin's camps. Intellectually and in terms of physical control, the mastery of the military party apparatus is total, but it is not realized through physical extermination; this is not a consolation for the creators, but as long as they are alive, this creativeness least flickers in them.

The differences are obviously sufficient to justify conflicts and different roads. But they are not so great as to make China a new, irresistible example.

According to its stated goals, the classless society that China is "constructing" does not differ from that of the USSR. Superficially there is no difference. But it is not so. Stalin, on the eve of the war, had proclaimed that in the USSR the first, socialist, phase of Communist society had been "constructed," in which were eliminated the exploiting classes but not all differences—for example, between manual and physical labor, between city and village. That was both a delusion and deluding oneself: dogmatic totalitarian tyranny had annihilated the autochthony of social groups and destroyed the bonds between the individual and his social group, thus creating the illusion of harmony and an absence of conflict. The functions of the shattered society were taken over by the party oligarchy and its organs of oppression. Although in the post-Stalin period from those monstrous edifices they renounced some of the gilding, the post-Stalin leaders—for reasons of high state and of caste—held to Stalin's basic position that the socialist society had been constructed in the USSR; this placed their country an entire epoch ahead of other "socialist" countries and concealed the emergence and mastery of the "new class" of party bureaucrats. But reality is otherwise. The "Communist society," which the Soviet Union should already be approaching, is in reality some kind of "consumption society," of course, a differentiated one. Today the only serious obstacles to the Soviet Union along that path are the ossified dogma and the monopolism and hegemony of the party bureaucracy.

The Chinese leaders have the same vision of society as did Stalin, but they are constructing it by different—less extreme—means. Those means are essential, in that the vision is utopian. In China society is not shattered but, rather, smothered with total dogma and compulsory uniformity. That offers China other possibilities, especially with the opening up of the rest of the world to it; although not in the immediate future, China could extricate itself from totalitarian forms more readily than the Soviet Union.

Although the Soviet system prevents the complete interestedness of the producers, the Soviet leaders have always emphasized and pointed to its significance for production. The Chinese leadership, however, emphasizes the moral factor as the most important for production. Such a viewpoint is not entirely new: all Communist countries have taken refuge in it whenever they fell into exceptional difficulties and distress. What was the exception for others became for China the rule: as a consequence of her backwardness and her inability in the foreseeable future to satisfy in some measure the individual desires of such a large number of inhabitants, the Chinese leaders transformed this misfortune into an ideal and embraced the moral factor as the leading, universal rule.

The so-called "cultural revolution" is likewise an expression of the submission to that principle. Mao Tse-tung perceived that the Soviet party bureaucracy was transformed into a "new class." Such a development could have been disastrous for China, not because it would mean the abandonment of ideas, but because the poor masses, their hopes aroused, would have deserted from the leadership which, weakened, would have fallen into a position of dependence on Moscow. Thus China became a nation in which poverty was most righteously apportioned, along with insignificant privileges of the Communist bureaucracy.

Mao again astounded the world with his revolutionary energy. But at the same time the creative intelligentsia was stifled and battered. The military section of the party and, with it, the army, acquired superiority and the unifying role. The unity of the country and its independence were preserved. That was not, however, a break with the party, but, rather, leaning on its "most revolutionary" part—in accord with Mao's teaching that "power comes out of the barrel of a gun." Mao took refuge in the renewal of the party. For only an ideological force—the party—can over the long run take the leading role in forming the "classless society." Harmony was re-established temporarily: power in fact was held by the army, the party and the representatives of the "revolutionary masses."

After Mao's death, the spirit of reform will probably revive, but radical changes are not in the offing for China, nor will China construct a conscious society of equality. Even if there were no other inducements, the particular characteristics of functions already force the party and other leaders to a special, *i.e.*, a privileged, way of life. The raising of production, linked with and competing with the rest of the world, the interests of those in power, and "human nature" will inevitably lead to a more differentiated—and a freer—society.

The revolution, without regard for slogans and symbols, has returned to China her trampled, dismembered body: Chinese Marxism is for the most part the substitute for the Confucian state religion and state idea. With time, with encounter with the world, China, like Russia before it, will enter its own, national currents. André Malraux once asked Mao Tsetung whether he was aware that he was the new emperor of China, to which Mao replied: What else could I be? The Chinese revolution, like the Russian before it, changed world power relations more than it did the Chinese people. And deep within himself Mao hides the knowledge that China is a page on which can only be written a continuation of its own history.

China has even less reason to peaceably tolerate the hazard and supremacy of others in zones that protect access to her, especially insofar as those zones are gripped by a kindred revolutionary ferment. And because the country is still struggling for its integrity and because it still feels called upon to unmask Soviet "revisionistic" imperialism, by now only external dangers can force today's China to dictate the direction of its "socialist" or other neighbors through military pressure. The disputes with India are still local in character, a question of prestige. China assists revolutionary movements, but up to now China has not threatened anyone with its army. North Korea and North Vietnam are more independent of Peking than any East European country (with the exception of Yugoslavia) is of Moscow. Vietnam, in addition, with its revolution and its war for unification, alone is taking care of its independence and its own forms.

The world is more complete and more unfettered with China—while for China the world was and remains necessity and hope.

November 4, 1971 (unpublished)

The Roots of Nationalism in Yugoslavia

The Yugoslav Communists are guided by the same doctrinal and practical considerations in handling the nationality question as in dealing with all other problems.

In orthodox Marxist terms nationalities are the product of capitalism, and national rivalry is a conflict among the bourgeoisies. Hence the belief that by eliminating capitalism and the bourgeoisie and by "constructing" the classless society, national contradictions should gradually disappear. A monolithic and international party directs this "construction," and as a result it both gives form to and is the embodiment of the same kind of national tendencies. Because this same doctrine holds that there are no differences between national groups except language, cultural traditions, psychological characteristics and economic conditions, the Communists—once they are in power—do not go beyond cultural and administrative autonomy when they recognize the rights of national groups.

The Yugoslav Communists abandoned this position only when they were forced to. But there is no denying that they have gone a step farther than their Soviet predecessors, who pioneered in this terrain, by giving official recognition to the rights and special characteristics of national groups. There is no "Big Brother" nationality among Yugoslavia's national groups, no single party bureaucracy leading the others.

This departure from Soviet practice stems not from principles but from the Yugoslav reality. If this reality is ignored there is no way of understanding the policy pursued by the Yugoslav Communists in handling national problems, or the nationalistic rivalries that are today shaking up and eroding socialist structures just as they once did in monarchist and bourgeois Yugoslavia.

What happened? What is happening today? How is it that there has been a resurgence in Yugoslavia of nationalist movements and antagonisms which have taken the whole world by surprise and even caused anxiety, especially among the Communists.

Yugoslavia came into being with the victory of the Entente over the Central Powers in World War I. However, the idea of the Yugoslav state—almost a hundred years older, sometimes weaker, sometimes stronger—found supporters among all the southern Slavs, including also the Bulgarians. The realization of the idea fell to the Serbian state of Royal Serbia, a member of the Entente, and to the Yugoslav-oriented members of other nations in today's Yugoslavia, primarily the Croatians. Exactly because it started from Croatian idealism and the Serbian state, Yugoslavia began its life with a Serbo-Croatian conflict. That is not the sole national conflict, but it is the most important one, the decisive one. The Serbs and the Croats constitute the largest national groups in Yugoslavia and have the most deeply rooted state traditions, ideas and pretensions. They are closest in their languages and their ethnic origins and they live side by side in Bosnia, Herzegovina and Croatia. These resemblances may well bring the groups closer together, but they also give rise to fears of assimilation.

The complexity of their relations is better seen against the background of their differences. Their traditions and their mentalities are different, as are their religions (the Serbs are Orthodox, the Croats Catholic). The ruling Serbian parties treated Yugoslavia like an extension of their own state, while the Croats, through their strongest party—the Croatian Peasant party of Stjepan Radić and Dr. Maček—incessantly demanded state autonomy. It was around this conflict that all political organizations were oriented, and the conflict unleashed irrational forces, revived old myths, destroyed legal order and delayed social progress. National strife and the failure to resolve the national question led to a weakening of freedoms, as much those freedoms of which the Kingdom of Serbia was proud as those freedoms the Croats and Slovenes had enjoyed in Austro-Hungary. In 1929, King Alexander tried to save the country from breaking up by resorting to personal dictatorship and he actively promoted the idea of a "Yugoslav nation" and of "Yugoslavianism." Disintegration was avoided, but the idea was dead: the entire Croat population united in opposition, the Serbian democratic parties went down in futile opposition. Extremists grew in number and lined up to await the day of settling accounts.

That day of reckoning came with the Nazi invasion. The legal structures of old Yugoslavia were overwhelmed by despair and confusion and they surrendered to the invaders almost without a struggle. The Croatian fascists (the Ustashi) got a "state" from the occupying forces and undertook to exterminate the Serbs from "their" territories. Chauvinistic and reactionary fanatics on the Serbian side responded with similar measures.

It is incontestable that in the massacres going on between Serbs and Croats the Yugoslav state would have disappeared had not the Communists appeared on the scene. They had all the conditions for such a role: vision, organization and leadership. The Communists were impervious not only to the demoralization of the ruling classes, but also to the chauvinistic excesses. They were the only party that was *Yugoslav* in the composition of its membership, in its political practice and—interpreted narrowly—in its internationalism.

The times were growing ripe for a revolution and also for the Communists to play a decisive role in preserving and restoring the Yugoslav state. As a result of the uprising against the invaders and against those forces who for one or another reason leaned on them, the Communists simultaneously accomplished the revolution and restored the Yugoslav state. It would be most accurate to say that the Communists won because they embodied—of course, in their own way—the Yugoslav idea, that is, the Yugoslav state community. Herein are to be found, let it be noted, also the roots of the conflict with Stalin in 1948 and of Yugoslavia's determined resistance to Soviet hegemony.

But the Communists could only establish a state and establish nationality relations within it according to their own image and abilities. Their intention was that all would have equal rights. But they came into conflict not only with the complexity of the national intermixture, with different gradations and traditions, with opponents of varying strengths, but also with the awakened appetites of their own organs. Thus, to borrow Orwell's phrase, "some became more equal than others."

The Communists had every reason to establish republics for the Serbs, Croats, Slovenes and Macedonians, because each was indisputably a distinct nation. For the first time in their history, the Slovenes and Macedonians were given their own states, and this could not fail to please each of them—the former because they were the most highly developed and they acquired new economic possibilities, and the latter because they were the least developed and they acquired more just and broader prospects. Serbian and Croatian nationalisms had been defeated as the major opponents of the revolution, and so the Serbs and the Croats accepted the same status—the former because it did not threaten Yugoslavia, and the latter because they got some kind of statehood.

But republican status was also given to the Montenegrins, although they are a part of the Serbian people. The Comintern and the Communist party of Yugoslavia had much earlier taken the position that Yugoslavia was an "artificial creation" of the Versailles Treaty and that the Montenegrins were a separate nation due to their existence up to 1918 as a separate state and due to their separatist movement in the prewar Yugoslavia. In Montenegro during the war there was a very powerful movement of Serbian counterrevolutionaries (Četniks), so that turning Montenegro into a state at the same time weakened the most serious opponent of the Communists—Serbian centralistic and hegemonistic nationalism. Besides, the party was organized on a Montenegrin basis, as was the administrative apparatus during the war, and those apparatuses were pleased with their equality in the new hierarchical structure with the apparatuses of other real nations. Thus a region for which administrative and provincial autonomy was justified was elevated to the status of a separate nation and a separate statehood. Such distinctiveness for Montenegro was not particularly important and created no special problems as long as an ideological and organizationally unified Communist party ensured *de facto* centralization. But today, with the disintegration of the party and with the republics having almost the status of sovereign states, for the awakened, expansive Croatian nationalism, the "Montenegrin state" becomes very important for its expansions, while the Serbs, even if they are not nationalist, see in it the dismemberment of their own nation.

Before the war the Communists envisioned autonomy for Bosnia and Herzegovina. Experience from the revolution led them to change their position and to give Bosnia and Herzegovina the status of a republic, despite the fact that Serbs and Moslems account for 40 per cent each, and Croats 20 per cent, of the population. Thereby the Communists were able to paralyze the demands of Croatian nationalism for their historical territories, and the demands of Serbian nationalism for their ethnic territories, and at the same time they were able to satisfy the yearnings of the Moslems for a separate state.

Apart from the six republics, the Communists formed within the Republic of Serbia two autonomous provinces, Vojvodina and Kosovo. The status of both provinces is the same, although in Vojvodina the majority of the population is Serbian and the significant minority is Hungarian, while in Kosovo the majority of the population is Albanian and only a little more than one-third are Serbs. As far as I can remember, concern for the Hungarian minority played a secondary role in the decision to give autonomy to Vojvodina. In Vojvodina in the past there had existed among the Serbs themselves those who favored autonomy, although it was a weak movement, and in addition the party developed an autonomous apparatus during the war. These were the decisive elements in the decision to give autonomy to Vojvodina. In Kosovo the situation was different. There also an autonomous apparatus had developed. In addition to that, Kosovo borders on Albania, and since at that time the Yugoslav and the Albanian Communists had visions of unification, autonomy for Kosovo was understood also as an intermediate step toward that goal. With the most recent constitutional changes (the "Amendments"), Vojvodina and Kosovo were nearly awarded the status of republics, over strong Serbian objections. A bizarre situation emerged: in order to satisfy the demands of the Albanians in Kosovo, the analogous rights were forced upon Vojvodina, although it had not asked for them. Thus the Serbian population in the Kosmet, despite the fact that Serbs constitute almost half the population of Yugoslavia, and despite the fact that Kosovo is an autonomous part of their own Serbian republic, are subject to pressures, and instead of visions of unification with Albania, the reality of Albanian irredentism has emerged.

Today's eruptions of nationalisms and national strife, however, do not mean that the Communists did not do anything to resolve the national question. Moreover, it would not be justified to say that the Communists made grave, essential mistakes in handling the national question. The problem cannot be presented that way because no one, not even Communists, can ever do anything beyond the scope of their ideas, interests and capacities. The revolution brought a change in the national question as well as in property relations and power.

The problem is primarily that even though social, and especially political, systems change, nations persist. That means that the national question in a multinational state can be resolved at best only for a specific period, in the framework of a specific political and social structure. Each change of the social and political order alters the relations among nations. And conversely: nations, changeable in their aspirations and potentials, influence the changing of the system.

This is what has happened in Yugoslavia.

In Yugoslavia, an ideological, monolithic party disintegrated or was transformed. It happened gradually, especially due to changes in the structure of society. Those changes revealed themselves most clearly in party crises. Analysis of those crises is beyond the scope of this article. But it is important to observe the present, ultimate crisis, which expresses itself in the absence of any organizational or operational unity. In Yugoslavia not only is there already no ideological unity, but also—if the present course of events continues, and it appears that it will—soon there will be no party at all. There will remain only the organs of authority and the various groups surrounding their hierarchies.

The Yugoslav leaders, secretly hankering for the former monolithicness, most frequently blame such a condition on "revisionists." But the "revisionists" are guilty only of observing the objective reality and of warning the party bureaucracy, blinded by power and dogma, in vain. And as far as monolithicness is concerned, in order to have it, one needs not only the right kind of revolutionary situation, but also a society different from what we have at present.

By the force of its needs and conditions, Yugoslav society developed contrary to the beliefs and intentions of Communists. Namely, instead of becoming less and less a class society, it became more and more a class society. It was nearest to being classless, in fact, immediately after the revolution: the particular characteristics and activities of social groups were smothered, and individuals were almost completely cut off from their social environment. Over this formless society and the isolated individuals in it the "new class"—the party bureaucracy—established its omnipotence. That led not only to Stalinist totalitarianism, but also to submission to Stalin. Rejecting the latter in its own selfish interests, Yugoslav Communists were forced to widen their base and, thereby, to move away from totalitarianism.

Critics from East Europe most frequently cite the market economy as the cause for the Yugoslav situation. The market economy doubtless plays an important role in the differentiation of society. But it is also true that the market economy is growing stronger in the East as well, and that is caused by the differentiation of social needs and the differentiation of society itself.

And what society has already been created in Yugoslavia? And what kind is in the process of being created in Eastern Europe?

The most visible characteristic is the disintegration of the party bureaucracy and at the same time the emergence of a particular kind of *middle class*. Cadres from the revolution, if they are not physically worn out, are replaced by less dogmatic, more talented pragmatics. The intellectual and social climate closely resembles that of Louis Philippe's time as seen by Stendhal and Balzac, with the difference that the middle class in Communist countries is not a bourgeoisie—because there is no bourgeois ownership—but it is in many ways similar to the bourgeoisie, especially in having as its "highest" ideals technical progress and a high standard of living. It is also recruited from all social strata—managers, the liberal professions, the pragmatic party bureaucracy, petty bourgeoisie, and even from among the workers and peasants. The beliefs and mentality of that class, with its modern "capitalist" mode of production, impregnate all the pores of "its" nation.

The transformation within society and within the party is built on the "natural," the only possible basis—a national basis. This can be seen above all in the pretensions of the national party bureaucracy, but also in other "bourgeois" forms of nationalisms. The Yugoslav party obviously disintegrated into republican branches, and those further divided themselves along the lines of the social orientation of its membership.

Along with the pretensions of the national bureaucracies, that is, of bureaucratic nationalisms, there emerges also an "ideology" of national superiority and national toleration. "Scientific" studies have been published about the exploitation of one nation by another and about the unlimited potential of one's own nation. This serves to arouse irrational impulses and to conceal one's own exploitative and hegemonistic intentions. Of course, there was exploitation. But not because of the hegemony of this or that nation, but because of the wastefulness and privileges of the party bureaucracy at the expense of everyone else. In that sense the criticism directed against Belgrade can be justified—not because it is the Serbian center, but because it is the bureaucratic center.

The reality of national relations and national aspirations is still hidden. This is valid for society as a whole as well as for the tendencies within it. For the changes in society have not been accompanied by changes in ideas and political institutions. The political structure in many ways remains just as it emerged from the revolution. The party bureaucracy could not halt social change, but it was strong enough and united enough to suppress new, democratic political currents. Each change in the bureaucracy turns out to be nothing more than a rearrangement of its own ranks. For that reason it recognized and made legal the quality of the independent nationalist bureaucracies. It suppressed or manipulated all other forms of liberalizing.

But its own nationalism is not sufficient for the national bureaucracies, and it is even less convincing to other groups. "National unity," that is, co-operation with other nationalistic currents, appears to the national bureaucracies as the easiest and most natural solution.

In Yugoslavia that process assumed the starkest and most serious forms in Croatia, as much because of traditional and legendary aspirations of the Croats for an independent state as because of momentary difficulties and potential capabilities of the Croatian economy. The "progressive" wing of the party bureaucracy switched to nationalistic positions. But it was weak and it opened the doors to traditional nationalism, leading to a union of the two nationalistic authoritarian structures—the party and the "bourgeois." Although democratic in appearance and paying lip service to "Yugoslavianism," Croatia in fact moved toward separatism and authoritarian nationalism. It could not have been otherwise: no democratic or pro-Yugoslav variant was either allowed or offered. In that partnership, the party's nationalism showed itself to be neither dynamic nor imaginative. The student strike of nationalists stunned the bureaucratic nationalists and finally forced Tito to the repression of the nationalists in the party and to the arrest of student nationalist leaders. The nationalist euphoria was halted. But the Croatian question and other questions of the system are only temporarily silenced.

Yugoslav society has been democratized to a significant extent, but the political structures are still predominantly authoritarian. And precisely because of this each crisis, including the eruption of nationalisms, appears as a crisis of the state community and the entire society.

But all this is superficial. The foundations of Yugoslav society are healthier and the Yugoslav state is more stable than might appear. The most obvious proof of this is the isolation and resistance that met the eruption of Croatian nationalism.

The Yugoslav state and Yugoslav society will be shaken by crisis—as long as power is in the hands of the existing bureaucratic structure. Crisis grows out of crisis. And it goes on and on. . . .

How long? And where to?

No renaissance and stabilization of the party bureaucracy appears possible. But neither does a political democracy as it exists in the West appear realizable. Yugoslavia is moving toward a nondogmatic, but still authoritarian political order. Civil liberties and the confederation of Serbs, Croats, Slovenes and Macedonians—so near as an ideal—remain still far away.

New version of "A Fly in the Federal Ointment," *Le Monde*,
Weekly English Edition, January 8, 1972

15
The Left Today

Young people—each in his own way—pose questions and seek answers. It would appear that the solution lies in this constant search. But everyone wants to find nothing less than the final solution in his own time—especially those among young people who are dissatisfied with the state of affairs they find, and who are sufficiently strong and serious to look social reality in the eye.

Land Without Justice, 1958
(Trans. Anon.)

On Alienation: Thoughts on a Marxist Myth

History repeats itself, so it seems, just as human destiny does. . . . If the Party bureaucrats of today remind one of those Renaissance princes for whom faith was a useful *décor*, Marxist theoreticians have much in common with those medieval Scholastic theologians who always found justifications for dogma, but never any for sin. If the former have given themselves over completely to the *civitas terrena*, the latter derive their delectation from dogmatic speculations and bitter meditations on life which has deviated from the one and only "scientific" and "redeeming" teaching. Hundreds of thousands of Communists have been purged by their own Party leadership as "traitors" and "renegades"; tens of thousands of "alien elements" have been purged because their attributes or their aspirations did not coincide with the teachings of the "infallible" teachers, or the practices of powerful leaders. Both under "capitalism" and under "socialism," life has taken to undogmatic channels. But faith has a diabolical side to it: the faithful will question everything but dogma, and so do our contemporary Marxist professors and theoreticians behave towards their sacred texts.

They have remembered the Teacher's saying that violence is the "midwife of history." Yet the violence of Stalinism, in spite of its senseless forms and proportions, did not turn out to be such a midwife. It did not bring about the "classless society," not to mention the "new man"; and it

403

was surely this disappointment, more than anything else, which made these "socialist humanists" bitter against Stalinism and neo-Stalinism. It has been a spiritual torture for them to have lived through the frightful moral and intellectual dramas of contemporary Marxism, and now they have to endure more trials and tribulations because of the purity and the perseverance of their beliefs.

The painful awakening started with the rejection of Stalin and the return to Lenin. Nevertheless, while Party bureaucrats satisfied themselves with Lenin's "infallibility" towards the Party, by the mythologizing of his role and personality, these pained but uncorrupted minds could not fail to notice the blood ties between Lenin and Stalin; and so they continued their reversion . . . back to Marx. But again, who could deny the relationship between Marx and Lenin? Had Marx not been mistaken in his prediction of revolution in industrial societies? Is it not blatantly obvious that socialist countries are as full of "contradictions" and other difficulties, different in nature but not in degree, as those that had beset those societies since destroyed by revolution or by Soviet military action? Has the chasm between modern science and the Marxist view of the world not turned out to be unbridgeable, in spite of the fact that this view justified its claims in and over society by its "scientific" nature?

There appears to be no end to the search for refuges and consolations. Just as Protestant dogmatists moved from the New back to the Old Testament, so have our hopeless Marxist dogmatists moved from the mature Marx back to the young Marx, and seized hold, in particular, of his theory of alienation. This was in no way fortuitous. The young Marx is essentially a moralist who, precisely through his theory of *Entfremdung* —the most unelaborated and most unclear of his doctrines—grew out of Hegel's philosophy and out of basic religious attitudes.

It is important to note that Lenin, Stalin and Mao do not even mention this theory of Marx's, and that, moreover, Marx himself, having matured, repressed it and considerably altered its form. This, however, does not in the least prevent the armchair revolutionaries of today from turning just to that theory for refuge from the gales which, although they have perhaps no more than shaken their reality, have nevertheless torn asunder their world ideals. . . . Marx's description of man's (more precisely, the proletariat's) alienation corresponds exactly to the medical description of the neurosis of the same name, although he finds social causes for it. Yet many things have changed since Marx's time, and one can well ask: is not the contemporary flight into the theory of alienation itself a symptom of alienation from reality and from one's own reason? Is it not, again, tantamount to the handing over of one's being to other forces?

Man's alienation in European thought has its roots in religious doctrines according to which the breaking of religious precepts is made tantamount to estrangement from god and his laws. Such ideas receive a more specific (though non-religious) aspect in Rousseau and in Goethe's *Faust*. For the sake of this essay, however, it is important to dwell on the philosophical ideas which directly influenced Marx, since it is to him alone that our uncritical and unoriginal discoverers of alienation have turned.

The dichotomy of Kant's man (*homo noumenon* and *homo phenomenon*) aimed at achieving moral perfection, and it developed with Hegel into a contradiction of the spirit for the achievement of an ideal being. Hegel's spirit, the Absolute Spirit, is synonymous with God. It is the inner being of the world. God-the-spirit and the world are one (*Weltgeist*). This God-spirit is not perfect as is the Christian God, but it develops gradually, from primal unconsciousness in the form of Nature, through historical man into his own self-consciousness. The organ through which God gradually becomes conscious of himself is the mind of man. God becomes fully God in man's knowledge of Him. Nature is God in space; history is God in time. The history of the world is the self-creation of God-spirit, the actualization of God in man. The process of God's self-consciousness, of man's discovery, is unending and develops by the activity of the mind through conflicts which are endlessly being transcended (*Aufhebung*). Thus God, or cognitive man, also fully appropriates the world to himself, since Hegel makes no fundamental difference between discovery and appropriation. By apprehending, Hegel's man—"finite self-conscious spirit"—conceives of himself as God.

But what is the self-alienation of the spirit, that is to say, of the cognitive man?

For Hegel, the object is alien and opposed to the subject. The spirit, as the only reality, is divided into conscious subject (man) and external object (the world). It is this relation that Hegel calls the self-alienation (*Selbstentfremdung*) of the spirit. Progressive cognisance, which is apprehension of the world, is the overcoming of alienation.

From the above it can be seen that Hegel's dialectic, his pattern of development through inner conflicts, is based on the division of the spirit against itself: its urge to be aware of itself as absolute, to possess the world by knowing it as itself. This contradiction of the spirit, and the transcending of it, Hegel has transplanted into history, which (for him) is the autobiography of God-the-self-conscious-man.

A new contribution to the theory of alienation was made by Ludwig Feuerbach. He rejected Hegel's system as so much speculative theology; but on the other hand, he discovered in it an "esoteric" content revealing the truth about man. Hegel's man is God in a state of self-alienation and of return to himself. But in reality—says Feuerbach—it is God who is man in a state of self-alienation, for there are not two worlds, but only one: the real material world. Hegel's self-alienated God-spirit is a mystical portrait of religious man. Being does not proceed from thought, but thought from being. Believing that he perceives God, man in fact perceives his own nature. Through his religious life, man is alienated from himself. History is not the process of God's achievement of full self-consciousness through man, but rather the contrary: the process of man's achievement of full self-consciousness through God. As far as man is concerned, the goal of history is for him to become fully human, to fulfil himself as man. God is only the prototype and the idealization of man. Instead of wasting his energy on God-the-illusion, man must return to himself, to productive work in real life.

Even from such an over-simplified exposition, the direct relation of Marx's thought to Hegel's and Feuerbach's system appears clearly. This was stressed by Marx himself, and moreover with unashamed youthful pride, at the very time of his formulation of the theory of alienation. In the course of intellectual growth, Marx's philosophy will draw upon other sources as well, notably upon the classical English political economy of Adam Smith, and on the French socialists. His theory of alienation, however, is mainly rooted in Hegel and Feuerbach.[1]

In Marx as in Feuerbach, man is the supreme being for man. He must strive for the realization of himself in the real world, and not in religious fantasies. For Marx, the solution to man's alienation in nature (Hegel), or in God (Feuerbach), is to be found in changing the existing world.

The existing world, for Marx, is essentially society. When in 1844, at the age of 25, he formulated in his *Economic and Philosophical Manuscripts* the theory of alienation, he already had well-established views on the world, and had accumulated significant experiences from revolutionary socialist groups. Hegel's spirit alienated in nature, and Feuerbach's man alienated in religion, became with Marx man alienated in society, man in the service of, and sacrificed to, inhuman social forces. And although he had not had any direct contact with the proletariat, Marx, inspired by Hegel's dialectic and by his new faith, came to see alienated humanity in the proletariat, devoid of property, devoid of rights, and embittered by exploitation.

The alienation of workers appears, according to Marx, in two forms—as alienation of the worker from the product of his labor, and as alienation of the worker from labor itself. Expressed very simply, the product does not belong to the worker, and labor itself does not belong to his essence as a man.

The more the worker spends himself, the more powerful the alien objective world becomes which he creates over-against himself, the poorer he himself—his inner world—becomes, the less belongs to him as his own. It is the same in

1. On the origins and contents of Marx's doctrine, see the scholarly and stimulating work of Robert Tucker, *Philosophy and Myth in Karl Marx* (Cambridge University Press, 1961), which I have found so illuminating.

religion. The more man puts into God, the less he retains in himself. The worker puts his life into the object; but now his life no longer belongs to him but to the object. . . . Whatever the product of his labor is, he is not. Therefor the greater this product, the less he is himself. . . . But the estrangement is manifested not only in the result but in the *act of production*. . . . Labor is *external* to the work, *i.e.* does not belong to his essential being; . . . in his work, therefore, he does not affirm himself but denies himself . . . does not develop freely his physical and mental energy but mortifies his body and ruins his mind. The worker therefore only feels himself outside his work, and in his work feels outside himself. . . . His labor is therefore not voluntary, but coerced; it is *forced labor*. . . . Just as in religion the spontaneous activity of the human imagination, of the human brain and the human heart, operates independently of the individual—that is, operates on him as an alien, divine or diabolical activity—in the same way the worker's activity is not his spontaneous activity. It belongs to another; it is the loss of his self.[2]

The mature Marx will keep an unbroken link with these views, although in an altered form, and with still other arguments:

There is a physical relation between physical thing. But it is different with commodities. There, the existence of the things *qua* commodities and the value-relation between the products of labor which stamp them as commodities, have absolutely no connection with their physical properties and with the material relations arising therefrom. There is a definite social relation between men, that assumes, in their eyes, the fantastic form of a relation between things. In order, therefore, to find an analogy, we must have recourse to the mist-enveloped regions of the religious world. In that world the productions of the human brain appear as independent beings endowed with life. . . . So it is in the world of commodities with the products of men's hands. This I call Fetishism which attaches itself to the products of labor, so soon as they are produced as commodities, and which is therefore inseparable from the production of commodities.[3]

Again:

Within the capitalist system . . . all means for the development of production transform themselves into means of domination over, and exploitation of, the producers; they mutilate the laborer into a fragment of a man, degrade him to the level of an appendage of a machine, destroy every remnant of charm in his work and turn it into a hated toil; they estrange from him the intellectual potentialities of the labor process in the same proportion as science is incorporated in it as an independent power. . . . It follows therefore that in proportion as capital accumulates, the lot of the laborer, be his payment high or low, must grow worse. The law . . . establishes an accumulation of misery corresponding with an accumulation of capital. Accumulation of wealth at one pole is, therefore, at the same time accumulation of misery, agony of toil, slavery,

2. Marx, *Economic and Philosophical Manuscripts of 1844* (Moscow: Foreign Languages Publishing House, 1961) , pp. 70–73.
3. Karl Marx and F. Engels, *Rani radovi* (Zagreb: Nepred, 1967) , pp. 246–249.

408 UTOPIA AND BUREAUCRACY

ignorance, brutality, mental degradation, at the opposite pole, i.e., on the side of the class that produces its own product in the form of capital.[4]

If we remember Hegel and Feuerbach, we shall at once see where Marx innovates. At the same time, his deep debt to them is also evident, especially in the schematic comparison between social and religious phenomena, and in the simplified, vulgarized explanation of religion.

Marx explains in a novel way the root of man's alienation. Although alienation reaches a turning point in the proletariat and developed commodity production, it did not start there. The original sin was in the division of labor and the birth of private property. Marx does not consider private property to be the original fount of alienation, but that the former materializes and affirms itself in the latter. The source of alienation is the division of labor which took place (as I understand Marx) in the pre-historical era, in primitive communities where new tools and crafts brought about occupational specialization and enabled production to rise above the bare needs of man's survival. It was then that the appropriation of man's labor became possible, that the ruling classes emerged, armed with instruments of domination for the defense of the system. But Marx, who in his youth had stressed the greed of man, did not clearly explain why it should have been that men had to invent new tools, and accept the expropriation of their labor, their subordination to other men. . . .

Man's (i.e., the proletarian's) alienation will be eliminated—according to Marx—with the coming of the communist society.

Communism as the *positive* transcendence *of private property,* as *human self-estrangement,* and therefore as the real *appropriation of the human* essence by and for man; communism therefore as the complete return of man to himself as a social (i.e., human) being—a return become conscious, and accomplished within the entire wealth of previous development. This communism . . . is the *genuine* resolution of the conflict between man and nature and between man and man . . . between freedom and necessity, between the individual and the species. Communism is the riddle of history solved, and it knows itself to be this solution.[5]

As can be seen (but the "new" theoreticians do not want to see), Marx's theory of alienation is his most general, and at the same time his most unelaborated—one could almost say, his least original—teaching on communism.

Communist society, however, is not the final goal of Marx's teaching, but the basis and precondition of Unalienated Man, i.e., of man in a new state, of man who will freely develop all his powers, who will produce

4. Marx, *Capital* (Moscow: Foreign Languages Publishing House, 1961), Vol. I, pp. 72, 645.
5. *Economic and Philosophical Manuscripts of 1844,* p. 102.

spontaneously according to the laws of beauty, who will fully achieve his human nature. To effect such a metamorphosis of man has been the aim of religions (to be sure, without "scientific" justifications of the type elaborated by Marx). Commenting on the Fall of Man (the sin of Adam and Eve), Hegel remarks that man, through his overwhelming desire to become like God in knowledge, lost his original harmony; he will achieve a "second harmony" through the philosophical quest for absolute knowledge. Is Marx's communism—"the complete return of man to himself as a *social* (*i.e.*, human) being"—not a return (albeit "on a higher level") to the lost "original harmony," *i.e.*, the proto-communist communities in which there was no division of labor or of property.

Just as medieval Christianity conceived itself and final salvation as a unity of dogma and good works, so Marx proclaims the unity of theory and practice. "The philosophers have only interpreted the world, in various ways; the point, however, is to *change* it," Marx wrote in his *Theses on Feuerbach*[6] one year after formulating his theory of alienation. In so doing, he does admittedly limit philosophy and science to utilitarian activities, and in precisely that does he differ from Hegel and Feuerbach, and finally achieve his "own self." Nevertheless, his insistence on the fulfillment of philosophy, and on the scientific character of his own doctrine, reminds one of Hegel and Feuerbach. The ghost of Hegel's Absolute Spirit, which apprehends the world by knowing it, continued to haunt Marx to the very end, as an integral part of his teaching.

The fact that Hegel's system is today irrelevant and faded does not in any way detract from the profound significance of his thinking for European culture and society. With his dialectic, Hegel introduced a creative tension and an irresistible dynamic which have not yet spent themselves, and some of his insights are among the most illuminating made by man. His theory of alienation, however, is a part of his system that, in spite of its complex splendor, had been undermined by the middle of the nineteenth century.

Something similar can be said of Marx today. His doctrine is kept alive mainly because it has evolved into the preservative of bureaucratic "socialist" structures. Since I have already dwelt upon this, and upon Marx's incomparable role in the development of humanity in my book *The Unperfect Society*,[7] I shall limit myself here to saying what I think of the theory of alienation, and of alienation itself.

The question is: what is unacceptable today, what is inexact, in Hegel's and Marx's theory of alienation? It is surely a question which can be faced by every person not confused and distressed by the disintegra-

6. Marx and Engels, *Selected Works* (Moscow: Foreign Languages Publishing House, 1962), Vol. II, p. 405.
7. Milovan Djilas, *The Unperfect Society: Beyond the New Class* (New York: Harcourt Brace Jovanovich, 1969).

tion of totalitarian ideologies, and by the unattainability of the perfect society and of the new, universal man.

First of all, no mentally balanced person feels "alienated" simply because nature is different from him, or because he cannot control the exchange of the products made by his own hands. He merely feels that he is not sufficiently qualified, or that he is inadequately rewarded.

Even this is too generalized to be entirely true. But it remains that Hegel's theory of alienation disintegrates if exposed to modern scientific inquiry and even to modern philosophical and religious thought. Can one find nowadays, in any science, references to a spirit which struggles within itself to overcome unconscious alien forces with its own self-conscious forces? Does any creative thinker in our age proceed from an intellectual position which opposes divine wisdom to nature, or one which starts from the absolute, aprioristic dichotomy of man? I know of no philosopher of any significance who would today endorse Hegel's system, of which the very theory of alienation is one of the central pillars. The fact that man apprehends nature ever more intimately can be interpreted more convincingly nowadays as an expansion of his condition in his own world than as the spiritual overpowering of alien forces.

The topical actuality of Marx's theory of alienation calls, however, for a fuller refutation.

In the manner of religious people, Marx started by adopting "truths" about the "inevitability" of communist society, a faith in a new, self-realized, and perfect "non-alienated" Man, and only then, carried away by the scientism of his age, did he go on to advance "scientific" proofs of this "inevitability" and of this faith—a task in which (it must be admitted) he invested much effort and passion.

There can be no doubt whatever that man, when he discovers a truth, or when he creates a work of art, or when he improves a skill, puts into his creations, i.e., "alienates" to them, his power, his feeling, his intellect. But he does so for the simple reason that he is *man*. Animals do perceive, and sometimes they innovate, but they are not able fundamentally to alter their condition; and that is precisely what man is doing all the time. He discovers new truths and new forms; he invents new tools, and he uses new materials. Man is man in so far as by his actions he moves away—"alienates" himself—from the conditions of life which nature has given him. With animals, adaptation is a gradual, long-term, instinctive process; but with man it is a conscious, daily process. If it were not so, man, as opposed to animals, would not be able to survive in nature. It is true that man's body predisposes him to this (his developed brain, upright position, agility of hands, etc.) ; but the most important is undoubtedly that man *thinks differently*. By thinking, he is able to evaluate his own capacities, and to adapt his activities to the change of circumstances. Therefore, it is not because this or that method of production (his social condition) has this or that characteristic that man "alienates" himself from it, but because (and perhaps only then) he cannot exist in such circumstances any longer. The ever-greater division of labor does increase alienation, and it makes it more complex; but this does not alter the fact that even primitive man alienated himself in the very act of "starting" to think, and act, differently than animals.

As with many other general truisms, Marx turned this one about the beginning of man and his humanism into a "class" truth, a "proletarian" and communist truth. Hegel was really nearer the truth, even though his conclusion—which was not accompanied by direct social action—had neither such an elaborate scientific appearance nor indeed such a great influence on society.

The industrial revolution signified an unprecedented scientific take-off. In Marx's eyes, it destroyed traditional structures and relations, and was accompanied by intense exploitation and unbridled brutality over workers and peasants. The class division was sharp and clear. The bene-fits of technological progress and of market expansion were grabbed by the owners of the means of production and exchange, *i.e.*, by the indus-trialists and bankers—the capitalists. It was also the age of the creation of a world market, of the triumph of commodity production over natural production. His faith in the inevitability of communism, his belief in the universal validity of Hegelian dialectic and in the absolute relevance of Feuerbachian materialism, even to society, led Marx to explain the laborer's (man's) alienation by the development of commodity produc-tion. And so he believed that, by doing away with commodity pro-duction, and with capitalist private ownership, the laborer's (man's) alienation would also be done away with.

The mature Marx does not fundamentally differ in that from the young Marx.

Let us now picture to ourselves . . . a community of free individuals, carry-ing on their work with the means of production in common, in which the labor power of all the different individuals is consciously applied as the combined labor-power of the community. . . . The social relations of the individual pro-ducers, with regard both to their labor and to its products, are in this case perfectly simple and intelligible, and that with regard not only to production but also to distribution.[8]

But how can one eliminate this execrable and ever-more articulated division of labor—the cause of commodity exchange of alienation? Marx is not very forthcoming on this point, and one can only surmise that in the communist future, technique will be so developed, and unalienated man so universal, that everybody, by spontaneous activity, will be able to carry out all functions, have all that he desires, and even create what he

8. *Capital*, Vol. I, pp. 78–79.

imagines. This is an attractive hope or vision, but it is devoid of scientific foundations, and modern technology, as well as the course of contemporary revolutions, points to a different conclusion. Division of labor is increasing. Man does less work, but is more specialized, more technical. And although it appears probable that exploitation and oppression did start with the division of labor, it is absolutely certain that the change of this or that set of social relations will not eliminate it, since the division of labor arose from man's needs, and from man's power to expand his own human (*i.e.,* non-animal) condition. For these very reasons, the division of labor proliferates.

For the young Marx, the "alienation of man" is basically another expression for the exploitation of labor. We have seen that the mature Marx kept the same views, albeit in generalized form. But alienation and exploitation are not, and cannot be, identical; the former is a human characteristic, a state of man, while the latter is an interhuman, a social relationship. Those theoreticians in "socialist" countries who maintain that "the task of socialism is to overcome those forms of human existence which create the alienated man" (*i.e.,* "Total state planning, but also the disposal of surplus-value by the state")[9] blur the real needs of their society, which are freedom of ideas, and freer forms of government and property. As for the "neo-Marxist" professors in the West, it is as though they were unhappy that the working class had lifted itself out of a state of suffering, and "thus" destroyed the conditions for revolution, for which very few of them, anyhow, seem to want to sacrifice themselves. The struggle for a more equitable distribution, and for freer forms, is possible; but it is surely obvious today that violence and injustice have not been eliminated with the abolition of capitalist private property.

The life of nations and men—"history" as Hegel and Marx would say—has not evolved according to Marx's "laws" and "inevitabilities," and certainly not according to his theory of alienation. Viewed in long-term perspective, the accumulation of wealth under capitalism has not meant for the workers an "accumulation of misery, agony of toil, slavery, ignorance, brutality, mental degradation"; they have acquired possibilities of attaining better standards and a higher position in society. The expansion of commodity production and the articulation of the production process (*i.e.,* the increased division of labor) have certainly not issued in bliss, but they have brought about an improvement of the human condition, and in that way they have reduced the alienation which Marx had in mind. The "neo-Marxist" theoreticians of alienation thus merely repeat the illusions of their exalted teacher, which have now become (as Marx would have said) farcical. The dogmatic constructions of Herbert

9. Predrag Vranicki in *Socialist Humanism,* ed. Erich Fromm (Penguin, 1967), pp. 282–283.

Marcuse about the "one dimensional man" of the "consumer society" are arbitrary and unattractive. Erich Fromm's assertions that "affluent alienation" (*i.e.,* alienation in a prosperous society) can be just as dehumanising as "impoverished alienation" (*i.e.,* alienation in conditions of poverty) are unreal and verbalistic. It has, finally, to come to this: although it cannot be denied that Marx, by coupling revolution and sociology, has contributed to the wider diffusion of socio-economic ideas, it is even truer to say that the aim of his ceaseless endeavors has been—to paraphrase Robert Tucker—not to set out the laws of society, ultimately of capitalism, but to confirm the faith of his youth in the inevitability of communist society, and of the new, universal, spontaneously active and "unalienated" man.

There is no alienation—and there cannot be any—in the sense intended by Marx. Marx has "alienated" the tormented life of men, and particularly of workers, in order to turn them into philosophical "weapons" for his *Weltanschauung.* As far as his New Man is concerned, I would today rather follow St. Augustine: better a sinful man than an automaton.

And yet, man does alienate himself—from society, from nature, from his own self.

Every time that man, by whatever action, achieves something fundamentally or radically new (it might be more exact to say: every time that something new is achieved in man), he alienates himself: estranges himself from the conditions and circumstances in which he has hitherto lived. In other words, whenever he creates, and in so far as he creates, he alienates himself. It is rare to find a great man—in politics, in science, in arts, or in any other sphere—whose work has not been a conflict with established conditions around him, and an estrangement from these. In reality, geniuses create new forms by moving away from the forms they have found. The alienation of great minds is, at the same time, a way for them of uniting with men and with the world. It is a sacrifice offered by them to their community, or even to humanity.

For such an alienation to come about, more is needed than talent: an inner, intellectual and emotive effort which no outside obstacle, social or material, is able to stop. Great men are like conflagrations; with their work they leave traces of fires in their spiritual homelands. For these reasons, great men are often considered to be mad. (In order that there should be no misunderstanding, I hasten to add that I do not refer here to insanity, to neurotic alienation, but only to alienation as an attribute of sane men.)

History records that, at times, in some nations, there was a dearth of great men, which coincided with periods of decadence. History nevertheless also indicates that the human species never ceases to give birth to geniuses, who are simply the protruding summits of its creative powers.

For creative alienation—in more humble and less striking ways—is also an attribute of more ordinary men, and a phenomenon of their everyday life. Every human action which creates something new is, at the same time, an alienation from the old, from the existing. No one has really loved a woman without separating from someone else. Nor has any designer, for instance, created a really new model without departing from existing fashion.

Such estrangement is visible, not only in its social aspect, but also as alienation from nature, and from one's own self.

Alienation from nature is obvious as a long-term process, and is nothing else but man altering, through technical and other improvements, the circumstances of his existence. Man alienates himself from the natural circumstances that he has found, at the same time as he adapts to new circumstances. In hitherto unprecedentedly artificial, i.e., alienated, circumstances, the astronauts of Apollo 11 have carried out the first human link-up with a celestial body.

In the process of such alienation, man does not stop being what he is, but becomes more independent, more alienated from nature. Man becomes man by alienating himself. "I alienate myself" means: "I am man." History offers innumerable instances of individual nations lagging behind, for various reasons, in technical and other forms of expansion of their conditions. These are, for them, periods of general decline and decadence. The technicalization of man's existence and the automation of social functions have altered the old, "idyllic" relations among men; but they cannot abolish these relations as such. On the contrary, alienation itself (i.e., the improvement of technique and of production) is the material condition for the unification of humanity, which thinkers ever since Kant have perceived and prophesied. The unification will take place one day, but not according to the plan of some genius or the action of a leader, but as a necessity of life, and through the living, conscious cooperation of nations. There is no end to this alienation from nature, and to that "purely" spiritual alienation, in the same way as there is no end to the universe of which we are part, and in which we exist.

The third aspect of man's creative alienation is alienation from himself, and to me this is its most mysterious aspect, although I am none the less convinced of its manifestation. To put it briefly, man does not achieve spiritual and technical creativeness without a transformation of his own self, i.e., an alienation from his previous self, from his thoughts, actions, dreams. I do not mean that man loses his personality: it is precisely with his personality that he carries out his work. But his personality evolves through a process of agonizing and dream-like, but inevitable, creativeness. And this takes place, it seems to me, in a way which makes the already created personality purer and more consequent in its creativeness, more capable of carrying out its work.

This alienation of one's own self, however, has nothing in common with the old-fashioned sermons about the need to change oneself in order to change the world. For that sort of "change" is simply the old promise of a "new" man, the perfect man. In the conditions of our time (for we cannot conceive and treat Marx's theories of alienation, and similar theories, independently of real, social, international and human circumstances), that sort of "change" is the unfortunate snare into which fall the innocent, misled by the not-so-innocent aims of their preachers and proctors. The change, the alienation of which I speak here, is personal and free—in so far as any human action can be. It has no other aim but the possible liberation of one's own and human creative potential. It is the confirmation of man's humanity—of a humanism based on the human self.

The human being thus manifests itself to us as creative, hence infinite in his creativeness and existence. Alienized, creative man is one of the aspects of mankind, just as Aristotle's man is "social," Smith's "economic," and Marx's "working." But in the same way as none of these aspects have turned out to be absolute, or even predominant, so man the alienized creator cannot be reduced to one aspect only. Even if he came to know what his Being and his Essence were, man could not return to them, for he has never departed from them. He is what he is. He feels and perceives his attributes, but remains, like the world, inaccessible. For man is also a world, endless within himself.

Finally, there would be no greater and more injurious illusion today than to see in that man a God, however much he may aspire to complete alienation—the absolute dominion over nature. For it is only an aspiration, part of the ceaseless movement into new circumstances and new possibilities. Man is not and cannot be a God. Not, however, because there is no God (and someone has to take his place) or because God does exist (and can have no replacement). Even his own spiritual works, man does not create out of his head alone, even less so Nature and his own self. God and Anti-God are also aspects of man's existence. We are part of the world, and in it we can subsist with our mind and work, and with our sacrifice.

New version of article in *Encounter*, May 1971
(Trans. Anon.)

The New Left—a Compound of Enthusiasm and Manipulation

No one was exactly surprised that the 1968 rebellion of young people, which spread like wildfire through the universities of Europe and America, caused resistance and concern among the keepers of social order and the theoreticians of change through reform.

Nor was it surprising that the majority of official Communist parties opposed these rebellions.

Insofar as there is any Marxism among the young rebels, it denounces the Moscovite (bureaucratic, Stalinist) and even the "oversimplified" Leninist "distortions." But that is merely one reason, and a secondary one at that, for the Communist resistance to the views and methods of disgruntled youth. The chief reason lies in the fact that the East European Communist parties are the major bulwarks of a bureaucratic and hegemonistic social order, and the parties in the West, particularly in Italy and France (the only two that have a significant influence), are no longer able to avoid dissolution into sects except at the cost of aligning themselves, albeit indirectly, with progressive technological developments in their own countries.

If the rebellion of youth was not looked upon with favor by the official Communist parties, it was welcomed by Trotskyites, Maoists and Castroists, anarcho-Communists, anarchists, disappointed Stalinists, and all kinds of intellectual, academic and salon revolutionaries. They all hastened too eagerly to warm themselves by the revolutionary fires, although they hadn't started them and did not have enough breath to keep them going. They were taken in by the ossified dogmatic belief that "capitalism" was pregnant with revolution, and they refused to recognize that the purges and the use of force and privileges in "socialism" had demolished their own revolutions. And while politicians and thinkers were busy with the problems caused by disorders in the universities and in the streets, the faithful and the survivors of former revolutions were quick only in flattering the rebellious youth and in imposing themselves on them. It could not have been otherwise: just as a jungle cry rouses the hunger, the mere thought of a revolution awakens in the former revolutionary a unique delight, but also the anxiety that he might be too late for the revolutionary train which is waiting to take him to power, and all humanity to the kingdom of peace and equality.

I compliment myself that I was not overcome by similar "weaknesses," although as a former revolutionary I ran the risk of being branded a traitor and a turncoat to capitalism, imperialism and counterrevolution. Nor did I rise to the defense of the existing order, which some might have interpreted as a sign that deep down I had not "settled my accounts" with the past. Others may have explained my position by saying that I had nothing to lose and that I could no longer feel enthusiasm for anything. I myself would maintain, however, that my position evolved from the recognition that no society is so just and open as to deserve unqualified defense from the attacks of the young, just as no young rebels are so idealistic and wise as to be beyond reproach or the need for sobering thought.

The current rebellion of the young is the first worldwide movement that did not originate in the mind of some genius or emanate from some leading center. Rather, it arose from a general resistance to bureaucratic aggrandizement, to consumer materialism and lack of idealism, to the atomic cataclysm, and to inhumane divisions—ideological, national, racial—on moral issues.

The roots of the moment lie not mainly in politics but in nonconformism, in dress, in morals and in behavior ("existentialists," beatniks, hippies, *et al.*). The Maoist and Castroite currents are either sporadic or, more often, are an expression of defiance and protest against official and prevailing views.

Nonconformism and humanistic beliefs are the most essential characteristics common to the young dissidents both in the West and in the East. And it is exactly what they have in common that was and will continue to be—at least as a tradition—the most inspiring and most creative factors in the spontaneous protest of contemporary youth.

And it is exactly that which weakens and pales the moment spontaneous movements become transformed into ideological and political movements. Institutionalization as such gives birth to caution, manipulation, dogmatic exclusivity and factional squabbles. That is exactly what happened to the contemporary movement of the young the moment ideologies—the idealized goals and manipulations of the leaders—began to unfold in them.

On top of everything else, like an evil omen the name "New Left" attached itself to the young rebels in the West. Although that appellation told us that the Old Left had missed its mark, it did not hint at some new, more attainable goals. The New Left merely promised to be more faithful to the ideal than the Old Left had been, but the ideal itself—the perfect (Communist-anarchistic) society—remained unchanged. And by not having the strength to cut the umbilical cord which tied it to the legends of the revolutionary tradition, the New Left was also unable to free itself from the sins of the old, outdated Left. More because of that dogmatic heritage than because of its diverse origins and its fragmentation into different currents, it was unable to create any more attainable and more inclusive programs. Although no one can deny that what it did aroused many a dormant conscience and raised a series of essential questions in the old structures (the war in Vietnam, race relations, reorganization of universities), the New Left in its spirit remains the Old.

Because of all of that, the movements of the New Left are short of breath. They are determined and effective in concrete situations and in the moral dilemmas of young intellectuals, but they are confused and powerless when it comes to society as a whole and the common problems of our planet.

From country to country, and in each one individually, the movements of the New Left are becoming more and more heterogeneous—torn into different factions and organizations. But from the beginning—and even more so later—it was apparent that there were differences between the views of the young dissidents in the West and those in the East. In the so-called consumer society in the West, because the broad masses are no longer subject to hunger or unemployment or the monopoly of power by one party, the young rebels are blinded by "more ideal" dogmas and utopias. Even in Yugoslavia, alongside the trend toward more effective production and political freedom, there also emerged, primarily at the universities, dogmatic groups of "humanistic" Marxists and egalitarians. But in Eastern Europe as a whole, the protest of the youth—if it succeeded in expressing itself at all (for example, in Czechoslovakia, Poland, Yugoslavia and among the Soviet intelligentsia)—was primarily of a freedom-loving, democratic character. It is not accidental that Rudi Dutschke, the keen restorer of "unspoiled Marxism" in West Berlin, was met with indignation by the Prague students, or that the able Daniel Cohn-Bendit, in his book *Obsolete Communism: The Left-Wing Alternative*,[1] does not even mention the events in Czechoslovakia. It was Kavan, the leader of the Czechoslovak students, who said: "For us the classic civil liberties are of the greatest significance. In socialist society, freedom of speech, freedom of the press, freedom of assembly and freedom of association are essential if the people are to exercise any control at all. . . . I have often told my friends in Western Europe that we are fighting only for bourgeois-democratic freedoms. But somehow I cannot seem to distinguish between capitalist freedoms and socialist freedoms. I can only recognize basic human freedoms."[2]

It is obvious that differences arise from the different structures and different tasks which confront the developed countries, and especially the intellectuals. This is true in the West as well as in the East (with the exception of China, which fell behind and where social and other differentiations are overshadowed by dogmatic enthusiasms, anathemas and bans). The inexhaustible and irresistible protests of young intellectuals emerge and will emerge anew—the increased role of knowledge and of educated cadres in the modern economy and contemporary technology makes this inevitable. Although everyday *labor* is not about to disappear, it is clear that industrial physical *work* diminishes.[3] The working class for the most part has merged with the middle class and incorporated itself into the "consumer society." The hopes of the young rebels in an alliance of workers and students has come to naught: even in France,

1. Daniel Cohn-Bendit & Gabriel Cohn-Bendit, *Obsolete Communism: The Left Wing Alternative* (New York: McGraw-Hill, 1969).
2. Cited from Stephen Spender, *The Year of the Young Rebels* (New York: Random House, 1969), p. 65.
3. This distinction between *labor* and *work* is based on Hannah Arendt, *The Human Condition* (Chicago: University of Chicago Press, 1958).

where students in June of 1968 served as the "detonator" of a general strike, the workers did not strike for the principles of the dogmatic wise men and young idealists, but, instead, for higher wages. Even in the West, private property is no longer the only (let alone the unconditional) form of ownership. Moreover, today it is clear that the form of ownership, although it can be a source of unjust differences, that is, lack of freedom, in itself is not the precondition of a better or a worse society. The modern economy can obviously function effectively under the management of technocrats. There is convincing evidence of that in the West (Volkswagen, Renault, INA, U.S. Atomic Energy Commission, etc.). But in the East the economy, precisely because it is nationalized, is stifled by the party and other bureaucracies. Educated people will soon become the most numerous and, judging by all signs, the most significant social stratum. Their increase occurred suddenly, in the course of a technological revolution, and neither they nor society as a whole has yet adjusted to the changes or even been able to comprehend them.

Stated most simply, the structure of society and politics in general is the same as before the present technological revolution. Such, by and large, are the ideas of young rebels—from the time of Marx, Bakunin, Lenin and W. D. Haywood. The problems of society are, however, more basic, the aspirations of intellectuals more far-reaching, and their role more indispensable.

It has been said that "the present generation of young people at our universities is the best-informed, the most intelligent and the most idealistic that this country has ever known."[4] I got the same impression of educated young Americans during my visit to the United States in the fall of 1968. The same can be said of young European intellectuals, whether in "capitalist" or in "socialist" states. One could think of other, even more beautiful, words to describe the new generation. But here we are talking about the new generation as a whole. And only the bitterest reactionaries and the most stubborn dogmatists would benefit by overlooking or ignoring the sterile dogmas with which the young rebels today throughout the world are not only destroying themselves but also making more difficult the emergence of genuinely new and attainable ideas and programs.

If the misfortunes of the Old Left did not end with the dissolution of its ideology, the misfortunes of the New Left just began with it. Therefore people like Sidney Lens are wrong when they maintain that the weakness of the New Left comes from the lack of a united, monolithic, "well-constructed" ideology.[5] No one can "construct" ideology—such a thing grows out of innumerable conditions and is finally synthesized in

4. *Crisis at Columbia* (New York: Vintage, Random House, 1969), p. 4.
5. "The Road to Power and Beyond," *Liberation* (New York), November, 1968.

the mind of some genius. Such a thing is especially "unfeasible" in a world that in all its aspects—the indeterminate structure of nature, the lack of idealism in all societies, the complexity of the human psyche and the infiniteness of the human mind—is daily discovered to be enormously varied and beyond definition. Modern society—like matter and man—can no longer be explained in terms of eighteenth- and nineteenth-century definitions, and even less by their simplified versions. Similarly, the rebellion of the young—the product of the atomic era and of present-day difficulties—cannot, even by the most skillful manipulation, be fitted into the ideologies of the nineteenth century. If it were possible to resurrect Marx and Bakunin today, it is clear that they would be neither Marxist nor anarchist. The changing of society is a creative and not an imitative process.

Today's social and political structures are in many ways outdated, owing in large measure to the fact that dogmas sanctified by revolution and by privileges played a large role in their creation. Therefore, much in contemporary societies is hermitic and static. Social, racial and other minorities have no opportunity to draw attention to their sufferings with legal measures, and even less to resolve them within periods of time that are of vital importance for them. Opponents of unnecessary and unjust wars, the poor and the slum dwellers, the underestimated intellectual masses, the unemployed workers, souls terrorized by dogmatic dictatorships, citizens without rights and oppressed peoples cannot wait until they gain power in parliament, until despots become benevolent, until totalitarian parties voluntarily renounce power and dogmas and until the conquerors voluntarily renounce their empires. Illegal and oppressive means are inevitable and justified whenever some group or community is forced to renounce its life and its visions. And because there are no perfect societies, such groups and communities, and hence even oppression itself, must exist.

But this does not justify movements in which force—the forcible destruction of society—is the essential component of the goals and the tactics. Today one can already find currents in the New Left for whom the war in Vietnam, the outdatedness of the universities, and the mistreatment of blacks are merely the legitimate causes for changing society —and such causes will always exist—but for whom the real essence is the destruction of the existing society and the "building" of "ideal" future societies. The New Left, or at least some of its most ideological elements, is already in conflict with society as a whole; these elements have already assumed their own form—their own methods and final aims. As a result, one has to speak about them as such, and not merely as a protest against specific and unjust relations.

The movements thus created have produced very few new ideas, despite the ingenuity and devotion of their leaders. For it is altogether irrelevant whether the "unspoiled" and "unrevised" Marxism of Rudi Dutschke is pure and ideal; the only relevant factor is whether modern society is in a condition to undergo the kind of revolutionary changes he has to offer. It is true that the revolutions betray themselves and devour their own children, but Cohn-Bendit's "uncontrolled spontaneity"—that is, "continuous change called Revolution,"[6] is not the remedy, for no society and no revolutionary could tolerate it. . . .

Modern developed countries, both in the West and in the East, are ill-suited to revolutions of the classic type, not so much because of the enormous power that governments have at their disposal as because human life in these countries has fused with modern technology, and the latter is so complex and refined that any permanent interference with it might have the same consequences as an atomic cataclysm. Moreover, modern production in those countries has already solved or is on the way to solving the basic material needs of the large majority of people, so that the center of social conflict has shifted in the direction of distribution of income and management of the state and the economy, and even in the direction of moral dilemmas. Sensitive to disturbances, modern systems succumb relatively easily to limited pressure and to reform of some of their institutions and activities. Thus, universities are in the process of being reorganized, Johnson gave up his candidacy, but the "student-worker" revolution did not materialize, and the "capitalist" society has not been destroyed.

To be a revolutionary is to be enthralled and romantic, especially if one does not have to pay for it with one's head or a jail term. But revolution is a very serious undertaking, a very responsible undertaking, and is justified only where it promotes the well-being of the nation. Revolutionary violence, like any other violence, transforms itself into insanity and tyranny the moment it ceases to be an instrument of change. Thus far revolutions have changed forms of power and ownership, but no revolution has ever changed either the nature of man or the character of nations. Property relations in developed countries are today less important than they were a hundred, or even fifty, years ago. This could not be said for power itself, whose role, especially in the co-ordination of the economy, has become more important.

Because of that, if anyone were to ask me to define the essence of today's revolution and the duties of contemporary revolutionaries, I would say: to examine the possibilities of human freedoms, both material and spiritual; to insist upon them publicly, honestly and unwaveringly; and to abandon dogmas and absolute truths. After so many sterile hopes and tragic temptations with both counterrevolutionary and revolutionary despotisms, at the beginning of a new era—in which mankind has

6. From a conversation of Daniel Cohn-Bendit with J. P. Sartre in *The Year of the Young Rebels*, p. 107.

been released from the confines of earth and fused with the cosmos—men
have become aware of their own value, which cannot be compensated for
or raised by any ideology or by any final form of authority and ownership.

Because of that, I believe that out of today's structures and today's
resistances will be born new, universal visions and new movements of
realizable and freer human conditions. If it were not so, I would not view
my past critically, nor would I have written these lines.

New version of an article that appeared in
newspapers throughout the world, 1969

16
In Lieu
of a Conclusion

[. . .]

It is my belief that society cannot be perfect. Men must hold both ideas and ideals, but they should not regard these as being wholly realizable. We need to comprehend the nature of utopianism. Utopianism, once it achieves power, becomes dogmatic, and it quite readily can create human suffering in the name and in the cause of its own scientism and idealism. To speak of society as imperfect may seem to imply that it *can* be perfect, which in truth it cannot. The task for contemporary man is to accept the reality that society is unperfect, but also to understand that humanist, humanitarian dreams and visions are necessary in order to reform society, in order to improve and advance it.

The Unperfect Society, 1969
(Trans. Dorian Cooke)

Is Communism Evolving into Democracy?

The answer to the question posed in the title of this discourse would be very simple if we derived it from Communism as an ideology and a social system. That answer without doubt could only be: No, no and again no. Communism is not evolving, nor is it by its nature capable of evolving, into democracy.

For Communism abstracts, or, more precisely, it molds the world, history and the human spirit into definitive "scientific" formulas. The essence of Communist teaching has not changed from Marx to the present, except in questions of political tactics, that is, the seizing and holding of power. Moreover, the essence of that teaching cannot change or be expanded, for the simple reason that it would thereby be destroyed: contemporary knowledge and experiences refute any validity, and especially the scientific validity, of the dialectical and materialistic schema.

The longer they last, the more obviously Communist teachings fall into ever more confined, ever more absurd dogmatism.

For our discussion it is necessary to emphasize that man, society and nation are not created according to any law, but grow out of the infinity of manifold conditions and human endeavors. People can and must expand their knowledge of these conditions and endeavors. But there is no fixed order; nor can there be. The classical order has been shaken even in the natural sciences, let alone in phenomena that exist precisely because they are unorderly—because they are alive and creative. The "scientificness" of Communists is the motivation for and the justification of their total mastery over society and over the individual.

Communist dogmatism is irresistible and effective where it can play the role of a new religion—in nations whose governmental and social structures are backward and retarded in the modern industrial transformation. After the coming of Communists into power, their utopia becomes the cruel reality exactly because it insists upon its "scientificness" and "idealness." "Building" the perfect, "classless" society and the "new" man, even though it is, and exactly because it is, an idealization of the power and the privileges of the party's bureaucracy, forces also a perfect, total means of oppression over society and the individual. Even in countries where Communism did not become totalitarian (for example, in Yugoslavia), Communism was always present as an idea in many undertakings.

And yet, the negative answer given to the question posed in the title of this discourse is so abstract and oversimplified that it itself falls into a dogmatic abuse of reality: the tendencies today being born in Communist countries, and even the tendencies emanating from Communism itself, are in such measure new and complex that their interpretation by means of existing theories and experiences would give a false picture and would lead into dead ends.

If we understand Communist ideology as a finalized, closed system of "truths" (and only thus should one understand it), then that ideology (with the exception of China and Albania) [1] either does not exist today or is hanging on with difficulty in specific areas, especially in the areas of authority and the economy. From the iron grip of the all-encompassing and omnipresent ideology first the arts begin to liberate themselves, and that mainly because the arts cannot be creative if they do not have the freedom to choose forms and—to some extent at least—themes. But even in Yugoslavia, because of the noninstitutionalization of freedom and of arbitrary limitations, the arts have limited possibilities. But there is improvement even in the Soviet Union. Despite all the strictness of party and police controls, the semilegal *"samizdati"* are thriving and—what is

1. I did not mention Cuba with China and Albania mainly because its totalitarianism —as I understand it—has the characteristics of Latin-American personal dictatorships.

perhaps even more significant—in the existing legalized forms there are emerging nonconformist interpretations and embarrassing initiatives (for example, the periodical *Novy Mir,* the well-known appeal of the scientist Sakharov, and others). After the arts come the sciences and scientific theories. Philosophy, it is true, almost does not exist. But also there are no ideological "purges." The obsoleteness of their own dogmas, however, force even the Soviet Communists to seek "supplements" for the holy of holies—Marxist ideology. . . . Two years ago in the USSR there was called a meeting of psychologists to provide "scientific" aid to the party in the struggle against religion. And there at that meeting, of all the explanations of religion, some even rational, but on the whole a bunch of stupidities, not a single one was Marxist. But this did not prevent the party from publicizing those explanations widely. Time and events have made the teachings of the party so meaningless that it is not afraid to accept other, "alien," teachings, if those offer greater security than its own.

The ferment and confusion in the economy are even deeper, although there is less talk about it. There are even economic theories (about the market economy, overemployment, convertibility, the world market as a measure of efficiency, etc.) which only superficially maintain their ties with Marxist dogma. But, most important, in Eastern Europe there are already emerging different (from country to country) property relationships and different means of managing the economy. Thus in Yugoslavia and Poland there are no collective farms, and all other Eastern European countries are characterized by the strengthening of the private service sectors and different kinds of "black markets." Even the Soviet Union had to give the collective farms the freedom to trade noncompulsory surpluses, and one per cent of the arable land, the portion of the collective farms comprising household plots, produces 69 per cent of the marketed surplus of potatoes, 40 per cent of the meat, and approximately the same per cent of fruits and vegetables. But what is most important is that the so-called socialist property in various ways is escaping from under the "planned management" of the party and the government bureaucracy. The recent disturbances on the Polish coast were in good measure the result of the tardiness in reforming the method of economic management. In all East European countries the parties are in a dilemma: if they allow independence of the economy—they will be proclaimed parasites; and if they retain control, even with the aid of the state—the waste, disproportions and inefficiency will threaten the nation with lagging behind and social unrest. The way of managing the economy in Eastern European countries moves with difficulty but constantly in the direction of Western effectiveness and profitability. In Yugoslavia the way today is different from the West only in that it is less developed and is still burdened by bureaucracy and dogmatism. Moreover, Yugoslavia has come so far that it is already very difficult to determine who is the real owner of the firm—the state (in the name of the nation), or the state and those who work in the firm ("group ownership"). Strikes are not rare, "incomprehensible" occcurrences in Eastern Europe, and in Yugoslavia the demands for legal regulations governing strikes have already been publicly presented.

The cited occurrences in the cultural sphere and in the economic sphere are not new. But they are today reaching such a volume and such maturity that the existing structure and everyday life cannot exist or be imagined without them.

That leads to new questions and to new conclusions: 1) In what measure are these occurrences the consequence of the conscious actions of leaders, that is, the liberalization of Communism? 2) What, under such conditions, are the possibilities of the so-called heretics of Communism?

1. In no single Communist country were the present reforms the fruit of the willing and conscious action of the leadership. The so-called liberalization of Communism is a very imprecise, inaccurate term which was invented by the Western press for the sake of simpler explanations of the retreat from the inflexibility and senselessness of "Stalinism." Even "Stalinism" was invented by the Western press for "practical" simplistic needs. "Stalinism" is Marxism realized, of course, in Russian conditions. And just as there is no, nor can there be, "Stalinism" as perverted Marxism, there is no, nor can there be, liberal Communism, but there are Communist regimes and Communist leaders who are more or less forced to abandon "Stalinist" methods.

"Liberalism" penetrates into the consciousness of Communists only when they have no other way out. Liberalism does not come forth as the result of their good will, but out of necessity, out of chaos, and primarily out of the fear of losing power. Concessions in culture, decentralization in the economy, introduction of some kind of legality and a more tolerant position toward religions—all those are the consequences of the resistance to totalitarian irrationality, terror and waste. . . . Yugoslavia is in this—as in many other things—an explicit example: thus the Yugoslav leadership carried out the collectivization of the economy after the conflict with Stalin (conflict, 1948; collectivization 1949–1950) and it abolished the collective farms ("working co-operatives") only after they proved to be catastrophic for agricultural production and had brought the state into dependence upon American food surpluses. True, the introduction of collective farms in Yugoslavia was in significant measure caused by the dogmatic reaction to Stalin's accusations about the kulak policy of Yugoslavia's leaders, and it was accompanied by reform measures in other areas. But the lagging in liberalization that occurred after Stalin's death and that lasted an entire decade cannot have any other explanation than the fear of new ideas and the new ideological rapprochement between Yugoslav and Soviet leaders. Obviously, the liberalization did not originate from liberalism, at least not the liberalism of the majority of the leadership, but from difficulties and fears. Even Khrushchev's reformism had its origin in the struggle with his rivals and in the horrible consequences of Stalin's terror.

But when reformism takes roots, it is nourished by life itself with inexhaustible juices and in countless inexplicable ways. Many Communists, and even entire groups and organizations of Communists (for example, in Czechoslovakia in 1968), are seized by doubts and inspired by new visions of freedom. But there always remains one part of the Communists who remain dedicated to the original totalitarian doctrine and ready to use totalitarian methods. Thus the change in Czechoslovakia began with the dissatisfaction of writers and authors, was inflamed by the actions of youths and workers, and only then was accepted by the majority of the leaders. But up to the end, that is, up to Soviet intervention, democracy was not institutionalized. People were enjoying nonlegalized freedoms; but the disillusion and nonorganized freedom became easy prey to the interventionists.

2. The significance of the heretics in the change of Communist structure can be, and often has been, very important, but only if they are—and may I be permitted to say with emphasis—"heretics" and not heretics, that is, if by criticism they point to exits from the enchained circle, and not just lament the betrayal of the dogma and the absence of egalitarianism. To no one, and especially politicians, is it very comfortable when someone uncovers his inconsistencies or his unclean conscience. But no politician has ever been destroyed by that; and least of all will that happen to a Communist, since his dedication to the movement justifies any inconsistencies and lack of scruples.

The heretics of Communism lead to doubts and to reflection. But they cannot destroy the Communist faith, for the simple reason that Communism is not a religion but an ideology, that is, a totalitarian movement. Communism is a world closed in itself, immune not only to any external, hostile criticism, but also to that of its own disillusioned: for genuine Communists, those who criticize their monopoly of power and privileges, are only inconvenient fools. . . . Because of that, the leftist publications and the leftist professors in Yugoslavia, despite all their erudition and despite the relative tolerance of the regime toward them, can only serve to confirm their own barrenness. . . . But Communism is vulnerable, defenseless against the critics who explain it without bias and who find possible exits from it. For that reason Solzhenitsyn in Russia and Kolakowski in Poland are indestructible and undefeatable despite their isolation. Their unbiased criticisms are at the same time also visions, not of some alien and unreal society, but, rather, of that which is just beginning to develop on the surface of Communism itself.

The time of heresies and heretical critics of Communism has already in the main passed. One does not deal here with the "betrayal" of leaders but with the change of the unsuitable and antiquated order. Democratic currents face the mapping out of realistic reform programs and corresponding actions, of course adapted to the requirements of each of the individual nations.

But what comes out of this process of the falling apart of the ideology and the economy of Communism? Are the Communist systems converging toward Western societies, since they obviously cannot endure any longer in isolation, nor can they adjust their own ideological and bureaucratic economies to the postindustrial technetronic epoch?

There are still Communist dreamers and bureaucrats who are convinced that "revisionists" will not come to the fore in China, Cuba and Albania, and that there will be no "capitalist" disintegration of society in those countries. But what those dreamers are unable to see in China, Cuba and Albania, and what heartens the party bureaucrats, in fact is not the lack of stratification, but the totalitarianism that hides and stifles it: Maoist shirts are of the same cut, but of different fabric; and underneath them some wear silk and others cotton. If in the societies of China, Cuba and Albania there were no tendencies toward a differentiated, stratified society, there would be no need for totalitarian mastery. . . . Stalin "built" the "classless" society, but in such a way that social differences, and with them the social dimension of the individual, were oppressed and destroyed by the terror. But even that was contrived and temporary: the "classlessness" of society was paid for by the total absence of freedom and was upheld by the privileged "new class"—the party bureaucracy.

Disintegration of Communist structure begins with the insistence upon national uniqueness (so-called national Communisms). Not even that happens because of the pure patriotism of the Communists, but mainly because of their fear for their own power, and because of the catastrophes induced by imitating and by forcing the Communist great powers—the USSR and China—as models in every respect. But disintegration and change are not stopped, nor can they be stopped, at "national" Communism: the strength and attraction of Communism lie, among other things, in its completeness, and in its renunciation and lopping off of any insignificant part that undermines the entire structure. And the moment one party separates itself, it creates new relations and forces, new possibilities and motivations. Ideology, which among Communists is more or less a means rather than a real ideal, loses the power to incorporate into itself the new reality and begins to spread and to seek escape in hitherto "alien" ideas. In Khrushchev's struggle against the "Stalinists," the conflict with Yugoslavia was one of his most potent arguments. The same thing is happening in the management of power and the economy. The rebellions of national parties also changed the position of the Communist great powers, the USSR and China. And not even the Communist great powers are internally unchangeable: in the USSR, for example, are occurring processes similar to those in other East European countries, but they are moving at a slower pace because of imperial interests and because of the more ingrained privileges of their party bureaucracy. The uniqueness of Russia lies therein, that it was always ruled by a centralized bureaucracy and that economic and technical progress were paid for by ever greater lack of freedom. There is hope that in the modern epoch the fate of Russia will change, although Soviet society is not as differentiated as was Czechoslovakia in 1968 or Yugoslavia at the present.

Communist societies do not differ in the forces that operate within them, but they do differ in the relations and forms of the operation of those forces. In all of Eastern Europe (including even the Soviet Union), totalitarianism is disintegrating in all its forms. In all of Eastern Europe there is not a single significant creative Marxist. Georg Lukács was once one. There was Leszek Kolakowski, the most subtle critic of dogmatism, but he is exiled from his country. Totalitarianism was able to make itself a reality only by destroying its own soul: all that is today creative in East Europe is critical of totalitarianism and of existing reality. But totalitarian forces and tendencies have not disappeared anywhere—and probably will not for a long time. Nor can one conclude that Communist structure is evolving into democracy, even if Communists no longer use totalitarian methods.

Of course, it occurs, and it will probably occur on a larger scale, that certain groups and factions of Communists accept democratic ideas and forms. . . . Because Communists, united against alien, hostile forms, are themselves "infected" by the disintegration of their own society and the dissolution of their own ideology. . . . But such groups and factions in reality are Communist only in their origins and because of ties (whether for reasons of conformity or of tactics) to outmoded but still ruling structures. And exactly because of these characteristics and possibilities and even because of their illusions, these groups and currents can play a very significant role. [. . .] Thus in Yugoslavia, even among the top leadership—and most expressly among the top leadership—besides Communist-bureaucrats, there are Communist-democrats and Communist-nationalists. [. . .]

The disintegration of totalitarianism liberates new, previously stifled forces. But all of them are not, nor can they become, democratic. Moreover, one cannot be sure that democratic forces will reign everywhere. As always, everything depends on people and on conditions. But this dissolution of Communist totalitarianism in any case does not lead to the restoration of the social relations destroyed by the revolution. After accomplishing its task, the oppression that grew up from the revolution is retreating—as after other revolutions—in the face of the growing needs of the people and the national particularities and possibilities.

From this it follows that at the moment there is no—and judging by everything there cannot be—political and social convergence of Communist structures with other, democratic structures. True, technologies in Communism and in the West are developing in the same general directions and are growing closer together in their levels and are even becoming linked. That, of course, brings the West and the East closer together. One could even conclude that such a process reduces the inflexibilities and softens the rigidity of Communist structures. But this does not transform it either into something Western or into anything else contrary to its essence. Communism falls into its own kind of chaos, and in that measure people become freer, but it does not transform itself into democracy. This is how the rejuvenation of nations and societies begins: the decay of one form is the foundation for the birth of a new one.

Obviously the structures growing on the soil of Communism will be more open and—potentially—more peaceful toward Europe and the United States. But they will, at least in the beginning, retain a course and characteristics in many ways different from those of the West. . . . Because even Communism, although in its dogma international, in reality had to become national. . . . The world is obviously unifying itself through free differentiation and not by forcing everything into the same mold. In our times nothing confirms this ancient truth more than the disintegration of Communist totalitarianism.

March 1971 (unpublished)

Toward the Coexistence of Ideologies

The visit of President Nixon to China seems to me so significant, indeed a turning point for the entire world, that it can only be compared to the outbreak of a major war or a revolution in an important country. But I will remark only upon its ideological significance—if I may call it that—because perhaps that aspect has not been sufficiently noted.

In the communiqué of the Sino-American talks what was most unusual and most noticeable was the exposition of the "ideological principles" of both sides. Thus the United States said that it "supports the individual freedom and social progress of all peoples of the world, and freedom from foreign meddling or intervention. [. . .] The United States believes that with the effort for reducing tensions it contributes to improving communications between countries which have different ideologies, and in that way reduces the risks of confrontation arising from miscalculation or misunderstanding." And China emphasized that "countries desire independence, nations desire liberation, and people desire revolution—that is the irresistible thrust of history." [. . .]

But what does that pompous exposition of ideologies really mean? Nothing else but that the national, state, interests of China and the United States have become more important than their ideologies. In accentuating and emphasizing adherence to ideologies, there are also "unquiet consciences." And why not, with this acceptance of the inevitable that state relations develop without regard for and even in spite of ideologies? That is finally a recognition of the reality that the already long-established groupings in the world are not centered around ideologies or based upon them, but are centered around great powers and based on national interest.

Their respective ideologies may remain irreconcilable, but the United States and China are not any longer irreconcilable. It will be thus in the future, because ideologies are intellectual creations, established once and for all, while the interests of nations are living and changeable.

Ideologies are repelling and hostile toward everything that does not fit into their framework, or that resists fitting into their "perfect" systems and becoming subject to their "absolute" truths. The characteristics of every ideology are such that a common life with another ideology with "alien" ideas is fatal. Contemporary ideologies cannot become reconciled, they can't even accept coexistence. But the coexistence of ideologies is already becoming a fact—despite ideologies, despite the fact that ideology denies that possibility. That coexistence appears and comes more alive with the co-operation of states of opposing ideologies, with the strengthening of the national interest over the ideological, international principle. The coexistence of ideologies is the right to "one's own" ideology. Ideologies, whether they like it or not, are retreating behind national borders. There one finds sterility and decadence—by which ideologies "coexist." And the truth of that will be confirmed by the fact that ideologies will be silent about it and will cover it up.

It would be very erroneous to conclude from that that the world will become less suited for wars and *coups d'état*. Ideologies darkened the conscience of the world, but they also created the self-illusion that they will prevail with their "tested truths" and their "perfect" systems. Now there will be fewer such illusions. The spiritual difficulties of co-operation among nations will also weaken. But it is possible to have an outbreak of "sacred national selfishness"; some great powers might seek somewhere in the world greater "rights" than they are entitled to on the basis of technology and culture. Not even in such a world will it be easy to maintain the balance and preserve the peace. . . .

The world was once—on the eve of World War I—"nonideological," that is, it had "national" ideologies. On the ruins of that world emerged ideology. The present world is more complex; great nations are forced to be dependent upon one another. The contemporary world does not have to relive the fate of earlier worlds if . . . if the common interests of nations, which have doubtless already broken through the brittle frames of ideologies, can be nurtured.

March 1972 (unpublished)

The Central Question Is Europe

[. . . In an interview in his Belgrade home with *World* correspondent Rudolph Chelminski, Djilas talked about the current Soviet-American rapprochement and its larger meaning for the future of Europe.]

Djilas: The Soviet-American rapprochement is a very positive trend in international relations, but there will be some complications because Europe is not in the game. The role of Europe in the future is not clear right now. Ideally, it should be neither anti-American nor anti-Soviet but participation with both. If this does not happen, the situation could be very bad. Even the relationship between American and Soviet Russia might not remain stable—they would both be trying to compete for the most influence over Europe. Other questions are of secondary importance. The central question is Europe.

Europe must unite; there is no other way. If she does not unite, she will be divided by the interests of Soviet Russia and America—not disunited by geography, as she is now, but by influence. I don't agree with the American papers that say Soviet Russia won more from this agreement than the United States did. This view is true only for the moment, in a superficial way. The Soviets will gain from technological developments in the U.S.A., and they have succeeded in definitively dividing Germany and so on. But when you evaluate the outcome with the future in mind, it is not correct to speak of who has won more. Such terms are not correct. It is not a question of who is victorious in these negotiations, because for once the United States and the Soviet Union have adopted an attitude of cooperation rather than political competition. America is not the loser in the light of the future. For me, what is important is the process of disintegration of ideology and totalitarianism that we are seeing throughout Soviet Russia and Eastern Europe. The rapprochement is helping this spontaneous process throughout the East. Ideology is dying: the totalitarian system does not exist any more in Eastern Europe.

Q: In what ways does the Soviet Union most need the United States?

Djilas: There are many obvious ways that we all know of. But we shouldn't forget that she also needs the United States in foreign relations, especially regarding a stronger position toward China. That's a factor. As for the question of arms, what is happening is of great importance; but, here again, the future is very uncertain. For example, war with atomic weapons is almost impossible, but if the United States and the Soviet Union forbid their use, then war becomes possible. They will be open not only to the use of traditional weapons but to classic Great Power policies as well, the spheres of influence and all that, as at the end of the nineteenth century. Ideology didn't cause World War I. Great Power influences did.

Q: Can you imagine Western Europe as a bloc ever turning against the United States?

Djilas: I don't believe that theory. Absolutely not. There will be discussions and disagreements and economic conflicts, but that sort of break could not occur, even superficially. It's not just a question of Western Europe's not being able to survive without American protection; now, or in the future, she may be able to do without that protection. But the problem is deeper than that. The American and Western European forms of life are too similar for them to turn against each other. The only thing Western Europe may ask is more equality with America.

Q: Should American troops remain on European soil?

Djilas: It isn't necessary for them to be there as an effective force; symbolic force is enough. Everybody must know that America will fight—that's all.

Q: Will Western Europe, in fact, unite?

Djilas: Unity is already on its way. A bit too slowly, but Western Europe is moving toward the goal. I believe in it. It is the only future for Europe.

Q: Are you surprised at how easily the American people accepted Nixon's pragmatic about-face in the government's foreign policy?

Djilas: No. The Americans are not as doctrinaire as the Communists. Personally, I think America has won the cold war, but that doesn't mean that they should blackmail the Soviets. The Soviet Union cannot be blackmailed. What Congress is doing with trade and the Soviet Jews is absolutely stupid. Senator Jackson's proposal is nonsense. The Soviets could instead trade with Japan or with Western Europe. Or they could even manage without foreign trade. What the Russians are doing with the Jews is bad. Every honest man must be against it. But Congress is falling back into an old-fashioned style of trying to blackmail Russia with bargains. It is as if the Russians demanded a settlement to the question of the American Negroes.

Q: Will the future be governed exclusively by commerce and pragmatism?

Djilas: I don't believe in ideology any more, but I do believe in new forms, new programs. Without some sort of faith, humanity cannot exist. This need is just something in human nature.

Q: What is your vision of the new faith?

Djilas: I call it existential humanism. The definition isn't clear and is open to different interpretations. But essentially it means that life must be more and more free and liberated from dogmatism. Everyone must be guaranteed housing and education and food. There must be free health care and old-age care. The application would be worked out differently in different countries, but it must include ethics in politics. Ethics and politics are not necessarily contrary to each other. For example, in ancient Greece and Rome, the statesmen were often very ethical men. In modern times there have also been some ethical men—I think of de Gaulle, for example, or Brandt. Of course, in politics it is difficult to be completely ethical. You must be canny, too, because to be cheated in politics means to be stupid.

Q: Do you see this new faith being applied anywhere in the world today?

Djilas: No. This is my utopia alone.

World, August 14, 1973

Index

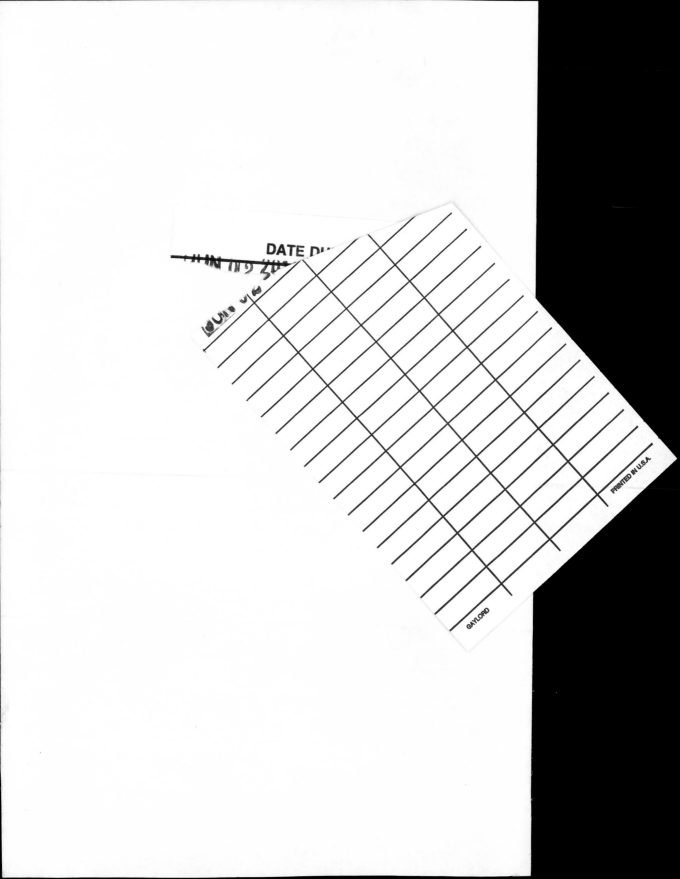

DATE DUE

GAYLORD   PRINTED IN U.S.A.